lonely planet

American South

p50

Texas
p264

Deep South
p130

Florida
p200

Regis St Louis, Jesse Scott

FROM LEFT: DIGIDREAMGRAFIX/SHUTTERSTOCK, MATT CUDA/SHUTTERSTOCK, BLUIZ70/SHUTTERSTOCK

Charlotte (p85)

CONTENTS

Plan Your Trip

The Guide

Black bear

Food truck, Atlanta (p152)

Toolkit

Storybook

JRTWYNAM/SHUTTERSTOCK

Lake Martin (p197)

THE AMERICAN SOUTH

THE JOURNEY BEGINS HERE

Some of my earliest travel memories revolve around national parks in the South: spotting alligators on boardwalk strolls through the Everglades, crawling through Mammoth Cave's chilly passageways and watching the fireflies dance around the family tent in the Great Smoky Mountains. Although I've traveled the globe since then, I'm convinced that the world's greatest treasures are right in my own backyard.

Regis St Louis

@regisstlouis

A Southerner by choice, Regis has spent half a lifetime exploring far-flung corners of the South, and he has written Lonely Planet guides to Texas, Florida, the Carolinas and the Great Smoky Mountains, among many other destinations.

My favorite experience is boating across the mirror-like waters of **Lake Martin** (p197), an aquatic wonderland of towering bald cypress trees, ostentatious lotus flowers and great blue herons silently stalking the shoreline.

WHO GOES WHERE

Our writers and experts choose the places which, for them, define the American South.

ELENA SUVOROVA/SHUTTERSTOCK

My home base of **Fort Lauderdale** (p230; pictured) truly lives up to its 'Venice of America' nickname. Within a five-minute wander along its Las Olas Boulevard artery, you can be gawking at superyachts coasting along the Intracoastal Waterway and neighboring canals; strolling a stretch of designer boutiques; and dipping your toes in the Atlantic Ocean. Beyond its white-sand-heaven reputation, I love how Fort Lauderdale's artistic edge is becoming more visible, too, with the Flagler Village neighborhood now rivaling Miami's Wynwood in terms of graffiti-art-draped pizzazz.

Jesse Scott

@jesserobertscott

A Fort Lauderdale resident and the founder of browardist.com, Jesse has been writing about entertainment, food, travel and their intersections for 20-plus years.

CONTRIBUTING WRITERS

Amy C Balfour
Joel Balsam
Dale Blasingame
Rachel Chang
Sarah Etinas
Caroline Eubanks
Mary Fitzpatrick
Bailey Freeman
David Gibb
Robert Isenberg
Adam Karlin
Stephen Lioy
Emily Matchar
Kevin Raub
Meena Thiruvengadam
Mara Vorhees
Terry Ward

Nashville
Dance with country fans at a honky tonk (p103)
Atlanta
Explore food halls and dynamic neighborhoods (p151)
Mississippi Delta
Discover the birthplace of the blues (p175)
San Antonio
Wander through beautifully preserved Spanish missions (p280)
Austin
Feel the creative spirit at live-music bars (p270)
New Orleans
Join the jazz-fueled party on Frenchmen St (p181)
0 1,000 km
0 500 miles
Minneapolis
St Paul
WISCONSIN
Rapid City
Pierre
SOUTH DAKOTA
Sioux Falls
Madison
Casper
Sioux City
IOWA
Cedar Rapids
Milwaukee
WYOMING
NEBRASKA
Des Moines
ILLINOIS
Cheyenne
Grand Island
Omaha
Lincoln
Denver
Kansas City
Colorado Springs
KANSAS
COLORADO
MISSOURI
Jonesboro
Brownsville
Fayetteville
Memphis
Amarillo
Little Rock
Mississippi River
Hot Springs
Clarksdale
OKLAHOMA
ARKANSAS
Lubbock
MISSISSIPPI
Fort Worth
Dallas
Longview
Shreveport
Jackson
Tyler
Abilene
Midland
LOUISIANA
Pecos
Odessa
Waco
San Angelo
Killeen
TEXAS
College Station
New Orleans
Baton Rouge
Marfa
Johnson City
Conroe
Beaumont
Austin
Presidio
San Antonio
Houston
Galveston
Del Rio
Eagle Pass
Laredo
Corpus Christi
Brownsville

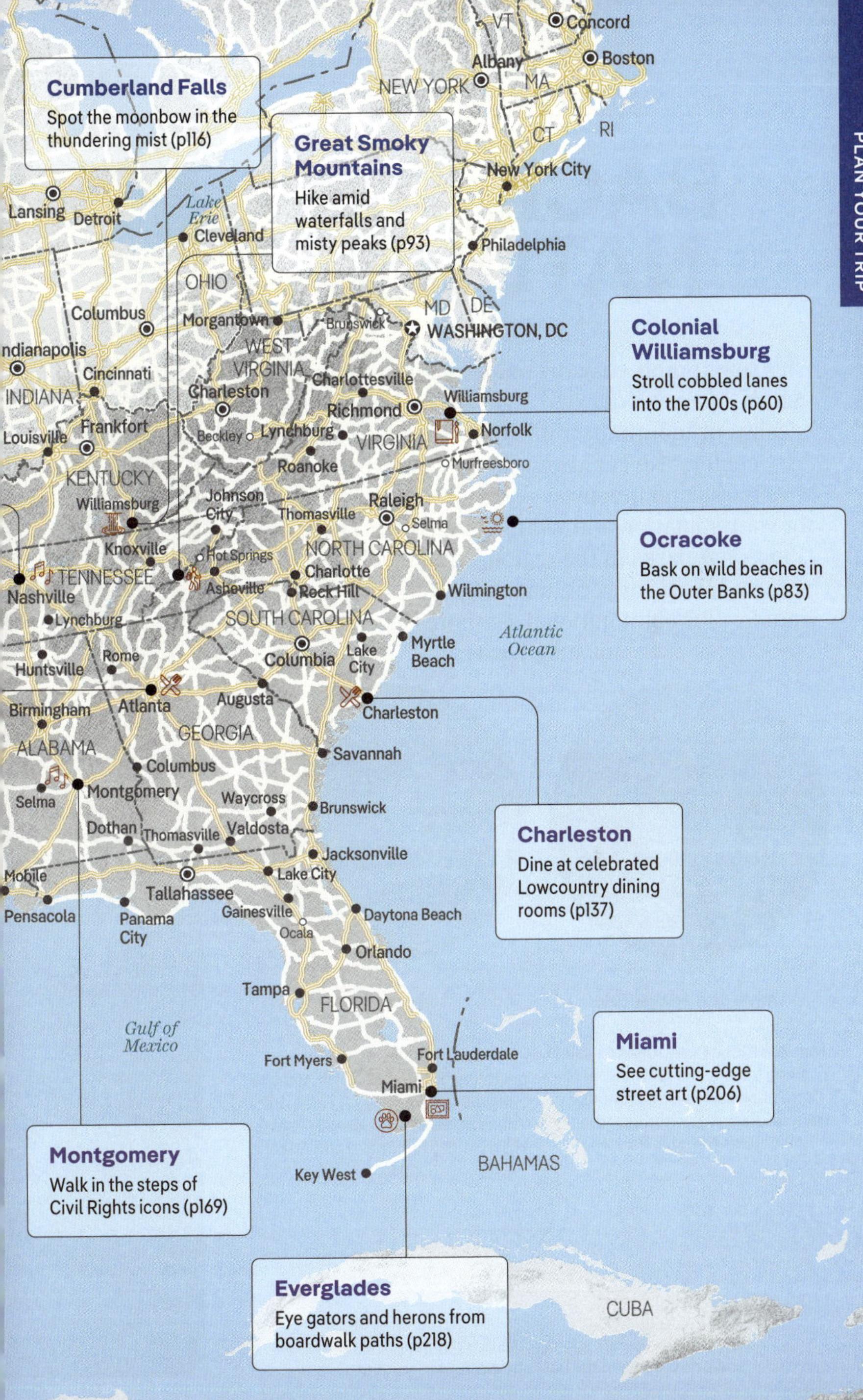
Cumberland Falls
Spot the moonbow in the thundering mist (p116)
Great Smoky Mountains
Hike amid waterfalls and misty peaks (p93)
Colonial Williamsburg
Stroll cobbled lanes into the 1700s (p60)
Ocracoke
Bask on wild beaches in the Outer Banks (p83)
Charleston
Dine at celebrated Lowcountry dining rooms (p137)
Miami
See cutting-edge street art (p206)
Montgomery
Walk in the steps of Civil Rights icons (p169)
Everglades
Eye gators and herons from boardwalk paths (p218)
Concord
Boston
VT
Albany
NEW YORK
MA
CT
RI
New York City
Lansing
Detroit
Lake Erie
Cleveland
Philadelphia
OHIO
MD
DE
Columbus
Morgantown
Brunswick
WASHINGTON, DC
Indianapolis
WEST VIRGINIA
Cincinnati
Charlottesville
INDIANA
Charleston
Williamsburg
Richmond
Louisville
Frankfort
Beckley
Lynchburg
Norfolk
VIRGINIA
Roanoke
Murfreesboro
KENTUCKY
Johnson City
Williamsburg
Thomasville
Raleigh
Selma
Knoxville
Hot Springs
NORTH CAROLINA
Nashville
TENNESSEE
Asheville
Charlotte
Rock Hill
Wilmington
Lynchburg
SOUTH CAROLINA
Atlantic Ocean
Huntsville
Rome
Columbia
Lake City
Myrtle Beach
Birmingham
Atlanta
Augusta
Charleston
ALABAMA
GEORGIA
Savannah
Columbus
Selma
Montgomery
Waycross
Brunswick
Dothan
Thomasville
Valdosta
Jacksonville
Mobile
Tallahassee
Lake City
Pensacola
Panama City
Gainesville
Ocala
Daytona Beach
Orlando
Tampa
FLORIDA
Gulf of Mexico
Fort Myers
Fort Lauderdale
Miami
Key West
BAHAMAS
CUBA
PLAN YOUR TRIP

BACK TO NATURE

It's remarkably easy to escape city crowds in the South – you can drive to secluded marshes, rivers, beaches or mountain trails in half a day from many city centers. No car? Even the largest urban areas have parks and greenways providing a quick escape for contemplation and wildlife-watching. There are 11 national parks in the region, which include a mix of sun-baked canyons, ancient peaks and remote islands, plus eight national seashores and hundreds of state parks.

FROM LEFT: PIERRE LECLERC PHOTOGRAPHY/GETTY IMAGES, LMPLATTI/SHUTTERSTOCK, DAMON SHAW/SHUTTERSTOCK

Drive the Ridgeline

The Blue Ridge Pkwy runs 469 miles along the crest of its namesake mountains, linking Shenandoah National Park, VA, with Great Smoky Mountains National Park, NC.

Birding

Each year over three billion migrating birds cross North America on one of four flyways. Three are found in the South: Central (Texas), Mississippi (Gulf Coast) and Atlantic (East Coast).

Night Skies

The International Dark Sky Reserve surrounding Big Bend National Park spans some 15,000 square miles, and offers some of the best stargazing in the country.

Buffalo National River (p126)

BEST NATURE EXPERIENCES

Spend the day paddling past towering cliffs and darting kingfisher's on a breathtaking stretch of Arkansas' ❶ **Buffalo National River** (p126).

Hike past the thundering ❷ **Rainbow Falls** (p96) in Great Smoky Mountains National Park en route to Lookout Lodge with its dramatic overlooks.

Enjoy stillness and shade while kayaking through a blackwater swamp home to turtles, barred owls and snakes in South Carolina's ❸ **Congaree National Park** (p148).

Admire the furry majesty of a bison (from a safe distance) while visiting ❹ **Caprock Canyons State Park** (p311) in Texas.

Walk boardwalk trails or go boating in search of gators, birds, manatees and crocs at ❺ **Everglades National Park** (p218).

JACQUE MANAUGH/SHUTTERSTOCK

Ground Zero (p176)

THE GREAT AMERICAN SOUND

From the soulful blues born in the Mississippi Delta to the bluegrass of Appalachia and Nashville's big country sound – plus jazz, funk, hip-hop and rock and roll – the South has invented sounds integral to modern music. You can walk in the footsteps of musical legends and hear tomorrow's future stars in concert halls, honky-tonks and music clubs across these 13 Southern states.

American Routes

For a deep dive into American music in all its beguiling forms, tune into American Routes *(amroutes.org)*, a weekly two-hour radio show (also a podcast) from New Orleans.

Price of Admission

Cover charge at many music clubs ranges from $10 to $20. Some places have free music, but don't forget to tip the musicians.

BEST LIVE MUSIC EXPERIENCES

Walk the music-filled strip of New Orleans' Frenchmen St, ducking in to bars like ❶ **d.b.a.** and the **Spotted Cat** (p189).

Join country lovers for a night of dancing in a Nashville honky-tonk – like ❷ **Tootsie's Orchid Lounge** (p105).

Listen to up-and-coming blues stars at ❸ **Ground Zero** (p176) in the Mississippi Delta town of Clarksdale.

Take in the legendary music scene of Austin, Texas, starting with a show at the long-running ❹ **Continental Club** (p277).

Head to Asheville, North Carolina for Sunday Bluegrass Brunch at the ❺ **Jack of the Wood Pub** (p89), a showcase of local musicians playing toe-tapping tunes.

BEHIND THE WHEEL

The open road awaits. As you hop into the driver's seat and hit the highway, you can chart a course through some of North America's most striking landscapes. Lofty Appalachian peaks, beach-dotted shores of the Carolinas and the sultry swamplands of Louisiana are a few fine starting points for the great Southern road trip.

FROM LEFT: BETTY SHELTON/SHUTTERSTOCK, KELLY VANDELLEN/SHUTTERSTOCK

Automobile Organizations

If you're not already a member, join an automobile organization, like AAA, which will provide 24-hour roadside emergency assistance, plus 10% savings at some motels and attractions.

Fill Up the Tank

Keep the fuel tank topped up when you head onto the backroads – especially in remote parts of Texas where service stations can be few and far between.

Wildlife Safety

Be mindful of driving around dawn or dusk when wildlife is most active, and deer and other animals can wander onto the road.

1 5 4 3 2

BEST ROAD-TRIP EXPERIENCES

Pass through sun-bleached towns and desert wilderness en route to the stunning canyons in the 1 **High Plains** (p311) of Texas.

Roll down the windows and feel the ocean breeze while island-hopping down the Florida Keys on the 2 **Overseas Highway** (p227).

Plan a mountaintop road trip following the 469-mile 3 **Blue Ridge Parkway** (p64), offering spectacular views across Virginia and North Carolina.

Breathe in the scent of forest while driving past rushing streams, scenic trailheads and old homesteads on 4 **Roaring Fork Motor Nature Trail** (p96) in the Great Smoky Mountains.

Experience a little-visited part of the South along the lovely 5 **Natchez Trace Parkway** (p180) crossing Mississippi up to Tennessee.

COASTAL TREASURES

Amid hundreds of miles of shorelines, you'll find islands, seaside towns and some of the USA's loveliest beaches. There are plenty of surprises en route, from herds of wild horses descended from shipwreck survivors to remote national parks reached only by boat. Wherever you roam, it's hard not to feel like you've left the modern world behind as you head out to a place where nature rules supreme in a salt-tinged realm of sea, sand and sky.

Queen of the Shore

Florida has more coastline than any other state in the contiguous US, including 825 miles of sugar-sand beaches and 350 miles of coral reefs.

Ocean Safety

A red flag flying on the beach means no swimming, due to dangerous conditions. To escape a rip current, swim parallel to shore.

Surfing

Some of the East Coast's best surfing spots are in the Carolinas. Visit Kitty Hawk, Cape Hatteras and Wrightsville Beach (NC) and Folly Beach (SC).

FROM LEFT: BILANOL/SHUTTERSTOCK, JUST DANCE/SHUTTERSTOCK, WILDNERDPIX/SHUTTERSTOCK

Wild horses, Chincoteague National Wildlife Refuge (p66)

BEST SEASIDE EXPERIENCES

Swim, snorkel, paddle or dive around Florida Keys reefs at the nation's first underwater park, ❶ **John Pennekamp** (p224).

Spot herds of wild horses trotting amid the forests and prairies at ❷ **Chincoteague National Wildlife Refuge** (p66) in Virginia.

Escape the crowds on remote and pristine beaches on ❸ **Ocracoke Island** (p83) in North Carolina.

Enjoy some beach time on the Texas Gulf Coast at Port Aransas, followed by birding at the ❹ **Aransas National Wildlife Refuge** (p305).

Spend the day frolicking in the waves, followed by a magnificent sunset at ❺ **Pass-a-Grille Beach** (p261) near St Petersburg, Florida.

Fairhope (p172)

SMALL TOWNS

Small towns have long occupied a large place in the national imagination – symbols of simplicity, nostalgia and neighborly pride. Across the US, these appealing settlements prove cities aren't the only havens of culture. Tight-knit art communities, mom-and-pop restaurants, and streets leading to mountain trailheads and pristine lakes: in these quiet corners, charm gets served in bite-size portions.

Escaping the Crowds

What's the smallest town in the South? There are several contenders, including Thurmond, West Virginia – population: five. It's also home to the least-used train station in the Amtrak network.

What's in a Town?

What qualifies as a small town is fairly subjective, though the US Census Bureau generally considers any place with a population of 5000 or more a city.

BEST SMALL TOWN EXPERIENCES

Chase over 250 cascades in ❶ **Brevard, North Carolina** (p91), known as the 'Land of Waterfalls', then celebrate your finds at a local brewery.

Take a stroll along the hilly streets of ❷ **Eureka Springs** (p124), an art-loving town of pretty Victorian houses in the Ozarks of Arkansas.

Explore the shops and creek trail in ❸ **Boerne** (p287), one of many photogenic small towns in Texas' Hill Country.

Road trip through the ❹ **Mississippi Delta** (p175), birthplace of blues legends like BB King.

Hop between galleries, shops and cafes in the Alabama settlement of ❺ **Fairhope** (p172) before heading to the seaside.

REMEMBERING THE PAST

Ancient peoples, revolutionaries and visionaries in the fight for Civil Rights have all played pivotal roles in shaping the American psyche. Today, hundreds of sites (many managed by the National Park Service) preserve the memory of watershed places and events in the nation's history, including 1000-year-old mound settlements, Spanish Missions and Civil War battlefields.

FROM LEFT: EWY MEDIA/SHUTTERSTOCK, SCOTT K BAKER/SHUTTERSTOCK

Talking History

American History Tellers is an excellent and highly engaging podcast with episodes that explore everything from the Lost Colony of Roanoke (Roanoke Island amphitheater pictured; p83) to the Great Mississippi Flood.

Artful Documentaries

Take a deep dive into history by watching a documentary by Ken Burns, whose wide-ranging output covers jazz, the American Revolution, the Civil War and much more.

Original Residents

People have occupied the American continent for 12,000 years, possibly longer. Remnants of ancient civilizations like Georgia's Ocmulgee Mounds (p158) tell tales of complex Indigenous societies.

BEST HISTORY EXPERIENCES

Gain insight into a once-flourishing civilization while visiting the massive earthworks of ❶ **Poverty Point** (p197), Louisiana's only UNESCO World Heritage Site.

Feel the clock spin backwards while walking the old lanes of ❷ **Colonial Williamsburg** (p60; pictured right) and seeing blacksmiths, carpenters and weavers plying their trades.

Unearth the nation's dark history of slavery at Montgomery, Alabama's ❸ **Legacy Sites** (p170), through memorials that confront the past and inspire reflection.

Learn about the blending of cultures while exploring the ❹ **Spanish Missions** (p285) in San Antonio, Texas.

Take the boat from Charleston out to ❺ **Fort Sumter** (p143) to step into the past – it was here on April 12, 1861 that Civil War erupted.

A MOVEABLE FEAST

Whatever your reasons for visiting, food is likely to play a starring role during your travels. This is the land of Gulf Coast seafood decadence, tender brisket in Texas smokehouses and decadent Creole cooking in New Orleans. You also won't go thirsty in a region known for its home-grown bourbon (Kentucky and Tennessee), vineyards (Virginia and Texas) and craft breweries (everywhere else) – not to mention Southern-style sweet tea and much-loved local coffee roasters all across the South.

Food & Culture

For insight into Southern food and culture, including recipes, restaurant reviews and interviews with makers, check out the Local Palate *(thelocalpalate.com)*.

Farmers Markets

All over the South, farmers markets abound, celebrating bounties of local veg, seafood, foraged mushrooms, inventive baked goods and more. Saturday morning is typically market time.

Closing Time

Some small-town restaurants have limited opening hours, even in communities that are tourism-reliant. Always check timings in advance, especially if you aren't staying somewhere with a kitchen.

FROM LEFT: JACEK CHABRASZEWSKI/SHUTTERSTOCK, KAD PHOTO/SHUTTERSTOCK, ANDRIY BLOKHIN/SHUTTERSTOCK

Cafe Du Monde (p193)

BEST FOOD EXPERIENCES

Munch on beignets and sip chicory coffee at ❶ **Cafe du Monde** (p193) in New Orleans' City Park, then take a stroll among the age-old live oak trees.

Taste melt-in-your-mouth brisket with a side of green spaghetti at woman-owned ❷ **Barb's BQ** (p287), one of the best joints in the fabled Texas barbecue town of Lockhart.

Indulge in a meal of African-influenced Low Country cuisine at long-running ❸ **Hannibal's Kitchen** (p140) in Charleston, South Carolina.

Discover top winemakers with a side of panoramic views in Virginia's stellar Ablemarle County. Start a tasting tour at notable wineries like ❹ **Blenheim Vineyards** (p62).

Explore Atlanta's boundless culinary creativity at ❺ **Politan Row** (p155) in Colony Square, ranked among America's best food halls.

FABLED FESTIVALS

From small-town parades to big-city blowouts, festivals showcase creativity, community and culture. These aren't just parties – they're bucket-list experiences worth planning a trip around. And although summer rules, you'll find major gatherings all year long. Whether honoring identity, celebrating history or joining a vast outdoor dance party, each event provides a glimpse of the loud, proud American spirit.

BEST FESTIVAL EXPERIENCES

Join the movers and shakers at ❶ **South by Southwest** (p277), a showcase of Austin's cutting-edge music, film, art and technology.

Dance through the bead-covered streets of New Orleans as brass bands blare and Carnival season crescendos into its bedazzling finale: ❷ **Mardi Gras** (p181).

Escape the winter chill by heading to Miami for ❸ **Art Basel** (p33), featuring artist talks, gallery openings, special exhibitions and loads of art-minded entertainment.

Discover new music from around the world at ❹ **Festival International** (p194), an entirely free event held on multiple stages in downtown Lafayette, Louisiana.

Join music lovers for three days of down-home authentic jams in Eureka Springs, Arkansas, at the ❺ **Ozark Folk Festival** (p121).

FROM LEFT: ROBERT DAVIS/ALAMY, BLUIZ70/SHUTTERSTOCK

Independence Day

July 4 commemorates the Declaration of Independence with barbecues, parades and fireworks. Myrtle Beach (p145), South Carolina, hosts loads of activities including live music, a 5k fun run and boat parade.

Pride Month

Cities and small towns fly rainbow flags at parties and parades throughout June. One of the South's biggest LGBTIQ+ celebrations (p326) happens in Atlanta, and there are lots throughout Florida.

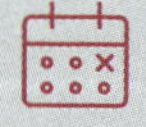

Federal Holidays

Check the calendar before making plans. On federal holidays, including US-specific holidays like Thanksgiving and Memorial Day, many businesses shut down, particularly in rural regions.

SEAN PAVONE/SHUTTERSTOCK

Cumberland Falls (p116)

OFFBEAT AMERICANA

Leave the well-worn path behind to uncover the weirdest and wildest corners of these Southern states. Under-the-radar destinations may take extra effort to reach, but even a tiny detour can sometimes reap big rewards: outdoor art installations, roadside folk monuments, oddball museums and surreal landscapes – some of which are as memorable as the nation's more popular attractions.

BEST OFFBEAT EXPERIENCES

Look for hidden small doors, part of the ❶ **Tiny Doors ATL project** (p154), near key attractions in Atlanta.

Wind through West Virginia's mountains in search of the ❷ **Mothman** (p73) and **Bigfoot** (p74) museums.

Clock the full moon at ❸ **Cumberland Falls** (p116) in Kentucky, when planetary alignment and mist form a moonbow – a rare after-dark rainbow.

Dig deep and dream big at ❹ **Crater of Diamonds** (p122) in Arkansas, and keep whatever sparkling gems you find.

Tuck into brunch while watching mermaids swim past at the extraordinary ❺ **Wreck Bar** (p234) in Fort Lauderdale.

Roadside America

You'll find plenty of ideas for an excursion to see oddball monuments and attractions on the Roadside America app. There's also ample (free) content on the website.

National vs State Parks

Federally recognized national parks get all the glory, attracting swarms of visitors, but lesser-known state parks can rival their beauty. Give these underdog destinations a try.

REGIONS & CITIES

Find the places that tick all your boxes.

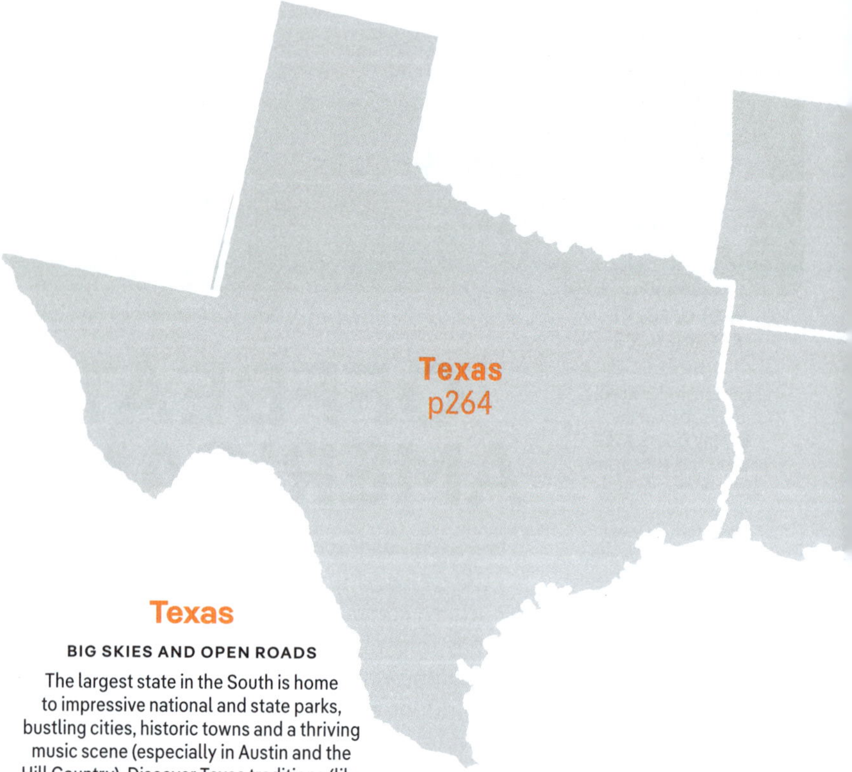

Texas
p264

Texas

BIG SKIES AND OPEN ROADS

The largest state in the South is home to impressive national and state parks, bustling cities, historic towns and a thriving music scene (especially in Austin and the Hill Country). Discover Texas traditions (like the longhorn cattle drive in Fort Worth), see the fabled missions of San Antonio and eat the world's best barbecue.

Deep South

BIRTHPLACE OF AMERICAN MUSIC AND CIVIL RIGHTS

The South's soulful rhythms echo from the jazz clubs of New Orleans up the Mississippi Delta to the juke joints of Clarksdale, and east to the buzzing heart of Atlanta. It's a land of aching history, with powerful sites dedicated to the fight for Civil Rights, and some of America's most captivating cities – including Savannah and Charleston.

Upper South

WIDE-RANGING ADVENTURES

Dramatic scenery and a heady cultural scene defines these six states, each bursting with personality. Fill your days with waterfall hikes in the Smokies, bourbon and horse-racing in Kentucky, white-water rafting on mountain rivers, and meandering road trips on the Blue Ridge Parkway and the Outer Banks. Come sundown, take in the region's country music, blues and bluegrass.

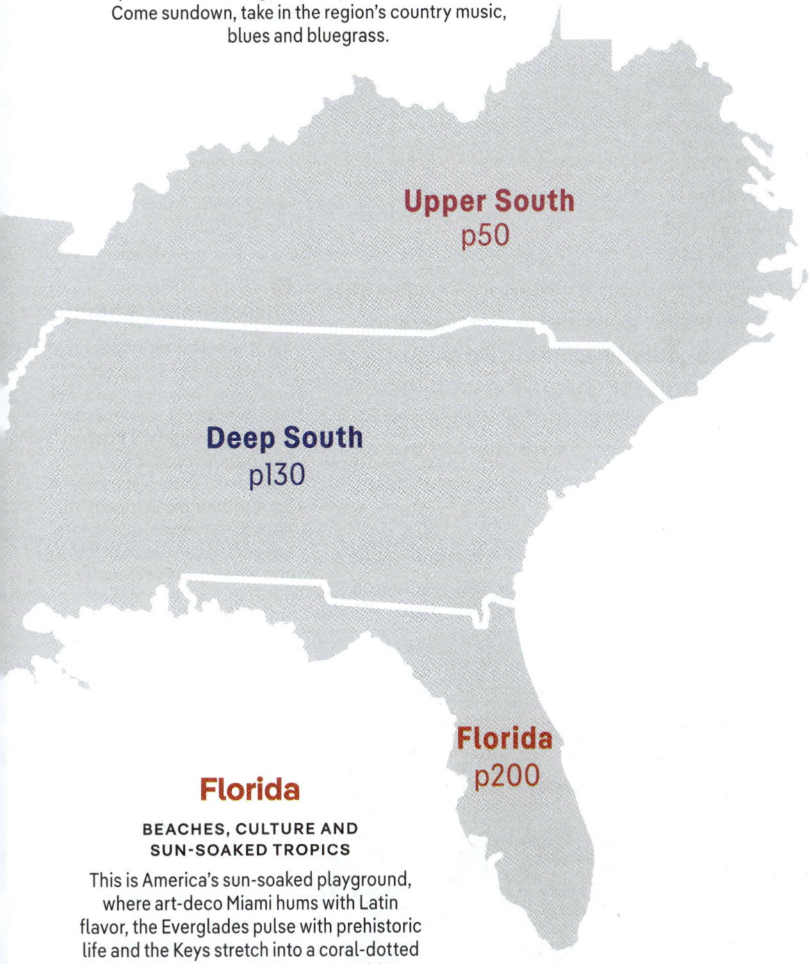

Florida

BEACHES, CULTURE AND SUN-SOAKED TROPICS

This is America's sun-soaked playground, where art-deco Miami hums with Latin flavor, the Everglades pulse with prehistoric life and the Keys stretch into a coral-dotted turquoise sea. Imaginations run wild in theme-park-happy Orlando, rockets launch along the Space Coast, and tales of Spanish colonists linger in towns lined with moss-laden live oaks.

ITINERARIES

The Southeast by Rail

Allow: 9 days

Distance: 1080 miles

Skip the hassle of driving and simply enjoy the view on this scenic train trip from Virginia to southern Florida. The South's oldest towns and neighborhoods beckon along the way, nestled among Spanish-moss-draped oak trees and beguiling architecture. There's ample amusement for visitors of all ages, including Orlando's renowned theme parks and the beaches of Fort Lauderdale and Miami.

Fort Sumter (p143)

1 RICHMOND 1 DAY

Virginia's capital has a trove of excellent museums, starting with the admission-free **Virginia Museum of Fine Arts** (p58). Afterward, check out the **American Civil War Museum** (p58), and explore the atmospheric **Shockoe Bottom neighborhood** (p58), ending with a meal at the **Tobacco Company** (p58).

Detour: *Continue by rail (a 90-minute trip aboard Amtrak's Northeast Regional) to Colonial Williamsburg (p60), for a time-warping wander through a town stuck in the 1700s.*

2 CHARLESTON 2 DAYS

Savor sweet tea on a side porch to settle into the slow pace of South Carolina's oldest city, and be sure to sample Lowcountry cooking – **Hannibal's Kitchen** (p140) is a great choice. Learn about Black history at the **International African American Museum** (p140), take a deep dive into Civil War history on a boat trip to **Fort Sumter** (p143) and get a glimpse of 19th-century finery at the **Aiken-Rhett House** (p140).

3 SAVANNAH 1 DAY

Georgia's oldest city drips Southern Gothic style, its moss-bedecked live oak trees lending each historic mansion a mysterious air. Get the lay of the land on a cinematic wander among **Savannah's Historic District** (p160), then tour one of the city's historic homes – like the haunting **Mercer-Williams House** (p160) or the **Owens-Thomas House & Slave Quarters** (p160). Afterward, head to the artfully designed **Plant Riverside District** (p160) for shopping and cocktails.

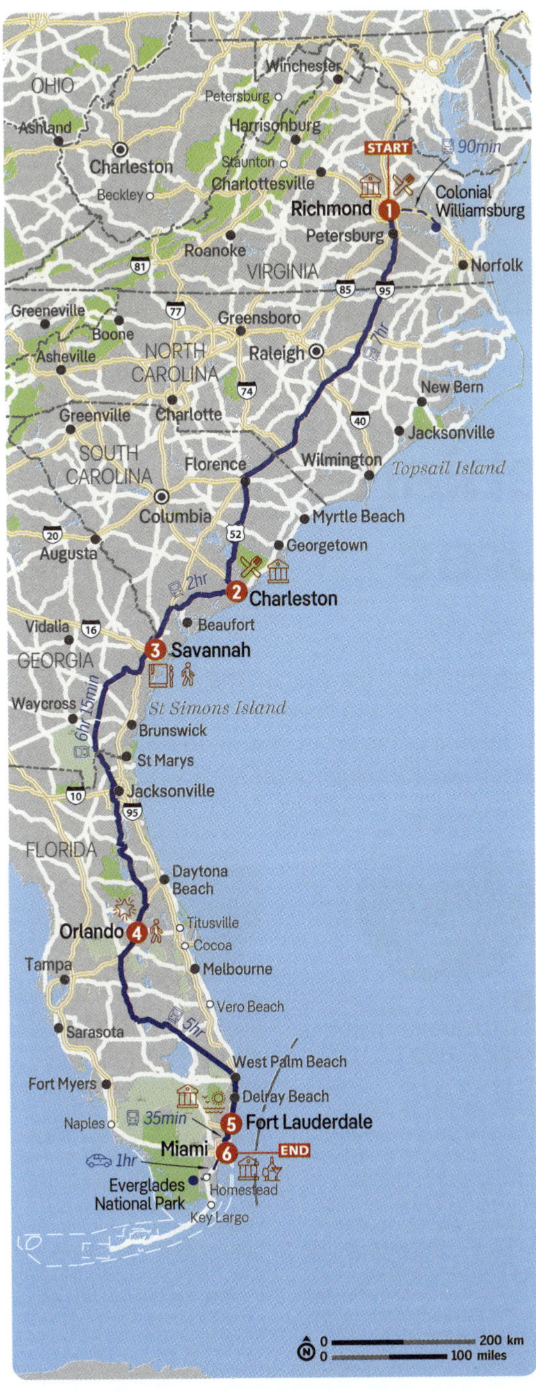

4

ORLANDO 2 DAYS

You could spend many days enjoying the attractions of **Disney World®** (p241), but be sure to prioritize blockbusters like Guardians of the Galaxy: Cosmic Rewind, Avatar: Flight of Passage and Star Wars: Rise of the Resistance. With more time, head to **Universal Orlando Resort** (p243), starting with Diagon Alley and the Wizarding World of Harry Potter. There's also the amazing **SeaWorld Orlando** (p244), which emphasizes education and conservation.

5

FORT LAUDERDALE 1 DAY

Stroll the promenade skirting **Fort Lauderdale Beach** (p230) amid bronzed beach bods, then spend some time breathing in the sub-tropical beauty of the **Bonnet House Museum & Gardens** (p233). In the afternoon, hop aboard the **Jungle Queen Riverboat** (p233) for a narrated cruise or get active and rent a kayak, SUP or bike for DIY adventures in **Hugh Taylor Birch State Park** (p232). Cap the day with an ocean-facing meal at **Takato** (p232).

6

MIAMI 2 DAYS

Take the Tri-Rail to Miami for several days of action-packed exploring. Admire art-deco architecture on a memorable stroll of **South Beach** (p206), go boating across **Biscayne Bay** (p211) and photograph Wynwood Walls' magnificent **outdoor murals** (p211). By night, have rooftop cocktails at **Sugar** (p211).

Detour: *Rent a car for a day to visit a wilderness of gators, birds and bromeliads at Everglades National Park (p218).*

Harpers Ferry (p76)

ITINERARIES

Appalachian Adventures

Allow: 8 days **Distance:** 720 miles

One of the oldest mountain chains on the planet, the Appalachians stretch across the eastern US. You could spend many days exploring this region with its trio of national parks offering rugged hiking trails and dramatic scenic drives, plus charming mountain towns.

1

HARPERS FERRY 1 DAY

Just two hours' drive from Washington, DC, the picturesque town of Harpers Ferry (p76) is a gateway into Appalachia. Take in the lay of the land on a morning hike up the **Maryland Heights Trail** (p76) for views over three states. In the afternoon, delve into America's tumultuous history preceding the Civil War at free National Park–run sites around town, including **John Brown's Fort** (p76).

2

SHENANDOAH NATIONAL PARK 1 DAY

Near the Virginia town of Front Royal, you'll reach the start of Skyline Drive, the roadway into the heart of Shenandoah National Park (p64). Take turnoffs to historic buildings, including the Massanutten Lodge. Or skip the scenic drive and focus on one of the park's most rewarding (and challenging) hikes: the climb to the top of **Old Rag Mountain** (p64).

3

BLUE RIDGE PARKWAY 1 DAY

Head to the town of Roanoke, a lively mountain town and handy access point for the Blue Ridge Parkway (p64) – among the most scenic roads in the Appalachian Mountains – and enjoy the views as you roll toward North Carolina. Before hopping on the road in Roanoke, head up to the Mill Mountain Star, a 90ft city icon that affords far-off views of mountain peaks.

FROM LEFT: KHAIRIL AZHAR JUNOS/SHUTTERSTOCK, OGPHOTO/GETTY IMAGES, JORDAN DELMONTE/SHUTTERSTOCK

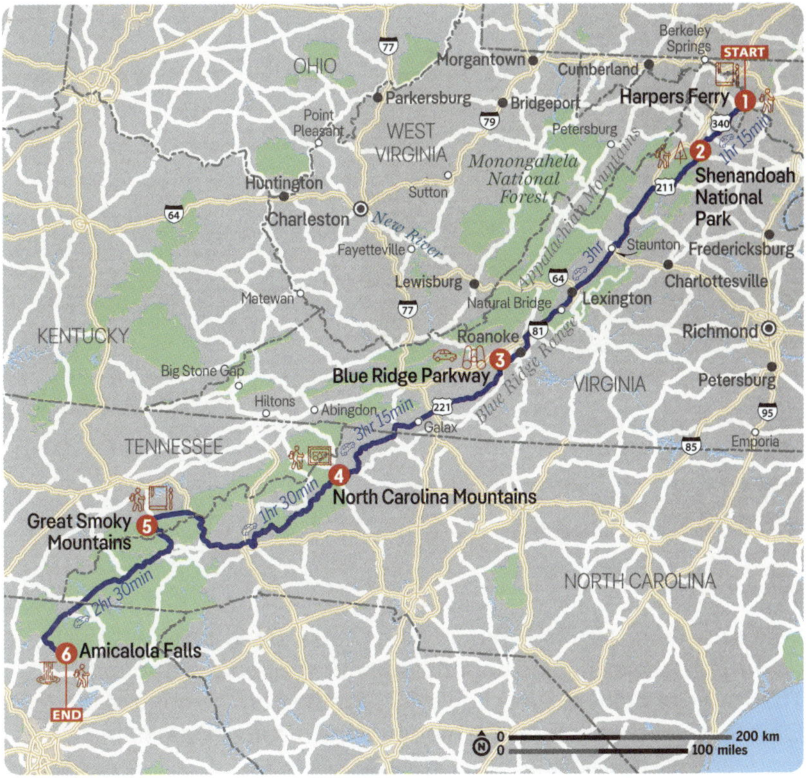

4 NORTH CAROLINA MOUNTAINS ⏱ 2 DAYS

Start off the North Carolina adventure in **Blowing Rock** (pictured; p91), a town of galleries and woodland walks. Continue to **Asheville** (p89) to explore the city's rich arts and crafts scene, and breweries. On your second day, visit the **Biltmore** (p90), America's grandest private estate, then continue to **Brevard** (p91) for more mountain craft culture and nature adventures.

5 GREAT SMOKY MOUNTAINS ⏱ 2 DAYS

Greet the day atop the observation deck on **Kuwohi** (pictured; p95), the highest point in the Smokies, then continue to the **Alum Cave Trail** (p94) for a rewarding hike. End the day with a drive along the **Roaring Fork Motor Nature Trail** (p96). On day two, visit the old farmsteads in **Cades Cove** (p96). If time allows, take in the Native American sights in **Cherokee** (p92).

6 AMICALOLA FALLS ⏱ 1 DAY

Northern Georgia has some impressive scenery, and it's well worth making the effort to see Amicalola Falls, the highest waterfall in the Southeast. Short trails lead to dramatic viewpoints of the cascade, though you can also opt for bigger hiking challenges – including the 8-mile approach to Springer Mountain, the southern terminus of the famous Appalachian Trail.

SIMPLY PHOTOS/SHUTTERSTOCK

Bourbon Street (p186), New Orleans

ITINERARIES

River City Rambles

Allow: 9 days **Distance**: 910 miles

Welcome to the heart and soul of the USA: a place of fabled music, down-home cooking and countless under-the-radar attractions. The journey begins in lively Louisville, perched on the edge of the Ohio River, and ends near the mouth of the mighty Mississippi in food- and festival-loving New Orleans.

1

LOUISVILLE 1 DAY

Start off by visiting the stellar **Muhammad Ali Center** (p112), which delves into the life of Louisville's most famous native son. Taste Kentucky's honey-colored liquor along **Whiskey Row** (p112) and see how the Louisville slugger gets made at its eponymous **museum and factory** (p112). The Kentucky Derby's horses run at **Churchill Downs** (pictured; p112) in May, but you can visit the connected museum year-round.

2

FRANKFORT 1 DAY

Immerse yourself in Kentucky's fascinating history in the charming small town and **state capital** (pictured; p114). See key episodes from the past at the excellent **Kentucky Historical Society** (p114) and the Capital City Museum, then stroll the brick lanes around town amid shops specializing in handicrafts, records, books and more.

***Detour:** Make the 1-hour drive southwest to Bardstown, for a half-day exploring the heart of bourbon country.*

3

NASHVILLE 2 DAYS

Wander through history at the interactive (and free) **Tennessee State Museum** (p103), then delve into Nashville's musical heritage at the **Country Music Hall of Fame & Museum** (pictured; p103). In the evening, follow the sound of twanging guitars to **Tootsie's Orchid Lounge** (p105). On day two, head to East Nashville for forest strolls in **Shelby Bottoms** (p106) and shopping in the **Fatherland District** (p106).

FROM LEFT: THOMAS KELLEY/SHUTTERSTOCK, ALEXEY STIOP/SHUTTERSTOCK, BRENDA KEAN/SHUTTERSTOCK

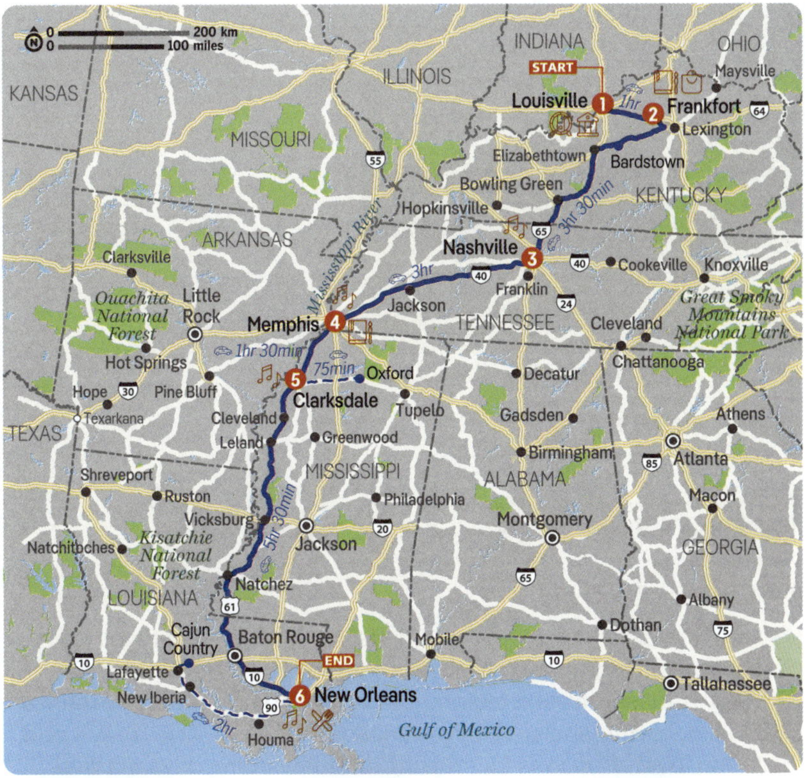

4 MEMPHIS ⏱ 2 DAYS

Dive into the city's legendary music sites, including **Sun Studio** (p99) and **Memphis Rock 'n' Soul Museum** (p99). That night, catch live music at **BB King's** (p101) on Beale St. On your second day, join Elvis fans at **Graceland** (p101), then immerse yourself in the past at the **National Civil Rights Museum** (p99). Later, take in the shops, cafes and bars of the creative **Cooper-Young district** (p101).

5 CLARKSDALE ⏱ 1 DAY

After crossing into Mississippi, learn about the famous innovators that changed musical history at the **Delta Blues Museum** (p175). Browse the selection of records and folk art at **Cat Head** (p176), then spend the night listening to live blues at clubs like **Red's** (pictured; p176) and **Ground Zero** (p176).

Detour: *Make the 75-minute drive east to Oxford to visit author William Faulkner's home and the leafy campus of Ole Miss.*

6 NEW ORLEANS ⏱ 2 DAYS

Spend your first day exploring the sights and sounds of the **French Quarter** (p184). In the evening, catch live jazz on **Frenchmen Street** (p189). On your second day, hop on the St Charles Avenue streetcar for a ride out to **Audubon Park** (p193). End the day over food and drinks in the backyard revelry of **Bacchanal** (pictured; p188).

Detour: *Visit Cajun Country (two hours west) for a Saturday morning dance party, followed by a swamp tour.*

DANIELLE BEDER/SHUTTERSTOCK, TLF IMAGES/SHUTTERSTOCK, WILLIAM A MORGAN/SHUTTERSTOCK

ALIZADA STUDIOS/SHUTTERSTOCK

Piedmont Park (p156), Atlanta

ITINERARIES

Crossing the South

Allow: 7 days **Distance**: 890 miles

Visit four states on this journey from Alabama's biggest city to North Carolina's enchanting barrier islands. Highlights include impressive Civil Rights museums and historic downtowns buzzing with life, plus a possible detour to ancient Native American mounds. At journey's end, you'll find lovely beaches for relaxing after rewarding days of travel.

1 BIRMINGHAM 1 DAY

Alabama's most dynamic city (p168) was the epicenter of the fight for Civil Rights in the 1960s. Learn about freedom fighters and harrowing tragedies in the **Civil Rights Institute** and **16th Street Baptist Church** (pictured). Watch the sunset from **Vulcan**, the city's famed hilltop statue, then catch a performance at the **Alabama Theatre** or live music at **Saturn**. End the night with drinks at the **House of Found Objects**.

2 MONTGOMERY 1 DAY

Get an early start visiting Montgomery's **Legacy Sites** (p170), which features memorials, sculptures and exhibition halls that take you through 400 years of Black history, from enslavement in Africa to racial injustice endured during the Jim Crow era, and up to the challenges of today. Add on a visit to Martin Luther King Jr sites, including the **Dexter Parsonage Museum** (p171), a time capsule from his years as a pastor.

3 ATLANTA 2 DAYS

Spend your first day exploring **downtown** (p151), including Centennial Park and the World of Coca Cola. On day two visit the **Martin Luther King Jr National Historical Park** (pictured; p153) to learn about the Civil Rights leader, and visit his boyhood home and the church where he was ordained a minister.

Detour: *Make the 90-minute drive southeast for a half-day exploring the Ocmulgee Mounds, a remarkable record of an ancient civilization in the South.*

FROM LEFT: PHILLIP FOSTER/SHUTTERSTOCK, JUSTIN SULLIVAN/GETTY IMAGES, MICHAEL GORDON/SHUTTERSTOCK

4 GREENVILLE 1 DAY

Stroll the streets and leafy parks in one of South Carolina's most charming little towns. Browse the shops, galleries and cafes, then rent a bike for a spin along the **Swamp Rabbit Trail** (pictured; p147). That night, have dinner and drinks at **Jianna** (p147) near Falls Park.

Detour: *Head two hours southeast to Congaree National Park for a boardwalk stroll or paddling trip through wildlife-rich wetlands.*

5 WILMINGTON 1 DAY

One day is plenty of time to fall in love with the dynamic and surprisingly diverse port city. Visit the **Battleship North Carolina** (pictured; p80), take a stroll through the splendid Airlie Gardens, then enjoy some downtime on the beach some 10 miles east of downtown. By evening, head back to the historic center for a sunset stroll along the RiverWalk and dinner of refined Southern fare at **Savorez** (p80).

6 OCRACOKE 1 DAY

After making the drive to Cedar Island, hop on the 2¼-hour ferry ride to Ocracoke (p83). Once there, ease into village life, visiting historic sites (including a museum and burial ground), as well as the Ocracoke Lighthouse and the pristine Springer's Point Preserve.

Detour: *Make the 70-minute ferry ride to Hatteras for more beach time and a look at the fascinating relics inside the Graveyard of the Atlantic Museum.*

PIETRO ANDREETTI/SHUTTERSTOCK, FRAME CRAFT 8/SHUTTERSTOCK, WILLIAM SILVER/SHUTTERSTOCK

TRAVELVIEW/SHUTTERSTOCK

Historic Market Square (p284), San Antonio

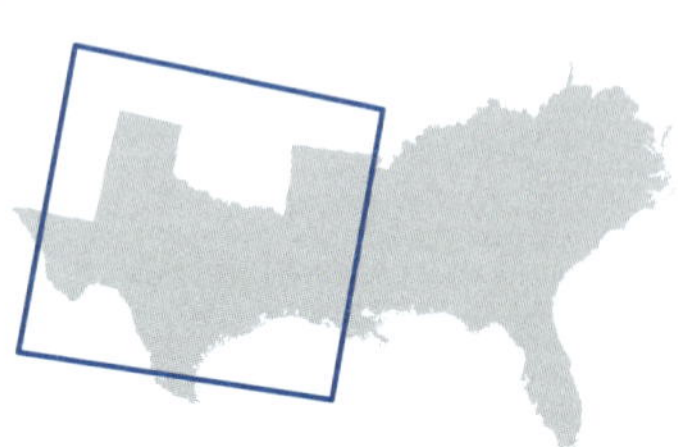

ITINERARIES

From the Mountains to the Desert

Allow: 10 days **Distance:** 1260 miles

The journey starts in an outdoors-loving town in the Ozarks, and ends in the high deserts of West Texas. Along the way, you'll see a mix of little-known historical treasures, Texan oddities and surprising natural wonders – including hot springs, ancient peaks and star-filled night skies.

1

BENTONVILLE 1 DAY

One of Arkansas' most captivating towns, Bentonville (p125) is famed for its art scene and its world-class mountain biking. Rent a bike and hit the trails of **Slaughter Pen** (pictured), then take in the latest exhibition at the forest-fringed **Crystal Bridges Museum**. Afterward, head to the Hub for craft beers and comfort fare.

Detour: *It's a one-hour drive to Eureka Springs, a charming town of architecture, galleries and hilltop vistas.*

2

LITTLE ROCK 1 DAY

Take a tour through the 1990s, and learn about one Arkansas boy's unlikely rise to high office at the **Clinton Presidential Center** (p117). Take a stroll along the nearby **riverfront** (p119), then learn about the brave students who helped end segregation at **Little Rock Central High School National Historic Site** (p122).

Detour: *Make the one-hour drive to Hot Springs National Park for a forest hike, followed by a soak.*

3

DALLAS & FORT WORTH 2 DAYS

Learn about Dallas' darkest day at the **Sixth Floor Museum** (p290), then have lunch at the **Farmers Market** (p291). Later, head over to **Bishop Arts District** (p292) for shopping and cafe-hopping. On day two, head to the **Fort Worth Stockyards** (p294) for the daily cattle drive, then go to the Cultural District to visit top-notch museums like **The Modern** (p294). After sundown, join boot-scootin' revelry at **Billy Bob's Texas** (pictured; p294).

FROM LEFT: TARA KENNY/SHUTTERSTOCK, E4 PLUS/SHUTTERSTOCK, ERIKA CRISTINA MANNO/SHUTTERSTOCK

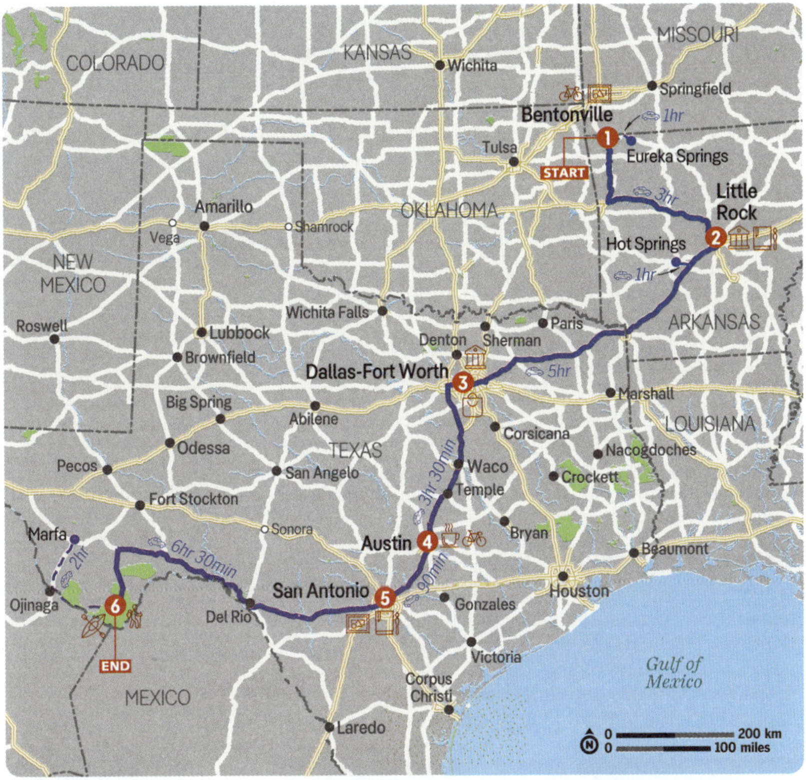

COLORADO
KANSAS
Wichita
MISSOURI
Springfield
Bentonville
1hr
Eureka Springs
Tulsa
START
3hr
Little Rock
OKLAHOMA
Amarillo
Vega
Shamrock
NEW MEXICO
Hot Springs
1hr
Wichita Falls
Paris
ARKANSAS
Roswell
Lubbock
Denton
Sherman
Brownfield
Dallas-Fort Worth
5hr
Big Spring
Abilene
Marshall
LOUISIANA
Corsicana
Odessa
TEXAS
Nacogdoches
Pecos
San Angelo
Waco
Crockett
3hr 30min
Temple
Fort Stockton
Bryan
Sonora
Marfa
Austin
Beaumont
2hr
6hr 30min
90min
San Antonio
Houston
Ojinaga
Gonzales
Del Rio
Victoria
END
Gulf of Mexico
MEXICO
Corpus Christi
Laredo
0 200 km
0 100 miles

4

AUSTIN 2 DAYS

Austin is Texas's capital of quirky cool. Dig into the neighborhoods that have shaped Austin's character. Linger over drinks and snacks at coffee shops and restaurants in **South Congress** (p271), walk or cycle the **Ann and Roy Butler Hike-and-Bike Trail** (p275) and beat the heat with a dip in **Barton Springs** (pictured; p275). Catch live music at the legendary **Continental Club** (p277) or at dance hall **Broken Spoke** (p277).

5

SAN ANTONIO 2 DAYS

Spend the first day exploring San Antonio's historic sites, including the **Alamo** (pictured; p280) and the **Mission Trail** (p285), a collection of 18th-century churches south of town. On day two, check out the Mexican crafts (and snacks) at **Historic Market Square** (p284), then take a stroll up the scenic Riverwalk, stopping to visit the collections at the **San Antonio Museum of Art** (p284), followed by dining and shopping at **The Pearl** (p284).

6

BIG BEND NATIONAL PARK 2 DAYS

Take a memorable hike in Big Bend (p308), a remote national park set amid mountains, desert and riverside. On day two, head off on a rafting or canoeing adventure along the **Rio Grande** (pictured), then rest your bones in **Boquillas Hot Springs** (p309).

Detour: *Make the two-hour drive northwest to Marfa for a dose of avant-garde art amid the cowboy country of West Texas.*

ALIZADA STUDIOS/SHUTTERSTOCK, 400TMAX/GETTY IMAGES, MARK TAYLOR CUNNINGHAM/SHUTTERSTOCK

WHEN TO GO

There's year-round appeal in the South: springtime blooms, autumn colors (Upper South), and beach fun in summer (the Carolinas) and winter (South Florida) alike.

The South is a multi-season showstopper. The warmer months are best for outdoor adventures, when beach towns boom with vacationers. In autumn (October to early November), fiery leaves light up the forests of the Upper South, particularly around the Great Smoky Mountains, the Blue Ridge Parkway and Shenandoah National Park. Winter, from December to March, can be a fine time to hit the beaches of southern Florida or South Padre Island, or catch one of the big festivals like Mardi Gras in New Orleans, Mobile or Galveston. Spring's April arrival is spectacular in the Upper South, where wildflower fields announce a new beginning.

Off-Season Deals

January through March is the cheapest time to book hotels in the Upper South, with many towns offering lower prices. The deals come with a catch: some rural businesses curtail hours or shut down for the winter. Prices drop around Florida and Gulf Coast states in August and September – the height of hurricane season.

I LIVE HERE

A COLD-WEATHER FEAST

Candi Vanardo is a sous-chef at Deelightful Roux School of Cooking in Central City, New Orleans. @deelightfulroux

In winter, it's time to gather with friends and family over a great meal. And in New Orleans that means gumbo – a rich stew of seafood, smoked sausage, hot sausage and filé (ground sassafras leaves). We don't cook gumbo in summer. As my grandmother would say, 'It'll spoil your stomach if you eat gumbo when it's hot.' So we look forward to those cold-weather days.

FROM LEFT: MICHAEL WARREN/GETTY IMAGES, ERIN WESTGATE/GETTY IMAGES

Great Smoky Mountains National Park (p93)

SPECTACULAR WILDFLOWERS

Home to more than 1500 types of flowering plant, the Great Smoky Mountains are a wildflower powerhouse, with more species than any other national park in the US. Thriving at elevations above 3500ft, the Catawba rhododendron blooms in June, flaming azaleas in early July.

Weather through the year in Atlanta

  JANUARY	FEBRUARY	 MARCH	 APRIL	 MAY	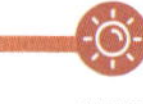 JUNE
Avg daytime max: 54°F	Avg daytime max: 58°F	Avg daytime max: 66°F	Avg daytime max: 74°F	Avg daytime max: 80°F	Avg daytime max: 86°F
Days of rainfall: 10	Days of rainfall: 8	Days of rainfall: 9	Days of rainfall: 9	Days of rainfall: 10	Days of rainfall: 12

HURRICANES

Every Gulf and Atlantic Coast resident in the South knows that June to November is hurricane season, though the worst storms tend to arrive in August or September. On average, each year sees about 18 hurricanes, with between two and six making landfall.

The South's Biggest Events

The mother of all street parties, **Mardi Gras** (p181) features several wild weekends of parades, costumes and merriment, plus other big celebrations on the weeks leading up to Shrove Tuesday. **February**

During the **Kentucky Derby Festival** (p112), five Kentucky 'princesses' preside over this two-week, party-packed, marathon-running, firework-exploding lead-up to America's longest continuously held sporting event where bold hats abound. **April–May**

Atlanta's native dogwood trees are celebrated at the **Atlanta Dogwood Festival**, first held in 1936. Today it's a full-on weekend of live music, arts and crafts, food and, of course, dogwoods. **April**

One of the biggest contemporary-art shows in North America, **Art Basel Miami Beach** showcases unique works from over 280 art galleries, representing some 40 different countries. **December**

Wacky & Wonderful Fests

A whimsical riposte to Houston's car-centric culture, the **Art Bike Parade** (p301) features beautifully tricked-out bicycles in an event celebrating creativity, sustainability and youth empowerment. **May**

At the **Chincoteague Pony Swim** 'saltwater cowboys' herd a horde of semi-feral swimming ponies into Virginia's Assateague Channel, then auction the foals on Chincoteague Island (p66). Onlookers coo over the cloppers' manes, bobbing above the water. **July**

After eating bowls of toot-inducing beans prepared in pots by local chefs, the **Bean Fest & Championship Outhouse Races** (p121) features a parade of outlandishly outfitted outhouses competing for the 'fastest privy' prize in the Ozarks. **October**

Practice saying 'Argh, matey!' for the four-day **Tybee Island Pirate Fest** (p162) in South Carolina, with a parade, costume contest, live music and lots of family-friendly programming. **October**

I LIVE HERE

SUMMER ESCAPES

Terry Ward is a Tampa-based travel writer. @terrywardwriter

Once the summer heat is firmly upon us, central Florida's incredible springs beckon me inland from the coast. The captivatingly turquoise waters stay a consistent 72°F (22°C) year-round. Spots like Itchetucknee Springs State Park are epic for tubing with friends. Ginnie Springs begs you to paddle a kayak between dips. And I love Rainbow Springs State Park for snorkeling through what I can only describe as a mermaid's dreamscape.

Ginnie Springs, Florida (p200)

SUNSHINE

Don't tell anyone, but Florida just barely scrapes into the top-10 list of America's sunniest states. Nevertheless, the Sunshine State averages over 230 days of clear skies each year. Fort Myers tops the charts with around 270 days of annual sunshine.

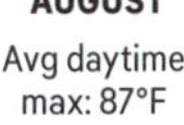
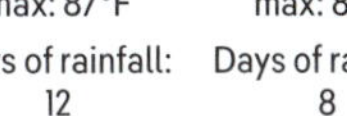

JULY	AUGUST	SEPTEMBER	OCTOBER	NOVEMBER	DECEMBER
Avg daytime max: 89°F	Avg daytime max: 87°F	Avg daytime max: 83°F	Avg daytime max: 72°F	Avg daytime max: 64°F	Avg daytime max: 55°F
Days of rainfall: 13	Days of rainfall: 12	Days of rainfall: 8	Days of rainfall: 6	Days of rainfall: 7	Days of rainfall: 9

FROM LEFT: GOODLUZ/SHUTTERSTOCK, BFA/WARNER BROS/ALAMY

Miami Beach (p206)

GET PREPARED FOR THE AMERICAN SOUTH

Useful things to load in your bag, your ears and your brain.

Clothes

Attire Outside the cities, shorts and T-shirts are fine for casual restaurants, cafes and bars. You'll want to dress things up a bit in the cities and at more formal restaurants and nightspots.

Footwear Sandals or flip-flops are great for the beach. Versatile walking shoes will serve you well on urban wanders, though you'll want decent hiking footwear if you're tackling tougher trails.

Rain Precipitation is a year-round possibility, so pack a lightweight rain jacket or an umbrella.

Cold weather November through March can bring chilly weather, so make sure you have a warm jacket, hat and gloves if visiting then. Snow is rare in the Deep South but not impossible (New Orleans received a record-breaking 12in snowfall in 2025).

Swimwear Pack swimming gear and a quick-drying towel for time on the beach or pool.

Manners

People often take the time to say hello in the South, and maybe have a chat. At the very least, it's polite to greet those you pass on the street and when entering a business (shop, restaurant, bar).

Things move a little slower down in the South, so don't lose your patience when things take longer than expected.

READ

Demon Copperhead (Barbara Kingsolver; 2022) Brilliant retelling of *David Copperfield*, set in an impoverished community in present-day Appalachia.

The 1619 Project (edited by Nikole Hannah-Jones; 2021) Groundbreaking collection that creates a powerful portrait of the Black experience in the US.

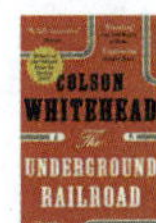

The Underground Railroad (Colson Whitehead; 2016) A Pulitzer Prize–winning masterpiece focused on enslavement in 1850s Georgia.

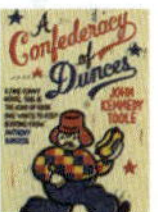

A Confederacy of Dunces (John Kennedy Toole; 1980) Quintessential and brilliantly funny New Orleans picaresque novel.

Words

For more insight into Southern speech, see p388.

About as useless as tits on a bull Something is worthless. Akin to 'ain't worth a hill of beans'.

Bless your heart Sometimes an expression of sympathy ('you poor thing'); other times a cutting insult ('you're a fool'). Context is key!

Britches Pants or trousers: 'They're getting too big for their britches' (undeservedly proud of themselves).

Dadgummit, Dagnabit Polite ways to curse.

Diddly squat Nothing. 'I ain't got diddly squat.' (I'm broke).

Don't poke the bear Don't provoke someone who's quick to anger.

Fixin' to Getting ready to do something.

Gussied up Dressed up as if for a special occasion.

Hankering A craving for something.

Hey Casual version of hello; often precedes 'y'all'.

Highfalutin' Fancy in a pretentious way.

I reckon I suppose.

Might could It's a possibility, but there's no commitment. 'We might could do that.'

Month of Sundays Long, boring, tedious. 'Visiting with them is like a month of Sundays.'

Moonshine Un-aged corn whiskey. Also called hooch, white lightning, corn liquor, rotgut and mountain dew.

Ruckus A big commotion.

Skedaddle To leave a place.

That dog won't hunt That idea or excuse won't work.

This ain't my first rodeo To have past experience with something.

Y'all Contraction of 'you all' – used when addressing a small group.

Yonder Over there in a direction indicated.

WATCH

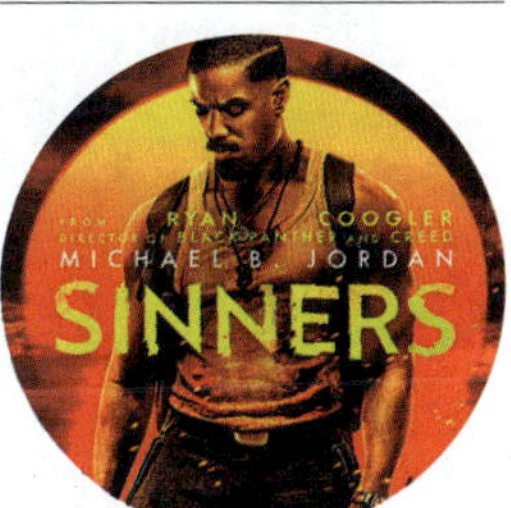

Sinners (Ryan Coogler; 2025) Thought-provoking, genre-bending film of blues, historical drama and vampires set in 1930s Mississippi.

Moonlight (Barry Jenkins; 2016) Poignant Oscar-winning coming-of-age tale set in a housing project in Miami.

Boyhood (Richard Linklater; 2014) A poignant drama shot over the course of 12 years around Texas.

12 Years a Slave (Steve McQueen; 2013) The most accurate and compelling cinematic portrayal of slavery in the American South.

Cold Mountain (Anthony Minghella; 2003) Civil War–era love story set in the North Carolina Mountains.

LISTEN

The New Orleans Collection (Jon Batiste; 2025) Acclaimed artist that channels feel-good vibes through soul, funk, gospel and brass.

Cowboy Carter (Beyoncé; 2024) Pioneering album of country music and Americana that celebrates lesser-known Black artists of the past.

662 (Christone 'Kingfish' Ingram; 2021) The musical ambassador from Clarksdale, Mississippi, represents the new generation of rising blues stars.

Rejuvenation (The Meters; 1974) A masterpiece – maybe the masterpiece – of 1970s funk led by legendary frontman Art Neville.

DENNIS W DONOHUE/SHUTTERSTOCK

Alligator, Everglades National Park (p218)

TRIP PLANNER

NATIONAL PARKS

The American South is home to 11 national parks, plus another 100-odd sites that are part of the national-park system. No trip would be complete without a visit to at least one of these remarkable natural treasures, offering the chance to hike, raft, drive or camp amid unspoiled wilderness.

FANTASTIC FLORA & FAUNA

Travel from craggy ridgetops to coastal swamps to experience the breadth of Southern biodiversity. Over 19,000 plant and animal species reside within the **Great Smoky Mountains** (p93) – more than any other US national park. Visit in spring when wildflowers paint green hillsides with pastel blooms. Bring binoculars to Florida's **Everglades** (p218), where alligators and manatees swim among mangrove waterways and myriad birds flit through the trees. At **Congaree** (p148) in South Carolina, synchronous fireflies light up forests around May, and the floodplain teems with turtles and river otters year-round.

GEOLOGICAL WONDERS

Misty mountains, parched deserts and underground cathedrals: the American South showcases millions of years worth of nature's handiwork. **Big Bend** (p306) is home to the only mountain range (the Chisos) entirely contained within one national park. **Shenandoah's** (p64) 105-mile Skyline Drive traces the Blue Ridge Mountains, where boulder-strewn hikes lead to panoramas of Virginia's rolling hills. Beneath Kentucky's forest floor, **Mammoth Cave** (p115) stretches over 400 miles – the world's longest cave system, featuring the stunning stalactites of Frozen Niagara.

PARKS APPS & PODCASTS

National Park Service *(nps.gov)* The NPS app features maps, self-guided tours, accessibility information and updates on park conditions.

AllTrails *(alltrails.com)* Lists of trails with user reviews, current conditions and real-time tracking while hiking. It's worth paying for AllTrails+ to download maps offline and get wrong-turn alerts.

Recreation.gov Reserve campsites, permits and day-use passes for national parks and other federal areas.

GuideAlong *(guidealong.com)* Self-guided audio tours – ideal for road-tripping through the Smokies and Shenandoah.

National Park After Dark *(npadpodcast.com)* Two friends investigate the dark underbelly of America's natural treasures, with fascinating histories, tragic events and firsthand anecdotes.

ADVENTURES ON THE WATER

Dive into parks where water plays a starring role. At West Virginia's **New River Gorge** (p72), rafting season begins around April, but daredevils don't arrive until September, ready to take on Class V rapids along the Gauley River. **Biscayne** (p222), near Miami, trades roads for reefs – 95% of the park is underwater, tempting snorkelers to take a plunge. Florida's remote **Dry Tortugas** (p224) lies 70 miles off Key West's coast, where day-trippers snorkel among coral and overnight campers get beaches to themselves.

RANGER PROGRAMS

Many national parks offer free activities led by park rangers. This might entail anything from stargazing out in Big Bend to taking a slough slog (walking through a swamp) in the Everglades. There are often talks about history, wildlife and archaeology, with daily offerings during the summer. Check out what's on offer before you head to a park (look up 'Things to Do' under the 'Plan Your Visit' tab on each park's website).

WISANU BOONRAWD / SHUTTERSTOCK

Stargazing, Big Bend National Park (p307)

KNOW BEFORE YOU GO

Fees & Reservations

Entrance fees vary from free (Hot Springs) to $35 per vehicle (Everglades). If you want to visit multiple parks and other federal recreational lands within 12 months, consider purchasing the America the Beautiful pass *($80; store.usgs.gov/pass)*, which provides access for four adults and all children under 16 at over 2000 federal recreation areas across the US.

Permits

Permits are required for overnight backpacking trips (or canoeing in the case of the Everglades). Generally, you don't need a permit to day hike in a national park. One exception is the popular day hike Old Rag Mountain in Shenandoah. Apply well in advance through recreation.gov.

Safety Tips

Consult a park ranger before tackling long trails. Always leave details of your route and expected return time with a responsible party. It's not wise to hike alone. Day hikers: allow ample time to complete a trail before nightfall.

Lodging

Some national parks have historic lodges, often located mere steps from iconic landscapes and major trailheads. There's even a place in the Smokies (LeConte Lodge, p95) reachable only by hiking up the mountain. Plan well ahead as all park lodging fills quickly.

Camping

The national parks are dream destinations for campers. Reserve nine to 12 months ahead of your trip, particularly for sites in the national parks themselves. Use recreation.gov.

RICKBERK/GETTY IMAGES

Newfound Gap Road, Great Smoky Mountains National Park (p93)

TRIP PLANNER

ROAD TRIPS

Motor past sun-baked fields, cross island bridges and wind along lofty ridge lines on a cinematic road trip through the South. Scenic byways and linear parks stitch the region together, creating a grand collage of tiny towns, historic sites and dazzling coastline. Whether you've got a day or a week, there's a route here worth roaming.

TAKE THE HIGH ROAD

The **Blue Ridge Parkway** (p64) ditches highway billboards for natural beauty while snaking from Virginia's Shenandoah National Park to North Carolina's Smokies. The speed limit never tops 45mph, giving drivers time to contemplate roadside vistas while cruising to towns like crafty Asheville, NC. Blast bluegrass tunes, stretch your legs on mountain trails and fuel up at folksy log diners for a taste of Southern hospitality. Once you reach the Smokies, turn onto Newfound Gap Road (northbound) for yet more stellar scenery amid the wonders of this vast national park.

THE BLUES HIGHWAY

Highway 61 follows the bends and twists of the Mississippi River for much of its journey from New Orleans to Minnesota. In the South it's known as the **Blues Highway** (p175), as it takes you through the heart of the Mississippi Delta, passing towns where some of the first great American music was born. You can stop at the Crossroads and contemplate the legend of Robert Johnson (who allegedly met the devil on this intersection), explore historic towns like Vicksburg, and ultimately make your way to music-loving cities like Clarksdale and Memphis, where live music is still a vital part of the culture.

ROAD TRIP CHECKLIST

Join an automobile club Organizations like AAA provide 24-hour emergency roadside assistance and discounts on lodging and attractions. Some international automobile associations have reciprocal agreements with US clubs: check if you can bring a member card from home.

Pack repair tools Make sure your vehicle has a spare tire, a tool kit (eg jack, jumper cables, ice scraper, tire pressure gauge) and emergency equipment (eg flashers).

Bring maps Don't rely solely on GPS – service is patchy in remote areas. A good map comes in handy when cell service fails.

Carry your driver's license and proof of insurance Never get behind the wheel without them.

SOUTHERN HISTORY

The **Natchez Trace Parkway** (p180) drifts from just outside of country-loving Nashville to the outskirts of lovely riverside Natchez. The journey along a serene two-lane road follows an ancient Indigenous route through Tennessee, Alabama and Mississippi. The roadway is a visual text-book of Southern heritage, passing sacred ceremonial mounds, Civil War battlefields, old homesteads and the watery wilderness of Cypress Swamp.

THE OVERSEAS HIGHWAY

Curving beneath southern Florida are the Florida Keys: a 106-mile-long archipelago of mangrove and sandbar islands, teal waters and magnificent sunsets. A memorable journey down the **Overseas Highway** (p227) takes you from the bustle of Key Largo to Key West, passing arts-loving villages, old-fashioned roadside eateries and stretches of verdant hardwood forest, crossing some 42 bridges along the way (including one that stretches 7 miles across open waters).

Overseas Highway (p227)

MIA2YOU/SHUTTERSTOCK

PLAN YOUR TIME

Blue Ridge Parkway
Visit between April and October, when most park facilities remain open. October is prime for peeping fall foliage (start early in the day to beat the heavy crowds); May brings bursts of wildflowers. Start: Front Royal, VA; End: Cherokee, NC. Distance: 469 miles. Budget a minimum of two days – though you may need four or five if you plan to do a lot of hiking and to explore towns just off the parkway.

Blues Highway
Take the trip any time. Spring and autumn are best, as summer can be awfully hot. Start: New Orleans; End: Memphis. Distance: around 470 miles. Budget two days for a quick tour – or take five days in order to enjoy nights of live music at key places along the way.

Natchez Trace Parkway
Spring and autumn are lovely. Summer is hot and winter can be chilly, but don't let the weather stop you. Start Nashville; End: Natchez, MS. Distance: 444 miles. Budget two to three days.

Overseas Highway
There's no bad time to make this trip, though be aware of sky-high prices from December through February, and pay close attention to weather forecasts if traveling during hurricane season (June to November). Start: Key Largo; End: Key West. Distance: 106 miles. Budget one day for a quick trip, or three days to see the sights.

BONCHAN/SHUTTERSTOCK

Shrimp and grits

THE FOOD SCENE

Stellar ingredients, culinary creativity and global flavors: wherever you roam, you're never far from a memorable meal in the South.

In a region of over 120 million residents, with immigrants hailing from every corner of the globe, the American South offers incredible diversity when it comes to cooking. Big cities are no longer the sole providers of great ethnic cooking, and you can find thoughtfully prepared Mexican, Thai and Indian dishes, among other fare, at small towns all across the region.

The South is also a land of plenty with richly productive farmland, vineyards and abundant coastlines. Every state offers unique cuisine, and its locals will proudly tell you the best places to go to find those unmatched specialties. While there are plenty of award-winning dining rooms, the South also has humbler but no less memorable spots where recipes have been passed down through the generations to sublime effect in traditional dishes featuring locally sourced ingredients. Indeed, one of the great rewards is seeking out these authentic, traditional spots which shine a light on unique recipes you simply won't find anywhere else.

Lowcountry Cooking

Along the South Carolina and Georgia coast, Lowcountry dishes are prevalent. A historically significant West African–influenced cuisine spawned from coastal estuaries thick with shrimp, crab and oysters, Lowcountry fare can be enjoyed everywhere from a weathered seafood shack overlooking a coastal marsh to a white-linen, reservations-required hot spot in

Best Southern Dishes

SHRIMP & GRITS
Locally caught shrimp mixed with hot, creamy stoneground grits.

GUMBO
Roux-based stew of chicken and shellfish, or sausage and often okra.

BRISKET
Beef cut seasoned and cooked for eight hours or more.

BRUNSWICK STEW
Tomato-based stew with lima beans, okra, corn and chicken.

Charleston or St Simons Island, where the chef is king. Shrimp and grits is a culinary mainstay.

While there are lots of takes on seasoning, the quintessential preparation features sautéed wild-caught local shrimp atop a bed of creamy stoneground grits. The beloved, rib-sticking staple can be enjoyed for any meal, though it was traditionally taken by coastal fishers at breakfast to fuel pursuit of the day's catch.

Soul Food & the African American Diaspora

When it comes to perceptions of cuisine from this part of the country, the distinction between what's known as 'Southern' food and 'soul' food can be blurry. While all soul food is Southern food, not all Southern food is soul food – the roots of the latter stem from what was developed by enslaved Africans in the Southeastern US as they made do with whatever was available to them. As their descendants migrated north and west after the Civil War and emancipation, they carried the recipes of their forebears with them.

The diaspora brought about what is known today as soul food, a true American immigrant cuisine – in Black communities outside the South it's a celebration of downhome, rural roots, with traditional dishes being served usually only at special occasions. Typical ones include fried chicken and fish, ham hocks, oxtail, chitlins, hush puppies (cornmeal fritters) and greens (collard, mustard or turnip).

Hush puppies

State Fair of Texas

FROM LEFT: BRENT HOFACKER/SHUTTERSTOCK, RAKSYBH/SHUTTERSTOCK

FOOD & DRINK-CENTRIC FESTIVALS

Jazz Fest (p181; nojazzfest.com; late April–early May) Locals will tell you: food plays a starring role in the celebrated music fest held in New Orleans.

Original Gullah Festival (p146; originalgullahfestival.org; May) Learn about traditional Gullah culture, while indulging in hearty Lowcountry cooking.

State Fair of Texas (p294; bigtex.com; late Sep–late Oct) Spend the day sampling classic and avant-garde snacks, from perfectly battered corny dogs to the deliciously mystifying cotton candy bacon on a stick.

Kentucky Bourbon Festival (p113; kybourbonfestival.com; Sep) Immerse yourself in Kentucky's best-loved spirit at this three-day gathering featuring over 60 different distilleries.

Atlanta Dogwood Festival (dogwood.org; Apr) Amid the springtime blooms in Piedmont Park, you can enjoy some of Atlanta's best food trucks while catching live music and browsing craft stalls.

COLLARD GREENS
Leaves of a dark-green vegetable eaten as a side dish.

FRIED GREEN TOMATOES
Unripe tomatoes covered in cornmeal and fried.

BISCUITS AND GRAVY
Buttermilk biscuits smothered in creamy sausage-flecked gravy.

PECAN PIE
Sugar, butter, eggs, vanilla extract, karo syrup and pecans.

HOT CHICKEN
Nashville's fried chicken: coated in a cayenne pepper sauce.

Gumbo

New Orleans Gumbo

The Crescent City has always been famous for its cuisine, which feature influences from Africa, the Caribbean and the American South – not to mention its longtime French connection and waves of immigrants from Vietnam to Honduras. There are lots of New Orleanian classics, but its most famous dish is gumbo, a spicy, full-bodied soup or stew. Ingredients vary from chef to chef, but gumbo is almost always served over starchy steamed rice. Coastal gumbo teems with oysters, jumbo shrimp and crabs, while prairie-bred Cajuns turn to their barnyards and smokehouses.

Texas Barbecue

Make no bones about it – Texas barbecue is an obsession. The best often comes from famous family dynasties that have been dishing up the same crowd-pleasing recipes for generations. Telltale signs that you've located an authentic barbecue joint include zero decor, smoke-blackened ceilings and laid-back table manners (silverware optional). At most places, you can order a combination plate or ask for specific meats to be sliced by the pound right in front of you.

Floribbean Cuisine

'Floribbean' cooking refers to Florida's tantalizing gourmet mélange of just-caught seafood, tropical fruits and eye-watering peppers, all dressed up with some combination of Nicaraguan, Salvadoran, Caribbean, Haitian, Cajun, Cuban and even Southern influences. Some call it 'fusion', 'Nuevo Latino', 'New World', 'nouvelle Floridian' or 'palm-tree cuisine', and it can refer to anything from a ceviche of lime, conch, sweet peppers and Scotch bonnets to grilled grouper with mango, adobo and fried plantains.

Dessert Time

There's hardly anything more Southern than pecan pie, and if you haven't had Georgia's famous pecan pie with sugar, butter, eggs, vanilla extract and karo syrup, you haven't lived. And don't forget the peaches. They're most famously associated with Georgia, but South Carolina actually grows more of them. Peach pie or cobbler is a can't-miss ending to a Southern meal. Other Southern staples you'll see on dessert menus include chess pie (flour or cornmeal, butter, sugar and eggs with flavorings such as vanilla, chocolate, lemon and buttermilk) and sweet-potato pie (mashed sweet potatoes with nutmeg and cinnamon along with sugar, eggs, milk and butter).

FINGER FOODS

In the American South some of the best meals require no silverware – just a big stack of napkins for mopping yourself up after the messy business of eating – quasi-barbaric table manners be damned! This might mean slapping on a bib at a crab restaurant along the Virginia coast, working your way through a small mountain of smoked barbecue ribs in Memphis, or biting into a massive Cuban sandwich while watching the world stroll past at an eatery in Miami. Of course there's so much more. Indeed, you could eat your way all across these 13 states without resorting once to those cumbersome table tools. There are donuts and croissants, cheeseburgers and French fries, freshly shucked oysters and peel-and-eat shrimp, plus tacos, burritos, po'boys (Louisiana sandwiches), fried chicken and ice-cream cones – not to mention all that delectable fresh fruit, from juicy strawberries to Georgia peaches – best conveyed to mouth by hand alone.

TOP: JOTAI/SHUTTERSTOCK, RFONDREN PHOTOGRAPHY/SHUTTERSTOCK;
FROM LEFT: BRENT HOFACKER/SHUTTERSTOCK, J.DII/SHUTTERSTOCK, BRENT HOFACKER/SHUTTERSTOCK, JOSHUA RESNICK/SHUTTERSTOCK

Specialities

Seafood

Oysters There are hundreds of varieties of these cherished bivalves. Some of the best come from Dauphin Island (Alabama), Cedar Key (Florida), Sapelo Island (Georgia), Grand Isle (Louisiana), Harkers Island (North Carolina), Beaufort (South Carolina), Anahuac (Texas) and Chincoteague Island (Virginia).

Blue crabs Crack into these crustaceans and get wrist deep in messy innards as you pick for bits of sweet meat. Some seafood markets sell 'em by the dozen and will steam them for you on the spot.

Grouper The mild, slightly sweet flavor of this fish makes for delicious blackened grouper sandwiches in Florida.

Peel-and-eat shrimp Old-school Florida treat, served boiled and pink in their shells; there's always cocktail sauce.

Conch fritters Popular in the Keys, this giant sea snail is battered and fried; a great late-afternoon snack.

Barbecue Styles

Texas Beef, especially brisket, slow-cooked over oak (and sometimes mesquite for added flavor).

Key lime pie

Memphis Known for its dry-rubs, though sauces are also used.

Carolina The love for pork shows no bounds; vinegar-based sauces are common.

Sweet Treats

Pecan pie Buttery nuts layered atop a caramel-like custard filling.

Peach cobbler A deep-dish dessert with a thick crust and peach filling; best served warm with a scoop of vanilla ice cream.

Key lime pie Boasts a creamy, tangy filling made with Key lime juice; best topped with a big meringue.

MEALS OF A LIFETIME

Grey (p160) An award-winning chef elevates family recipes in a former Greyhound bus station in Savannah.

Franklin Barbecue (p278) Bite into some of the world's best brisket at this legendary Austin spot.

Paradise Grille (p261) Dig your heels in the sand while munching a grouper sandwich and watching a Florida sunset.

Leon's Oyster Shop (p140) A former Charleston auto shop turning out delicious plates of oysters and perfectly cooked fried chicken, best enjoyed with rosé on tap.

Buck & Johnny's (p196) Tuck into eggs and boudin (spicy sausage), then join revelers on the dance floor at the famous zydeco breakfast in Louisiana's Cajun Country.

THE YEAR IN FOOD

SPRING

Foragers head into the woods in search of tasty, tender fiddleheads and ramps (a kind of wild leek). In many places the first local farmers markets begin (though in warmer parts there are year-round markets). (April–May)

SUMMER

Farmers' markets fill with a bounty of fresh fruits and vegetables, and this is the prime season for food festivals. It's a popular time for heading to the coast for feasting on lobsters, clams and other delectable seafood. (June–August)

AUTUMN

These are months of abundant autumn harvests (apples, squash, pumpkins, sweet potatoes) – a prelude to the biggest feast of the year during Thanksgiving (turkeys, cranberries, pumpkin pie). (September–November)

WINTER

In the region's north the punishing winter doesn't bring an end to culinary riches since farming innovations allow for winter growing (cold-hardy fresh greens). Make the most of long nights with hearty feasts. (December–March)

FROM LEFT: JOEL CARILLET/GETTY IMAGES, ONLYBOUNDARIES/SHUTTERSTOCK

Appalachian Trail, Tennessee

THE OUTDOORS

Flower-draped mountain meadows, wildlife-rich wetlands and golden beaches fronting shimmering seas: the American South has no shortage of spectacular settings for a bit of adventure.

Nearly 3000 miles of coastline stretch along the Atlantic and Gulf coasts from Virginia south to Florida and across to Texas. The Appalachian Mountains ripple across five Southern states, with other ancient mountain ranges crossing Arkansas and the western reaches of Texas. Churning rivers, crystal-clear streams and island-dotted bays create an aquatic landscape ideal for exploring by raft, canoe or kayak. When it comes to hiking, mountain biking or water sports, you'll find world-class places to commune with nature all across the American South.

Walking & Hiking

Outdoors-loving Southerners take great pride in their formidable network of trails – over 15,000 miles at last count – and there's no better way to experience the countryside than up close and at your own pace. A focal point is the Appalachian Mountains, protected by numerous state parks, forests and even three national parks. This is home to the legendary Appalachian Trail (AT), where you can hike anything from a short section to over 1000 miles.

West Texas has the only mountain-desert habitats in the South. Find hundreds of miles of epic trails in Texas' two national parks, Big Bend and Guadalupe Mountains. In the Panhandle, Palo Duro is the second-largest canyon in the country after the Grand Canyon, and offers a good range of scenic hikes.

Alternative Activities

SCUBA DIVING
Flip your fins to see coral reefs and a shipwreck, waiting underwater at **Biscayne National Park** (p222).

SANDBOARDING
Rent a board and glide your way down the dunes of **Jockey's Ridge State Park** (p84).

BIRDING
Spot species you've never seen before in the birding paradise of **Aransas National Wildlife Refuge** (p305).

FAMILY ADVENTURES

Watch marine life glide under the boat or take a closer look while snorkeling in **John Pennekamp Coral Reef State Park** (p224).

Look for alligators and turtles on a guided boat ride through **Okefenokee Swamp** (p159).

Make a family trip to **Big Bend** (p306), with river rafting, nightly stargazing and rewarding hikes (including short ones to hot springs).

Turn on your headlamp to tour the subterranean karst wonderland of **Mammoth Cave** (p115).

Climb up into the saddle for a ride through forests with **Smokemont Riding Stables** (p94) in the Great Smoky Mountains.

Rent mountain bikes (kids' bikes available) and hit the green (easy) trails around **Bentonville** (p125).

Cycling & Mountain Biking

Cycling's popularity increases by the day, with numerous cities (including Atlanta, with its leafy, ever-growing Beltline) adding cycle lanes each year and becoming more bike-friendly. Smaller places are catching on, too, like South Carolina's Greenville, home to the picturesque (and delightfully named) Swamp Rabbit Trail.

Mountain bikers have some excellent options, especially in the Bentonville area of Arkansas, which is the most extensive network (and home to the most avid and supportive riders) east of the Rockies. Western North Carolina is another big draw, with numerous good trails in Dupont State Forest near Brevard.

Everglades National Park (p218)

Aquatic Activities

Florida's seascape is synonymous with aquatic adventure. The state's coast also holds the largest coral reef system in the continental US – most magical around John Pennekamp Coral Reef State Park, a diver's delight.

For canoeing and kayaking, the Everglades is a prime spot, for both short and multiday adventures. You can also kayak or canoe through a swamp in Congaree or float through marshes and along estuaries on barrier islands in South Carolina and Georgia.

West Virginia has an arsenal of legendary white water. First, there's the New River Gorge National River, where you paddle through a deep gorge sometimes dubbed the Grand Canyon of the East. There's also the Gauley, which is revered for its ultrasteep and turbulent chutes. Six more rivers, all in the same neighborhood, offer training grounds for less-experienced river rats. North Carolina has two choice places for paddlers: the US National Whitewater Center outside Charlotte, and the Nantahala Outdoor Center near the Smokies.

In Texas, tubing is a great way to beat the heat. Floating along sparkling rivers is a must when visiting Hill Country towns like New Braunfels in the summer. There's also excellent rafting in Big Bend National Park: rapids up to Class IV alternate with calm stretches on the Rio Grande.

STARGAZING
Peer deep into outer space at the **McDonald Observatory** (p307), home to some of America's clearest night skies.

ZIPLINING
Enjoy the view while soaring through the treetops of eastern Tennessee at **High Point Zip Adventure** (p108).

CAVE KAYAKING
Paddle through a flooded limestone mine beneath prime Kentucky wilderness with **Gorge Underground** (p116).

SKIING
Explore the varied terrain on 60 different runs at West Virginia's **Snowshoe Mountain Resort** (p77).

ACTION AREAS

Where to find the American South's best outdoor activities.

Walking/Hiking

1. Old Rag Mountain (p64)
2. Harpers Ferry (p76)
3. Nags Head Woods Preserve (p84)
4. Red River Gorge (p116)
5. Alum Cave Trail (p94)
6. Rainbow Lake Wilderness Area (p108)
7. Palo Duro Canyon State Park (p311)

Swimming/Pools

1. Cumberland Island (p163)
2. Cape Hatteras National Seashore (p82)
3. John Pennekamp Coral Reef State Park (p224)
4. Dry Tortugas National Park (p224)
5. Barton Springs Pool (p273)
6. Folly Beach (p144)
7. South Beach (p206)

Cycling

1. Ann and Roy Butler Hike-and-Bike Trail (p275)
2. Swamp Rabbit Trail (p147)
3. Jekyll Island (p163)
4. DuPont State Forest (p91)
5. Slaughter Pen (p125)
6. Cades Cove Loop (p96)
7. Mon River Trail (p76)

National Parks
1 Great Smoky Mountains (p93)
2 Everglades (p218)
3 Congaree (p148)
4 Shenandoah (p64)
5 New River Gorge (p72)
6 Big Bend (p306)
7 Mammoth Cave (p115)
Kayaking/Canoeing
1 Rachel Carson National Wildlife Refuge (p80)
2 Biscayne National Park (p222)
3 Congaree National Park (p148)
4 New River Gorge National Park (p72)
5 Everglades (p218)
6 Buffalo National River (p126)
7 Nantahala River (p92)
Concord
Boston
VT
Albany
NEW YORK
MA
CT
RI
New York City
Lansing
Detroit
Lake Erie
Cleveland
Philadelphia
OHIO
Columbus
Morgantown
Brunswick
MD
DE
WASHINGTON, DC
Indianapolis
Cincinnati
WEST VIRGINIA
Charlottesville
INDIANA
Charleston
Richmond
Williamsburg
Louisville
Frankfort
Beckley
Lynchburg
VIRGINIA
Norfolk
KENTUCKY
Roanoke
Murfreesboro
Williamsburg
Johnson City
Raleigh
Thomasville
Selma
Knoxville
Hot Springs
NORTH CAROLINA
TENNESSEE
Nashville
Asheville
Charlotte
Rock Hill
Wilmington
Lynchburg
SOUTH CAROLINA
Rome
Columbia
Lake City
Myrtle Beach
Atlantic Ocean
Huntsville
Birmingham
Atlanta
Augusta
Charleston
GEORGIA
ALABAMA
Savannah
Columbus
Selma
Montgomery
Brunswick
Waycross
Dothan
Valdosta
Jacksonville
Mobile
Tallahassee
Lake City
Pensacola
Panama City
Gainesville
Ocala
Daytona Beach
Orlando
Tampa
FLORIDA
Gulf of Mexico
Fort Myers
Fort Lauderdale
Miami
Key West
CUBA
0 1,000 km
0 500 miles

THE AMERICAN SOUTH

THE GUIDE

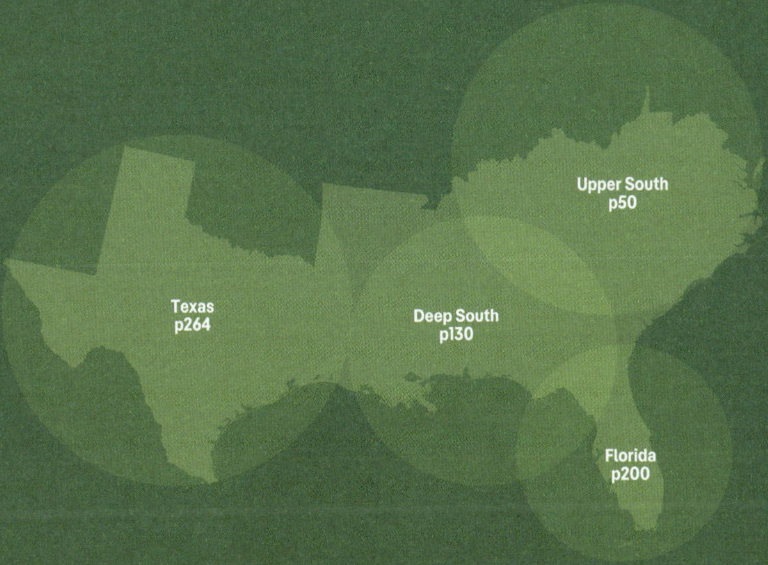

Chapters in this section are organized by hubs and their surrounding areas. We see the hub as your base in the destination, where you'll find unique experiences, local insights, insider tips and expert recommendations. It's also your gateway to the surrounding area, where you'll see what and how much you can do from there.

Higgs Beach (p228)

LUNAMARINA/SHUTTERSTOCK

Researched and curated by
Regis St Louis & Mary Fitzpatrick

The Upper South

WIDE-RANGING ADVENTURES, PEPPERED WITH WILDLIFE AND NIGHTLIFE

Two mountain chains, beach-covered shorelines and rolling fields form the backdrop to a region rich in history and culture.

The Upper South is a land of ancient mountains, primeval forests and remote islands where wild horses still roam. It's home to five national parks, the highest peaks in the eastern US, and the longest cave system on the planet. Outdoor adventure comes in many forms, from watching the sunrise over blue-tinged mountains in North Carolina, to rafting along churning rapids in West Virginia – not to mention limitless opportunities for hiking, including some 935 miles of the Appalachian Trail.

Despite the wild beauty of these six states, the Upper South is perhaps better known for its history and cultural treasures. Some of the earliest European settlements in North America survive in well-preserved Jamestown and Colonial Williamsburg. Pastoral landscapes transformed into battlefields serve as unchanged monuments to harrowing wars of the past. Music pilgrims come to visit famous sites like Graceland and Sun Studio to connect with the visionary artists who shaped history. Meanwhile fans of country, rock and blues fill the clubs of Nashville, Memphis and Louisville to hear the great performers of today.

Urban and rural settlements alike offer plenty of chances to experience the heart of the Upper South – whether catching authentic mountain jams in Appalachia or exploring the gallery scene in an arts-loving town in the Ozarks. You'll also eat and drink well in a region known for its wineries, bourbon distilleries, fresh seafood and classic barbecue.

RUSH JAGOE/LONELY PLANET

THE MAIN AREAS

VIRGINIA
Cauldron of American history. **p56**

WEST VIRGINIA
Adventure-filled gateway to Appalachia. **p70**

NORTH CAROLINA
Enchanting cities, mountains and islands. **p78**

For places to stay in the Upper South, see p128

JARED LLOYD/ALAMY

Left: Blues singer, Memphis (p99); Above: Wild horse, Rachel Carson National Wildlife Refuge (p80)

TENNESSEE
The epicenter of country and blues. **p97**

KENTUCKY
Bourbon distilleries, racehorses, wilderness. **p110**

ARKANSAS
Mountain biking, hiking and kayaking. **p117**

Find Your Way

Six different states make up this large region with its diverse mix of attractions – from presidential estates (Monticello, Mount Vernon) to rugged national parks (Shenandoah, Great Smoky Mountains). Plan carefully to avoid time-consuming journeys between far-flung destinations.

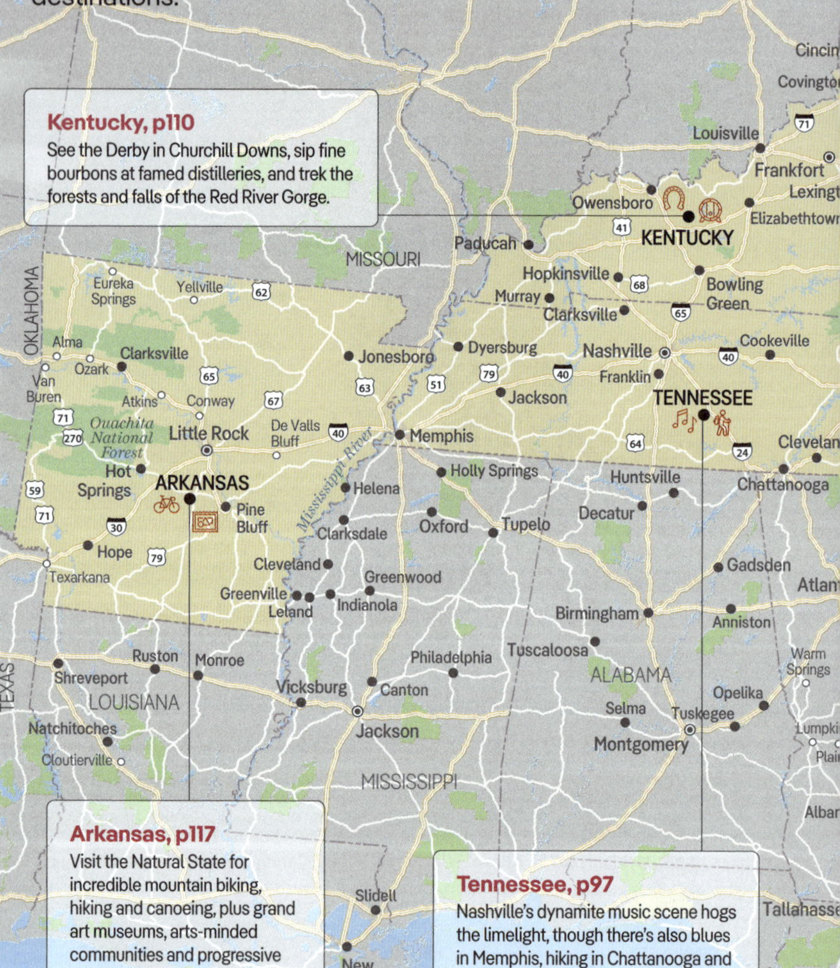

Kentucky, p110
See the Derby in Churchill Downs, sip fine bourbons at famed distilleries, and trek the forests and falls of the Red River Gorge.

Arkansas, p117
Visit the Natural State for incredible mountain biking, hiking and canoeing, plus grand art museums, arts-minded communities and progressive college towns.

Tennessee, p97
Nashville's dynamite music scene hogs the limelight, though there's also blues in Memphis, hiking in Chattanooga and ridgetop adventures in the Smokies.

West Virginia, p70

Raft wild rivers, hike rugged trails, and lose yourself in the forests and small towns of the resilient and oft-underestimated 'Mountain State'.

North Carolina, p78

Go island-hopping in the Outer Banks, get active in the Appalachian mountains, and explore the arts in Asheville, Charlotte and Durham.

Virginia, p56

Feel the past come to life in 400-year-old colonial settlements and grand presidential estates, then immerse yourself in mountain and coastal beauty.

CAR

Driving is often the only way to reach out-of-the-way places and to enjoy the region's many scenic roads. Within urban areas, heavy traffic and parking challenges make walking, cycling, and local buses or ride-haling services better options.

TRAIN

A handful of towns in Virginia, West Virginia and North Carolina are connected by rail. With careful planning you can hop on trains like Amtrak's Floridian, which links Harpers Ferry (WV) with Richmond (Virginia), and several eastern North Carolina cities.

BUS

Major carriers like Greyhound, Megabus and Flixbus link key towns and cities across the region. You'll also find regional operators like Virginia Breeze that travel various routes from towns and cities in Virginia to Washington, DC, and beyond.

Plan Your Days

Don't try to cram in too much, though with a week or more to spare, you can see a few different regions of the Upper South, including coastline, mountains and music-filled city neighborhoods.

ALEKSANDR DYSKIN/SHUTTERSTOCK

Oconaluftee Indian Village (p92)

Pressed for Time

Start the day in **Colonial Williamsburg** (p60), where costumed interpreters and 1700s architecture immerse you in the world of Revolutionary-era Virginia. Have an early lunch of authentic 18th-century recipes at the **King's Arms Tavern** (p62), then drive an hour northwest to **Richmond** (p58), and pay a visit to the renowned **Virginia Museum of Fine Arts**, home to an impressive permanent collection and blockbuster temporary shows (hint: the galleries are open until 9pm on Wednesday through Friday). If time allows, learn about America's most fraught period at the **American Civil War Museum**. Afterwards, indulge in comfort smokehouse fare at **Lunch. SUPPER!** and then catch a concert while sampling craft beers at the **Richmond Music Hall at Capital Ale House**.

Seasonal Highlights

For outdoor activities, time your visit for the warmer months (May to September). It's also when you'll catch the region's biggest festivals. Beat the crowds by coming in early spring or late autumn.

MAY

With spring in full bloom, pull out the pastel hues and head-turning hats for a trip to the Kentucky Derby. The exciting race is preceded by two weeks of celebration during the Kentucky Derby Festival (p112).

JUNE

Summer days offer unrivaled adventures, especially in the mountains of North Carolina and Tennessee, where there's great mountain biking and hiking, as well as white-water adventures down the Nantahala.

JULY

On the last Wednesday of the month, watch the wild horses of Virginia's Chincoteague Island (p66) plunge into Assateague Channel (driven by saltwater cowboys) during the annual pony swim. Catch the pony auction the following day.

Five Days to Travel Around

Start off in the pretty town of **Charlottesville** (p62). Stroll the leafy campus of the **University of Virginia**, explore Thomas Jefferson's estate of **Monticello**, and take a wine tour through the vineyards of **Albemarle County**. Get behind the wheel for a scenic drive along the **Blue Ridge Parkway** (p64), then continue to **Shenandoah National Park** (p64) for rewarding mountain hikes. More adventures await in West Virginia's **New River Gorge National Park** (p72), with ridgeline trails and white-water rafting. Cross over Appalachia's western side to visit Kentucky's dramatic **Red River Gorge** (p116). Next up is bourbon tasting and horse racing near **Lexington** (p113), followed by the inspiring museums and buzzing eating and drinking spots of **Louisville** (p112).

A 10-Day Road Trip

Begin in **Wilmington** (p80), North Carolina, with its vibrant river district. Drive to Cedar Island and take the ferry to **Ocracoke** (p83), gateway to beaches and island lore on the Outer Banks. Next is **Asheville** (p89), a bohemian town of crafts and breweries in the North Carolina Mountains. Enjoy outdoor adventures near **Brevard** (p91), then learn about the **Cherokee** in the town named for them (p92). Nearby, the **Great Smoky Mountains National Park** (p93) offers hikes amid forests, streams and waterfalls. Dust off your cowboy boots (or buy a pair) in **Nashville** (p103), America's country music capital, then continue west to **Memphis** (p99) for blues and barbecue. End in Arkansas with mountain biking and art-gazing in the Ozark town of **Bentonville** (p125).

AUGUST

Head to Virginia Beach for the big Coastal Edge East Coast Surfing Championship (p66) to see mad skills on the waves, take part in a 5k run and catch live music on the beach.

SEPTEMBER

With the summer crowds subsiding, it's a great time to head to the coast (but be mindful of hurricanes). You'll still find warm, pleasant temperatures along Cape Lookout National Seashore (p81) in North Carolina's Outer Banks.

OCTOBER

The forests in the Upper South blaze with red, yellow and orange during the height of autumn. A great place to experience the beauty is on the trails in the Smoky Mountains (p93).

DECEMBER

It's a festive time of year, with holiday events at estates like Monticello and the Biltmore. On the weekend before Christmas, Mount Vernon (p69) hosts a winter market followed by fireworks over the Potomac.

Virginia

BEACHES | HISTORY | SHENANDOAH MOUNTAINS

Places

TOP TIP

Plan a few days in each region – the coastal plains and Virginia Beach, the central Piedmont region and Richmond, the Blue Ridge Mountains and points west – to experience Virginia's unique zing.

In a famous line from the musical *Hamilton*, Thomas Jefferson celebrates returning home from France in the late 1700s by proclaiming his love for his sweet home, Virginia. Anyone who spends any time exploring Virginia and engaging with Southern-charm-filled locals will surely fall in love with the state, too.

From the misty peaks of the Blue Ridge Mountains to the serene ripples of Chesapeake Bay, the state offers an array of natural beauty. Virginia's past is as varied as its geography: it's where the first English settlement of Jamestown was established, and the site of crucial Civil War battles. Bustling urban epicenters, from the capital of Richmond to the DC-adjacent Arlington, brim with architectural landmarks, while Virginia's coastal towns exude a nautical heritage that's a mix of quaint and captivating.

Whether you're tracing the founding fathers' footsteps, exploring wine country or hiking Appalachian trails, Virginia will enchant with its stories and scenery.

GETTING AROUND

Renting a car is the easiest way to navigate the state's entirety. Take note, particularly in Northern Virginia and along major highways, of HOV lanes (often requiring two or more passengers per vehicle) and snag an E-Z Pass toll pass to navigate rush-hour traffic. Amtrak connects the entire state, from Roanoke and Danville in the southwest to Norfolk in the southeast and Alexandria in the north. The trains connect with other major Virginia systems, including Virginia Railway Express and Metro.

Richmond and Charlottesville have bikeshare programs and the Greater Richmond Transit Company (GRTC) has free Pulse buses serving most tourist routes.

VIRGINIA
0 100 km
0 50 miles
PENNSYLVANIA
MARYLAND
DELAWARE
OHIO
WEST VIRGINIA
KENTUCKY
VIRGINIA
TENNESSEE
NORTH CAROLINA
Union Town
Gettysburg
Wilmington
Newark
Middletown
Havre De Grace
Hagerstown
Westminster
Cumberland
Martinsburg
Frederick
Baltimore
Romney
Charles Town
Winchester
Leesburg
Dover
Annapolis
Milford
WASHINGTON, DC
Arlington
Alexandria
Mt Vernon
Easton
Georgetown
Front Royal
Woodbridge
Waldorf
Cambridge
Shenandoah National Park
Lexington Park
Salisbury
Fredericksburg
Ridge
Pokomoke City
Lancaster
Morgantown
New Martinsville
Washington Court House
Chillicothe
Athens
Parkersburg
Clarksburg
Canaan Valley State Park
Moorefield
Hillsboro
Jackson
Weston
Elkins
Gallipolis
Portsmouth
Wayne National Forest
Huntington
Charleston
Monongahela National Forest
Monterey
George Washington National Forest
Harrisonburg
Morehead
Louisa
Staunton
Charlottesville
Fayetteville
Oak Hill
Calvin Price State Forest
Douthat State Park
Waynesboro
Blue Ridge Parkway
Tappahannock
Chincoteague National Wildlife Refuge
Chesapeake Bay
Lewisburg
Lexington
Ashland
Saluda
Exmore
Prestonburg
Williamson
New Castle
Bent Creek
Richmond
Princeton
Appalachian Trail
Lynchburg
Farmville
Williamsburg
Bluefield
Blacksburg
Roanoke
Petersburg
Kiptopeke
Kingdom Come State Park
Rocky Mount
Smith Mountain Lake
Roanoke River
Newport News
Virginia Beach
Harlan
Big Stone Gap
Wytheville
South Hill
Norfolk
Abingdon
South Boston
Emporia
Suffolk
Chesapeake
Middlesboro
Galax
Martinsville
John H Kerr Reservoir
Franklin
Kingsport
Bristol
Mount Airy
Danville
Roanoke Rapids
Murfreesboro
Roxboro
Winton
Elizabeth City
Johnson City
Reidsville
Oxford
Morristown
Boone
Elkton
Hertford

LIVE-MUSIC VENUES IN RICHMOND

The National: Has large capacity, an intimate feel, stunning architecture and a state-of-the-art sound system.

The Camel: Catch up-and-coming local talent in a cozy setting, with yummy smashburgers, too.

Canal Club: Industrial chic, adjacent to Canal Walk, with indoor and outdoor performance spaces.

Richmond Music Hall at Capital Ale House: Mid-size venue with a big sound that's attached to a craft-beer haven.

Altria Theater: Historic space with opulent features and arguably the best sight lines and acoustics in town.

Richmond

Museum hop in the downtown

Begin at the **Virginia Museum of Fine Arts** *(vmfa.museum; free)*, where a highlight is the permanent 'Fabergé and Russian Decorative Arts' exhibit, with nearly 300 gold and precious-metal-draped objects. Hit also the free Institute for Contemporary Art (ICA) at Virginia Commonwealth University, with its modern sculpture garden.

The **Branch Museum of Architecture and Design** *(branchmuseum.org; suggested $5)*, housed in a stately brick castle of sorts on Monument Ave, has rotating exhibits focusing on a range of topics, including the origins of Richmond's cityscapes and international women's-rights posters. The hands-on **Science Museum of Virginia** *(smv.org; adult/child $18/15)* captivates curious minds of all ages. You can generate tornadoes, or test your reflexes against the speed of light in interactive labs. The **American Civil War Museum** *(acwm.org; adult/child $18/9)* includes personal artifacts and narratives conveying various wartime characters, with its exhibits often focusing on one of three perspectives – the north, the south or African American. The museum is housed in the former Tredegar Iron Works building; cannons made on its grounds fired the first shots at Fort Sumter in South Carolina to kick off the Civil War.

Stroll the cobblestoned Shockoe Bottom

From your first step on Shockoe Bottom's cobblestones, you know the streets have been a setting for the extraordinary through the centuries. This is where George Washington mapped out a national system of transportation canals, laying the groundwork for America's infrastructure. It's where Thomas Jefferson signed the Virginia Statute for Religious Freedom, a cornerstone of American civil liberties. And it's where Abraham Lincoln famously arrived by canoe to witness the historic fall of the Confederacy. Knowing Shockoe Bottom's lore makes it a magical stop.

The neighborhood's hub is **17th Street Market**, which regularly hosts art shows as well as a bimonthly farmers market. A communal favorite is the Richmond Night Market (second Saturday of every month), with an artisan village, live art activations and jam sessions from local bands. The **Tobacco Company** *(www.thetobaccocompany.com)* is a three-level, charm-filled restaurant that was once a – you guessed it

EATING IN RICHMOND: OUR PICKS

Stella's: Intimate Greek eatery with authentic flavors evoking a homemade charm in every bite. Reservations recommended. *11:30am-3pm Mon-Fri, plus 4-10pm Mon-Sat* $$$

Lunch.SUPPER!: Southern fare featuring locally sourced ingredients. You can't miss the deer-antler chandelier and ornate decorations. *11am-9pm Mon-Fri, from 10am Sat & Sun* $$

Pho Tay Do: Vietnamese cuisine in a quirky house setting, with authentic pho and other dishes. Cash only. *10am-6pm Mon, Tue & Thu-Sat, to 5pm Sun* $$

Hot for Pizza: A divey den, boasting drink deals and a lineup of pies with ingredients like fennel sausage and oyster mushrooms. *11am-2am Mon-Sat, from noon Sun* $$

HIGHLIGHTS
1 Poe Museum
2 Science Museum of Virginia
3 Virginia Museum of Fine Arts

SIGHTS
4 American Civil War Museum
5 Branch Museum of Architecture and Design

SLEEPING
6 Linden Row Inn

EATING
7 17th Street Market
8 Hot for Pizza
9 Lunch.SUPPER!
10 Stella's
11 Tobacco Company

DRINKING & NIGHTLIFE
12 Capital Ale House

ENTERTAINMENT
13 Altria Theater
14 Canal Club
15 The Camel
16 The National

WILLIAMSBURG WALKING TOURS

Ultimate Pirate Tour: All-ages tour that delves into the history of pirates and their impact on early colonies.

Murder Tour and Pub Crawl: Learn about the town's seedy, murderous history while sipping on a libation at each pub.

Haunted Williamsburg: Candlelight tour in which you get to enter historic buildings in Colonial Williamsburg.

We Shall Overcome: Hear inspiring stories of African Americans while visiting the Williamsburg landmarks connected to their stories.

Taste of Williamsburg: Williamsburg's best bites and craft drinks are the focus of this tasty tour.

– tobacco warehouse. The pecan-crusted lollipop lamb chops, brass elevator and central walnut staircase dazzle 'round the clock. The **Poe Museum** *(poemuseum.org; adult/child $10/free)* is a living homage to famed Richmond resident, Edgar Allan Poe, offering insights into his enigmatic life and the theories surrounding his demise. The courtyard space – dubbed the Enchanted Garden, which was inspired by Poe's 'To One in Paradise' poem – is a quiet oasis and regularly hosts 'Un-Happy Hours' sponsored by local breweries.

Williamsburg

Hitch a wagon ride in Colonial Williamsburg

Williamsburg was Virginia's capital during the American Revolution and today's **Colonial Williamsburg** *(colonialwilliamsburg.org; adult/child $32/9)* is a living time capsule that transports locals and visitors alike to the 1700s. Throughout the 300-plus-acre area, historical reenactors with powdered wigs and tricorn hats wander about as horse-drawn carriages roll by. For a carriage ride *(from $10),* head to the Colonial Williamsburg Visitor Center.

By wagon or foot, prioritize a stop at the Governor's Palace. Amid its three-story brick grandeur, note all the pineapple accents – an emblem of hospitality and wealth in the mansion's 1700s heyday and beyond. From the palace, head just west to the Capitol building – this is where the House of Burgesses initially proposed US independence from the British in 1776. A final stop is the Public Gaol, where you can learn about colonial-era crime and punishments. Take note of the historic pillory, a wooden structure with slots for criminals' heads and hands. It was common for passersby to hurl tomatoes and other objects at criminals, so come to this photo op – and the other pillories scattered about Colonial Williamsburg – creatively.

Unexpected historical pizzazz

Don't let Williamsburg's generally refined vibe fool you – there's some quirkiness to explore here. Hit the **Virginia Musical Museum** *(virginiamusicalmuseum.com; free),* which celebrates the state's musical heritage through a collection of rare musical instruments and memorabilia celebrating Virginia-bred icons. Learn all about the likes of country-pop legend Patsy Cline and the 'Queen of Jazz,' Ella Fitzgerald. Among the more unique items is the country's first talking doll and a 1790 Joshua Shudi harpsichord – one of two in existence today. The **College of William & Mary** is the US's second-oldest institution of higher education (Harvard is the oldest). Stop at the Crim Dell Bridge – local lore promises eternal love to those who kiss atop its burgundy-and-gold-railed steps and, if you cross the bridge alone, well, you're doomed to solitude. While at William & Mary, check out the Wren Building, which has survived three major fires since its 1700 inception and is the oldest college building still in use in the country.

When hunger inevitably beckons, **Charly's Airport Restaurant** is a quirky and unexpected find. Situated at Williamsburg Jamestown Airport, it allows you to watch smaller and

BILL CHIZEK/SHUTTERSTOCK

Colonial Williamsburg

TIPS FOR NAVIGATING WILLIAMSBURG

At approximately 9 sq miles, Williamsburg is compact and largely walkable. Colonial Williamsburg is particularly easy to stroll, with wide, pedestrian-friendly expanses.

Beyond its colonial core, the Williamsburg Area Transit Authority (WATA) serves key tourist attractions such as Jamestown, Busch Gardens and the College of William & Mary. WATA has an all-day pass for $3 and is particularly handy for venturing beyond Colonial Williamsburg. Pay cash for the all-day pass on the bus (credit cards are not accepted).

There's a fee to enter buildings and experience educational programming in Colonial Williamsburg. Odds are that you may want to pair your visit with a Yorktown trek, a Busch Gardens trip or more, and a variety of discounted packages are available at *colonialwilliamsburg.org*.

sometimes vintage aircraft depart and land as you nosh on homestyle plates. Round out a day of the extraordinary at the **Archaearium** *(historicjamestowne.org; adult/child $15/5)*, an archaeology museum dedicated to America's first English colony, Jamestown. The museum has more than 2000 artifacts,including Native American arrowheads and tobacco pipes bearing the names of prominent settlers.

Charlottesville

Exploring past and present

In the foothills of the Blue Ridge Mountains, Charlottesville is as ahhhh-worthy visually as it is historically. It is home to the **University of Virginia**, which was founded by Thomas Jefferson in 1819 and remains a centerpiece of the city's architectural and cultural story. The university's Rotunda and vast lawn are quintessential landmarks, embodying Jefferson's vision of an 'academical village.' President James Monroe's home, **Highland** *(highland.org; adult/child $18/13)*, is notably in Charlottesville as well. Just outside of town is **Monticello** *(monticello.org; adult/child from US$22/8)*, Jefferson's historic home with graceful grounds that you can stroll on your own, capped by the main house, for which you'll need to take a guided tour. Afterwards, spend time exploring Charlottesville's pedestrian-friendly **Downtown Mall**. It's a brick- and column-draped experience with pops of energy coming in the form of buzzing breweries, the facade of the ever-glowing **Paramount Theater** *(theparamount.net)* and more. The mall is a seven-block stretch, with the Ting Pavilion and Omni Charlottesville Hotel as its east and west anchors. Between them, hit **Lone Light Coffee** for a coffee concoction or sweet treats such as bourbon vanilla-infused ice cream.

Uncork Virginia's wine wonderland

Charlottesville wasn't named *Wine Enthusiast*'s Wine Region of the Year in recent times for no reason. The city and surrounding Albemarle County are home to more than 40 wineries, producing everything from the heartiest of merlots to light hybrids. Companies such as **Central Virginia Wine Tours** *(centralvirginiawinetours.com)* offer transportation and winery hops. If you're plotting your own wine adventure, start at **Blenheim Vineyards** *(blenheim vineyards.com)*. The property dates to 1730 and was started as a sustainable winery by world-renowned musician

EATING IN WILLIAMSBURG: HISTORIC TAVERNS

King's Arms Tavern: Authentic colonial dining, blending 18th-century recipes with modern flavors. *11am-2pm daily, plus 4:30-8pm Thu-Mon* **$$$**

Christiana Campbell's Tavern: George Washington's favorite local seafood spot. Come for the crab cakes, stay for the balladeers. *4-8pm Tue-Sat* **$$$**

Chowning's Garden Bar: Relaxed open-air dining with a colonial twist, offering classics such as burgers and hot dogs. *11am-5pm Thu-Sat* **$$**

Raleigh Tavern Bakery: Fresh ginger cake, sandwiches and baked treats from this bakery with wood-fired ovens. *9am-5pm* **$**

DRIVE THROUGH WARTIME & COLONIAL HISTORY

This tour takes you through some of Virginia's most historic sites against a scenic tidewater backdrop.

START	END	LENGTH
Yorktown Battlefield	Historic Jamestowne Island Loop	30 miles; 4-5 hours

Begin at ❶ **Yorktown Battlefield** to soak in Revolutionary War history seeped into the ground. This 1781 battle was a turning point in the war, leading to its end and the USA's independence from Great Britain. Make your way towards ❷ **Nelson House**, one-time residence of Thomas Nelson Jr, a signatory of the Declaration of Independence. Most features in the Georgian home are original. If you visit when enough staff are present, a tour of the interior is possible. Wind your way through the streets of ❸ **Yorktown's historic waterfront**, where restored 18th-century homes line the streets. Water St leads to the ❹ **French Memorial**, a tribute to the French soldiers who lost their lives in battles in and around Yorktown. Hop on the ❺ **Colonial Parkway** from here. This 23-mile scenic drive weaves its way through pine and hardwood forests, tidal estuaries along the James and York rivers and through Williamsburg on its way to Jamestown. Overlooks dot the parkway. Head to Jamestown Island where you'll find the ❻ **Jamestown Settlement**. Exhibits and outdoor re-creations tell the story of America's beginnings, including its Indigenous people and the arrival of English colonists in 1607. Around the corner from the settlement, you'll find ❼ **Jamestown Glasshouse**, where modern glassblowers hold demonstrations while utilizing tools and techniques similar to those used in the 17th century. Just a bit further and you can cruise the ❽ **Historic Jamestowne Island Loop**, discovering the beauty of the island's marshy landscape.

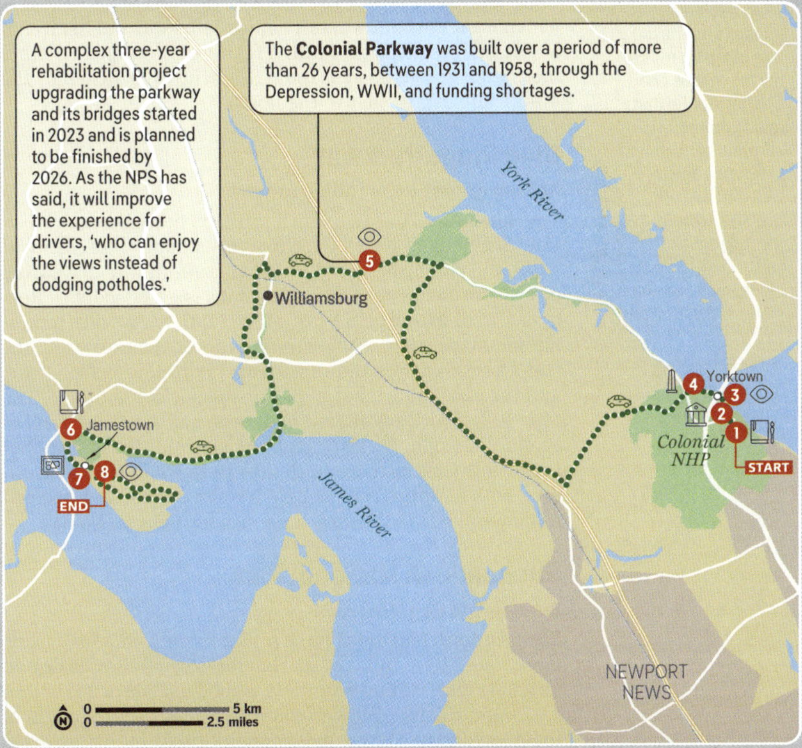

A complex three-year rehabilitation project upgrading the parkway and its bridges started in 2023 and is planned to be finished by 2026. As the NPS has said, it will improve the experience for drivers, 'who can enjoy the views instead of dodging potholes.'

The **Colonial Parkway** was built over a period of more than 26 years, between 1931 and 1958, through the Depression, WWII, and funding shortages.

York River
Williamsburg
Yorktown
Colonial NHP
START
Jamestown
END
James River
NEWPORT NEWS
0 5 km
0 2.5 miles

PROFESSOR O'KEEFFE

We can thank the hallowed halls of the University of Virginia for inspiring Georgia O'Keeffe to be the artist we recognize today. O'Keeffe spent summers at UVA studying art, eventually teaching some courses herself. It was under her teachers' mentorship that she began exploring the abstract, drawing inspiration from the Blue Ridge Mountains and campus life. O'Keeffe endured many trials over those years, including her mother's death, but it was camping trips in the mountains near Charlottesville that reinvigorated her, allowing her painting to flourish again. UVA and Charlottesville provided the foundation from which O'Keeffe's art blossomed, leaving a mark on the art world.

ANDREW GITTIS/SHUTTERSTOCK

and local icon Dave Matthews. Others to take in include **King Family Vineyards**, situated on a former thoroughbred horse farm; **Pippin Hill** *(pippinhillfarm.com)*, which is a rolling-hills staple with farm-to-table dinners and estate tours; and **Jefferson Vineyards** *(jeffersonvineyards.com)*, which is on the land where Thomas Jefferson and his friend and Italian winemaker Philip Mazzei grew grapes together more than 250 years ago. Today, the winery is owned by the Monticello estate, just to the north.

Blue Ridge Parkway

Rolling greens upon rolling greens

The Blue Ridge Parkway, which runs 469 miles through Western Virginia and North Carolina, has a handful of standout stops and can be accessed less than a 10-minute drive from downtown Roanoke. Among the stops is an offshoot to Roanoke's **Mill Mountain Star** (at 90ft tall, the world's largest human-made star), with a viewpoint over Roanoke from the star's base. Sunrises and sunsets are breathtaking from here, and the star lights up at night for the perfect photo op. The Blue Ridge Parkway is free to access, and its speed limit is typically 45mph. Parkway regulars say mid- to late October is the best time to drive it, thanks to its vivid foliage. However, with its springtime pops of flowers and the snowcapped mountain vistas in winter, it's a visual treat year-round.

Shenandoah National Park

Summit Old Rag Mountain

Shenandoah National Park *(nps.gov/shen, $15-$30)* spans more than 310 sq miles of soaring forests, wildflower-dotted meadows and tinkling waterfalls. A good portion of it is within a 45-minute drive of downtown Harrisonburg. A highlight of the park, and one of the most popular hikes in the region, is

Old Rag Mountain

Old Rag Mountain. You'll need to snag a day-use ticket in advance during peak season (March 1 through November 30). Allow seven hours for the hike – there are two different routes you can take, amassing approximately 2500ft in elevation. Along the way, count on some rock scrambles and boulder hiking. On completion, you'll be rewarded with 360-degree views of the valley, which glows yellow and orange during the fall foliage season.

Appreciate views on Skyline Dr

With 105 miles of mountain bliss, this public road through Shenandoah National Park provides awe-inspiring views from the crest of the Blue Ridge Mountains. There is no shortage of opportunities for snapping photos, with 75 overlooks along the way.

Virginia Beach

A non-bored walk

This much is certain: you might be on vacation, but you'll still want to wake early, plop it on the **Virginia Beach Boardwalk** adjacent to white sands and take in a sunrise. Beyond that, there is so much to explore along the boardwalk. Starting in the south at 2nd St and running north to 40th St, it

THE JM IN JMU

James Madison, born in Virginia in 1751 and nicknamed 'Father of the Constitution,' helped write the US Constitution and the Bill of Rights. Madison also cowrote the Federalist Papers, pushing for the Constitution's approval. As the fourth president, he led the nation during the War of 1812 and helped negotiate the Treaty of Ghent. Back home in Virginia, he was involved in founding the University of Virginia and served in the state's House of Delegates and the US House of Representatives. His legacy is closely tied to Virginia's history and politics. Today, Harrisonburg's own James Madison University bears his name as tribute.

EATING IN HARRISONBURG: FARM-TO-TABLE RESTAURANTS

Rocktown Kitchen: Locally sourced, seasonal American cuisine in an elevated yet casual dining venue. *11am-2:30pm & 5-9pm Tue-Sat* $$$

Local Chop & Grill House: Organic ingredients from neighborhood farms in the historic City Produce Exchange building; extensive whiskey selection. *4-11pm Mon-Sat* $$$

Magpie Diner: A 1950s service station turned modern diner, with locally roasted coffee and craft cocktails alongside seasonally inspired classic dishes. *8am-2pm Tue-Fri, from 9am Sat & Sun* $$

Little Grill: Cozy spot offering a menu for vegetarians and those seeking locally sourced organic-meat options. *hours vary* $

SURF'S UP, DUDE

Virginia Beach is home to the world's oldest continuously run surfing competition, the Coastal Edge East Coast Surfing Championship, locally known simply as ECSC. For more than 60 years, competitive surfers have flocked to the area to claim their place on the podium, creating an event that has morphed into so much more. The weeklong festival, typically held in August, delights with showcases in longboard, shortboard and stand-up paddleboarding. Through the years, other beach-favorite activities such as volleyball and street skating, live music, arts-and-crafts vendors and more have been added to the festival lineup, making ECSC an event for more than just wave riders.

spans 3 miles and is nearly 30ft wide in most spots. Among its quirkier highlights: just north of 30th St is Neptune's Park, where you'll find a large statue of the Roman god. At 38th St is the Navy Seal Monument, a life-size statue of a serviceman donning a swimsuit, flippers and weapon. At 25th St is the *Norwegian Lady* statue, commemorating a nearby shipwreck from the 19th century. For bird enthusiasts, the Atlantic Wildfowl Heritage Museum is housed in a small cottage near 12th St and is loaded with waterbird art, relics and exhibits, leaving you to surely say, 'What the...duck!' by the end.

Climb Cape Henry Lighthouse

There are many firsts pertaining to the 90ft-tall, red- and tan-bricked **Cape Henry Lighthouse**. Beyond being near the first landing site of English settlers in the US, the lighthouse also marks the first public-works project of the US government, overseen by Alexander Hamilton. The lighthouse is on the Fort Story military base, so you'll need to provide ID at the base's gate and then shuttles (which run every 15 minutes) take non-military civilians directly to the lighthouse. On arrival, there are 191 steps to climb to enjoy 360-degree coastal views from the cozy lantern room.

Norfolk

Explore naval history

It's only appropriate that Norfolk, about a 20-minute drive from Virginia Beach, has a naval museum on a ship. Part of the **Nauticus** maritime discovery center, the Battleship *Wisconsin* includes interactive spaces that you can stroll through, including an on-ship hospital with a surgery center, barber shop and even a brig where misbehaving sailors were temporarily jailed. There's also a sailing center on-site where you can take a craft for a guided spin on the water, with a unique perspective on downtown Norfolk's skyline. For a more relaxed time on the water, Half Moone Cruise and Victory Rover Naval Base Cruises are next door and offer narrated cruises of the city's coastline.

Chincoteague National Wildlife Refuge

Horsing around on the Eastern Shore

It's an otherworldly scene here, with wild horses roaming, chomping on marsh grasses and slurping up water from ponds, and **Chincoteague National Wildlife Refuge** *(fws.gov; pedestrian & cyclist/vehicle per day free/$10)* is the epicenter

DRINKING IN VIRGINIA BEACH: ORANGE CRUSHES

Waterman's Surfside Grille: The OG – Waterman's vodka, fresh OJ, a splash of Sprite, enjoyed at the beach. *hours vary*

Shack on 8th: Crush on Classic Orange to Honey Habanero among patio vibes with fire pits and yard games. *4pm-late Thu & Fri, from noon Sat & Sun*

Back Deck: Indulge in refreshing crush variations at this laid-back bayside waterfront venue. *11am-10pm*

Chix on the Beach: Beachfront crushes with the personal touch of lime and cranberry. *11am-10pm Sun-Thu, to 2am Fri & Sat*

ANTON_IVANOV/SHUTTERSTOCK

Arlington National Cemetery

of the action. In the refuge, which is located mostly on the Virginia side of Assateague Island, about a two-hour drive from Virginia Beach, nearly 300 ponies wander through the forests and prairies and it's not uncommon to see colorful shorebirds and bald eagles soaring in the sky. **Assateague Explorer** *(assateagueexplorer.com)* has a Pony Express Nature Cruise, which lasts about two hours and coasts safely up to the horses. Perhaps the most unique pony spectacle in the region, held on the last consecutive Wednesday and Thursday in July, is the annual Pony Penning, where the area's ponies are guided to swim across the Assateague Channel to Chincoteague Island, where select foals are auctioned off. This sale helps to humanely control the pony population and proceeds benefit veterinary care for the herd.

Arlington

In solemn tribute

Arlington National Cemetery *(arlingtoncemetery.mil; free)* is a 693-acre military cemetery where over 400,000 people, including more than 300,000 veterans, lie at rest. The country's most famous cemetery isn't just a place to reflect or grieve – it's also a solemn but scenic walk through the nation's military history. Main sites include Arlington House, the former residence of Robert E Lee, and the gravesite of President

NAVIGATING IN & AROUND VIRGINIA BEACH

If you're sticking to the beach, strolls and a periodic rideshare (Uber or Lyft) will do the trick. Hampton Roads Transit operates an Atlantic Ave trolley that runs parallel to the boardwalk. There are plenty of touristy bike shops along the boardwalk area with hourly rentals as well as day packages in the $40 range.

For ventures beyond Virginia Beach, you'll need a car. Norfolk is an east-west straight shot along Interstate 264. The drive to Virginia's Eastern Shore has at its core a 17-plus-mile journey across the Chesapeake Bay Bridge-Tunnel. Within the over-under-water stretch, there are two 1-mile sections of tunnel. There's a $22 fee (round trip) on the Bridge-Tunnel, which is best navigated with an E-Z Pass.

EATING IN CAPE CHARLES: OYSTERS

Oyster Farm Seafood Eatery: Raw and steamed offerings, with a deck overlooking Chesapeake Bay. *4-8pm Wed & Thu, 11:30am-8pm Fri & Sat, to 3pm Sun* $$$

The Shanty: Cottage vibe with local oyster selections, rice bowls and orange miso-glazed calamari. *11:30am-9pm* $$

Hook @ Harvey: Open for dinner, with a bistro setting, rotating fare and ever-fresh seafood catches. *5-9pm Tue-Sat* $$$

Coach House Tavern: Tucked into a golf community, this neighborhood restaurant has fresh oysters served on the half shell. *hours vary* $$

John F Kennedy, with its eternal flame. The most notable site, however, is the Tomb of the Unknown Soldier, a tribute to the unknown fallen soldiers of the US's major wars. The neoclassical white-marble sarcophagus is guarded 24 hours a day.

To find a specific grave or memorial, download the ANC Explorer app, which has maps and photos down to individual tombstones.

WHY I LOVE FREDERICKSBURG

Jesse Scott, Lonely Planet writer

Consider me one of those dudes that's ultra-proud to be where he's from. Hint: it's Fredericksburg. In my 37 years, I've seen this town blossom from a sleepy Civil War town to one with a rockin' culinary scene, a broadminded and artsy vibe and rad public spaces. Rte 3 is now nuts with shopping and there's even a baseball team. Who woulda thought? Hurkamp Park has the giant word LOVE to take photos with – it's painted a different vibe each season. This town is full of love – people say hi to you on the streets, and generations want to tell you how proud they are to be from 'the 'Burg.' I don't blame them.

Fredericksburg

Historic-house hopping between revolutionary residences

The 'midpoint between Washington, DC and Richmond' and George Washington's boyhood home, beautifully preserved, heritage-filled Fredericksburg is home to numerous historic homes, some of which are open to the public and host regular tours.

Chatham Manor *(nps.gov)* looms over the Rappahannock River and dates back to 1771. During the Civil War, it was a hospital and Union headquarters, with famous visitors such as Abraham Lincoln and Walt Whitman. There are free walking tours of the grounds, including a stop with views of Fredericksburg's steeple-filled skyline. **Mary Washington House** *(washingtonheritagemuseums.org)* is a larger, white-paneled downtown home where George Washington's mother lived toward the end of her life (from 1772–1789). Beyond rooms set up to replicate Mary's lifestyle, the lush-yet-quaint gardens offer a lovely and colorful stroll, particularly in springtime.

Kenmore *(kenmore.org)* is another standout residence, constructed in 1775 by Fielding Lewis and his wife, Betty, who was George Washington's sister. At the time of its construction, it was an architectural marvel for its ornate plasterwork and ceilings, which have been tastefully restored through the years. If you plan to visit both Kenmore and Mary Washington House, buy a combo ticket at Kenmore for discounted entry.

Alexandria

A walk fit for a king

Old Town Alexandria is a nationally designated historic district and its core, King St, puts much of its zest on display, particularly between the King St Metro station and the Potomac River waterfront. Among the highlights is **Torpedo Factory Art Center**, a former munitions plant and now an art gallery. Inside, you can weave through the galleries of 70-plus local artists. For Alexandria-themed tchotchkes, the **Old Town Shop** has Americana-inspired ornaments, puzzles and charms. The **Alexandria Visitor Center** has some fun keepsakes, too, including an ever-evolving collection of history-themed candles. Eastward, King St culminates at a waterfront park with views of DC's skyline.

MATTARISTUDIO/SHUTTERSTOCK

Mount Vernon

Mount Vernon

Walk in Washington's footsteps

Mount Vernon *(mountvernon.org; adult/child $28/15)* was George Washington's most famous home, built by his dad in 1734. George and his wife, Martha, lived here for 40-plus years, with George dying here in 1799. To enter the grounds, you'll need to purchase a pass, with an additional fee to access the main mansion. There are a number of add-ons available from there – the best are a 45-minute boat excursion on the Potomac River and, for *Hamilton* lovers, a look at how Washington's life correlated with the famed Broadway show's songs.

Highlights in the mansion include Washington's private study and the majestic New Room. You'll also want to check out the farm space, with costumed interpreters depicting how Mount Vernon's workers sheared sheep, harvested crops and more. Mount Vernon was also once home to hundreds of enslaved people and among the more moving moments at the mansion is a small, replica slaves' cabin.

COBBLE, COBBLE

Embracing the historical whimsy of Old Town's cobblestone streets is no challenge. It's like stepping back in time. This style of paving wasn't chosen for its charm – during construction, cobblestones were affordable and readily available as merchant ships used river-rounded rocks as ballast in Alexandria. However, their durability posed challenges. Alignment issues and erosion meant ongoing maintenance, which eventually became unsustainable. Cobblestones eventually became a thing of the past in Alexandria as brick and other sturdier materials became more common. Ongoing preservation efforts, including the repaving of some cobblestones in 1979, have contributed to local conservation.

EATING IN ALEXANDRIA: BEST RIVER VIEWS

Vola's Dockside: Premier riverfront dining, with seafood, tacos, American classics and a mid-century-modern throwback in the Hi-Tide Lounge. *hours vary* **$$$**

Ada's on the River: Seafood and steaks surrounding a custom wood-burning oven with views of the Potomac. *hours vary* **$$$**

BARCA: Mediterranean fare, tapas and a wine bar situated on a pier. *hours vary* **$$**

Jula's on the Potomac: American classics on the 4th floor, with a terrace overlooking the river. *hours vary* **$$$**

West Virginia

WHITE-WATER | APPALACHIA | FORESTED SLOPES

Places

'The sun doesn't always shine in West Virginia,' President John F Kennedy once said, 'but the people do.'

Kennedy wasn't alone in his affection for the Mountain State. 'Take Me Home, Country Road' is one of John Denver's most enduring ballads, and countless writers have waxed poetic on this wild and wonderful land. Yes, West Virginia has seen plenty of drama over the years, from the Hatfield-and-McCoy blood feud to the complicated legacy of coal mining, but open-minded visitors will find the best of Appalachia in these textured highlands. Nearly 80% of West Virginia is blanketed in forest, and its six national parks are a paradise for temperate wildlife – as well as birders, hikers and anglers. West Virginia's reputation for hospitality is also well earned, and locals tend to wear their hearts on their sleeves. As you fall into its down-home rhythms, you'll likely find yourself shining, too.

GETTING AROUND

With its odd shape and rolling topography, West Virginia is best explored 1 mile at a time. Drives can be long and service stations scattered, so keep an eye on the fuel gauge. While Greyhoud connects most major towns, tickets aren't cheap and the winding routes burn time: Morgantown to Charleston takes almost 10 hours. A car makes things easier and is necessary to really explore southern West Virginia. The tougher your vehicle, the better – while highways are well maintained, secondary roads have their share of potholes, and you don't have to stray too far to hit gravel and severe inclines. Central Charleston and Morgantown are walkable, and there are local buses.

Charleston

A dusty district turned hip

Charleston, West Virginia's low-key capital, stands at the confluence of the Elk and Kanawha rivers and is hours from any major city, yet it packs a lot into its walkable central area. **Capitol St** is a tree-lined commercial strip with vintage storefronts, brick-paved sidewalks, brewpubs and restaurants. You can amble across downtown Charleston in no time, but the neighborhood is rich in historic architecture and commemorative plaques. The most recent addition is **Slack Plaza**, a beautiful pedestrian concourse, playground and splash pad. Two whimsical sculptures of fiddling musicians welcome you to the plaza, and real-life instrumentalists play here in the warmer months. Downtown Charleston is best enjoyed in the summer, when the streets are busy and food trucks are out, but Slack Plaza also has a skating rink in the winter. Just a few blocks away is the **Clay Center for the Arts and Sciences** *(theclaycenter.org; free)*, where you'll find a theater, art museum and planetarium in one facility – perfect for families and kids.

TOP TIP

Driving from Virginia, you can explore West Virginia's history in roughly chronological order – from the colonial getaway of Berkeley Springs (p77), head to Harpers Ferry (p76) for a lesson in abolitionism or Morgantown (p75) for a course on the Industrial Revolution. Then hike in the footsteps of Hatfield and McCoy (p73) before finishing at Charleston.

NEW RIVER GORGE'S TOP ONE-DAY ACTIVITIES

Fayette Station Rd: This one-way road spirals 8 miles through the gorge. The 40-minute drive includes a trestle bridge over the New River.

Endless Wall Trail: The hiking is tame; the views are epic. This popular 2.4-mile walk skirts a spectacular series of cliffs.

Bridge Walk: Join this tour *(bridgewalk.com)* to conquer acrophobia and cross the New River Gorge Bridge on a narrow catwalk. Don't worry; you're safely clipped in.

Cathedral Falls: Twenty minutes' drive from the bridge, this waterfall makes for a spectacular selfie. Park in the lot and you're steps away.

Bridge Day: Mark your calendars: the bridge is closed to motor traffic on the third Saturday of October. Pedestrians, vendors and BASE jumpers rejoice.

ZACHARY HOOVER/SHUTTERSTOCK

New River Gorge Bridge

New River Gorge

Hit the trails...and rocks...and water

About a 70-minute drive from Charleston, you'll come to the iconic steel **New River Gorge Bridge** arcing over New River Gorge. It's one of the most resplendent sights in West Virginia, with its image recreated on T-shirts, mugs and more. The architectural masterpiece, completed in 1977, is 3030ft in length, making it the longest single-span arch bridge in the Western Hemisphere. It's also a fitting gateway to the **New River Gorge National Park and Preserve**, a 70,000-acre wooded wonderland. The park is a magnet for hikers, campers, rock climbers and mountain bikers, especially in summer. Motor activities are also common here, with routes for 4WDs and snowmobiles and, after a good winter storm, snowshoers and cross-country skiers take over the trails. But even in the busiest months, you can find peace and solitude among the corrugated hills. The New River itself extends 53 miles through the protected landscape, with waters that range from calm and glassy to frothing class III rapids. The waterway's length attracts kayakers and white-water rafters from around the world, and the varying conditions appeal to both newbies and veterans. Many tour operators are based in Fayette County, but the largest and most dynamic is **Adventures on the Gorge**

EATING & DRINKING IN CHARLESTON: OUR PICKS

Adelphia Sports Bar: Bustling bar and dining room with a diverse pub menu and lots of TVs. *11am-11pm Mon-Wed, to midnight Thu-Sat, 1-10pm Sun* $$

Black Sheep Burrito & Brews: Upmarket Mexican fusion restaurant with reasonable prices, plus cocktails. *11am-9pm Mon-Thu, to 10pm Fri & Sat, 11am-3pm Sun* $$

Hale House: Refined bistro with a brick dining room and menu of 240 varieties of bourbon. Head downstairs to the Volstead speakeasy. *4-10pm Mon-Sat* $$

Fife Street Brewing: Lively taproom with high ceilings and big windows, on a lively pedestrian walkway. *11am-10pm* *(adventuresonthegorge.com),* based in Lansing. This outfit can arrange class-V rafting trips, family ziplining and accommodations in its luxury cabins.

Fayetteville, a tiny historic town on the western side of New River Gorge, is just a mile from the bridge and makes a good base. Its Court St is lined with bistros, outfitters and antebellum houses, and visitors typically stop here to grab lunch and get their bearings. The town is ringed with hotels, lodges and campgrounds, and plenty of visitors bed down in Fayetteville while spending daylight hours in the park.

Hatfield-McCoy Trails

Hike through history

It's strange to think that these peaceful paths were once the backdrop for a bitter blood feud, with members of the Hatfield and McCoy clans spending 28 years treading these very routes in their quest for shotgun justice. What started as an argument over land rights in the 1860s ballooned into an interfamilial conflict, and at least 20 lives were lost in West Virginia's woodlands before its ceasefire in 1891. Founded in 2000, the **Hatfield-McCoy Trails** *(trailsheaven.com; permit $50)* extend more than 1000 miles through the southwestern quarter of the state, spanning nine counties.

Such a vast network has plenty of segments and trailheads, but the closest to Charleston is the **Ivy Branch trail system**. An entry point in the town of **Julian** stands about a half-hour drive from the capital, and you'll find a sizable parking lot and welcome center. From here, you can access 60 miles of rugged, wending paths.

Point Pleasant

A living folk hero?

West Virginia has many folk heroes, but none of them excites the imagination like the Mothman. This insect-human hybrid made its debut in *The Mothman Prophecies,* a 1975 memoir by John A Keel, which takes place in the small riverside town of Point Pleasant, about an hour's drive northwest of Charleston. The Mothman has gone on to win worldwide attention among cryptozoologists, and many a local has claimed to spot this winged, 10ft-tall critter in the wild. The legend inspired a 2002 feature film, *The Mothman Prophecies*, starring Richard Gere. A year later, a Mothman statue was unveiled in the middle of Point Pleasant. The statue stands directly in front of

OUTDOOR EXCURSIONS IN NEW RIVER GORGE

Bill Chouinard, pilot, vacation-rental operator and owner of Wild Blue Adventure Co *wildblueadventure company.com*

Fayette County is the epicenter of multisport days in the US. I moved here nearly 30 years ago, dropping out of college with $300 and a one-way ticket to the world-class climbing at New River Gorge.

I've spent almost three decades climbing, kayaking, mountain biking, running, paragliding, BASE jumping and now flying here. This place is more than just our home. It's fuel for daily inspiration, exploration and adventure. The thing that really makes this place stand out is the people – an incredible mix of locals and transplants drawn here by a common interest in the outdoors and everything it offers.

EATING IN FAYETTEVILLE: BEST GRUB

The Stache: Come for the toys and knickknacks; stay for the eclectic ice cream and candy. *11:30am-6pm* $

Wanderlust Creativefoods: Elegant and sophisticated plates in a cozy setting, with decor highlighted with attractive woodwork. *4-9pm Thu-Sun* $$

Southside Junction Tap House: LGBTIQ+-friendly corner bar in an old brick building. Craft beers, burgers and live music. *3-11pm Mon, Tue, Thu & Fri, 2-11pm Sat, to 9pm Sun* $$

Pies & Pints: Funky pizzas and a dizzying range of beers on tap in a polished modernist venue. *11am-9pm Sun-Thu, to 10pm Fri & Sat* $$

YARNS SPUN ABOUT THE HATFIELD-MCCOY FEUD

Blood Feud: The Hatfields & McCoys Novelist Lisa Alther presents an authoritative nonfiction biography of the Hatfields and McCoys and their multigenerational feud.

The Feud: The Hatfields & McCoys Dean King describes the peaceful coexistence between the two families before the Civil War wrenched them apart.

The McCoys Before the Feud: A Western Novel This fictional account by author Thomas A McCoy imagines his ancestors' less-known exploits in the American West.

The Coffin Quilt Ann Rinaldi's young-adult novel illustrates life in 1870s Appalachia through the eyes of young Fanny McCoy.

Hatfields & McCoys Kevin Costner and Bill Paxton star as rival patriarchs in this action-packed History Channel miniseries.

GEORGINA BURROWS/SHUTTERSTOCK

the **World's Only Mothman Museum** *(mothmanmuseum.com; adult/child $5/2)*, a small storefront that houses newspaper clippings, artwork and other ephemera. In the third week of September, the whole thing is commemorated with the annual Mothman Festival.

Sutton

Supernatural sightings and Bigfoot

About an hour's drive northeast of Charleston, in Sutton, is some more food for the imagination. The **Flatwoods Monster Museum** *(braxtonwv.org/the-flatwoods-monster; free)*, a former soda fountain, features the Flatwoods Monster, a 10ft-tall extraterrestrial with a red face and flowing gown that locals claimed to have spotted in 1952. The town embraces this strange episode with a sign that reads 'Home of the Green Monster,' a reference to the creature's green outfit. Just a block away is the **West Virginia Bigfoot Museum** *(wvbigfootmuseum.org; free)*, a roomy exhibition space dedicated to all things Sasquatch. This newest addition opened in 2021 and displays art, artifacts and testimonials from Bigfoot lore.

DRINKING IN CHARLESTON: LOCAL HAUNTS

Red Carpet Lounge: Local favorite, with a sizable patio out back and bargain prices. *11am-midnight Mon-Wed, to 1am Thu, to 2am Fri, noon-2am Sat, 1pm-midnight Sun*

Bar 101: Busy bar with craft beer, pub menu, regular DJs and throbbing dance floor. *11:30am-12:30am Mon-Thu, to 2am Fri, 1pm-2am Sat, to midnight Sun*

ROQ: Atmospheric lounge specializing in cocktails, live music and salsa dancing. Thoughtful menu, including flatbreads. *4pm-late Tue-Fri, from 5pm Sat*

Vino's Bar & Grill: Upstairs is a West Virginia lounge with a Manhattan streak; downstairs is a casual hangout. DJs, pool and pinball. *4pm-2am Tue-Fri, from 8am Sat*

Morgantown Rail Trail, Mon River Trail (p76)

Morgantown

Stroll High St

Most of the culture and nightlife in Morgantown, former coal capital and home of West Virginia University (WVU), is squeezed into High St, a long commercial corridor just east of the Monongahela River. On the north end, WVU campus crowns a hilltop with stately brick buildings, and students trickle down steep walkways to the restaurants, bars and galleries below. Weekends can get rowdy, as WVU has a long-standing party-school rep. One exception is First Friday, a family-friendly showcase of local artists and gourmands. The lynchpin of First Friday is the **Monongalia Arts Center** *(MAC; monartscenter.com)*, an historic gallery and performance venue.

The **Metropolitan Theatre** *(morgantownmet.com)* is an active show space for concerts, plays and comedians. Each year, some 35,000 theatergoers travel from across the tristate area, most to catch touring musicians. The auditorium dates back to 1924, when it served as a vaudeville stage. Nearby stands a statue of TV star Don Knotts, a beloved native son.

THE ORIGINAL MORGAN

Morgantown is named after its tough-as-nails founder, Colonel Zackquill Morgan, who was born in Wales and fought in both the French and Indian War and the American Revolution. Morgan and his wife, Catherine Garretson, weren't just early settlers in the region; they were the first known colonists to build a home on the land that would become West Virginia. In his postwar life, Morgan commissioned a courthouse and public square, and he personally opened the town's first tavern. In 2016, some 221 years after his death, a statue of Morgan was unveiled on Spruce St. It was sculpted by artist Jamie Lester, who also created the Don Knotts monument around the block.

DRINKING IN MORGANTOWN: BEST BARS

Gibbie's Pub & Eatery: Deep hangout with multiple bars, an impressive local beer selection and generous patio. Lots of local regulars. *11am-2:30am*

Apothecary Ale House & Cafe: Hip pub with vintage interior and wide selection of brews on tap. *11am-midnight Mon-Thu, to 1am Fri & Sat, noon-8pm Sun*

Metropolitan Billiard Parlor: Basement pool hall with a small bar and lots of vintage decorations. A local institution since Prohibition. *5-11pm Sun-Wed, to midnight Thu-Sat*

Sports Page: Immensely popular sports bar with TVs, wings baskets and a locally famous iced tea. *7pm-3am Thu, from 5pm Fri, 11am-3am Sat, noon-3am Sun*

OUTDOOR ACTIVITIES AROUND HARPERS FERRY

Maryland Heights Trail: This 6.5-mile trail has some tough climbs, but hikers are rewarded with unparalleled views of the town and valley.

River tubing: The lazy currents are ideal for floating downriver in an inflatable tube. Come summer, make arrangements with **River Riders** *(river riders.com)*.

Ziplining: Fly along seven ziplines through the canopy, or walk an elevated skybridge, at **Harpers Ferry Adventure Center** *(harpersferry adventurecenter.com)*.

C&O Canal towpath: This segment of rail trail is part of a 333-mile bike route between Pittsburgh and Washington, DC.

Bolivar Heights Battlefield: These peaceful meadows and forest were hotly contested during the Civil War. See the cannons, fences and still-visible trenches.

The river itself – the 'Mon' – has always been the lifeblood of Morgantown, first for industry and now for recreation. Cycle or jog along the **Mon River Trail**, which snakes along the river for 19.5 miles, ending in the town of Reedsville, or rent a kayak or stand-up paddleboard from **Morgantown Adventure Outfitters** *(adventurewv.wvu.edu)* between April to October.

Harpers Ferry

Explore a Blue Ridge paradise

To call Harpers Ferry, about a three-hour drive from Morgantown, a special place is a serious understatement. Here, the beloved Shenandoah River merges with the Potomac on its journey to Chesapeake Bay. Three states – Maryland, Virginia and West Virginia – huddle together, and you can hopscotch across multiple borders without breaking a sweat. This valley has received more than its share of natural and structural beauty, thanks to rolling hills, soaring cliffs and two railroad bridges that span the wide waters. Even its architecture excels: the Historic District's stone houses, federalist brick facades and cobbled streets look virtually unchanged since hoop skirts were in fashion.

Harpers Ferry was also the backdrop for John Brown's final standoff. In 1859, the radical abolitionist attempted to attack the town, raid its armory and free enslaved people across the region. Instead, Brown's men embedded themselves in a local engine house and clashed with the US Army. Brown was tried and executed, but he became a hero of the antislavery movement.

You can see this story in three dimensions at the **John Brown Wax Museum** *(johnbrownwaxmuseum.com)*, which vividly brings this final struggle to life. Check before visiting, as the museum's fate was uncertain at the time of research. The center of the action was **John Brown's Fort** *(nps.gov; free)*, the name given to the little brick firehouse he used as a stronghold. The 'fort' has been moved slightly from its original location, but visitors can still tour the structure, and Harpers Ferry is packed with other monuments from the era. The town was literally designed for walking, but note that some streets are steep and not ideal for wheelchairs.

EATING IN HARPERS FERRY: UNIQUE VENUES

Rabbit Hole Gastropub: Craft cocktails and gourmet dining in a discerning country-charm setting. Beautiful porch and stone walls. *noon-8pm Mon-Thu, 11am-9pm Fri-Sun* $$

Kelley Farm Kitchen: West Virginia's first plant-based restaurant, set in a farmhouse. Riffs on traditional entrees and great ramen. *4-8pm Wed, from 11am Thu-Sat, noon-4pm Sun* $$$

Barn of Harpers Ferry: Converted barn with regular live concerts and creative libations. Food served Fridays and Saturdays. *4-11pm Wed-Sun* $$

Yatai Hibachi Food Trailer: Pan-Asian food truck. Claim a picnic table and watch chef Made Sudira work the hibachi. *11am-8pm Wed-Sat, noon-7pm Sun* $$

JON BILOUS/SHUTTERSTOCK

Harpers Ferry

Berkeley Springs

Soak in waters fit for a president

Not only did George Washington sleep here, he also bathed in Berkeley Springs – indeed, he was such a fan of the area, he bought up much of its real estate. Travelers have flocked to the town's 74°F thermal pools since colonial times, and Indigenous people likely enjoyed the mineral-rich waters long before that. Berkeley Springs is a two-hour drive from Morgantown and an hour's drive northwest of Harpers Ferry, but the mineral baths and quaint downtown are well worth the trip.

The town has two full-service retreats: **Atasia Spa** *(atasiaspa.com)* and Renaissance Spa at the **Country Inn** *(thecountryinnwv.com)*. You can also find warm waters in **Berkeley Springs State Park** *(berkeleyspringssp.com)*, home to the Old Roman Bath House. This historic brick structure contains a 750-gallon private mineral bath, where four adults can soak for up to an hour. All facilities offer a complete menu of facials, massages and other wellness services.

The town's main drag is, naturally, named Washington St, and its handful of shops and restaurants should occupy most visitors for an afternoon or two.

TOP SKI RESORTS OF WEST VIRGINIA

Canaan Valley: This state park has a sizable lodge, cabins and tent sites. There are 47 ski trails in the winter, plus an 18-hole golf course in summer. *canaanresort.com*

Snowshoe Mountain Resort: A beloved resort modeled on Alpine villages, boasting 14 lifts and 60 ski trails. Fire-tower visits and mountain biking are popular in summer. *snowshoemtn.com*

Winterplace Ski Resort: An intimate four-season resort in southern West Virginia, with 28 trails, nine lifts and 16 lanes of snow tubing. *winterplace.com*

Timberline Mountain: A great place for beginners and crowd-shy skiers. Timberline has 37 easygoing trails and a 20-room boutique hotel. *timberlinemountain.com*

EATING AROUND BERKELEY SPRINGS: BEST BITES

Naked Olive Lounge: This Berkeley Springs olive-oil tasting room triples as a gourmet food market and LGBTIQ+-friendly cocktail lounge. *11am-11pm Fri & Sat, noon-6pm Sun* $$

Cacapon Mountain Brewing: Follow your spa session with a craft beer in an upbeat Berkeley Springs taproom. Kitchen window available for bites. *4-8pm Thu, noon-8pm Fri & Sat, to 6pm Sun* $$

Lot 12 Public House: Savor chef Damien Heath's masterful dishes and thoughtful wine pairings in a converted, century-old Berkeley Springs house. *5-9:30pm Fri & Sat, to 9pm Sun* $$$

Prima Marina: Riverside restaurant in Moundsville serves up hoagies, freshwater-fish platters and beautiful Ohio River sunsets. *11am-8pm Tue-Sat, to 3pm Sun* $$

North Carolina

WILD COASTLINE | APPALACHIAN PEAKS | ARTS & CRAFTS

Places

TOP TIPS

On the Outer Banks, many restaurants have limited hours or close from November to March; call ahead to ensure your destination is open.

Blessed with islands and mountains, dynamic cities and arts-loving small towns, North Carolina seems to have it all. The state of 11 million residents also boasts astonishing diversity and a road trip here can take in everything from famous Civil Rights sites (Greensboro) to communities with deep-rooted Native American heritage (Cherokee).

The coast is synonymous with the Outer Banks – affectionately dubbed OBX – the chain of barrier islands that remain largely underdeveloped despite their popularity with summer vacationers. This is the region for visiting landmark lighthouses, seeing herds of wild horses and exploring hundreds of miles of windswept beaches.

Central North Carolina, also known as the Piedmont, is home to buzzing cities and appealing college towns (like Durham and Chapel Hill). West of there, the Appalachian Mountains hold some of the tallest peaks east of the Mississippi, and make a memorable setting for hiking, mountain biking, wildlife watching, rafting and numerous other outdoor adventures.

GETTING AROUND

Charlotte and the Triangle cities (Raleigh, Durham, and Chapel Hill) all have public bus systems, though using them takes some planning as they may be infrequent or limited. There are also intercity buses operated by Greyhound. Amtrak has several rail lines through North Carolina, connecting Raleigh, Durham, Greensboro and Charlotte by train. The North Carolina Ferry System *(ferry.ncdot.gov)* runs the state's ferry routes, including three to Ocracoke Island. Island Express Ferry Service *(islandexpressferryservices.com)* provides additional boats to the islands of the Cape Lookout National Seashore. Once on the islands, getting around by bicycle is an excellent option (especially in summer, when vehicular traffic can be a nightmare).

NORTH CAROLINA
KENTUCKY
TENNESSEE
VIRGINIA
NORTH CAROLINA
SOUTH CAROLINA
GEORGIA
ATLANTIC OCEAN
Lynchburg
Blacksburg
Roanoke
Petersburg
Virginia Beach
Norfolk
Danville
Kerr Lake
Currituck Sound
Corolla
Elizabeth City
Kingsport
Mt Airy
Hyco Lake
Roanoke Rapids
Henderson
Roanoke River
Hertford
Bodie Island
Kitty Hawk
Nags Head
Manteo
Albemarle Sound
Grandfather Mountain (5964ft)
Boone
Blowing Rock
Winston-Salem
Greensboro
Carrboro
Durham
Rocky Mount
Williamston
Roanoke Island
Knoxville
Mt Mitchell (6684ft)
Pisgah National Forest
Hickory
Statesville
Saxapahaw
Raleigh
Chapel Hill
Wilson
Greenville
Belhaven
Outer Banks
Cape Hatteras National Seashore
Cherokee
Waynesville
Asheville
Morganton
High Rock Lake
Asheboro
Bryson City
Lake Norman
Mooresville
Uwharrie National Forest
Goldsboro
Washington
Hatteras Island
Avon
Brevard
Shelby
Concord
Kinston
Pamlico Sound
Hatteras
Southern Nantahala Wilderness
Charlotte
Southern Pines
Fayetteville
New Bern
Ocracoke
Ocracoke Island
Croatan National Forest
Portsmouth Island
Spartanburg
Monroe
Morehead City
Greenville
Broad River
South River
Cape Lookout National Seashore
Laurinburg
Jacksonville
Beaufort
Toccoa
Great Pee Dee River
Cape Fear River
Lumberton
Whiteville
Wilmington
Florence
Carolina Beach
Athens
Columbia
Atlanta
Myrtle Beach
Bald Head Island
Augusta
Savannah River
Georgetown
0 100 km
0 50 miles
N
40
81
77
85
95
26

VENUS FLYTRAPS

Anybody who has seen *The Little Shop of Horrors* might be alarmed to learn that carnivorous plants grow wild in the wetlands of North Carolina. But never fear – real Venus flytraps and their brethren feast on insects and arachnids, not human flesh. A 'trap' is located at the end of each leaf; tiny hairs detect movement on the leaf and trigger its 'jaws' to clamp shut on the prey.

The Venus flytrap is cultivated around the world, but this unique plant is native only to the coastal bogs in North and South Carolina (specifically, within a 60-mile radius of Wilmington). See them in late spring and early summer, when the plants are blooming and actively trapping.

Wilmington

Bustling riverside city

Perched at the edge of the Cape Fear River, Wilmington grew prosperous on trade, especially after the arrival of the railroad in the 1840s. Nowadays, the historic downtown area is packed with handsome 18th- and 19th-century houses, plus colorful boutiques, craft-beer bars and classy restaurants, making it perfect for a wander.

Locals and visitors alike flock to the scenic riverfront boardwalk for waterside dining and sunset views. Docked on the west bank of the Cape Fear River, the mighty **Battleship North Carolina** *(battleshipnc.com; adult/child $14/6)* is an impressive sight from your vantage point across the river. Take the Bizzy Bee water taxi across to learn about the history and engineering of this storied WWII vessel.

Among Wilmington's most beloved destinations, **Airlie Gardens** *(airliegardens.org; adult/child $10/3)* is a 67-acre expanse of lawns, flowers and forest, bursting with blooms and dotted with artworks. Walking trails wind through the grounds and around a lagoon, connecting formal gardens and ungroomed forests.

Just 10 miles east of downtown are the sandy shores and crashing surf of **Wrightsville Beach**. Occupying a barrier island, this is a classic beach town, complete with windblown houses, seafood shacks, fishing piers and ice-cream stands, all lined up along the sandy lanes.

Beaufort

Discover the old town

Not to be confused with the similarly named town in South Carolina, Beaufort is one of North Carolina's oldest cities (c 1709), and it has the historic charm to show for it. In the heart of town, the delightful **Beaufort Historic Site** *(beaufort historicsite.org; tours adult/child $15/6)* includes seven 18th- and 19th-century buildings clustered around a shady green. Three historic houses are packed with period furnishings and artifacts, depicting daily life back in the day. There's also a jail, a courthouse and a 19th-century apothecary.

Wilderness of Rachel Carson Reserve

Beaufort overlooks a mosaic of scenic islands, marshlands and waterways that comprise the **Rachel Carson National Wildlife Refuge** *(fws.gov/refuge/rachel-carson)*. Here, ever-shifting

EATING & DRINKING IN WILMINGTON: OUR PICKS

Dixie Grill: Classic retro diner with retro diner fare, especially Southern classics like biscuits and gravy. *8am-3pm Mon-Sat, to 2pm Sun* $

Savorez: Its walls covered with artwork, this classy spot serves creative Southern food with Latin flair. Tops for Sunday brunch. *11:30am-10pm Mon-Sat, 10am-2pm Sun* $$

Fork 'N' Cork: Convivial bar with a dozen decadent burgers on the menu, plus craft cocktails and a daily-changing special mac and cheese. *11am-11pm* $

Flytrap Brewing: Sample American and Belgian-style ales alongside food-truck fare (and weekend live music). *3-10pm Mon-Thu, noon-midnight Fri & Sat, noon-10pm Sun*

Battleship North Carolina

islets and shoals provide refuge for wild horses, river otters and water birds. The best way to experience this blissful place is to rent a kayak or take a tour with **Beaufort Paddle** *(beaufortpaddle.com; half-day rental single/double $60/75, tour adult/child $65/45)*. Pull your kayak up onto the sandy beach at the western end of Town Marsh to explore several different habitats on two 1-mile loop trails. Be sure to bring water, as there are no facilities and little shade in the reserve.

You can also visit the Rachel Carson Reserve in the comfort of a covered boat with **Water Bug Tours** *(waterbugtours.com; adult/child $20/10)*. No paddling required!

Cape Lookout National Seashore

Explore the rugged coastal beauty

The most rewarding day trip from Beaufort, **Cape Lookout National Seashore** *(nps.gov/calo)* is a 56-mile stretch of windswept, wave-beaten barrier islands. The jumping-off point is Harkers Island, which is 17 miles east of Beaufort. There's a visitor center with a few exhibits, but most folks just hop on the Island Express Ferry Service *(islandexpressferryservices.com; adult/child $30/20)* and head out to the islands.

Your first stop is **Shackleford Banks**, a starkly beautiful place strewn with wildflowers and home to wild 'Banker'

BLACKBEARD THE PIRATE

Fierce and fearsome, Blackbeard terrorized ships up and down the East Coast in the early 18th century. In 1718 his fleet blockaded the port of Charleston, SC, demanding food and supplies and holding the city hostage for several weeks. Shortly thereafter, Blackbeard surrendered to the North Carolina governor, promising to change his ways. The reformed pirate settled down with his new wife in Bath.

This period of respite did not last long, however. Blackbeard soon returned to piracy, with the Royal Navy in hot pursuit. On November 22, 1718, Lieutenant Robert Maynard ambushed the pirate at Ocracoke Inlet, arresting or executing his crew. Blackbeard's head was cut off and hung from the bow of Maynard's ship, an ignominious end for a notorious swashbuckler.

EATING & DRINKING IN BEAUFORT: OUR PICKS

Turner Street Market: A quick, central place for fresh sandwiches, salads or hot breakfast. *7am-2pm* $

Black Sheep: A lovely waterfront setting to nosh on crusty pizzas with tasty toppings. Extensive drink menu too. *11am-9pm Wed-Sun* $$

Beaufort Grocery: Cozy, convivial bistro serving homemade soups and sandwiches by day, fancy dinners by night. *11:30am-9:30pm Thu-Sat & Mon, 10am-2pm Sun* $$$

Backstreet Pub: Cool cubbyhole with a breezy courtyard. Weekend live music, midweek 'Hoot Nite' jam sessions. *noon-close Mon-Sat, from 5pm Sun*

BEST ART GALLERIES IN OCRACOKE

Village Craftsmen: Run by the 10th generation of Howards on Ocracoke, this gallery features local arts and crafts and plenty of history.

Down Creek Gallery: This place overlooking Silver Lake offers fine art by Ocracoke and Hatteras artists, including paintings, pottery, glasswork and more.

Bella Fiore: Creative gifts and accessories, including scarves, bags, hats and exquisite handcrafted jewelry.

Over the Moon: Packed with quirky and clever gifts, art from recycled materials and funky arts and crafts.

Art Ocracoke: Island-inspired pieces, especially paintings of lighthouses, beaches and resident creatures.

CHANSAK JOE/SHUTTERSTOCK

Ocracoke Lighthouse

ponies. Trails crisscross the island, but they can be marshy depending on the tide. Pack a picnic and spend a few hours birding, pony-spotting and snapping pics of the supremely picturesque landscape.

From here it's a short ride to **Cape Lookout** with its distinctive diamond-patterned lighthouse. Wide and wild, the beach here is prime for swimming and beachcombing. 'Beach shuttles' take passengers around the abandoned buildings of Cape Lookout Village and down to the Point, the southernmost tip of the cape.

Outer Banks

Shipwrecks and wild beaches

Hatteras and neighboring Ocracoke Islands make up the **Cape Hatteras National Seashore**, a preserve of sand dunes and salt marshes, including 70 miles of glorious, undeveloped beaches. At the southern end of Hatteras, a few laidback beach towns cater to families, fisherfolk and surfers, but it's pretty quiet outside of the summer months.

The seafloor here is strewn with thousands of shipwrecks, earning it the nickname 'Graveyard of the Atlantic.' Every wreck has a story, and many are told at the **Graveyard of the Atlantic Museum** *(graveyardoftheatlantic.com; free)*

EATING ON HATTERAS ISLAND: OUR PICKS

Buxton Munch: Cheerful longtime favorite serving up nosh-worthy fish tacos, avocado wraps and crabby patties. *11am-3pm Tue-Sat* $

Orange Blossom Bakery: Filling breakfast sandwiches and irresistible pastries. A Buxton institution and worth the wait. *6:30-11am* $

Tavern on 12: Wildly popular local spot for elevated pub fare, including crab cakes, po' boys and Hatteras-style clam chowder. *11am-8pm Tue-Sun* $$

Oceanas Bistro: Islanders congregate at this Avon haunt for delectable 'grillers' (open-faced quesadillas), many featuring local seafood. *8am-10pm* $$

in Hatteras. Artifacts, photographs and video footage bring the history to life – not just the disasters but also the heroic lifesaving efforts of local villagers.

The **Hatteras Island Ocean Center** *(hioceancenter.org; free)*, is an indoor-outdoor nature center that's all about life in the marsh. See it up close as you walk along the scenic boardwalk and trail that wind through the salt marsh and maritime forest. Look for birds including herons, egrets, kingfishers, ibises and ospreys, as well as turtles, snakes and skinks. It's particularly lovely in the early morning and late afternoon.

Go carefree (and car-free) on Ocracoke

Take the ferry to Ocracoke Island to frolic on untamed beaches, explore the historic village and immerse yourself in local lore. The island's unofficial historian, Philip Howard, is a descendent of William Howard, the first European owner and settler of Ocracoke. Howard narrates two entertaining walking tours that are available for download at Ocracoke Navigator *(ocracokenavigator.com)*. Follow the tour 'Around Creek' to see the historically important sites northeast of Rte 12, such as the **British Cemetery** and the **Ocracoke Preservation Museum** *(ocracokepreservation.org; free)*. Southwest of Rte 12, the tour 'Down Point' includes the **Ocracoke Lighthouse** and grand **Berkley Manor**, built by inventor, industrialist and local icon Sam Jones. Packed with anecdotes and quirky characters, the tours offer fascinating insights into Ocracoke history, culture and island life. Both tours start at the Village Craftsmen (*villagecraftsmen.com*).

A well-groomed (but poorly marked) half-mile trail traverses **Springer's Point Preserve** *(coastallandtrust.org)*, a lush and scenic area of maritime forest, salt marsh and sandy beach. Look for the side-by-side graves of the former property owner, the aforementioned Sam Jones, and his beloved horse Ikey D. The route ends at the waterfront, where herons, egrets and ibises nest nearby.

Searching for the Lost Colony

In the 1580s – more than two decades before Jamestown – English settlers came to Roanoke Island to establish the first British colony in the Americas. The first English-American baby, Virginia Dare, was born in 1587. The site of this settlement is part of the **Fort Raleigh National Historic Site** *(nps.gov/fora)*. Unfortunately, the colony struggled from the get-go, and the governor had to return to England for supplies. By the time he made it back, his 116 compatriots had disappeared, almost without a trace. The fate of the 'Lost Colony' remains one of the United State's greatest mysteries.

Exhibits at the visitor center delve into the settlement's backstory and the theories behind its disappearance. Nearby are the remains of the earthen fort that was constructed by colonists in 1585. The next stop in your 'Lost Colony' experience is **Roanoke Island Festival Park** *(roanokeisland.com; adult/child $11/8)*, an indoor-outdoor living history museum on the Manteo waterfront. Back at Fort Raleigh,

FREEDMEN'S COLONY

Mike Anderson is an interpretive park ranger at Fort Raleigh National Historic Site *@fortraleighnps*

While Fort Raleigh National Historic Site is best known for the 16th-century Lost Colony, my favorite piece of the park's history is the 19th-century Freedmen's Colony, which was a safe haven for thousands of freedom-seekers during the Civil War. The goal of the Freedmen's Colony was to help formerly enslaved people claim their rights, by reuniting families, providing education, creating jobs and giving opportunities for property ownership. This story sheds light on the role of Roanoke Island in the struggle for freedom from slavery. Visitors can learn more by participating in a ranger program, exploring the exhibits at the visitor center or walking the Freedom Trail.

BEST HIKES IN THE OUTER BANKS

Nags Head Woods Preserve: Eight trails cross the maritime forest, thick with ancient oaks, hickories and birch.

Kitty Hawk Woods: Nearly 2000 acres of maritime forest, swamp and freshwater wetlands, rich with bird and animal life.

Dogwood Trail: A 5-mile paved path loops around Duck Woods Country Club, alongside a picturesque creek in Southern Shores.

Currituck Banks Maritime Forest Trail: A 1-mile trail snakes through salt marsh and maritime forest, ending at Currituck Sound. Lovely for sunsets.

Freedom Trail: This 1.3-mile route connects Fort Raleigh to Croatan Sound, with signposts detailing the history of the Freedmen's Colony.

the highlight of Manteo's historical experiences is surely the Tony-winning play the **Lost Colony** *(thelostcolony.org; adult/child from $25/12; late May-Aug)*, performed at the outdoor theater. This extravagant musical dramatization features Native American dance, Elizabethan costumes and epic battle scenes.

Flounder and dunes on Nags Head

Many a fisher has been known to while away a summer day (or a summer) waiting for a bite at **Jenette's Pier** *(jennettespier.net; adult/child fishing $14/7, walk-on $2/1, rod rental $12)*. Anglers of all ages and backgrounds line the rails, nurse cold drinks, cast their lines and share stories about big catches and near misses. It's fun to watch and even more fun to join in. All-inclusive 'family fishing' lessons (adult/child $20/10) are available for first-timers.

Five miles north of the pier, **Jockey's Ridge State Park** *(ncparks.gov/jockeys-ridge-state-park)* is a vast, desert-like landscape comprising the tallest dune system on the East Coast. Miles of sandy hills roll all the way to Roanoke Sound. Tracks in the Sand is an out-and-back, 1.2-mile trail that traverses the dunes. For a bit more adventure, rent a sandboard from **Kitty Hawk Kites** *(kittyhawk.com; $25)* and sled down. The steeper the hill, the faster you go. Prepare to get sandy.

Powerful winds mean that kite-flying at Jockey's Ridge is a popular pastime. The summit is also a premier spot to watch the sunset over the sound.

Historic flight from Kitty Hawk

On December 17, 1903, Wilbur and Orville Wright launched the world's first successful airplane flight at Kitty Hawk (now Kill Devil Hills). The 12-second flight is memorialized at the impressive **Wright Brothers National Memorial** *(nps.gov/wrbr; adult/child $10/free)*. The First Flight Boulder marks the takeoff point, with additional markers showing the distances of their four increasingly successful flights that day. The on-site visitor center has a full-size reproduction of the 1903 flyer, as well as excellent exhibits about Wright family life, the brothers' scientific process and their competitors in the race to fly.

Village and equine life in Corolla

The centerpiece of this little village is **Historic Corolla Park** *(visitcurrituck.com)*, a pleasant manicured space dotted with museums and historic buildings, including a

EATING & DRINKING IN THE OUTER BANKS: OUR PICKS

Art's Place: Fab local spot in Kitty Hawk for beers and burgers, plus live music on the outdoor stage. *7am-9pm* **$$**

Kill Devil Grill: In a historic diner car, this casual place serves sophisticated Southern-influenced fare. *11:30am-9pm Tue-Sat* **$$**

Corolla Beer Garden: Tiny wooden shack with a big shady garden and 14 beers on tap, plus occasional live music. *2pm-sunset Apr-Oct* **$**

Blue Moon Beach Grill: Not on the beach but still a fabulous stop in Nags Head for seafood and sandwiches. *11:30am-9pm Wed-Mon* **$$**

ACESHOT1/SHUTTERSTOCK

Whalehead Club

fabulous art-nouveau 'cottage,' dubbed the **Whalehead Club** *(adult/child $7/5)*. A 45-minute audiotour of the house gives insights about the history of the property and shows off its art-nouveau ornamentation. Nearby, the red-brick **Currituck Beach Lighthouse** *(obcinc.org; adult/child $13/free)* still shines its beacon to warn ships away from the barrier islands. You can climb the 220 steps to the top, which offers 360-degree views of sea and sound.

Wild mustangs roam freely on the beaches and dunes north of Corolla. If you don't have a 4WD, **Corolla Outback Adventures** *(corollaoutback.com; $68)* and **Wild Horse Adventure Tours** *(wildhorsetour.com; $65)* offer excursions that bounce you down the beach and over the dunes in the back of an open-air truck in search of the feral creatures.

WILD-HORSE HISTORY

Nobody knows exactly how the wild Spanish mustangs ended up in the Outer Banks, but historians believe they arrived with the first Spanish explorers, as early as 1526. Others theorize that some horses swam ashore from shipwrecks – or were deliberately offloaded as extra weight when ships ran aground on the sandbars. In any case, the so-called Banker horses have flourished on the Outer Banks for hundreds of years, with a peak population of 5000 animals in the early 20th century.

Nowadays, the **Corolla Wild Horse Fund** *(corollawildhorses.com)* manages and protects the herd of about 100 members in Corolla. Visitors can learn more (and meet rescued and rehabilitating horses) at its Betsy Dowdy Equine Center *(10am-2pm Wed Jun-Sep)* in Grandy.

Charlotte

Museums and galleries galore

North Carolina's largest city, Charlotte has an increasingly big and boisterous arts scene, with once-empty industrial zones now teeming with record stores, galleries, vintage boutiques and concert venues. A single block holds three of the best art spaces, all under the umbrella of the Levine Center for the Arts. The impressive **Mint Museum Uptown** *(mintmuseum.org;*

EATING IN CHARLOTTE: OUR PICKS

Mert's Heart & Soul: Homey soul food and Lowcountry cuisine diner. Don't miss the salmon cakes or the shrimp and grits. *11am-8pm* $$

Optimist Hall: Buzzy food hall with global offerings; crispy okra fries at Botiwalla and buns at Bao & Broth are highlights. *7am-9pm* $

Alexander Michael's: In an old blue house, this beloved Uptown tavern has welcoming vibes and comfort food with a twist. *11am-10pm Tue-Sat* $$

Supperland: In a former church, 'Supperland' describes itself as 'Southern steakhouse meets church potluck.' *5-10pm Mon-Thu, to 11pm Fri & Sat, brunch 10:30am-1:30pm Sat & Sun.* $$$

THE GREENSBORO SIT-INS

On February 1, 1960, four Black college students sat down at a whites-only lunch counter at Greensboro's Woolworth's department store. When asked to leave, they refused; they sat until the store closed that night. The next day, more students joined. Soon, hundreds of Black students were participating in what became known as the Greensboro Sit-Ins. These sit-ins quickly spread to other cities in the South, where segregation persisted in stores, restaurants, buses and schools. Sit-ins became boycotts of stores with segregated lunch counters, and owners began losing revenue. By July the Greensboro Woolworth's had taken a major financial hit and agreed to desegregate. Sit-ins as a form of nonviolent protest would continue throughout the Civil Rights movement.

JAY YUAN/SHUTTERSTOCK

Duke University

adult/child $15/free) has galleries surrounding a four-story atrium. Just across the way is the **Bechtler Museum of Modern Art** *(bechtler.org; adult/child $10/5)*, with a small-but-mighty collection of work by mid-20th-century modernists like Giacometti, Miró and Picasso. A block away is the ochre modernist building of the **Harvey B Gantt Center** *(ganttcenter.org; adult/child $9/7)*, with a small permanent collection and rotating exhibitions of contemporary Black works.

Raft the urban environment

Northwest of Charlotte, on the banks of the Catawba River, the **US National Whitewater Center** *(whitewater.org)* is all about outdoor adventure – especially the kind that gets you extremely wet. The main attraction is the artificial river, where visitors run rapids in kayaks or guided rafts *($59)*. But an all-access day pass *(adult/child $79/69)* will also get you climbing, ziplining, stand-up paddleboarding, doing yoga and more. Reserve your rafting time when you buy tickets, ideally for the first trip of the day – these can fill up.

EATING IN DURHAM: OUR PICKS

Guglhupf: Crowds pack the patio of this German-style bakery-cafe for schnitzel and *schnecken* (sweet rolls), washed down with pilsner. *8am-8pm Tue-Sat, to 3pm Sun* $$

Little Bull: Creative Mexican-American comfort food like *birria* (stewed meat) dumplings and steak with peanut salsa draw raves. *5-10pm Wed-Sun, plus 11am-2:30pm Sun* $$$

King's Sandwich Shop: Order at the window and take your chili dog and milkshake to a picnic table at this 82-year-old institution. *11am-4pm Mon-Sat* $

Zweli's: Bright cafe in a renovated tobacco warehouse serving Zimbabwean classics like piri piri chicken and greens in peanut-butter sauce. *5-9pm Tue-Thu, 11am-8pm Sun* $$

Winston-Salem

Peer back to the 18th century

Members of a German-speaking Protestant sect called the Moravians settled in what's now Winston-Salem in the late 1700s. Today, **Old Salem** *(oldsalem.org; adult/child $30/16)* is a living history museum extending across several blocks south of downtown. It's free to admire the architecture, shop for crafts or buy cookies at the wonderful, wood-fired Winkler Bakery. But you'll have a much richer experience if you pay for access to the on-site museums, houses and workshops, where costumed guides demonstrate Moravian traditions such as gardening, doctoring and gunsmithing.

Greensboro

Pioneers of the Civil Rights

In the Woolworth's building that was the site of the original Greensboro Sit-Ins, the powerful **International Civil Rights Center & Museum** *(sitinmovement.org; self-guided tour $15)* is dedicated to the history and legacy of the USA's Civil Rights movement. You can take a self-guided tour of the permanent exhibit, with pictures, videos and artifacts including the original Woolworth's lunch counter, but spending the extra $5 for the guided tour is well worth it.

Durham

A Day at Duke

In the town of Durham, **Duke University** is one of the country's most prestigious institutions of higher learning, with a splendiferous Gothic-style campus to match. The main attraction for visitors is **Sarah P Duke Gardens** *(gardens.duke.edu; free)*, an expansive 55 acres of koi ponds, terraced flower gardens and magnolia groves. Descend the original terrace where seasonal flowers are planted in luscious tapestries, wander the graceful bridges and stone paths of the Asiatic Garden, and picnic on the wide lawns.

Durham's coolest attraction has to be the **Duke Lemur Center** *(lemur.duke.edu; adult/child $17/12)*, a research and conservation institute that's home to the largest collection of lemurs outside their native Madagascar. Visits are by guided tour only, and must be reserved weeks if not months in advance.

Chapel Hill

College days

Strolling along a brick path through a shady quad surrounded by antebellum buildings: this is the **University of North Carolina** *(unc.edu)*, the US's oldest public university. You can easily spend half a day walking the historic campus, visiting photo hot spots like the Old Well (drinking from it is said to bring straight As), the flower-filled Coker Arboretum, and the Davie Poplar, which was already a century old when UNC was founded in 1793.

THE TRIANGLE

Raleigh, Durham, Chapel Hill: three points on the isosceles triangle that give the region its name. The three cities are deeply interconnected but also have their own identities. **Raleigh** has all the things you'd expect of a state capital: government workers bustling around downtown on their lunch hour, big museums full of kids on field trips, steak houses serving rib eyes to movers and shakers. **Durham** is diverse and progressive, with a downtown of old brick tobacco warehouses now full of restaurants, bars, bookshops and tech-company offices. College town **Chapel Hill** has long been nicknamed 'The Southern Part of Heaven,' and in the spring when the dogwoods and cherry trees bloom on campus and the sky is Carolina blue, it's easy to see why.

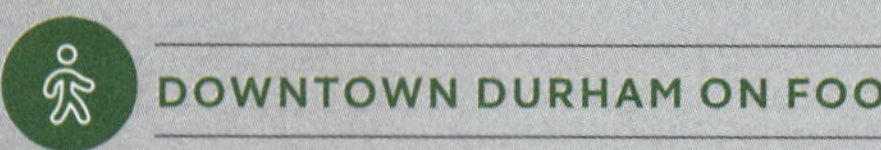

DOWNTOWN DURHAM ON FOOT

Wander among the stylishly renovated warehouses of this tobacco town turned arty hot spot.

START	END	LENGTH
Brightleaf Sq	Durham Bulls Athletic Park	1.2 miles; 2 hours

Begin at 1 **Brightleaf Square**, where two historic brick tobacco warehouses are home to restaurants, boutiques and a charming antiquarian bookstore.

Walk southeast down Main St, noting the massive 1948 2 **Chesterfield Building**, one of the last cigarette factories to be built in Durham.

After 0.5 miles you'll come to 3 **Five Points**, where Main St meets Chapel Hill St. Continue past the pretty brick and stone storefronts and restaurants on Main until you reach Corcoran St. Here you'll find the 4 **21c Hotel**, with edgy public art in an old bank tower designed by the architects of the Empire State Building.

Go north on Corcoran to CCB Plaza, where the iconic bronze 5 **bull statue** (its official name is *Major*) is the subject of thousands of Instagram posts.

Half a block east on Chapel Hill St is the 6 **Durham Hotel**, in a mid-century modern bank building.

Turn right on charmingly cobblestoned 7 **Orange St**, then again on 8 **Parrish St**, once known as 'Black Wall St' for its many Black-owned banks and businesses in the late 1800s and early 1900s.

Two blocks south, at 201 Pettigrew St, is the splendid Italianate 9 **Old Bull Building**. Finished in 1874, it's downtown's oldest edifice. Continue south to the restaurant- and shop-filled 10 **American Tobacco Campus**, across from the beloved 11 **Durham Bulls Athletic Park**.

The Five Points area has some of Durham's best restaurants, from Italian to tapas to fried chicken and waffles.

The *Life is So Beautiful. Life is So Hard* mural in the Brightleaf Sq parking lot is a quote from author and Duke professor Kate Bowler.

On the American Tobacco Campus, the iconic Lucky Strike water tower has presided over downtown since the 1930s.

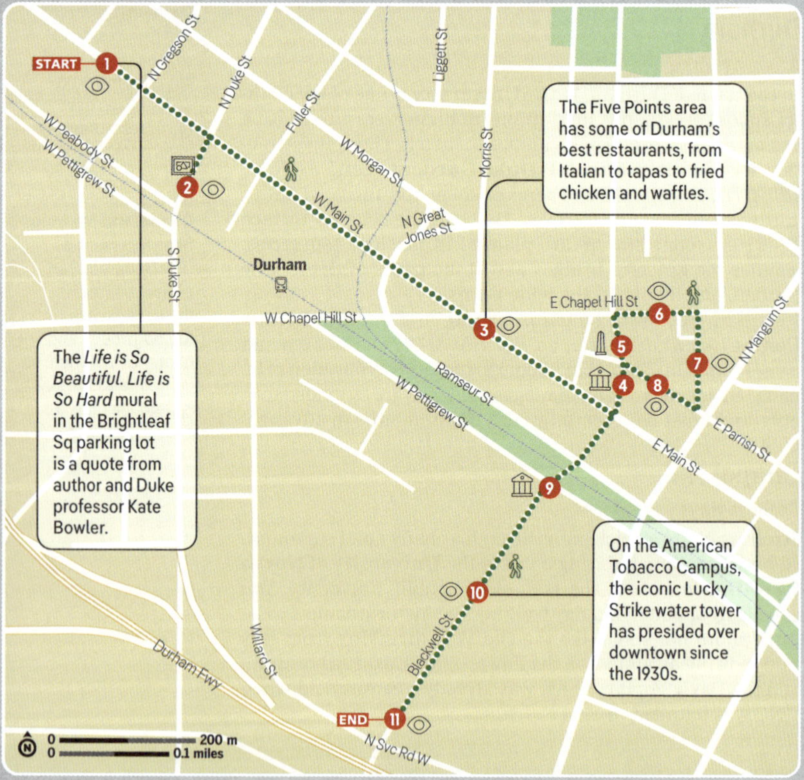

Carrboro

NC's most charming small town

Chapel Hill's little sister, Carrboro, is a former mill town turned progressive paradise. It's adjacent to Chapel Hill – get there by walking west on Franklin St. Once called West End, it was long the working-class neighbor to the wealthier college town next door. But things have changed. Today the old mill is Carr Mill Mall, whose co-op grocery, the **Weaver Street Market**, is the spiritual center of town, with locals eating and dancing on the lawn all day. Other major attractions of Carrboro include the **farmers market**, which draws crowds on Saturday mornings and Wednesday afternoons, the many coffee shops and bars, and the two-day Carrboro Music Festival, with some 100 bands playing at venues around town in early fall.

Saxapahaw

Explore a mill village

On the Haw River west of Chapel Hill, the village of Saxapahaw was a cotton mill town until the 1990s, when it was largely abandoned. It's been redeveloped now, and is a popular weekend destination for lunch and river activities like stand-up paddleboarding. Draws include the **Haw River Ballroom**, a music venue with a riverside deck in the mill's old dye room; the biscuits at **Saxapahaw General Store**, a laid-back gourmet cafe in an old gas station; and the trails and whale-shaped slide at **Saxapahaw Island Park**.

Asheville

Artists and artisans

The North Carolina Mountains have deep craft-making traditions. See the imagination on full display by heading to the galleries and collectives of Asheville. Occupying a prime position on Pack Sq and Biltmore Ave, the **Asheville Art Museum** *(ashevilleart.org; adult/child $20/10)* has a stellar collection of 20th- and 21st-century American art, with a focus on the Southeast.

Nearby, the **Noir Collective** *(noircollectiveavl.com)* is a pillar of the historic Black business district, and a great place to discover emerging and established artists, artisans and designers from Asheville's Black community. You'll find paintings, graphic T-shirts, jewelry and incense, as well as books.

BEST LIVE MUSIC SPOTS IN ASHEVILLE

Orange Peel: A showcase for big-name indie bands since 2002. Seats a thousand-strong crowd.

Asheville Music Hall: Upstairs is AMH; One Stop is downstairs. Diverse sounds from funk, reggae and jazz to rock tribute bands.

Grey Eagle: All-ages club that's a great place to catch rising and established stars playing bluegrass, rockabilly, folk and blues.

Jack of the Wood Pub: Welcoming tavern with a small stage where you can catch Irish folk and Appalachian music jams.

Highland Brewing Co: A 10-minute drive from downtown, Asheville's largest independent brewery hosts mountain music and other sounds.

EATING & DRINKING IN ASHEVILLE: OUR PICKS

Huli Sue's: Perfect barbecue stars in smokehouse salads and pulled-pork sandwiches. Also blackened-fish tacos, poke bowls and tropical cocktails. hours vary *hours vary* $$

Chai Pani: Like a colorful Bollywood film, with small plates perfect for sharing; try the okra fries or kale *pakoras* (fritters). *11am-3pm & 5-9pm* $$

Cúrate: Convivial hangout celebrating the elegant simplicity of Spanish tapas, with an occasional Southern twist. *4-10:30pm Tue-Thu, from 11am Fri-Sun* $$$

Battery Park Book Exchange & Champagne Bar: Raise a glass in Asheville's most atmospheric drinking den. *hours vary*

BLACK CULTURE IN ASHEVILLE

Alexandria Ravenel, co-founder of Noir Collective (p89), shares insight on the heritage of Black Asheville *@noir collectiveavl*

The YMI Cultural Center has been here for over 130 years, and it sits central to what is now called the historic Black business district. Before my time there were a lot of Black-owned businesses on South Market St and Eagle St. YMI was at the heart of all that activity, and it still plays a vital role in what's sometimes called 'the Block.' It offers extensive programming on workforce development and housing opportunities, with space for youth projects. With a beautiful gallery space and a state-of-the-art ballroom, YMI also does a great job in keeping the culture going strong in Black Asheville, with lecture series, town halls and jazz nights.

Some of the old buildings of downtown now hold galleries. At the **Woolworth Walk**, you can browse works by dozens of creators in a 1938 Woolworth store.

Badly affected by flooding from Hurricane Helene in 2024, the **River Arts District** *(RAD; riverartsdistrict.com)* nevertheless continues to play a vital role in the city's creative community. Start the journey through RAD at the **Odyssey Gallery of Ceramic Arts** *(odysseygalleryofceramicarts.com)*, which features the wide-ranging work of nearly two dozen artists.

Beer City USA

A walk through the South Slope Brewing District is an easy introduction to 'Beer City USA' – an apt nickname for a metropolitan area with more than 50 breweries and cideries catering to a population of just 95,000. The massive **Wicked Weed** *(wickedweedbrewing.com)* mothership, with over two dozen taps, is a stalwart of Biltmore Ave. Never mind the menacing logo at **Burial** *(burialbeer.com)*: this friendly joint whips up some of Asheville's finest and most experimental Belgian-leaning styles. Step inside the multistory **Green Man** *(greenman brewery.com)* for English-style ales. Its original Dirty Jack's taproom has a scruffy, everybody's-welcome appeal; it's also a favorite of soccer fans.

Beyond the city limits you'll find some appealing options. Some 18 miles south of Asheville, **Sierra Nevada** *(sierranevada.com/visit/mills-river)* is a massive brewery from the California-based icon with great food, 23 taps, daily tours, a patio and live music on weekend afternoons from 2pm to 5pm.

America's grandest mansion

The largest privately owned home in the US, Biltmore House was completed in 1895 for shipping and railroad heir George Washington Vanderbilt II, and modeled after a French Renaissance–style chateau. **Biltmore** *(biltmore.com; adult/child from $85/50)* is extraordinarily expensive to visit, but you could spend the better part of a day exploring this 8000-acre estate with its dazzling art-filled house (which you'll see on a self-guided tour), gardens and satellite areas including the farmyard and winery, plus 22 miles of hiking trails. Buy your tickets in advance, and arrive right at opening time to make the most of the experience. You can also eat at the Biltmore: there are numerous options around the estate, from casual cafes and bustling taverns to decadent, multicourse meals at the Dining Room.

EATING & DRINKING IN BREVARD: OUR PICKS

Square Root: Award winner with a creative menu including local mountain trout, cedar plank salmon and wok-fried brussels sprouts. *11am-9pm Tue-Sat* **$$$**

Oskar Blues: Wide variety of brews (and food-truck burgers) on a spacious covered patio, plus live music weekends. *noon-8pm Sun-Thu, to 9pm Fri & Sat* **$**

185 King Street: Proudly calls itself 'Brevard's Backyard,' with outdoor seating, craft beers and live music. *4-9pm Tue-Fri, noon-9pm Sat & Sun* **$**

Wood & Vine: Atmospheric spot for innovative wines, plus oysters, wood-fired pizzas and truffle ravioli. *4:30-8pm Tue-Sat* **$$**

KONSTANTIN L/SHUTTERSTOCK

Biltmore

Blowing Rock

Forested beauty

The stately and idyllic mountain village of Blowing Rock makes a scenic base for exploring North Carolina's forests and mountains – among the tallest in the Eastern USA. Just a few minutes' walk from Main St, the **Glen Burney Falls Trail** takes you past a series of waterfalls, where you can admire the silvery streams pouring over slick smooth boulders amid birdsong and rhododendron.

The highest of the Blue Ridge Mountains, **Grandfather Mountain** *(grandfather.com; adult/child from $25/10)* is famous for the Mile High Swinging Bridge (though a mile above sea level, the bridge stretches just 80ft above a chasm). There's also a nature center with rescued wildlife, and plenty of walks. The challenging Grandfather Trail to Calloway Peak (2.4 miles one way) takes you scrambling up ladders and holding on to cables as you ascend steep slopes.

If you're just here to hike, you can head instead to **Grandfather Mountain State Park** *(ncparks.gov; free)*. Access its 13 miles of wilderness trails at Mile 300 on the Blue Ridge Pkwy.

Brevard

Hiking, biking and gallery-hopping

It's easy to fall for Brevard, a charming little mountain town with a downtown full of indie shops, craft breweries, cafes and wine bars. Take in the art scene at the **Lucy Clark Gallery** *(lucyclarkgallery.com)*, with works in fabric, metal, textiles and ceramics by 45 artists.

Serious mountain bikers give high marks to the 86 miles of trails in **DuPont State Forest**, a 10,000-acre reserve located about 11 miles southeast

READING THE NORTH CAROLINA MOUNTAINS

Cold Mountain: (Charles Frazier; 1997) Adventure, savagery and heartache as a soldier journeys home during the Civil War.

The Caretaker: (Ron Rash; 2023) Friendship, love, betrayal and the legacy of war in 1950s Blowing Rock.

Even As We Breathe: (Annette Saunooke Clapsaddle; 2020) Set in the 1940s and focused on a young Cherokee man on a journey of discovery.

When These Mountains Burn: (David Joy; 2020) Masterfully told tale of addiction and redemption against the devastating fires of 2016.

Big Lies in a Small Town: (Diane Chamberlain; 2020) Mystery and murder in a small NC town; narrated by two women born in different times.

DRIVING THE BLUE RIDGE

The scenic **Blue Ridge Parkway** (p64) winds its way past overlooks and hiking trails for 469 miles in North Carolina and Virginia. Sections of the NC side were badly damaged by Hurricane Helene in 2024. Check road closures on *nps.gov/blri*.

SEQUOYAH'S SYLLABARY

Although he could neither read nor speak English, Sequoyah (1770–1843) became obsessed with the 'talking leaves' (words on paper) and felt they were somehow key to white settlers' power. After working assiduously for nearly a decade, he invented a writing system for the Cherokee language, which he unveiled in 1821. Consisting of 86 characters, the Cherokee Syllabary became widely adopted by the tribe within a decade. Literacy spread quickly, and five years after the appearance of the syllabary, thousands of Cherokee could read and write – far surpassing the literacy rates of the white settlers around them. Sequoyah became something of a folk hero for the Cherokee, and his achievement is astonishing: it's the only recorded instance of one person single-handedly creating a system of writing.

of Brevard. Rent bikes and enjoy a post-ride craft brew at the **Hub** *(thehubpisgah.com)*.

For more great outdoor experiences, head to **Pisgah National Forest**. Pick up maps at the Pisgah Visitor Center, a 10-minute drive from Brevard, then take a hike. Among many options, the trail to **Looking Glass Rock** is a strenuous, mostly uphill journey (around 6 miles round trip) to a sweeping panorama over the Blue Ridge Mountains. Afterwards, cool off by zipping down **Sliding Rock** *($5)*, a natural 60ft slide of smooth, gently sloping granite into an 8ft deep pool at the bottom.

Cherokee

Vibrant native community

North Carolina's westernmost tip is blanketed in parkland, sprinkled with tiny mountain towns and rich in Native American history. At the **Museum of the Cherokee People** *(motcp.org; adult/child $15/8)*, you can learn about Cherokee history and see works by living Cherokee artists and craft makers. Across the street, **Qualla Arts & Crafts** *(quallaartsandcrafts.org)* sells high-quality baskets, beadwork, wooden carvings, copper jewelry, pottery, finger weavings and paintings. There's also a small gallery displaying the work of legendary makers of the past.

Run by the nonprofit Cherokee Historical Association, the **Oconaluftee Indian Village** *(cherokeehistorical.org/oconaluftee-indian-village; adult/child $25/15)* transports visitors back to the 1700s in a recreated settlement. Cherokee guides will take you through the open-air space, stopping at various stations where you can learn about tribal craft traditions, hunting and weapon-making.

Bryson City

Taking a scenic train ride

The **Great Smoky Mountains Railroad** *(gsmr.com)* chugs from Bryson City out into the wilderness on one of two memorable train trips *(from $65)*, each lasting around four hours. Special seasonal excursions are offered throughout the year, including a holiday-themed Polar Express from early November through December.

Rafting and other adventures

A true crossroads for adventure, the **Nantahala Outdoor Center** *(noc.com)* specializes in wet and wild rafting trips down the Nantahala River. The center's 500-acre main campus also offers ziplining and mountain biking, and it has its own lodging and dining options. The standard, three-hour guided trip (**$70**) sweeps eight-person groups on yellow rafts through the dramatic Nantahala Gorge. The scenery is superb, with dense forest lining both banks of the broad, ever-frothing river.

ZACK FRANK/SHUTTERSTOCK

Mountain Farm Museum

TOP EXPERIENCE

Great Smoky Mountains National Park

The Smokies are a magical place to reconnect with nature. Days here are spent hiking past shimmering waterfalls and picnicking beside boulder-filled mountain streams, followed by evenings watching fireflies on the move. Lofty summits offer mesmerizing viewpoints over the rolling mountains, while the dense forests and open valleys create memorable opportunities for spotting elk, black bears and numerous bird species.

DON'T MISS

- Oconaluftee Visitor Center
- Mountain Farm Museum
- Charlies Bunion
- Alum Cave Trail
- Kuwohi
- Roaring Fork Motor Nature Trail
- Rainbow Falls
- Cades Cove Loop

Gateway to the Southern Smokies

Just 2 miles north of Cherokee, NC, the inviting, modern **Oconaluftee Visitor Center** straddles a vast open meadow by the Oconaluftee River. Inside, interpretive displays inform visitors about the area's attractions, and volunteer staff give suggestions about hikes and present talks on wildlife.

Out back, the open-air **Mountain Farm Museum** *(free)* is a recreation of a Great Smokies farmstead, providing a glimpse into the everyday lives of hardworking mountain people in the 19th and early 20th centuries. The field beyond the fence is a prime grazing spot for elk – come early or late in the day to spot them.

PRACTICALITIES

- nps.gov/grsm
- admission (parking pass) $5/15 per day/week
- 24hr

OVERNIGHT HIKES

There are scores of options for overnight hikes in the Smokies, including the granddaddy of backpacking trips, the Appalachian Trail. There are few dedicated loop routes in the Smoky Mountains, though the many intersecting trails allow you to plan a loop without having to end far from your starting point. A backcountry permit and campsite reservation are required for all backcountry stays in the park *(nps.gov/grsm/planyourvisit/backcountry-camping.htm)*.

RETURN OF THE ELK

Before European settlement, an estimated 10 million elk ranged across the future United State, including southern Appalachia. By the mid-1800s the region's elk were wiped out by habitat loss and overhunting. In 2001 after years of study and planning, the park reintroduced a small herd of elk to the Smokies. Today the population numbers around 300, and they range throughout the park; look for them in the Oconaluftee Valley.

THERON STRIPLING III/SHUTTERSTOCK

Alum Cave Trail

Horseback Rides & Wagon Trips

Smokemont Riding Stables *(smokemontridingstable.com)* offers two different rides. On the one-hour River Crossing Trail *($50)*, you will indeed get to splash through the water during a scenic 3-mile loop. The 2½-hour Waterfall and Riverside Trail *($125)* visits Chasteen Creek Cascade. Smokemont also offers a 40-minute wagon ride *($30)*. Reserve ahead.

Hiking to Charlies Bunion

For a taste of the US' oldest long-distance trail, make the journey to **Charlies Bunion**, which offers a stunning panorama over a vast swath of the Smokies. From **Newfound Gap**, this 8-mile out-and-back jaunt follows the Appalachian Trail along the North Carolina–Tennessee border before reaching an outcropping with an awe-inspiring overlook.

Ascent to Alum Cave

The 4.6-mile (out-and-back) **Alum Cave Trail** is one of the Smokies' most popular, thanks to its scenic beauty and variety. A few steps off the busy main road you'll find yourself in a gorgeous green forest where canopies of rhododendrons overhang the rushing waters of Walker Camp Prong. The path's wide and flat first mile offers a delightful stroll with minimal exertion. At 1.4 miles the route crosses a log bridge and spirals up through Arch Rock, a photogenic cleft navigated by graceful stone steps. From here a more pronounced climb, punctuated by breathtaking views of the valley below, leads to Alum Cave (2.3 miles), a dramatic overhang of sandy-hued stone that contrasts fetchingly with the surrounding forest and serves as a convenient umbrella during rainstorms. Most people retrace their steps from here, but you can continue

2.7 miles further on the steep trail toward the summit. The views just keep getting better, while strategically placed cables serve as handholds for navigating slippery stretches of rock underfoot. At trail's end (5 miles), turn right on the Rainbow Falls Trail to reach LeConte Lodge, Mt LeConte's summit and a pair of classic viewpoints: Cliff Tops and Myrtle Point.

Overnighting on the Mountain

Spending the night in the **LeConte Lodge** is a bucket-list goal for many in-the-know Smokies visitors. The rustic cabins clustered at 6400ft above sea level offer the national park's only indoor accommodation. While amenities are generally simple – bunk beds, kerosene lamps, front-porch rockers, a washbasin and a shared outhouse – the effort of getting here makes it all the sweeter. The only way in is on foot, tackling one of several steep trails – none less than 5 miles – to reach your accommodation.

Reservations are awarded by lottery. In September the lodge accepts reservation requests (via *lecontelodge.com/reservations*) for the following season (March through November), with winners notified on October 1. Lodging and meals per person costs $190 ($104 for children).

Greet the Dawn at Kuwohi

At 6643ft, **Kuwohi** (formerly known as Clingmans Dome) is the highest point in Great Smoky Mountains National Park. In 1959 the National Park Service added a space-age viewing platform near the summit, which affords 360-degree views of the Smokies' grandeur. A magical time to visit is in the early morning on a clear day, when the sun crests the mountains' eastern slopes and mists hang in the valleys below. You'll also enjoy the experience without the sizable crowds that come

GHOST TOWN IN THE FOREST

From 1910 until the creation of the park in 1934, Elkmont saw the rise of small vacation homes, complete with large porches, bold colors and plenty of natural wood details. Today you can experience a remnant of the whimsical world created a century ago with a visit to **Daisy Town** (aka Elkmont Historic District), a painstakingly restored cluster of structures near the Elkmont Campground. Afterwards, continue uphill and onto the **Jakes Creek Trail** to see more ghostly ruins, including solitary chimneys, moss-covered steps and low stone walls, as well as one restored two-story house you can enter.

SK TANNER PHOTOGRAPHY/SHUTTERSTOCK

Kuwohi

TOP TIPS

- Gatlinburg (Tennessee) and Cherokee (North Carolina) are the closest towns to the park, and good places to arrange last-minute lodging.
- There are no restaurants in the park so be sure to pack a picnic.
- Arrive early in the morning at popular trailheads (like Alum Cave). Parking lots can fill up by 8am, leaving you out of luck. Alternatively, book a ride on a shuttle with **A Walk in the Woods** *(awalkinthewoods.com)* from Gatlinburg.
- The best way to travel the 11-mile Cades Cove loop is by bicycle on vehicle-free Wednesdays (mid-June to September). You can rent bikes on site.

later in the day. Kuwohi is reached from Newfound Gap via a 7-mile spur road. From the parking lot it's a taxing half-mile climb (up a paved trail) to the viewing platform, with an elevation gain of 300ft.

The Climb to Ramsey Cascades

For those with the stamina to tackle it, the beautiful climb to **Ramsey Cascades**, the park's highest waterfall, is one of the Smokies' most rewarding hikes. Ascending 2280ft over 4 miles, the Ramsey Cascades Trail starts in the remote Greenbrier section of the park, 11 miles east of Gatlinburg via the mostly unpaved Greenbrier and Ramsey Prong Rds. Along the way, you'll pass through old-growth forest with some massive tulip trees.

Driving the Roaring Fork Motor Nature Trail

The Roaring Fork area is named for one of the park's biggest and most powerful mountain streams and is well loved for its waterfalls, glimpses of old-growth forest and excellent selection of preserved cabins, gristmills and other historic structures. The one-way 5.5-mile **Roaring Fork Motor Nature Trail** begins and ends a short distance from downtown Gatlinburg.

A worthwhile add-on is the hike to **Rainbow Falls**, one of the park's most dramatic – and one sure to give you a good workout. From the trailhead, it's a 2.8-mile uphill trek with 1600ft of elevation gain. Your reward is one of the Smokies' highest waterfalls, cascading 90ft down a cliff immersed in forest. The fine stone-slab bridge over LeConte Creek makes for a delightful place to soak up the view.

Other fine routes here include the walk to **Grotto Falls**, most easily accessed via a 1.4-mile section of the **Trillium Gap Trail**. Beyond the beauty of the falls themselves, this outing offers two unique features: the chance to walk behind the 25ft cascades (a classic Smokies photo op) and the rare opportunity to cross paths with llamas carrying supplies to and from LeConte Lodge. Llamas travel the Trillium Gap Trail on Monday, Wednesday and Friday.

Time Travel on Cades Cove Loop

Thanks to its history, wildlife and pastoral scenery, the 11-mile **Cades Cove Loop** has become one of the Smokies' most sought-after tourist destinations. Alas, its popularity all too often translates into traffic congestion. To fully appreciate Cades Cove's majesty without the crowds, set off at dawn or in the late afternoon.

The one-way road encircles land used as a hunting ground by the Cherokee before English, Scots-Irish and German settlers arrived in the 1820s. These determined newcomers built cabins and churches while clearing the valley's trees for farmland. Mills, forges and blacksmith shops soon followed, creating a thriving community. Today the creaky cabins, mossy spring houses, weathered barns and tidy cemeteries whisper the stories of the families who made this place their home.

Tennessee

BLUES & COUNTRY | FORESTED PEAKS | CAPTIVATING CITIES

Most states have one official state song. Tennessee has 11 – and for good reason: this place has music deep within its soul. Here, you can find the mountain twang of folk music in Appalachia, bluesy rhythms of African American communities in the western Delta, and those polished country chords for which Nashville is famed.

The state's three geographic regions are represented by the three stars on the Tennessee flag. Each has its own unique beauty: the heather-colored peaks of the Great Smoky Mountains; the lush green valleys of the central plateau around Nashville; and the sultry lowlands near Memphis.

Apart from visiting fabled recording studios and hallowed Graceland, the Volunteer State is the place for art and culture, dining and nightlife, from Memphis to Chattanooga. Follow this with some nature time amid forested trails, shimmering waterfalls and rocky overlooks – the perfect complement to big-city rambles.

Places

TOP TIPS

While traveling through Tennessee, be sure to tune in to its excellent radio stations. The nonprofit, community-run WYXR (91.7 FM) in Memphis plays blues, hip-hop, jazz and indie rock. In Nashville, WNXP (91.1 FM) plays wide-ranging grooves with a focus on Music City's local talent. In Chattanooga check out WUTC (88.1 FM) for live local music.

GETTING AROUND

In Memphis, MATA *(matatransit.com)* operates buses as well as a vintage trolley line that runs up Main St (passing Beale St along the way). In Nashville, WeGo Public Transit *(wegotransit.com)* has decent service for getting around town (Rte 4 is useful for getting from downtown to East Nashville). You can also get around town on Nashville's good bikesharing network *(nashville.bcycle.com)*. Memphis and Nashville both have Uber and Lyft. For city-to-city transport, Greyhound is about your only option, though you can take the scenic train to New Orleans if you're heading south from Memphis.

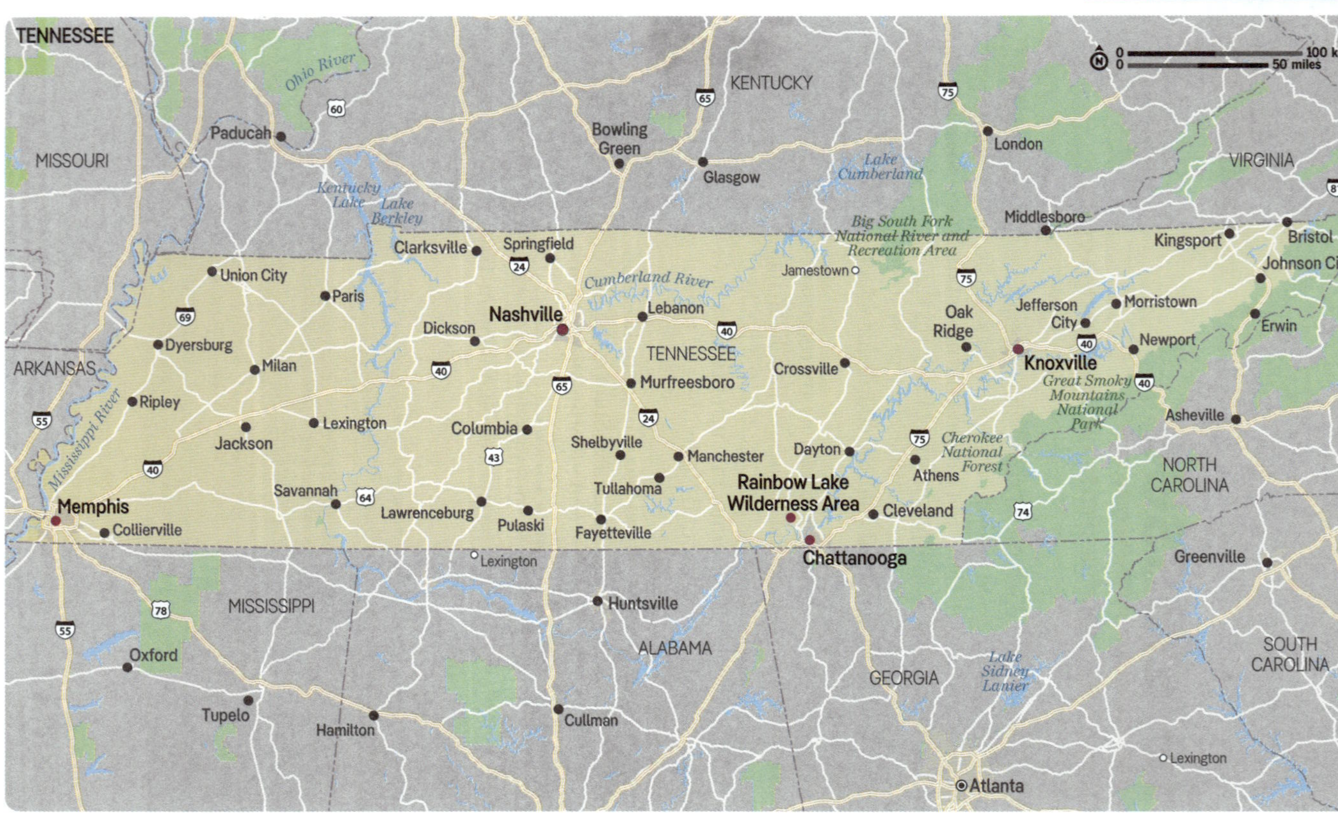
TENNESSEE
0 100 km
0 50 miles
KENTUCKY
MISSOURI
VIRGINIA
ARKANSAS
TENNESSEE
NORTH CAROLINA
MISSISSIPPI
ALABAMA
GEORGIA
SOUTH CAROLINA
Ohio River
Kentucky Lake
Lake Berkley
Lake Cumberland
Cumberland River
Mississippi River
Big South Fork National River and Recreation Area
Great Smoky Mountains National Park
Cherokee National Forest
Lake Sidney Lanier
Paducah
Bowling Green
Glasgow
London
Middlesboro
Kingsport
Bristol
Johnson City
Erwin
Morristown
Jefferson City
Newport
Asheville
Knoxville
Oak Ridge
Jamestown
Clarksville
Springfield
Union City
Paris
Nashville
Lebanon
Dickson
Dyersburg
Milan
Murfreesboro
Crossville
Ripley
Jackson
Lexington
Columbia
Shelbyville
Manchester
Dayton
Athens
Tullahoma
Rainbow Lake Wilderness Area
Cleveland
Savannah
Lawrenceburg
Pulaski
Fayetteville
Memphis
Collierville
Chattanooga
Greenville
Lexington
Huntsville
Oxford
Tupelo
Hamilton
Cullman
Atlanta
Lexington
60
65
75
81
24
40
69
55
43
64
74
78

Memphis

MAP P100

The fight for Civil Rights

Housed partly inside the Lorraine Motel, where Martin Luther King Jr was fatally shot on April 4, 1968, is the gut-wrenching **National Civil Rights Museum** *(civilrightsmuseum.org; adult/child $20/17)*. Its engaging and compelling exhibits chronicle the struggle for African American freedom and equality from the earliest days of slavery in the United States. Both Dr King's cultural contribution and his assassination serve as prisms for looking at the Civil Rights movement, its precursors and its continuing impact on American life. The turquoise exterior of the 1950s motel and two preserved interior rooms, which are on view, remain much as they were at the time of King's death.

Musical pioneers who changed history

Memphis draws music-loving pilgrims who come to pay their respects in a city famed for its connection to rock and roll. A good place to start is the **Memphis Rock 'n' Soul Museum** *(memphisrocknsoul.org; adult/child $14/11)* which takes you through the evolution of the genre, from the rural music of Black Americans singing gospel, field hollers and work songs, through the early days of blues recordings and into the emergence of rock and roll itself. Exhibitions and objects (a sharecropper's wagon piled high; an early vinyl-playing juke box; dazzling costumes worn by performers) bring the past to life, and there are lots of listening stations along the way where you can hear songs by innovators like BB King, the Staple Singers and Carl Perkins.

At **Sun Studio** *(sunstudio.com; adult/child $20/15)*, you can see (and hear) where the magic happened. Starting in the early 1950s, Sun's Sam Phillips recorded blues artists such as Howlin' Wolf, BB King and Ike Turner, followed by the rockabilly dynasty of Jerry Lee Lewis, Johnny Cash and, of course, the King himself (who started here in 1953). Packed 45-minute tours (hourly from 10:30am to 4:30pm) take you into the tiny studio, where you'll hear original tapes of historic recording sessions. Guides are full of great stories, and you can pose for photos on the 'X' where Elvis once stood and touch the microphone used by so many legends. Go early; tours sell out.

Wanna feel the funk? Head to the **Stax Museum of American Soul Music** *(staxmuseum.com; adult/child $20/16)*, aka Soulsville USA, a museum on the site of the old Stax recording

BACKSTAGE PASS

If you want to visit all of Memphis' major music sites, be sure to buy the **Backstage Pass** *($108)*, which is sold at **Rock 'n' Soul** and **Stax**. It gives admission to Graceland, Stax, Sun Studio and the Memphis Rock 'n' Soul Museum (saving you 20% vs buying tickets individually), and you can use it over multiple days. Elvis fans have plenty of other options, including VIP tours with a private guide and access to special collections *($145 to $250)*. You can further the experience by staying at the **Guest House at Graceland**, a 450-room resort featuring lots of Elvis touches (Priscilla Presley had a big hand in the design).

EATING IN MEMPHIS: OUR PICKS

MAP P100

Charlie Vergos' Rendezvous: Tucked along a downtown alley, this place has been serving its famous dry-rub ribs since 1948. *11am-9pm Tue-Sat* $$

Blues City Cafe: Buzzing spot on Beale St with a big menu, including turnip greens, skillet shrimp and juicy ribs, plus live music nightly. *11am-1am* $$

The Four Way: A 1940s landmark serving the best soul food in Memphis, from fried green tomatoes to catfish filets with yams, greens and cornbread. *11am-5pm Wed-Sun* $

Majestic Grille: This classy former 1913 movie palace has a broad menu of flatbreads, steaks and seared tuna, as well as weekend brunch. *11am-9pm* $$

HIGHLIGHTS
1 Graceland
2 National Civil Rights Museum
3 Stax Museum of American Soul Music
4 Sun Studio

SIGHTS
5 Cooper-Young
6 Crosstown Concourse
7 Formal Gardens
see 5 Jay Etkin Gallery
8 Memphis Brooks Museum of Art
9 Memphis Rock 'n' Soul Museum
10 Memphis Zoo
11 Old Forest State Natural Area
12 Overton Park
13 Overton Park Shell
14 Overton Square

SLEEPING
15 Arrive
16 Guest House at Graceland
17 Peabody

EATING
18 Blues City Cafe
19 Charlie Vergos' Rendezvous
20 Four Way
see 5 Imagine Vegan Cafe
21 Majestic Grille

DRINKING & NIGHTLIFE
see 5 Bar DKDC
see 5 Celtic Crossing
22 Earnestine & Hazel's
23 Eight & Sand
see 5 Java Cabana
24 Loflin Yard
25 Memphis Chess Club
26 Silky O'Sullivan's
see 5 Young Avenue Deli

ENTERTAINMENT
27 BB King's
28 Blues Hall
see 14 Lafayette's Music Room
see 28 Rum Boogie
29 Wild Bill's

SHOPPING
see 5 901 Comics
see 5 Burke's Book Store
see 5 Goner Records

studio. Dive into soul-music history with photos, displays of '60s and '70s stage clothing, a Soul Train dance floor complete with musical accompaniment and video, and Isaac Hayes' 1972 Superfly Cadillac, outfitted with shag-fur carpeting and 24-karat-gold exterior trim.

The world of Elvis Presley

Some 8 miles south of downtown, **Graceland** *(graceland.com; adult/child $84/48, parking $10)* is hallowed ground for Elvis lovers, who come to visit the King's former home and the sprawling museum complex adjoining it. Though born in Mississippi, Elvis Presley was a true son of Memphis, raised in the Lauderdale Courts public-housing projects, inspired by blues clubs on Beale St, and discovered at Sun Studio. In the spring of 1957, the already-famous 22-year-old spent $100,000 on a colonial-style mansion, named Graceland by its previous owners. A visit here starts with a short film, after which you'll receive a video tablet and headphones, then hop on a shuttle and head to the mansion. The tablet gives audio commentary (by John Stamos) as you make your way through the ostentatiously decorated home, complete with a 15ft couch, numerous TVs and some wildly imagined rooms (like the Jungle Room, which has shag carpet on floor and ceiling alike and a once-functioning artificial waterfall). The self-guided house tour ends near his grave. Next, you'll head to the entertainment complex, which houses Elvis' car museum, an exhibit on his time in the army, and a near-exhaustive lineup of memorabilia – including a beautifully displayed collection of his jumpsuits, in all their bedazzled glory. Don't miss Elvis' planes parked nearby.

Exploring Cooper-Young & Overton

Some 5 miles southeast of downtown, **Cooper-Young** *(cooperyoung.com)* is a vibrant district sprinkled with restaurants, shops and drinking spots. Everything is within a few blocks of the intersection of Cooper and Young Sts. You can browse for new and used vinyl at **Goner Records** *(goner-records.com)*, find some fresh or vintage comics and/or action figures at **901 Comics** *(facebook.com/901comics)* and discover new authors around the corner at the famed **Burke's Book Store** *(burkesbooks.com)*, which opened back in 1875. It has a special section on Memphis authors and local history, with used and new titles. You'll find works from artists with a Memphis connection as well as African carvings at **Jay Etkin Gallery** *(jayetkingallery.com)*.

LIVE MUSIC SPOTS

Beale St's music clubs draw mostly tourists, but this is the place for classic blues. Check the Memphis Flyer *(memphisflyer.com)* for shows elsewhere.

BB King's: The original Beale St nightclub from the blues legend brings a fine lineup of talented performers.

Rum Boogie and Blues Hall: Two adjoining spots on Beale St host popular blues nights; one cover *($5)* gets you into both.

Silky O'Sullivan's: Dueling pianos (and requests) make for a kitschy fun time on Beale St.

Lafayette's Music Room: Famous venue for quality performances (and good Southern fare) in an intimate setting near Overton Sq.

Wild Bill's: A gritty hole-in-the-wall juke joint with utterly authentic original blues. It's 4 miles northeast of downtown.

DRINKING IN MEMPHIS: OUR PICKS

MAP P100

Memphis Chess Club: Inviting rainy-day escape with good coffees, snacks and craft beer, plus board games including, of course, chess. *7am-8:30pm Mon-Sat, from 8am Sun*

Earnestine & Hazel's: This brothel turned dive bar has a 2nd floor of claw-foot tubs and tattered furniture. The Soul Burger is legendary. *5pm-late Wed-Sun*

Eight & Sand: DJs spin vinyl beneath a soaring record wall in this lounge-bar in the Central Station Hotel. *4-11pm Sun-Thu, to 1am Fri & Sat*

Loflin Yard: A massive junkyard-aesthetic beer garden with local beers on draft, barrel-aged cocktails, smoked brisket and other temptations. *4-10pm Wed & Thu, 11am-1am Fri & Sat, 11am-10pm Sun*

BEST ATTRACTIONS IN OVERTON PARK

Old Forest State Natural Area: Get a taste of the wilderness on the paved (1.4 mile) and unpaved (4 miles) trails lacing through this verdant old-growth forest.

Overton Park Shell: Spread a picnic blanket on the grass and enjoy free concerts from May through October, with food and drink for sale.

Formal Gardens: See what's in bloom or join a free yoga or tai chi class.

Memphis Brooks Museum of Art: Tennessee's oldest museum has excellent temporary exhibitions, plus live music, film screenings and art workshops (nude drawings, watercolors, printmaking).

Memphis Zoo: Earns high marks for its well-organized layout, fair prices and chance to feed giraffes.

FOTOLUMINATE LLC/SHUTTERSTOCK

Bicentennial Capitol Mall State Park

Stop for coffee at **Java Cabana**, a welcoming gathering place day and night (especially Thursdays at open mic from 7pm to 10pm). Grab a bite in the neighborhood. **Imagine Vegan Cafe** *(imaginevegancafe.com)* serves meat-free versions of Memphis classics, including a decadent barbecue sandwich. There's live music and good pub fare at spots like **Young Avenue Deli** *(youngavenuedeli.com)*, and cocktails and live bands (especially soul) at **Bar DKDC** *(bardkdc.com)*, plus some fine bars with terraces – like **Celtic Crossing** *(celticcrossingirish pub.com)* for nursing cold drinks amid a laid-back crowd.

About a mile north of Cooper-Young, Overton is another restaurant- and bar-filled district, with a dozen spots – many with patios. The epicenter is **Overton Square** *(overtonsquare.com)*, where you can catch free film screenings, food festivals and other periodic events.

Seven blocks north of the neighborhood is **Overton Park** *(overtonpark.org)*, a beloved green space that draws a wide cross section of Memphis to walking trails, sports fields, outdoor concerts, a zoo and more.

Wander a vertical village

One of Memphis' best-loved recent developments, the **Crosstown Concourse** *(crosstownconcourse.com)* transformed a massive (and long abandoned) Sears distribution center (built

EATING IN NASHVILLE: OUR PICKS

MAP P104

Acme Feed & Seed: A multilevel original on Broadway with Southern cooking, live music and rooftop parties (plus Sunday yoga). *4:30-11pm Mon-Thu, 11am-2am Fri-Sun* $$

Puckett's Restaurant: The Nashville original of this small chain boasts a barn-like decor, huge menu (breakfasts, Southern, sandwiches, barbecue) and nightly concerts. *7am-10pm* $$

Peg Leg Porker: Fall-off-the-bone ribs and tender pulled pork at this barbecue icon in the popular Gulch neighborhood. *11am-9pm Mon & Tue, to 10pm Wed-Sat* $

Black Rabbit: Beautifully prepared local rainbow trout, bone-in pork chop, creative cocktails and happy hour specials. Reserve ahead. *4-11pm Mon-Fri, 10am-midnight Sat* $$$

in 1927) into a live-work-entertainment complex with indie restaurants, shops and community organizations. Stop in the Memphis Listening Lab *(memphislisteninglab.org; free)* to hear rare grooves on vinyl; it also hosts music-related listening sessions, artist talks and book signings. On the same level (2nd floor), you can peek in a few galleries, or catch a periodic concert at the intimate Green Room *(crosstownarts.org/music/green-room)*. Next door, you can order cocktails from the small stylish drinking den, the Art Bar *(5pm to midnight)*. Restaurants and snack spots are sprinkled along the 1st floor. Top choices include the beautifully designed Bao Toan *(baotoanmemphis.com)* for elevated Vietnamese fare and creative cocktails, and Global Cafe *(globalcafememphis.com)* with cuisine from far-flung regions of the world. At Crosstown Brewing *(crosstownbeer.com)*, you can linger over microbrews (including their excellent IPA Traffic), munch on pizza and burgers, and catch trivia nights, live music and adult spelling bees.

Nashville

MAP P104

Discovering downtown Nashville

Tennessee's biggest city and capital is packed with intriguing attractions – not all of which revolve around Nashville's dynamic music scene. Before hitting the country-music bars, start your explorations at the **Tennessee State Museum** *(tnmuseum.org; free)*, where you'll find free parking and excellent multimedia exhibits spanning the ages (including well-done short films introducing different periods). You could spend several hours time-traveling through displays on natural history, First Peoples, the Civil War, World Wars and the battle for Civil Rights.

Next door is the **Nashville Farmers Market** *(nashvillefarmersmarket.org)*, where a large food hall has wood-fired pizza, Korean bowls, crepes, hot chicken, vegan tacos and more. Across the street, you can stroll through **Bicentennial Capitol Mall State Park** with its history-laden plaques and fountains, and make your way (up a steep hill) to the **Tennessee State Capitol** *(capitol.tn.gov; free)*. There you can wander through the lavishly decorated rooms or take a guided tour *(free, departing on the hour)* for more insight into Tennessee history and governance.

A few blocks south of the capitol, head inside the grand **Nashville Public Library** on Church Street *(library.nashville.org;*

TOP MUSIC SITES IN NASHVILLE

Country Music Hall of Fame & Museum: At the great cathedral of country music, you can gaze at Carl Perkins' blue suede shoes, Elvis' gold Cadillac and Taylor Swift's tiered gown from the Eras Tour.

Grand Ole Opry: Hosts the *Grand Ole Opry*, a lavish tribute to classic Nashville country music, every Tuesday, Friday and Saturday night from February through October.

Ryman Auditorium: See a show in the fabled venue where countless legends have performed.

Station Inn: Catch live bluegrass nightly at this long-running venue.

Johnny Cash Museum: Small but comprehensive collection of Johnny Cash artifacts and memorabilia.

Bluebird Cafe: Never mind the strip mall location, some of the best up-and-coming singer-songwriters in country music play here. Reserve ahead.

DRINKING IN NASHVILLE: OUR PICKS

MAP P104

6th & Peabody: Always a lively time at this sprawling indoor-outdoor space with a moonshine distillery, microbrewery and taco shop. *11am-10pm Mon-Wed, to 11pm Thu-Sun*

Close Company: In a redesigned candlelit warehouse in hip Germantown, you can sip inventive elixirs and munch on pastry pockets. *4pm-midnight*

Monday Night Brewing: Another favorite in Germantown, with an industrial-chic interior, huge patio and delicious house-made brews. *noon-10pm Mon-Sat, noon-8pm Sun*

Patterson House: Go early to score a spot at this intimate lounge with a Gatsby-esque vibe serving Nashville's best cocktails. *4pm-2am*

HIGHLIGHTS
1 Country Music Hall of Fame & Museum

SIGHTS
2 Bicentennial Capitol Mall State Parkl
3 Johnny Cash Museum
4 Riverfront Park
5 Tennessee State Capitol
6 Tennessee State Museum

ACTIVITIES
7 Nashville Public Library

SLEEPING
8 Union Station Hotel

EATING
9 Acme Feed & Seed
10 Assembly Food Hall
11 Black Rabbit
12 Peg Leg Porker
13 Puckett's Restaurant

DRINKING & NIGHTLIFE
14 6th & Peabody
15 Patterson House

ENTERTAINMENT
16 Robert's Western World
17 Ryman Auditorium
see 16 Stage on Broadway
18 Station Inn
19 Tootsie's Orchid Lounge

SHOPPING
20 Boot Country
21 Nashville Farmers Market

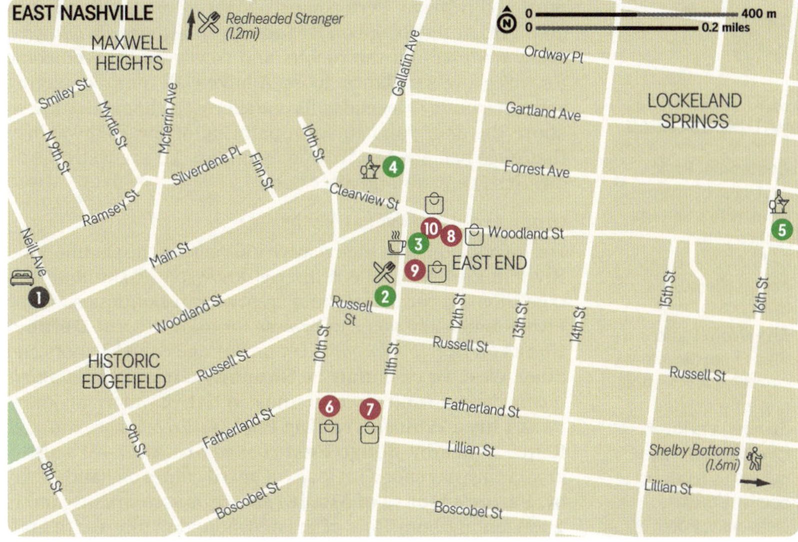

free). Head up to the 2nd floor to check out the Civil Rights Collection, a permanent exhibit with a symbolic lunch counter and various on-demand videos you can watch that spotlight different aspects of the movement.

From there it's an easy walk to Lower Broadway, which is thumping with shops, restaurants and honky-tonks. If you're in the market for Nashville's quintessential footwear, visit **Boot Country** *(twofreeboots.com)*, where it's 'buy one pair, get two pair free.' There are loads of dining options nearby, but for the indecisive, head to **Assembly Food Hall** *(assembly foodhall.com)* with dozens of vendors (and several bars) firing up a wide array of high-quality delicacies.

Hit the honky-tonks

The heart of Nashville's live music scene is Lower Broadway, a four-block stretch of downtown lined with music-filled bars, their bold neon signs lighting the way. The most venerated of the honky-tonks, **Tootsie's Orchid Lounge** *(tootsies.net)*, is a blessed dive oozing boot-stomping, hillbilly, beer-soaked grace with stages on each of its three floors. Nearby, **Robert's Western World** *(robertswesternworld.com)* is a cut above other joints, and a must for folks making a country

EATING & DRINKING IN EAST NASHVILLE: OUR PICKS

Urban Cowboy Public House: Stylish lounge and inviting patio make a memorable setting for inventive cocktails and wood-fired pizzas. *4-11pm* $$

Redheaded Stranger: Nashville's finest tacos, topped with ingredients like brisket, red hatch chilies and poblano peppers. Best enjoyed on the front terrace. *10am-10pm* $

Red Door Saloon East: Classic dive in bar-dotted Five Points with indoor and outdoor seating and plenty of love for the (Chicago) Bears. *11am-3am*

Bad Idea: Strange and wonderful mashup of Lao cuisine meets wine bar, set (naturally) in a converted church sanctuary. *5pm-midnight* $$$

BEST NASHVILLE NATURE ESCAPES

Centennial Park: Just west of downtown, with a full-size replica of the Parthenon and an easy trail around a lake.

Riverfront Park: Steps from downtown, you can go for a stroll or a run along the Cumberland River.

Cheekwood: The numerous gardens combine themes (Japanese, water, wildflower) with art, and surround a straight-out-of-a-Jane-Austen-novel house, where exhibitions are held regularly.

Shelby Bottoms: Boasts over 10 miles of multi-use trails including a paved trail that winds alongside the scenic Cumberland River.

Warner Parks: Picturesque overlooks, 200-year-old stone walls, old-growth forest and over 60 miles of trails, plus a nature center, play areas for kids, and regular events.

music pilgrimage. Performances start at opening and goes all night. At the **Stage on Broadway** *(thestageonbroadway.com)*, you can join the rockin' and rowdy crowd who come for three levels of dance floors. A huge wall mural depicting some of country's legends fills one side of the honky-tonk, and above the door you can see a painting of the Highwaymen that once belonged to Waylon Jennings. All are welcome by day; it's age 21 and up after 6pm.

Urban exploring in East Nashville

For inspiration, join the creative kids across the Cumberland River in East Nashville, a district known for its unique vintage shops, record stores and creative gift boutiques. At the Five Points Alley, you can browse for used titles at **Defunct Books** *(defunctbooks.com)*, try on vintage cowgirl boots and other Western essentials at **Goodbuy Girls** *(goodbuygirlsnashville.com)* and discover unusual Native American jewelry at **Three Wolves Trading Post** *(@threewolvestrading)*. Refuel at nearby **Bongo East** *(bongojava.com)* – it's also a great rainy-day spot with loads of board games on hand. Nearby, **Fanny's House of Music** *(fannyshouseofmusic.com)* is a welcoming bungalow of music where down-to-earth staff can you help you find your next new or vintage guitar, banjo or ukulele. There's also a small collection of vintage clothing and accessories.

Several blocks south of there the Fatherland District *(fatherlanddistrict.com)* is another indie shopping spot. Pick up western and retro-styled clothing at **Ellie Monster** *(elliemonster.com)*, hunt for old vinyl at **Daydream Records** *(@daydreamrecordshop)* and pick up assorted gifts (fragrances, jewelry, whimsical socks) at **Abode Mercantile** *(abodemercantile.com)*.

Chattanooga

Art and river life in downtown Chattanooga

It's easy to fall for the charms of Chattanooga, a Tennessee River town with a dynamic arts scene and a great love of the outdoors. At the **BluffView Art District** *(bluffviewartdistrictchattanooga.com)*, you can wander through a sculpture garden overlooking the river. Amid the greenery are over a dozen works, including pieces by Richard Serra and Leonard Baskin. Nearby, the **River Gallery** *(river-gallery.com)* showcases paintings, ceramics, glasswork and jewelry by numerous artists, many with local

EATING & DRINKING IN CHATTANOOGA: OUR PICKS

Niedlov's Cafe & Bakery: Heavenly pastries, outstanding coffees and flavor-rich sandwiches on perfectly baked breads. *7am-6pm Mon-Fri, to 4pm Sat* $

STIR: Artfully designed space in the historic Chattanooga Choo Choo complex, serving oysters, fish tacos, veggie bowls and steak frites. *11am-midnight Mon-Fri, from 10am Sat & Sun* $$

Hi-Fi Clyde's: Play ping pong, catch live music on weekend nights or linger over smoked wings and brisket nachos at this friendly corner bar. *11am-midnight Sun-Thu, to 2am Fri & Sat* $

1885 Grill: Tuck in to shrimp and grits, rainbow trout or fried chicken while relaxing on the tree-shaded patio opposite the Incline Railway station. *11am-9pm* $$

SEAN PAVONE/SHUTTERSTOCK

View from Lookout Mountain

ties to Chattanooga. Take a break at various restaurants in the area, including **Rembrandt's Coffee House** *(@rembrandts coffeehouse),* with its shaded courtyard.

Anchoring the district is the **Hunter Museum of American Art** *(huntermuseum.org; adult/child $20/free),* set in a striking building of elegant curving steel (like a mini Bilbao Guggenheim) adjoining an early-20th-century mansion. There's a fine permanent collection of 19th- and 20th-century works, along with Chattanooga's best temporary exhibitions.

It's a short stroll from here, via a pedestrian bridge over the Parkway, to the **Tennessee Aquarium** *(tnaqua.org; adult/child $40/30).* This impressive destination spotlights the inhabitants and ecology of the Tennessee River as it flows from the Appalachian Mountains to the Mississippi Delta. Exhibits in the Ocean Journey building display saltwater marine life. Crowd-pleasers include river otters, penguins and leaping lemurs.

Next to the aquarium, take the Passage, a lane that leads down to the river. Here, water cascades down the steps and into a small wading pool. It's a great spot for kids to cool off. Just below is **Ross's Landing** *(nps.gov/places/ross-s-landing.htm),* a stretch of greenery that was the starting point of the Trail of Tears. Artwork memorializes the forced removal of the Cherokee in 1838.

For hands-on adventures in downtown, head to the nearby **High Point Climbing** *(highpointclimbing.com; adult/child $31/29),* a requisite stop for rock climbers. The large center has bouldering walls and dozens of routes for top-rope climbing as well as auto-belay climbs covering a wide range of levels.

Trails and rails on Lookout Mountain

Some of Chattanooga's oldest and best-loved attractions are 6 miles southwest of downtown at Lookout Mountain, near the Georgia state line. Visitors come to ride the **Incline Railway**

GATEWAYS TO THE SMOKIES

Eastern Tennessee is a popular base for visiting Great Smoky Mountains National Park (p93).

Gatlinburg: At the entrance to the national park. Lures visitors with pancake breakfasts, moonshine distilleries and various odd museums and campy attractions, plus the mountaintop adventure park of Anakeesta.

Pigeon Forge: Some 10 miles north of the park entrance, the buzzing, often congested town of Pigeon Forge is another handy base, with myriad amusements, including the Dolly Parton theme park of Dollywood.

Townsend: A smaller settlement to the park's west; handy for reaching the Cades Cove section, some 16 miles away.

You can also access the park via the scenic North Carolina town of Cherokee (p92).

BEST ADVENTURES IN CHEROKEE NATIONAL FOREST

The 660,000-acre **Cherokee National Forest** in Tennessee's east offers unrivaled adventures.

Cherokee Rafting: Splash through family-friendly rapids on the Ocoee River or go epic on class III and IV rapids of the Olympic section.

Cherohala Skyway: See spectacular mountain scenery on the 43-mile drive from Tellico Plains (TN) to Robbinsville (NC).

Conasauga River Blue Hole: Snorkel the clear waters of the Conasauga River, home to over 39 different fish species.

Raft One: A one-stop shop for rafting trips, ziplines, horseback riding and mountain bikes for hire.

Benton Falls Trail: One of countless hikes in Cherokee, this 3-mile out-and-back route takes in Appalachian forests and a 65ft waterfall.

KEVIN RUCK/SHUTTERSTOCK

Rock City trail

(ridetheincline.com; adult/child $22/10), which chugs up a steep slope to a lofty neighborhood. From the top, you can stroll (head right 0.3 miles) to **Point Park** *(adult/child $10/free)*, a 10-acre site full of monuments and fine views that played a pivotal role in a Civil War battle. It's part of the Chickamauga & Chattanooga National Military Park *(nps.gov/chch)* run by the National Park Service, and you can learn more about the battle at the free visitor center and museum facing the entrance to Point Park. There are also numerous scenic hikes in the area, including the 3-mile out-and-back journey along the Bluff Trail to Sunset Rock. Access the trailhead in Point Park or start at the base of the hill at Cravens House (free parking) – the oldest surviving structure on Lookout Mountain and a major focal point during the battle.

Other attractions on Lookout Mountain include stunning **Ruby Falls** *(rubyfalls.com; adult/child $29/19)*, the world's longest underground waterfall. Next to it is **High Point Zip Adventure** *(rubyfalls.com; $22)* with some 700ft of ziplines and a 40ft climbing tower. Four miles south of there (in Georgia) is **Rock City** *(seerockcity.com; adult/child $43/33)*, a garden marked by dramatic rock formations and a clifftop overlook.

Rainbow Lake Wilderness Area

Waterfalls and lookouts

Near the settlement of Signal Mountain, some 20 minutes' drive north of downtown Chattanooga, the **Rainbow Lake Wilderness Area** *(free)* is home to bouncy suspension bridges, waterfalls, scenic overlooks and many miles of trails lacing through the area. Those out for a short-ish, easy-going excursion to the reserve's highlight can start at the Ohio Ave trailhead and make the 1.5-mile (round-trip) hike to Rainbow Lake. After rains, the water cascades 20ft over the dam, creating a lovely waterfall, and you can swim in the pool below.

For a longer outing, instead of heading straight to the lake, take the Bee Branch Trail, which will take you over an Indiana Jones–style suspension bridge. Turn left right after crossing the bridge and follow it down to Rainbow Lake. Afterwards, continue along the Cumberland Trail. This will take you past the spur trail to Rainbow Falls. For adventurers only, this super steep descent (0.1 miles) along slippery terrain has ropes that you'll need to hold on to to make it safely down and back. The reward: one of the region's most beautiful waterfalls, an 80ft cascade into a shimmering pool that you may have entirely to yourself (don't forget swimwear). Continuing on the Cumberland Trail you'll pass the Julia Falls overlook with its jaw-dropping views over the Tennessee River as it winds past Raccoon Mountain. The trail ends near Signal Point (another parking area/trail access point), where you can complete the loop by walking 0.5 miles on the road (it's a pleasant, little trafficked neighborhood).

Knoxville

Delving into the past in a World's Fair city

Dubbed a 'scruffy little city' by the *Wall Street Journal* before the 1982 World's Fair, Knoxville is these days a polished destination when it comes to the arts and outdoor attractions. The visual centerpiece is the **Sunsphere** *(worldsfairpark.org/sunsphere; adult/child $10/5)*, a golden orb atop a tower built for the Fair. You can take the elevator to the 4th-floor observation deck to see the skyline. Nearby, you'll find green space, fountains and a waterway, along with the **Knoxville Museum of Art** *(knoxart.org; free)*, well worth visiting for its impressive collection of East Tennessee artists. Seek out the turbulent works by the Delaney brothers, as well as spiritually charged mixed-media pieces by Bessie Harvey and the miniaturized wonderland of the Thorne Rooms.

Next, stroll a few blocks east to the **Museum of East Tennessee History** *(easttnhistory.org; adult/child $10/free)*. Interactive displays cover the Civil War (when many in the region sided with the Union against the Confederacy), 'hillbilly' stereotypes and mountain music, and the little-known role East Tennessee played during WWII, when the 'secret city' of Oak Ridge was created to refine uranium for the atomic bomb.

Afterward, walk through the sculpture-filled Charles Krutch Park and up to **Market Square**, where you'll find an assortment of outdoor cafes, restaurants and bars with tables on the plaza.

About 1.5 miles east of Market Sq, the **Beck Cultural Exchange Center** *(beckcenter.net; free)* is a great place to learn about African American history in Knoxville. The converted mansion houses rooms full of historic photos and artifacts, and kindly staff will put on a documentary about the destruction of Black neighborhoods owing to urban renewal. Next door, a museum dedicated to the artist Beauford Delaney is in the works.

MOONSHINE

Eastern Tennessee has deep ties to moonshine – un-aged whiskey, often sourced from corn. Moonshine earned its modern reputation during Prohibition, when alcohol production and consumption was banned in 1920. Enforcement, however, was difficult, and making illegal spirits provided extra income for Appalachian home distillers. To hide the smoke from their stills, the distillers made their corn liquor at night, under the light of the moon, hence the name moonshine. Although Prohibition was repealed in 1933, moonshining was a good way for families to make extra cash during the Depression, which continued across the 1930s. NASCAR racing is a descendant of the wild automobile chases of the era, when federal agents chased the souped-up cars used by the bootleggers to deliver their product.

Kentucky

THOROUGHBREDS | BOURBON | RUGGED WILDERNESS

Places

Horses thunder around racetracks, bourbon pours from distilleries and banjos twang in Kentucky, a geographical and cultural crossroads that's part North, part South, part genteel and part country cousin. Every corner is easy on the eye, but there are few sights more beautiful than the rolling limestone hills around Lexington, where long-legged steeds nibble under poplar trees on multimillion-dollar farms. Bourbon distilleries also speckle the countryside, prime for scenic road tripping to swirl and sniff a dram at the source. It's like an offbeat version of California's Napa Valley, but with fewer crowds and headier alcohol. Outdoor adventures prevail in the state's unspoiled parks and forests, which offer some dazzling attractions – including the world's largest caverns and thundering waterfalls that glisten with moonbows at certain times of the month. And while big cities like Louisville have farm-to-table restaurants, cocktail bars and a vibrant music scene, most of Kentucky is made up of small towns, including its delightful state capital, Frankfort.

TOP TIPS

Kentucky's farmers markets offer great ways to experience the state's bounty. Louisville has two excellent ones: **Bardstown Road** *(bardstownroadfarmersmarket.com; Sat year-round)* and **Douglas Loop** *(douglassloopfarmersmarket.org; Sat Apr-Dec)*. Lexington also has several farmers markets *(lexingtonfarmersmarket.com)* including a **downtown market** *(Sat year-round)*.

GETTING AROUND

Kentucky is generally a tough place to get around without a car. In Louisville **TARC** *(ridetarc.org)* runs a decent bus network that can get you around town (though not always all that quickly). Downtown is quite walkable, and route numbers 4, 6 and 29 run from there to Churchill Downs (with frequent service during the Kentucky Derby). In Lexington, there's a smaller bus network run by Lextran *(lextran.com)*. During racing season in April, buses connect Lexington's transit center (Vine St) with Keeneland. You'll find decent rideshare service from both Uber and Lyft in Louisville and Lexington.

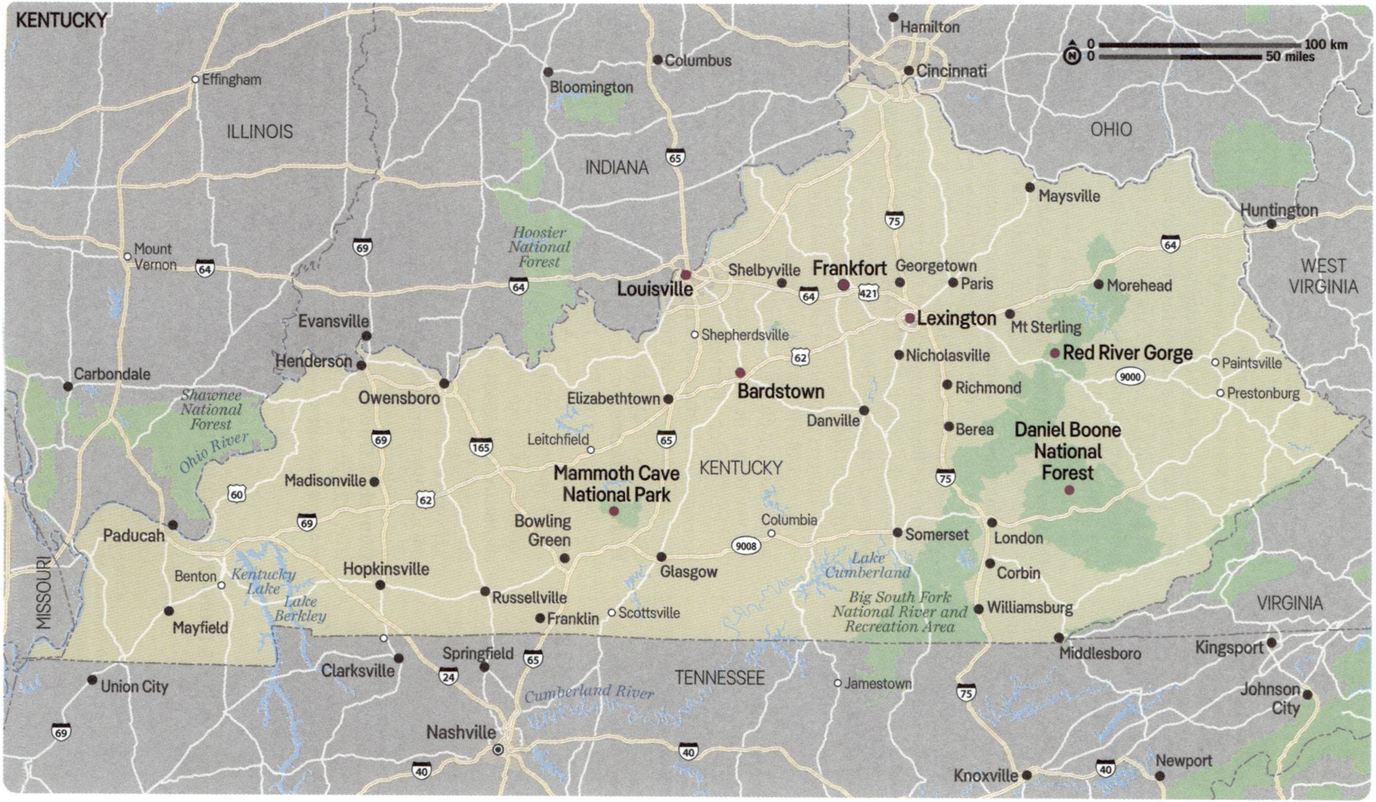

KENTUCKY

0 100 km
0 50 miles

ILLINOIS
INDIANA
OHIO
WEST VIRGINIA
VIRGINIA
TENNESSEE
MISSOURI
KENTUCKY

Hamilton
Columbus
Cincinnati
Effingham
Bloomington
Maysville
Huntington
Mount Vernon
Hoosier National Forest
Louisville
Shelbyville
Frankfort
Georgetown
Paris
Morehead
Evansville
Shepherdsville
Lexington
Mt Sterling
Henderson
Nicholasville
Red River Gorge
Paintsville
Carbondale
Owensboro
Bardstown
Richmond
Prestonburg
Shawnee National Forest
Elizabethtown
Danville
Berea
Daniel Boone National Forest
Ohio River
Leitchfield
Madisonville
Mammoth Cave National Park
Paducah
Bowling Green
Columbia
Somerset
London
Benton
Kentucky Lake
Lake Berkley
Hopkinsville
Glasgow
Lake Cumberland
Corbin
Russellville
Big South Fork National River and Recreation Area
Mayfield
Franklin
Scottsville
Williamsburg
Middlesboro
Kingsport
Springfield
Clarksville
Union City
Cumberland River
Jamestown
Johnson City
Nashville
Knoxville
Newport

75 64 65 69 64 64 421 62 9000 69 165 65 75 60 62 69 9008 65 24 75 69 40 40 40

THE KENTUCKY DERBY

On the first Saturday in May, a who's who of upper-crust USA put on their seersucker suits and most flamboyant hats and descends for the 'greatest two minutes in sports': the Kentucky Derby, the longest-running continuous sporting event in North America, when 20 horses thunder around the track at **Churchill Downs** for the race of a lifetime.

After the race, the crowd sings 'My Old Kentucky Home' and watches as the winning horse is covered in a blanket of roses. Then everyone parties. Actually, they've been partying for a while by this point. The **Kentucky Derby Festival**, which includes a balloon race, a marathon and the largest fireworks display in North America, starts two weeks before the big event.

Louisville

Kentucky legends

The must-see museum of downtown Louisville, the **Muhammad Ali Center** *(alicenter.org; adult/child $20/10)* tells the tale of the city's most famous native: a local boxer full of poetry and fearless conviction who earned the nickname The Greatest. Evocative exhibitions cover not just his sporting triumphs but his spirituality, humanitarianism and heartfelt generosity. There are also interactive exhibits, including a ring where you shadowbox with Ali, and a punching bag to practice your rhythm.

Nearby, a massive 120ft baseball bat marks the entrance to the **Louisville Slugger Museum & Factory** *(sluggermuseum.com; adult/child $24/16),* where you can see how baseball's most famous bat is made. Admission includes a plant tour and a hall of baseball memorabilia that features Babe Ruth's 1927 record-setting bat and Hank Aaron's 700th home run bat. A take-home mini-slugger bat is included with the entrance fee.

Across the street, the **Frazier History Museum** *(fraziermuseum.org; adult/child $16/10)* covers 1000 years of history in the land now known as Kentucky. Illuminating exhibitions detail famous expeditions like Lewis and Clark, the bourbon industry, Colonel Sanders (founder of KFC) and Corvettes (made exclusively in Bowling Green).

If you're not heading to the distilleries in the countryside, you can explore Kentucky's finest on the mile-long Whiskey Row. At **Kentucky Peerless Distilling Co** *(kentuckypeerless.com),* you can book a 75-minute behind-the-scenes distillery tour and tasting *($32)* at a small-batch distillery. **Evan Williams** *(evanwilliams.com)* offers memorable tours and tastings (from $20) that take visitors from the late 18th century to the present. **Angel's Envy** *(angelsenvy.com)* is a micro-distillery that lives up to its name, with high-quality bourbons you can learn about (and taste) on the hour-long signature tour ($30). Wherever you go, reservations are recommended, as these places are popular.

If you can't make it to the world's most famous horse race, the next best thing is visiting the **Kentucky Derby Museum** *(derbymuseum.org; adult/child $20/12).* On the grounds of **Churchill Downs** you'll explore derby lore through immersive, interactive exhibits including a jockey's-eye view of the race while atop a thoroughbred model.

EATING & DRINKING IN LOUISVILLE: OUR PICKS

Merle's Whiskey Kitchen: Buzzing, anytime spot for tacos, burgers and southern hits (like fried chicken), plus live music on weekends. *11am-10pm Tue-Thu, to midnight Fri & Sat* $

Holy Grale: Drink Trappist ales and slurp mussels in a Belgian gastropub and former chapel complete with stained-glass windows. *5-10pm Mon-Fri, from 2pm Sat & Sun*

Garage Bar: In buzzing bar-lined NuLu (New Louisville), this former auto garage fires up delicious brick-oven pizzas best enjoyed with an Atrium craft beer. *hours vary* $$

Proof on Main: Indulge in charred octopus, chicken Milanese and creative cocktails in an art-filled downtown space. *8am-10pm* $$$

JOSEPH HENDRICKSON/SHUTTERSTOCK

Muhammad Ali Center

Bardstown

On the bourbon trail

The elegant streets of Bardstown in Central Kentucky make an excellent base for exploring the nearby bourbon distilleries. Learn about the spirit's history from pre-colonial days through Prohibition and up to today at the **Oscar Getz Museum of Bourbon History** *(facebook.com/whiskeymuseum; free)*, then head to top-notch distilleries in the area like **Willett** *(kentuckybourbonwhiskey.com)*, where you can learn about production methods and family history on a 75-minute tour *($27)*, with samples throughout the experience. On a former tobacco farm, **Preservation Distillery** *(preservationdistillery.com)* offers intimate tours *($24)* of its small-batch operations. Plan your visit around the **Kentucky Bourbon Festival** *(kybourbonfestival.com)*, featuring three days of tastings, panel discussions and workshops in early September. If you don't have a designated driver, consider booking a tour with **Mint Julep Experiences** *(mintjuleptours.com; from $200)*, which includes three distillery tours and tastings, lunch and transportation.

Lexington

Horsing around

Kentucky's second largest city is often dubbed the horse capital of the world, owing to the staggering number of thoroughbred farms in the area. Some 10 miles north of downtown Lexington, you can get a deeper understanding of equine culture at the **Kentucky Horse Park** *(kyhorsepark.com; adult/child $28/14)*. Apart from the excellent museum documenting horses and their deep impact on human history (warfare, colonization, farming, transportation), the sprawling complex has shows and activities throughout the day – from horse-drawn trolley rides to draft horse and champion presentations, where you

THE LAND OF BOURBON

Silky, caramel-colored bourbon whiskey was likely first distilled in Bourbon County, north of Lexington, around 1789. Today 95% of the world's bourbon is made in Kentucky, thanks to the state's pure, limestone-filtered water, which contains a high proportion of minerals (like calcium and magnesium) that are optimal for distilling. Bourbon must contain at least 51% corn, and be stored in charred oak barrels for a minimum of two years. The char is essential for imparting those notes of vanilla, caramel and toffee, not to mention the smokiness. While connoisseurs drink it straight or with water, you must try a mint julep, the archetypal Southern drink made with bourbon, simple syrup and crushed mint.

A LEGENDARY FRONTIERSMAN

Lee Muncy, historical interpreter and member of the Sons of the American Revolution *@sar.org*

Before the Revolution, Daniel Boone was an employee of the British-run Transylvania Company, and he helped cut out a trail through the Cumberland Gap of the Appalachian Mountains down in Virginia. He ultimately founded Boonesborough, one of the first settlements in Kentucky. After the Revolutionary War, Boone moved to Missouri, which is where he was living when Lewis and Clark came to see him before their great expedition in 1802. They told him they were going in search of the Pacific Ocean. Boone said he'd already been there. Sure enough, when Lewis and Clark met various Indian tribes, a lot of them talked about that guy from Kentucky.

WANGKUN JIA/SHUTTERSTOCK

Mammoth Cave National Park

can meet the four-legged stars of the park. Check the schedule before heading here to avoid missing out.

Lexington is also home to **Keeneland** *(keeneland.com)*, with exciting thoroughbred races run in April and October, and opportunities to watch morning training sessions *($22)* or take a behind-the-scenes tour *($50)*.

Frankfort

Small-town charm

One of the south's most appealing little towns, Frankfort lies along the banks of the idyllic Kentucky River and its brick streets are dotted with indie shops, cafes and local restaurants. The diminutive capital of Kentucky also has a handful of museums where you can explore the past. Start off at the **Kentucky Historical Society** *(history.ky.gov; adult/child $8/6)*, where you can spend an hour or more learning about the lives of its former inhabitants, including Native Americans, pioneers, enslaved people, Civil War soldiers and moonshiners. There are lots of curious items here, like the pocket watch President Abraham Lincoln carried in 1860. Your admission ticket gives you access to two other nearby sites: the **Old State Capitol**, which was the seat of power from 1830 to 1910, and the **Kentucky Military History Museum** – the best place to find out about the state's involvement in wars dating back to the 1800s.

It's also worth visiting the **Capital City Museum** *(capitalcitymuseum.org; free)* for its displays on surprising events, like the assassination of Senator William Goebel, with accurately detailed mannequins gathered around the supine figure, who died in this building back in 1900.

When you need a break, take a stroll along West Broadway and intersecting St Clair Street. You can browse for regionally made crafts and artwork at **Completely Kentucky** *(completelykentucky.com)*, pick up new (and secondhand) reading material at **Poor Richard's Books** *(poorrichardsbooksky.indielite.org)* and purchase new and used records – as well as guitars – at **Musket's Music Station** *(musketsmusicstation.com)*. Enjoy coffee, snacks and yet more books at the **Kentucky Coffeetree Cafe** *(kentuckycoffeetree.com)* or head 1½ blocks southwest of there to **Engine House** *(enginehouse1868.com)*, a former fire station that today serves Frankfort's best lattes and cold brews.

Frankfort also has some distilleries near town. The legendary **Buffalo Trace** *(buffalotracedistillery.com)*, the nation's oldest distillery, has lovely grounds you can wander, in addition to free tastings. **Castle & Key** *(castleandkey.com; tour $30)* is among the most photogenic distilleries with its medieval-looking buildings.

Mammoth Cave National Park

Caving, hiking, horseback riding and canoeing

Home to the longest cave system on earth, **Mammoth Cave National Park** *(nps.gov/maca)* has more than 400 miles of surveyed passageways. It's at least three times longer than any other known cave, with vast interior cathedrals, bottomless pits and strange, undulating rock formations.

Excellent ranger-guided tours *(adult/child from $23/19)* explore the subterranean expanse. Book ahead if possible *(at recreation.gov)* as they do sell out, especially in summer and on weekends, and some tours are offered only at specific times on certain days of the week.

Jaunts range from hour-long strolls to strenuous, day-long spelunking adventures *(adults only)*. The **Frozen Niagara Tour** is the easiest of the bunch. There are several options that take place by lantern light, including **Star Chamber**, **Great Onyx** and **Violet City** – a nostalgic way of experiencing these caverns.

If you're short on time, opt for the self-guided **Discovery Tour** *(adult/child $12/9)*, where you can explore at your own pace through large open passageways dotted with artifacts from the cave's early days. There's also one accessible tour, where you can visit (via elevator) several impressive formation-filled rooms with no stairs involved.

In addition to the caves, the park contains 85 miles of trails. You can head off on memorable hikes, like the moderate 2.5-mile loop along the **Green River Bluffs** and **Heritage Loop** trails, where you'll enjoy some wonderful views over the dense forests. You can also experience the woodlands by horseback: family-owned **Double J Stables** *(doublejstables.com; rides $40-75)* offers scenic one- and two-hour trail rides.

Some 30 miles of the Green and Noilin Rivers wind through the national park. Several outfitters rent out kayaks and canoes, including **Adventures of Mammoth Cave** *(adventuresofmammothcave.com; canoe or kayak $65)*. They'll provide shuttle transport to the launch, where you can leisurely paddle your way along a 7.5-mile stretch of forest-lined riverside. Allow three to four hours to complete the journey.

RED RIVER GORGE ESSENTIALS

Info & Dining: Tiny Slade has a handy visitor center *(gopoco.org/visitor-center)* with maps and trail recommendations. Fill up at **Miguel's** *(7am-9:45pm)* on breakfasts, pizza and sandwiches, or cabin-like **Sky Bridge Station** *(noon-9pm Mon-Sat, to 6pm Sun)* for burgers and craft beer.

Roads: Many trailheads are reached off Hwy 77 and Hwy 715, which form a 33-mile loop near Slade.

Trails:

Rock Bridge Arch A 1.5-mile loop passing a small waterfall and shallow pool, where kids (and dogs) love to splash about.

Chimney Top This easy 0.7-mile trail is a scenic outing for all levels, as is the neighboring Princess Arch Trail.

Auxier Ridge A 4.5-mile out-and-back hike with great views. Many nearby trails too. Access it via Tunnel Ridge Rd.

THE MOONBOW

Cumberland Falls is one of the few places in the world to see a moonbow. Also called a lunar rainbow, this brilliant display forms in the water's mist when conditions are right. It can only happen during a full moon and on the two days before and after the full moon. There must also be clear skies and abundant mist (with decent wind). None of this would be possible without the atypical location of the falls – they face north with water cascading in a northward direction. Plan your visit sometime between dusk and midnight when the moon hangs low in the sky. The park website has dates for when the phenomenon occurs each month and it can happen throughout the year.

Red River Gorge

Hikes and cave paddles

A vast tract of cliffs, trickling streams and natural arches set amid dense forests, the **Red River Gorge** *(redrivergorge.com)* is Kentucky's top spot for outdoor activities. Hikers will find numerous trails traversing the forest of hemlock and white pine, past wild rock formations and thickets of rhododendron. Bordering the gorge area is the **Natural Bridge State Resort Park** *(naturalbridgestatepark.com; free)*, where you can hike a 1-mile trail up to the 65ft high, 78ft wide sandstone bridge. Take the narrow stairs up to the top and keep going (along the Laurel Ridge Trail) to reach a sweeping overlook across the forested landscape. From here, you can complete the loop via the Battleship Rock Trail, which will take you past high cliffs and fern-covered rock shelters. Alternatively, you can ride the **Sky Lift** *(naturalbridgeskyliftandgiftshop.com; adult/child $17/14)* up to a viewpoint near the natural bridge.

For a different perspective on this unusual geological region, book an excursion with **Gorge Underground** *(gorgeunderground.com; tour $55)*. You'll take a one-hour guided kayaking visit through a century-old, now-flooded limestone mine where you might see bats winging past and massive trout swimming below. Helmet and headlamp included, but dress warmly (thick socks) for the chilly subterranean temperatures.

Daniel Boone National Forest

Natural wonders in Cumberland Falls

Part of the vast Daniel Boone National Forest in eastern Kentucky, **Cumberland Falls State Resort Park** *(cumberlandfallsstatepark.com; free)* is a verdant expanse of densely forested ridges on either side of the meandering Cumberland River. The star of the show is the thundering **Cumberland Falls**, a 69ft tall, 125ft wide cascade that's sometimes dubbed 'the Niagara of the South.' Viewing platforms run along the east side of the falls, and some 17 miles of trails wind through the pristine forests surrounding them. One of the best short hikes is the 1.5-mile (round trip) out-and-back hike to **Eagles Falls**, a hidden cascade on the west side of the river. You can also tack on another half mile by following signs for the loop trail. A short drive (or walk) from the falls (and also part of Cumberland Falls State Resort Park), you'll find camping, cabins and lodge rooms as well as a simple old-fashioned restaurant. Just up the road, **Sheltowee Trace Adventure Resort** *(ky-rafting.com)* offers many activities: rafting, kayaking and ziplines. Also in the area, **Cumberland Falls Horse Stables** lead 45-minute rides *($25 per person)* through the forests. These depart hourly from 10am to 6pm.

Arkansas

MOUNTAIN BIKING | HIKING | ARTS & CULTURE

Bridging the Midwest and the Deep South, 'the Natural State' exemplifies its nickname with swift-rushing rivers, dark leafy hollows and the crenelated granite outcrops of the age-old Ozark Mountains. The most impressive scenery lies in Arkansas' upper half, but the entire state is blessed with exceptionally well-presented (and generally admission free) state parks and tiny, empty roads crisscrossing dense woodlands and rolling farm fields.

Adventure comes in many forms, from paddling the Buffalo River on day-long or multiday excursions to mountain biking the rugged woodland trails in Bentonville. There are caves to explore and forested paths that lead to towering waterfalls and dramatic overlooks. You can even dig diamonds in one of the state parks – or take it easy with a bit of hydrotherapy in the rejuvenating waters of Hot Springs. Nature aside, Arkansas' towns and small cities are a delight to explore, especially Little Rock, Fayetteville, Bentonville and Eureka Springs.

Places

TOP TIP

Be sure to visit at least one Arkansas state park *(arkansasstateparks.com)* while you're here. The state's 52 parks (most admission free) have an outstanding reputation, and many offer camping and good-value cabin accommodations. Some also have restaurants – like Petit Jean, with its fireplace and sweeping views.

Little Rock

MAP P119

See Clinton's legacy

Former President Bill Clinton served nearly 12 years as governor of Arkansas, so it's fitting that Little Rock houses the **Clinton Presidential Center** *(clintonlibrary.gov; adult/*

GETTING AROUND

Amtrak's *Texas Eagle* train, which runs from Chicago to Los Angeles, makes stops in Arkansas, including in Little Rock (the station is about 1.4 miles west of the River Market District). Greyhound buses also connect a few cities, but having a car is essential if you plan to explore beyond town centers. Arkansas' roads are generally in good shape, though take things slowly when traveling the narrow mountainous thoroughfares in the north of the state. Parking is free in most places, with the exception of downtown Little Rock and Fayetteville, as well as the streets near Hot Springs National Park.

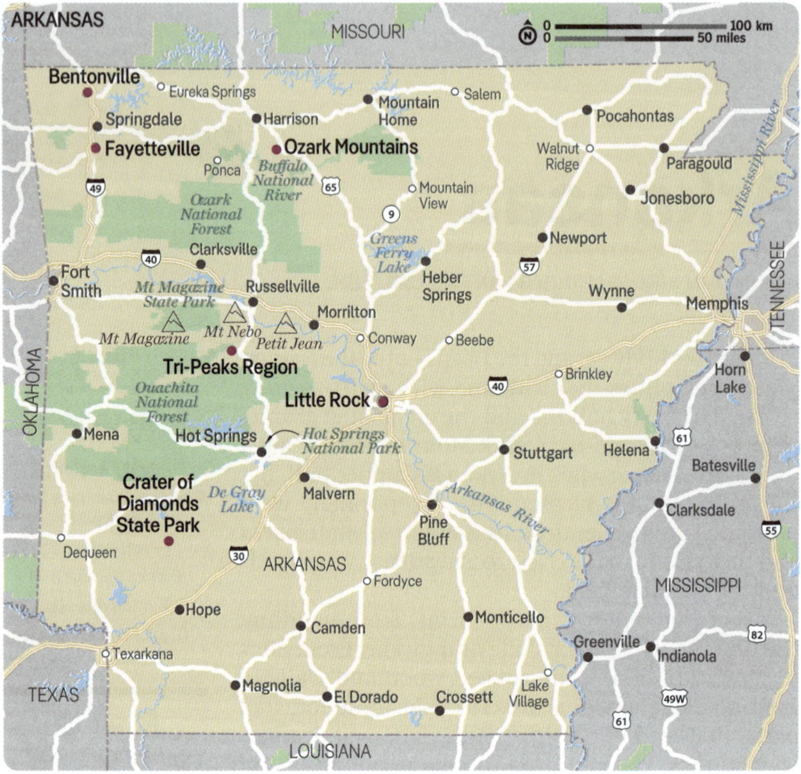

child $12/7). The excellent museum serves as a time capsule of the 1990s when the boy from Hope (Arkansas) was in the White House. Start off with a video about Clinton (narrated by the man himself), then check out the displays of photos and videos highlighting different aspects of his presidency, from his successes bringing down the national debt to his relationships with world leaders (including Nelson Mandela). Speaking of relationships, there's scant attention paid to a certain affair with a White House intern, though his impeachment is mentioned in passing. You can also wander through full-scale replicas of the White House Cabinet Room and the Oval Office, and see gifts from visiting dignitaries

EATING & DRINKING IN LITTLE ROCK: OUR PICKS

Community Bakery: A well-loved gathering space for coffees, flaky bakery items and soups, sandwiches, quiches and daily specials. *7am-8pm* $

Flying Fish: Feast on catfish, barbecue shrimp and fried oyster po'boys at this Cajun-style seafood joint with a vintage diner interior. *11am-9pm* $$

Brood & Barley: Atmospheric gastropub in North Little Rock serving bistro fare (steamed mussels, sliders) along with creative cocktails. *11am-11pm Mon-Sat* $$

Lost Forty Brewing: Little Rock's top craft brewer has a rotating array of IPAs, seasonal brews and Belgian-style ales, plus good pub grub. *11am-9pm* $$

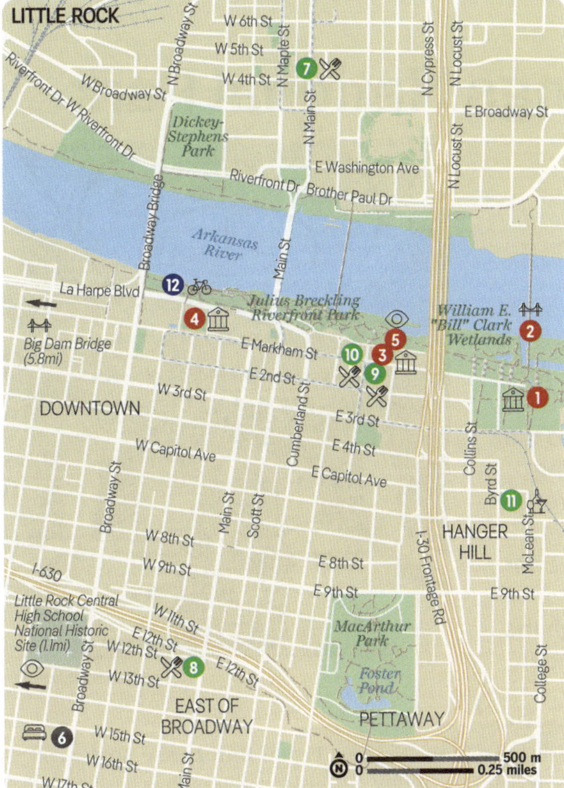

SIGHTS

1 Clinton Presidential Center
2 Clinton Presidential Park Bridge
3 Museum of Discovery
4 Old State House Museum
5 Witt Stephens Jr Nature Center

SLEEPING

6 Rosemont Cottages

EATING

7 Brood & Barley
8 Community Bakery
9 Flying Fish
10 Ottenheimer Market Hall

DRINKING & NIGHTLIFE

11 Lost Forty Brewing

TRANSPORT

12 Arkansas River Trail

NEIGHBORHOODS OF LITTLE ROCK

River Market District: Waterfront trails, playgrounds and nearby attractions (a theater, restaurants, cafes) on President Clinton Av.

Main Street Corridor: Running south of the waterfront, this stretch of Main St has restaurants and a pocket park that hosts occasional events.

North Little Rock: Just across the Arkansas River from the Riverfront District. Stroll across the pedestrian-only Junction Bridge and head over to Main St, which is filled with shops and eateries (between West Broadway and East 6th Sts).

SoMa: Short for South Main, SoMa is a vibrant neighborhood of galleries, indie shops, restaurants and even a distillery; it's best between West 12th and West 16th Sts.

(and also look at menus from state dinners). Don't miss those metal binders – you can peruse Clinton's schedule for every day he was in office.

Explore the riverfront

Stretching along the south bank of the Arkansas River, Little Rock's **River Market District** contains sculpture gardens, playgrounds and even a small wetlands sanctuary. Pedestrian paths wind along the riverfront, providing fine views for the strollers and cyclists passing through. Various bridges cross the river, including the **Clinton Presidential Park Bridge**, a scenic car-free path located near the Clinton Presidential Center.

TOP EXPERIENCE

Hot Springs National Park

Famed for its warm geothermal waters, Hot Springs is both a tiny national park and a charmingly low-key mountain town. Native Americans called this region the Valley of the Vapors, while Euro-American settlers were drawn to the springs' alleged healing powers. Today, restored bathhouses offer insight into the past (several offer old-school treatments), and trails lace through the surrounding woodlands.

EWY MEDIA/SHUTTERSTOCK

Fordyce Bathhouse

TOP TIPS

- Free ranger-led tours from Fordyce Bathhouse happen Thursdays to Mondays (typically 10am and 2pm).
- Behind Bathhouse Row, the **Grand Promenade** passes flowing springs (and a hot-water fountain off Reserve St).
- Near Bathhouse Row, **Maxine's** *(maxineslive.com)* has deep dish pizzas, burlesque shows and live music.

PRACTICALITIES

- nps.gov/hosp
- Fordyce Bathhouse Visitor Center 9am-5pm Thu-Mon
- free

Bathhouse Row

The heart of the National Park is **Bathhouse Row**, a collection of architecturally striking buildings where the upper class once came for several weeks of treatments. Get the lowdown at the 1915 **Fordyce Bathhouse**, which serves as the NPS visitor center and a museum. The well-preserved building has stained-glass, Greek statues and a vintage gymnasium. To experience it for yourself, book an old-fashioned hydrotherapy treatment a few doors down at the **Buckstaff Bathhouse** *(buckstaffbaths.com; from $45)*; reserve well ahead.

Hiking Trails

The park has 26 miles of trails, many of them are short and scenic, and they link up to form a network across the town's mountains. For a pleasant outing, you can hike up from Bathhouse Row via the Peak Trail (0.6 miles) to **Hot Springs Mountain Tower** *(hotspringstower.com; adult/child $14/11)*; there an elevator goes up to a 216ft observation deck. Or skip the expense and continue along the Hot Springs Mountain Trail, the Gulpha Gorge Tail, the Goat Rock Trail and the Upper Dogwood Trail, before completing the loop on the Hot Springs Mountain Trail – all in, a 5-mile (2½-hour) loop.

Cyclists and runners can put in some mileage along the **Arkansas River Trail**, which hugs both sides of the river for 15.6 miles (the **Big Dam Bridge** to the west and the Clinton Presidential Park Bridge to the east are key anchors).

A prime spot for learning about Arkansas' natural world is the **Witt Stephens Jr Nature Center** *(agfc.com/things-to-do/nature-centers/little-rock; free)*. Exhibits explore all of the state's ecological zones, and include small aquariums with fish and even an alligator.

Young travelers will also enjoy the nearby **Museum of Discovery** *(museumofdiscovery.org; adult/child $14/12)*. The fun science-and-natural-history center is perfect for families. Inside hands-on galleries, you can lie on a bed of nails, meander through a kaleidoscope tunnel, climb amid netting and tunnels in a tower, and feel the rumble and roar of a tornado.

For a dose of Arkansas history, visit the **Old State House Museum** *(arkansasheritage.com/old-state-house-museum; free)*, which covers key events of the past since the 1830s. There's a special collection on dresses worn by first ladies, and several galleries devoted to Arkansas governors, including Sarah Huckabee Sanders, who spent time in the governor's mansion as both a teenager (as daughter of Governor Mike Huckabee) and in more recent years as the state's first female governor.

When hunger strikes, stop in the **Ottenheimer Market Hall** *(10am to 2pm Monday to Saturday)*. The spacious food hall has some tempting good-value lunch options, including sushi, Thai cuisine, Middle Eastern cooking, barbecue and fish and chips.

Tri-Peaks Region

Trails, waterfalls and scenic drives

Stretching between the Ouchita and Ozark mountain ranges in the verdant Arkansas River Valley, the Tri-Peaks region is home to three impressive mountains, each protected by its own state park – there's no admission fee at any of them, though you'll have to pay extra for camping or overnighting in a rustic cabin.

The easternmost is **Petit Jean**, which is Arkansas' oldest state park (founded 1923). This is a great place for a hike, followed by a meal with a panoramic view in the old lodge (you can also overnight in a cabin). Some 20 miles of trails wind through this 2658-acre park. The most famous is the moderately challenging Cedar Falls Trail, a 2-mile out-and-back excursion leading to an impressive 90ft waterfall. To see the falls from overhead, you can drive to the Cedar Falls Overlook. Speaking of drives, don't miss the short ride along Red Bluff Dr, which has several fine viewpoints including the Mary Ann Overlook offering glimpses of Mt Nebo and Mt Magazine.

A twisting 25 miles northwest of Petit Jean, **Mt Nebo** may lack vertical glory (topping out at 1350ft) but the valley views are still outstanding from this leafy state park. There are some 32 miles of hiking and biking routes here. On foot, the moderate Rim Trail (a 3.5-mile loop) offers grand views that stretch nearly 100 miles on clear days. The mountain biking is excellent (though you'll need to BYO bike since there's no rental nearby);

TOP FESTIVALS IN ARKANSAS

Ozark Folk Festival: Eureka Springs' big jam fest features flat-picking, mandolin playing and jig dancing over three days in early September.

Hot Springs Documentary Film Festival: Nine days of innovative films in October, plus discussions, parties and even wellness events like hiking and meditation.

Bentonville Bike Fest: Held in May, this major cycling event features competitions, skill workshops, demonstrations, kid activities and group rides.

Bentonville Film Festival: In June, this is a week-long showcase of under-represented voices in cinema. Don't miss outdoor screenings at The Momentary.

Bean Fest & Championship Outhouse Races: Live music, bean feasting and people-powered potty races happen in Mountain View one weekend in October.

THE LITTLE ROCK NINE

In 1954, the US Supreme Court issued a landmark decision that outlawed segregation in public schools. Despite the ruling, many cities, including Little Rock, bucked the law and kept African Americans out of all-white schools. Change came when nine brave Black students – later known as the Little Rock Nine – enrolled at Central High School in 1957. The backlash was severe. Arkansas governor Orval Faubus sent the state's National Guard to block their entrance. They also faced an angry mob. President Dwight Eisenhower eventually got involved and sent the US Army to guard the students. Learn more about those tumultuous times by visiting the small **Little Rock Central High School National Historic Site** *(nps.gov/chsc; free)* near the still-functioning high school.

RCHAT/SHUTTERSTOCK

you'll find everything from the beginner friendly Miller's Goat Trail (5.3 miles) to the experts-only Lizard Tail (1.9 miles), not to mention the rewarding intermediate-level Chickalah Loop Trail (4.8 miles), among the best in the park.

Another 35 miles west of Mt Nebo, you'll reach **Mt Magazine**. Home to Arkansas' highest point (at 2753ft), this state park is a draw for hikers seeking bragging rights. The climb up Signal Hill takes you there, and it's a fairly easy 1.8-mile loop, with just over 250ft of elevation along the way. If you don't have time for a walk, the **Mt Magazine Scenic Byway** traverses the park and includes some memorable vistas of forests, lakes and valleys along the way as it connects Havana with Webb City along Hwy 309.

Crater of Diamonds State Park

Dig for diamonds

Some 60 miles southwest of Hot Springs, the **Crater of Diamonds State Park** *(adult/child $15/7)* is a one-of-a-kind place where you can dig through a 37-acre field (a former volcanic crater) in search of rocks, minerals and gemstones. Some 35,000 diamonds have been unearthed here, including an 8.5 karat one in 2015 worth a cool $1 million. On the downside, you'll be digging in the dirt on an exposed field in often scorching temperatures. You can bring your own gear, or rent tools from the park (shovel, box screen, bucket).

Fayetteville

Arts and culture

Nestled in the woodsy hills of the Ozarks, Fayetteville is the state's third largest town, fueled by the youthful energy of the **University of Arkansas**. On Fayetteville's west side, the leafy campus has wide-ranging cultural offerings, from classic and cutting-edge plays at the **University Theater**

Crater of Diamonds State Park

(theatre.uark.edu/productions) to concerts at the **Faulkner Performing Arts Center** *(faulkner.uark.edu)*.

The town's love of the arts isn't limited to the university. In the center, the **Walton Arts Center** *(waltonartscenter.org)* stages Broadway musicals, comedy shows, rock concerts and even puppet theater. Nearby, **TheaterSquared** *(theatre2.org)* stages more avant-garde shows, with a packed calendar of more than 350 performances and events each year.

Walkng around downtown Fayetteville

Fayetteville's attractive downtown is has plenty of indie shops, restaurants and cafes. A good place to begin the exploration is at **Fayetteville Historic Square** – especially lively on Saturday mornings during the weekly **farmers market** *(fayettevillefarmersmarket.org; 7am-2pm)*. Nearby, you can browse for quality home items, outdoor gear and gourmet provisions at **City Supply** *(citysupplyfayetteville.com)*. You can also pick up some vinyl at **Block Street Records** *(facebook.com/blockstreetrecords)*, and recharge over lattes and bakery items at **Little Bread Company** *(littlebread.com)*.

Later in the day you can enter a hallowed electric realm at **Pinpoint** *(pinpointfayetteville.com)*, a bar full of pinball machines, or drink quality bourbon cocktails at **Vault** *(vault.bar*; the mint juleps are ideal warm-weather refreshment).

PRIME MOUNTAIN BIKING SPOTS

Dave Neal, owner of Mojo Cycling, shares his favorite rides for first-time visitors to the Bentonville area *@mojocycling.com*

A good starting point is Bella Vista, just north of Bentonville. In the Back 40, there's a little entry park called Blowing Springs. It has numerous short trails that vary in technicality. There are beginner trails, where I taught my kids to ride, and more robust and tough trails too. There's also camping in the middle of it. So you can stay there and roll right out of your tent and on to a trail. Another great spot is called the Castle, found in Slaughter Pen. There are trails for all different levels here, and also a skills park where you can really progress as a rider.

EATING & DRINKING IN FAYETTEVILLE: OUR PICKS

Hammontree's Grilled Cheese: Inviting spot for elevated comfort food: panko-fried artichoke hearts, French onion soup and decadent sandwiches. *11am-9:30pm Mon-Sat* $

Cheers at the OPO: Upscale Southern comfort fare (fried green tomatoes, wood-fired meats) inside a grand building that was a former post office. *11am-10pm Wed-Sun* $$

Farmer's Table: An old house turned restaurant with outstanding locally sourced dishes. Best choice for breakfast. *7am-3pm Tue-Sun, plus 5-9pm Fri & Sat* $$

Maxine's Tap Room: An atmospherically lit drinking den with well-crafted cocktails and regional microbrews. *4pm-2am Mon-Sat, from 6pm Sun*

STROLLING EUREKA SPRINGS

One of the Ozarks' most photogenic towns, Eureka Springs is a hilly enclave of winding streets, Victorian architecture and eye-catching shops.

START	END	LENGTH
Crescent Hotel	Eureka Springs Historical Museum	1 mile; 1½ hours

Park just above the town at the 1 **Crescent Hotel**. Step inside this still-functioning 1886 grande dame, which is full of vintage character. Head to the top-floor Skybar for a bite or drinks on the terrace. Walk out the back through the hotel grounds and cross the street to 2 **St Elizabeth**, a striking limestone church built in 1909. Turn left out of the church, and find the 3 **Magnolia Path**. Descend through the trees and keep going downhill (at times on a wooden sidewalk). You'll eventually end up on Spring St, which takes you past vine-draped 4 **Harding Spring**, one of many picturesque springs for which the town is famed. Further along, you can pick up handmade watercolors and other creative supplies at 5 **Adventure Art**. Across the road, 6 **MoJo's Records** stocks quality vinyl, and there's a cafe attached.

Keep following Spring St as it winds and curves down the hillside, and you'll soon be in the heart of town, with colorful shops and galleries, cafes and restaurants. Finish at the 7 **Eureka Springs Historical Museum**, where you can learn about local history. If you don't want to walk back up the hill, hop on the trolley (red line; $4), which will take you back to your starting point.

For the unadulterated student-life experience, head a few blocks northwest to **Dickson Street**. Between University and Thompson Aves, you'll find live music spots (**George's Majestic Lounge**, the **Piano Bar**), buzzing little cafes and inviting stores – like the excellent **Dickson St Bookshop** *(dicksonstreetbooks.com)*.

Bentonville

Ride the fabled trails

One of the best places for mountain biking in the US east of the Rockies, the Bentonville area has over 160 miles of pathways and bikeways, streetside bicycle paths and looped trails. You could spend many days happily exploring this system with its free well-marked trails, each rated beginner (green), intermediate (blue) or expert (black diamond).

With limited time focus your attention on **Slaughter Pen**, with its 40-plus miles of single track of all levels. Between berms, big rocks and forests, you'll get a great taste of local nature. You can access the Pen via the All American Trail, a mountain-biking route that connects to the Crystal Bridges Museum. Another highlight is **Coler Mountain**, with its 17 miles of varied trails (best accessed via NW 3rd St, about 1.8 miles west of Bentonville City Sq).

Pick up a free map of the entire network at the visitor center or at outfitters like **Mojo**, which rents high-quality mountain bikes *(mojocycling.com; 4hr rental $40-100)*.

Be sure to also check out the **Ledger**, a rare bikeable building (follow the jewel-carrying insect mosaics up six stories of ramps). Stop for a pick-me-up on the ground floor at **Airship Coffee**.

See cutting-edge art in the Crystal Bridges Museum

Sprawling across a series of creek ponds fed by mountain streams, the enormous **Crystal Bridges Museum** *(crystalbridges.org; free; closed Tue)* is an unexpected find, to say the least. The curved pavilions, designed by acclaimed architect Mosh Safdie, house extensive collections that are connected by glass-encased tunnels, and the experience consistently filters sunlight through and across the grounds. The permanent collection focuses on artists active in the USA – everyone from Harlem Renaissance painter Jacob Lawrence to Osage photographer Ryan RedCorn. Special exhibitions (with admission prices) roam the globe, with recent retrospectives devoted to Yayoi Kusama, KAWS and Diego Rivera. Surrounding the museum, sculptures by renowned artists punctuate several leafy trails, including the **Art Trail**.

BENTONVILLE'S BEST ART & CULTURE EXPERIENCES

Skyspace: James Turrell's sky-centric circular chamber features a mesmerizing light installation beginning 45 minutes before sunrise and 10 minutes before sunset.

Bachman-Wilson House: Wander through this small, ingeniously designed home, dreamed up by the great Frank Lloyd Wright. Reserve a free ticket through *crystalbridges.org/calendar/frank-lloyd-wright-tours*.

Museum of Native American History: Impressive collection of artifacts made by cultures across the Americas.

Amazeum: A huge kids' museum with loads of fun, hands-on activities.

Walmart Museum: Learn the story behind Walmart.

Momentary: The factory-turned-creative hub has art exhibitions, live music and a top-floor cafe-bar.

EATING & DRINKING IN BENTONVILLE: OUR PICKS

Meteor Cafe: Sunny, anytime spot with well-pulled espressos and tasty breakfast tacos, plus pizzas and margaritas later on. *7am-10pm* $

Wright's Barbecue: The famed destination for brisket, pulled pork, fall-off-the-bone ribs and other smoky decadence. *10:30am-8pm Tue-Sat* $$

Hub: A favorite post-ride gathering spot for Tex-Mex, craft beers and events (live music Fridays, trivia night Wednesdays). *11am-10pm Tue-Sun* $$

Table Mesa Bistro: One of many appealing spots overlooking Bentonville's photogenic main square, serving creative bowls, Mexican fare and burgers. *8am-9pm Mon-Sat, 9am-8pm Sun* $$

Ozark Mountains

On the trail in Devil's Den

Tucked in the lush Lee Creek Valley, some 25 miles south of Fayetteville, the **Devil's Den State Park** *(free)* is a favorite getaway for hiking, trail running, mountain biking and camping. The route not to miss is the relatively straightforward 1.5-mile Devil's Den Trail, which courses past waterfalls (flowing after the rains), dense greenery and the eerie rock formations that give the state park its name.

Paddle the Scenic Buffalo National River

Designated the nation's first national river, the **Buffalo** rolls west to east for 135 glorious miles through the heart of northern Arkansas. Along the way, the rushing waters pass by ochre cliffs and granite outcroppings, while lapping at small sandy beaches that fringe deep tracts of Ozark forest. For a memorable DIY adventure, rent a kayak or canoe for the day *($72 to $102)* from **Buffalo Outdoor Center** *(buffaloriver.com)* in Ponca and make the 10-mile paddle to **Kyle's Landing**. They also offer shuttle service *(from $46)*, which means they'll drive your car to your arrival point, so you can head off when you finish the day's paddle. This wild river is also a great spot for multiday trips, and you can camp at designated campsites along the way. Check the National Park site *(nps.gov/buff)* for more details.

Into the Underworld at Blanchard Springs Caverns

The spectacular **Blanchard Springs Caverns** *(blanchardsprings.org)*, 15 miles northwest of Mountain View, were carved by an underground river. It's a little-known, mind-blowing spot in Arkansas. Guided tours *(adult/child $15/10)* like the accessible one-hour Dripstone Trail and the 1½-hour Discovery Trail (more challenging, with its 700 steps) are offered regularly. Reserve ahead through *recreation.gov.*

TOP HIKES IN THE OZARKS

Go after the rains to see waterfalls in all their flowing majesty.

Hemmed-in Hollow Falls: From the Compton Trailhead, make the 2.5-mile descent to this stunning 209ft waterfall. It's a challenging return (over 1300ft elevation gain).

Big Bluff & the Goat Trail: Start at the Centerpoint Trail to eventually reach (via exposed ledges in places) a fantastic view over the Buffalo River (6 miles return, with 1000ft elevation gain).

Hawksbill Crag: A moderate 2.7-mile out-and-back hike to cinematic Hawksbill Crag (aka Whitaker Point).

Glory Hole Falls: This moderate 2-mile return hike takes you to an unusual waterfall that pours through a hole in a rockface.

Alum Cove: Make the fairly easy 1.2-mile loop to see a natural rock bridge spanning over 130ft.

CAVAN IMAGES/GETTY IMAGES

Buffalo National River

Places We Love to Stay

$ Budget $$ Midrange $$$ Top End

Virginia

MAP P59

Linden Row Inn (Richmond) $$ Victorian-style inn with modern comforts. Enjoy the terrace and garden before making your way on foot to bustling Broad St.

Cedars of Williamsburg (Williamsburg) $$ Georgian architecture, cozy rooms, friendly service and walkable to downtown.

Liberty Trust (Roanoke) $$ Restored downtown bank incorporating original features such as a tasting room in the original vault.

Hotel Madison (Harrisonburg) $$ Comfortable accommodations with refined touches close to downtown. Catch views of the city or the mountains and nods to James Madison.

Ironclad Inn (Fredericksburg) $$ Historic residence turned inn walkable to downtown, with an Ironclad Distillery bourbon tasting room.

Boar's Head Resort (Charlottesville) $$$ Modern amenities and outdoor activities with a classic appeal, surrounded by the rolling foothills of the Blue Ridge Mountains.

Hilton Virginia Beach Oceanfront (Virginia Beach) $$$ Private balconies, panoramic ocean views, prime boardwalk location and a rooftop pool and bar.

West Virginia

Outpost (Fayetteville) $ Cabins, tent platforms and RV hookups – this Outpost is ready for almost any kind of outdoors enthusiast. Regular fireside jams for music fans.

Brass Pineapple Inn (Charleston) $$ This century-old inn was formerly a private home, and rooms retain an Edwardian homeyness. Some have claw-foot tubs. Room service on silver trays.

Glen Ferris Inn (Glen Ferris) $$ A lovely way station for travelers for nearly two centuries, just a stone's throw from photogenic Kanawha Falls. Home-style restaurant.

Country Inn (p77; Berkeley Springs) $$ Built in 1933, this Greek Revival–style estate is Berkeley Springs' keystone. Two restaurants, live music and a firepit.

Hotel Morgan (Morgantown) $$$ Distinguished flagship hotel in the middle of Morgantown, fully renovated in 2020. Anvil + Ax is a gorgeous cocktail lounge on the 1st floor.

1799 Inn (Harpers Ferry) $$$ When the Harpers Ferry armory was being built in 1799, workers stayed in this very house. The beautiful rooms thoughtfully blend old and new.

North Carolina

Crews Inn (Ocracoke) $ An authentic old island home, with five lovely light-filled rooms named for its original inhabitants, plus the delightful innkeeper's cottage out back.

Dunhill Hotel (Charlotte) $ Small, historic Uptown hotel with a quiet lobby and rooms that nod to the 1920s.

Arrive (Wilmington) $$ This stylish boutique operation has modern, bright rooms, a creative restaurant and an inviting courtyard, complete with lawn games.

Atlantic Inn (Hatteras Island) $$ A century-old property in Hatteras that's been revamped and reopened as a classy, comfortable lodging with a vintage vibe.

Princess Anne Boutique Hotel (Asheville) $$ Offers handsomely furnished rooms and spacious suites in a quiet, leafy neighborhood.

Tennessee

MAPS P100, P104, P105

Crash Pad (Chattanooga) $ Nicely run hostel with dorms and private rooms, guest kitchen-lounge and a courtyard in a great Southside location near restaurants and bars.

Arrive (Memphis) $$ Beautiful redesign of an industrial building just steps from the train station. Great ground-floor cafe and bar.

Peabody (Memphis) $$ A 464-room downtown property with classically furnished rooms and a lobby where ducks are marched in daily to swim about in the fountain.

Waymore's (Nashville) $$ In uber-hip East Nashville, this 93-room hotel hits all the right notes, with artfully minimalist rooms and a rooftop bar with skyline views.

Hotel Chalet (Chattanooga) $$ On the grounds of the historic train station, this revamped classic has stylish rooms set in Victorian railcars.

Union Station Hotel (Nashville) $$$ This soaring Romanesque gray-stone castle (and former train station) boasts grand common areas and contemporary rooms with playful accents.

Kentucky

DuPont Lodge (Daniel Boone National Forest) $ Near Cumberland Falls, this forest-fringed lodge has pleasant rooms, and you can also bunk in a rustic cottage with a fireplace.

Jailer's Inn (Bardstown) $$ In a former jail from 1819, you'll find a B&B kitted out with wallpaper-covered rooms with antique furnishings. Good cooked breakfasts.

21c Museum Hotel (Louisville) $$$ Art-focused option featuring edgy design details and changing exhibitions in common areas, plus inviting rooms with ample natural light.

Arkansas

MAP P119

Gold-Inn (Hot Springs) $ A delightfully renovated vintage hotel with colorful rooms and a swimming pool less than a mile from Bathhouse Row.

Bike Inn (Bentonville) $ A welcoming base for mountain bikers, with suites and simple cabins with shared bathrooms, and there's a sauna and gear for hire.

Rosemont Cottages (Little Rock) $$ In the vibrant Soma district, you can stay in attractive, uniquely designed cottages and suites that ooze southern charm.

Treehouse Cottages (Eureka Springs) $$$ Amid pine forest, these delightful stilted wooden cottages make a charming hideaway. Some boast Jacuzzi tubs and wrap-around decks.

RANDY DUCHAINE/ALAMY

Union Station Hotel, Nashville

Researched and curated by Regis St Louis

The Deep South

BIRTHPLACE OF AMERICAN MUSIC AND CIVIL RIGHTS

Explore the nation's most misunderstood region, a dynamo of music, culture and history, set against a backdrop of vibrant towns and diverse landscapes.

The Deep South is one of the first regions of the US to be considered its own distinct place, not merely for its geography, but its literature, cuisine, lilting accents and above all its history – one that is long and beautiful in places, cruel and harrowing in others.

Human presence in the South dates back thousands of years, evident in places like Georgia's Ocmulgee Mounds and Poverty Point in Louisiana. Native American tribes still retain strong ties to the land, while national park sites preserve the battlefields of the Civil War, as well as pivotal places in the fight for Civil Rights.

Despite all its heartache, the Deep South has always been a hotbed of creativity, particularly when it comes to music. In Mississippi, the Blues Highway rolls by pastoral landscapes little changed by time, and past towns where musical legends like BB King got his start. Clarksdale, meanwhile, keeps the blues alive with the next generation of artists dazzling the crowds at juke joints around town. Further south in New Orleans, it's all about jazz, which plays a starring role in the city's fabled nightlife and big festivals (Mardi Gras included).

Apart from the sights, sounds and cuisine of the Deep South, it's the people you meet who will likely leave the deepest impression. Southerners are cordial to a fault and often pleased to lay out the welcome mat and share their food and culture with visitors from near and far.

JEFFREY M FRANK/SHUTTERSTOCK

THE MAIN AREAS

SOUTH CAROLINA
Coastal allure and vibrant Charleston. **p136**

GEORGIA
Urban attractions and seaside beauty. **p150**

ALABAMA
The heart of the Civil Rights Movement. **p164**

For places to stay in the Deep South, see p198

RICK LORD/SHUTTERSTOCK

Left: Ocmulgee Mounds (p158), Macon; Above: Trumpet player, New Orleans (p181)

Alabama, p164

Journey into the past at Civil Rights sites in Birmingham and Montgomery, then launch into the future in Huntsville (aka Rocket City).

Louisiana, p194

Walk where ancient mound-builders dwelled, work the floorboards at a Cajun dancehall, and spy alligators and ibises on a wildlife-filled swamp tour.

New Orleans, p181

Home to French and Spanish colonial architecture and fiery jazz clubs, Nola captivates with its decadent cuisine, buzzing nightlife and music-fueled festivals.

Mississippi, p173

The birthplace of the blues has juke joints and heritage museums, Civil War sites and serene towns perched alongside America's mightiest waterway.

Find Your Way

The five states of the Deep South encompass flatlands (in the southernmost regions), uplands (in the north) and alluvial plains, with both urban and rural communities planted among the landscape. Throughout you'll find an excellent road network.

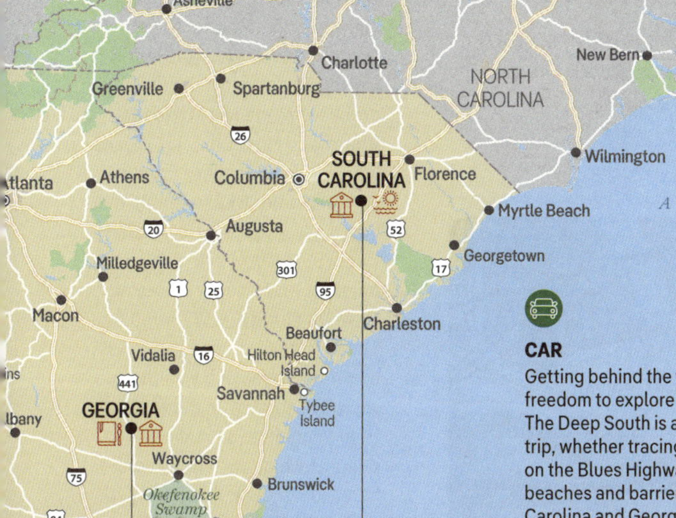

South Carolina, p136

Enchanting beaches are a big draw, as is charming Charleston. There are also islands, Gullah culture and paddling adventures in Congaree National Park.

Georgia, p150

Explore vibrant neighborhoods of Atlanta, see the Ocmulgee Mounds, get a taste of Savannah and unwind on picturesque islands like Jekyll and Cumberland.

CAR

Getting behind the wheel gives you the freedom to explore beyond city centers. The Deep South is a fine place for a road trip, whether tracing the Mississippi on the Blues Highway or exploring the beaches and barrier islands of South Carolina and Georgia.

BUS

Without a car, your best bet for navigating this vast region is Greyhound *(greyhound.com)*, which links major towns across the South. Megabus *(us.megabus.com)* also operates a few routes, mostly in Georgia and South Carolina.

TRAIN

Various long-haul routes operated by Amtrak pass through the South. While not all that practicable, these train journeys offer outstanding scenery. One route links New Orleans with Memphis, while an eastern route links Savannah and Charleston with cities north and south.

Plan Your Days

Start off in one of the key hubs (New Orleans, Atlanta, Savannah or Charleston) and think local: each region has its own unique food and arts scene.

MARIANNE PFEIL/SHUTTERSTOCK

New Orleans Pharmacy Museum (p183)

24 Hours in the Big Easy

Head straight for **New Orleans** (p181), one of the most fascinating cities in the country. Start with a morning stroll in the **French Quarter** (p184). Get a dose of history at the **Historic New Orleans Collection** (p183) and learn about primitive medical practices at the **New Orleans Pharmacy Museum** (p183). Have lunch at the legendary Creole spot of **Dooky Chase** (p188), then board a vintage streetcar along Canal St to **City Park** (p193). Have beignets and chicory coffee at **Cafe Du Monde** (p193), stroll the Spanish moss-draped live oaks lining the bayou and visit the sculpture garden. In the evening, treat yourself to a meal in the delightful hideaway of **N7** (p189). Later, join the jazz-loving crowds on **Frenchmen Street** (p189).

Seasonal Highlights

The Deep South is a year-round destination, with festivals throughout the year – especially in the springtime. Be prepared for intense heat and humidity if visiting from June to September.

FEBRUARY

Head to the South to escape the winter chill. It's the most festive time of the year in New Orleans and Mobile, which hosts ample revelry (parades, costuming, music, merriment) leading up to **Mardi Gras** (p181).

APRIL

Clarksdale, Mississippi, draws blues fans from far and wide to its fabulous **Juke Joint Festival** (p176). You can catch outdoor concerts at stages around town and keep the party going at old-school music joints by night.

MAY

New Orleans' celebrated **Jazz Fest** (p181) features a packed lineup of diverse sounds on 14 different stages, plus countless food temptations. It happens over two weekends (Thursday to Sunday) in late April and early May.

Seven Days in the Heart of the Deep South

Spend a full day exploring **Atlanta's downtown** (p151), including the **National Center for Civil & Human Rights**, the **World of Coca-Cola** and the **Georgia Aquarium**. On day two, On day two, visit the **Martin Luther King Jr National Historical Park** (p153) before heading to Alabama. See the powerful exhibits of the **Legacy Sites** (p170) in Montgomery, followed by the **Birmingham Civil Rights Institute** (p168). Keep north to Huntsville for a journey beyond our planet at the **US Space & Rocket Center** (p166). Head west to Clarksdale, Mississippi, for live blues at juke joints like **Red's** and **Ground Zero** (p176). Follow the famous river south to the historic towns of **Vicksburg** (p178) and **Natchez** (p179) before ending your journey in **New Orleans** (p181).

10 Days Circling Georgia & South Carolina

Start off in photogenic **Savannah** (p160) with a stroll through the **Historic District** and a tour of the **Owens-Thomas House & Slave Quarters**. Crossing into South Carolina, visit **St Helena Island** (p144) to learn about Gullah culture, then enjoy some beach time at **Hunting Island State Park** (p144). Continue to **Charleston** (p137), one of the South's most beguiling cities. Explore the past at the **International African American Museum** (p140), then see where war erupted at **Fort Sumter** (p143). Next head to **Congaree National Park** (p148) for a kayaking excursion through the wetlands. Get a dose of small town culture in lovely **Greenville** (p146), then loop back through Georgia to the impressive **Ocmulgee Mounds** (p158), a testament to thousands of years of Indigenous history.

JULY

Gain a deeper insight into the Gullah Geechee people during the Sweetgrass Festival held in Mount Pleasant near Charleston. You can browse the fine handicrafts (especially basketry) and indulge in rich Lowcountry cooking.

AUGUST

It's one of the hottest months in the South, making it a great time to head to the beach – though stay weather alert, since this is peak hurricane season (which runs from June to November).

OCTOBER

Dust off that eyepatch and tricorn hat and get yourself to Tybee Island's **Pirate Fest** (p162). The four-day celebration includes a pub crawl, parade, live music and costume contests, with lots of kids' activities.

NOVEMBER

In the south, college football is practically a religion. Seeing a home game at any SEC stadium is not something you'll forget, especially if you watch the Alabama Crimson Tide take the field in **Tuscaloosa** (p169).

South Carolina

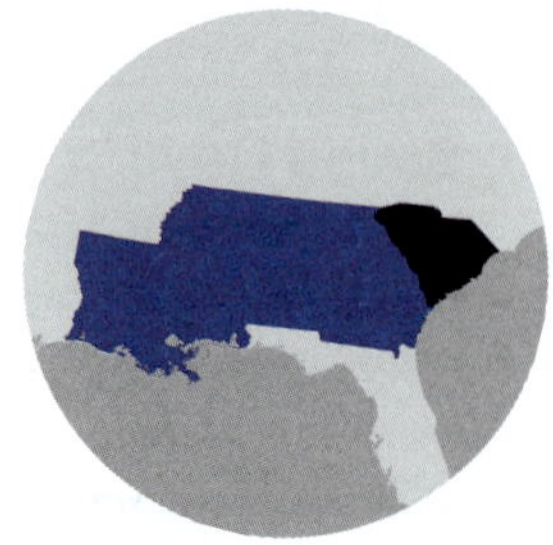

CULTURE & HISTORY | GOLDEN BEACHES | SOUTHERN CHARM

Places

TOP TIP

Dress up like greenskeeper Carl Spackler and jump into the ocean on January 1 during the Bill Murray Look-a-Like Polar Plunge on Folly Beach. This subzero swim pays homage to Charleston's most distinguished resident, Bill Murray, with participants attempting to resemble him in various roles.

There's a reason South Carolina ranks among the country's fastest-growing states. Yes, affordable housing and the low cost of living are factors, but the state's natural beauty and welcoming vibes surely play a part too. Most travelers begin along the Lowcountry coast, home to splendid historic cities such as Beaufort and Charleston as well as wide sandy beaches studded with dunes and palms. Along the barrier islands you can immerse yourself in Gullah culture, its language and stories created by the formerly enslaved, who held onto West African traditions through centuries of hardship.

Innovative cities including Greenville and Columbia are hubs of culinary and cultural expression in the state's interior. Museums, plantations and galleries in these destinations and along the coast are re-examining the state's past and sharing more comprehensive accounts. There's also plentiful scope for outdoor adventure amid landscapes ranging from rugged state parks in the mountains to spooky blackwater swamps to sun-kissed salt marshes.

GETTING AROUND

Driving your own vehicle is the best way to explore the state, though if you're just stopping through Charleston, you can explore its compact and pedestrian-friendly downtown on foot.

Amtrak *(amtrak.com)* runs through South Carolina on four routes. The *Silver Meteor* links NYC and Miami, with stops in Florence, Charleston and Savannah, GA. The *Palmetto* connects Charleston with New York City and Savannah. The *Silver Star* stops in Columbia, while the *Crescent* links Greenville and Clemson.

Greyhound *(greyhound.com)* has stations in Charleston, Columbia, Florence, Georgetown, Greenville and Myrtle Beach. Megabus *(us.megabus.com)* stops in Florence and Columbia.

Charleston

MAP P138

Step back in time

Cobblestone streets, hidden alleyways and photogenic homes straight from the 1800s set the stage for rewarding exploring in Charleston, one of the South's most fascinating cities.

The **Charleston Museum** *(charlestonmuseum.org; adult/teen/child $15/12/6)* may be the oldest museum in the country – it opened in 1773 – but it certainly isn't stuffy. Exhibits spotlight various periods of the city's long and storied past. Artifacts include a whale skeleton, tags worn by the enslaved and the 'secession table' used for the signing of the state's secession documents before the Civil War.

EATING IN CHARLESTON: SOUTHERN FARE

MAP P138

Marina Variety Store: A long-standing, down-home kinda place, with harbor views and Southern hospitality as warm as the buttermilk biscuits. *7am-9pm Wed-Sat, to 2pm Sun* $

Poogan's Porch: The homemade buttermilk biscuits are out of control and the chicken and waffles are second to none. Boozy brunchers have plenty of options. *9am-3pm & 4:30-9:30pm* $$

Slightly North of Broad: Lowcountry comfort dishes reinvented with flair. Try the peach salad with prosciutto, goat cheese and pecans. *11am-2:30pm & 5-10pm* $$$

FIG: Foodie favorite known for welcoming staff, efficient but unrushed service and sustainably sourced nouvelle Southern fare. *5-10:30pm Tue-Sat* $$$

HIGHLIGHTS
1 Old Slave Mart Museum

SIGHTS
2 Aiken-Rhett House
3 Charleston Museum
4 International African American Museum
5 Marion Square

ACTIVITIES
6 Gateway Walk

SLEEPING
7 Andrew Pinkney Inn

EATING
8 Chez Nous
9 FIG
10 Marina Variety Store
11 Poogan's Porch
12 Slightly North of Broad
13 Ordinary

DRINKING & NIGHTLIFE
14 Bin 152
15 Blind Tiger
16 Citrus Club
17 Fiat Lux
18 Henry's on the Market
19 Palmetto Lobby Bar
20 Pavilion Bar
21 Prohibition
22 Rooftop at the Vendue

SHOPPING
23 Charleston City Market

INFORMATION
24 Fort Sumter Visitor Education Center at Liberty Square

With its grand homes and manicured gardens, Charleston is awash in aesthetic charms. But the city owes much of its beauty and success to an economy that was once driven by enslaved labor. On the grounds of an open-air market that auctioned men, women and children, the simple but powerful **Old Slave Mart Museum** *(oldslavemart.org; $7)* spotlights the day-to-day realities and horrors of the slave trade in the years leading up to the Civil War. It was the largest of 40 or so similar auction houses in the city.

More than 250,000 enslaved Africans entered the United States in Charleston, and many disembarked at Gadsden's

Charleston City Market (p140)

FIIPHOTO/SHUTTERSTOCK

AFRICAN AMERICAN HERITAGE IN CHARLESTON

For a list of Black-owned restaurants and businesses, pick up the free Explore Black History booklets found around town or visit *exploreblack charleston.com.* The website has an interactive map, and it shares itineraries that spotlight destinations with connections to Black history. Located 1 mile north of the International African American Museum, **Hannibal's Kitchen** *(hannibalkitchen. com; 11am-8pm Mon-Sat)* serves soul food, including Gullah-Geechee standards such as shrimp-and-crab rice (its signature dish) and collard greens. Opened by family patriarch Robert 'Hannibal' Huger in 1985, the restaurant is now managed by his granddaughters.

Wharf beside the Cooper River. The wharf is now home to the striking **International African American Museum** *(iaamuseum.org; adult/child $22/10),* which shares the stories of the African American diaspora through interactive exhibits, firsthand recollections, eye-catching artifacts and compelling art. Gullah-Geechee culture is also featured – be sure to step into the recreated Praise House and watch the short film about the uplifting Moving Hall Star Singers, a multigenerational gospel group from Johns Island.

The only surviving urban townhouse complex in the city, the 1820 **Aiken-Rhett House** *(historiccharleston.org; adult/ child $15/7)* gives a fascinating glimpse of antebellum life on a 45-minute self-guided audiotour. The Historic Charleston Foundation has conserved but not restored the home, so when you step through the ornate doors of this tangerine-colored mansion, once home to South Carolina governor William Aiken, it feels like time-traveling to 1858. The collection of books, furnishings, art and architectural details, though worn, is largely intact.

Be sure to also take a peek in the **Charleston City Market** *(thecharlestoncitymarket.com),* which stretches four blocks along Meeting St in the French Quarter. It's one of the nation's oldest markets, getting its start in 1804.

Ghosts in the graveyard

If you're a fan of spooky Southern Gothic fiction, welcome to your unhappy place. The **Gateway Walk** is a loose, natural-feeling corridor that ribbons through downtown's hustle and bustle, but the weathered headstones, walled pathways and live oaks are an instant portal to another, quieter time. The silence is occasionally broken by church bells ringing in the distance. Defying the melancholy? Wildflowers deliver bursts of color in spring.

The western entry is on Archdale St at St John's Lutheran Church. If the gate is closed, begin next door at the Unitarian Church. A memorial to the enslaved workers who built the church rises near the entrance. The path winds through the graveyard and its intentionally overgrown foliage and concludes at St Philips Episcopal.

Afterwards, take a breather from the Gothic intensity by heading south to the Battery. A promenade follows along the harbor and offers views of Fort Sumter, while live oaks provide shade for cannons and statues of military heroes in the adjacent garden. Flanked by historic homes and the harbor, the area is a pretty spot to relax.

EATING IN CHARLESTON: OUR PICKS

MAPS P138 & P142

Edmund's Oast: Charleston's highest-brow brewpub serves Southern faves and a long list of cocktails and draft beers. *11am-10pm* **$$**

Leon's Oyster Shop: In a converted old body shop reimagined as an industrial-chic eatery, Leon's is a local favorite for oysters, fried chicken and scalloped potatoes. *11am-10pm* **$$**

Ordinary: Inside a cavernous 1927 bank building, this buzzy seafood hall and oyster bar feels like the best party in town. *5-10:30pm Wed-Mon* **$$**

Chez Nous: A diminutive restaurant with a short menu of dishes and wines from southern France, northern Italy and northern Spain. *11:30am-3pm & 5-10pm* **$$**

STROLLING HISTORIC CHARLESTON

Three centuries of history jostles for attention between Broad St and the Battery, which means wandering off course is entirely expected.

START	END	LENGTH
Old Exchange & Provost Dungeon	Four Corners of Law/ St Michael's Church	1.5 miles; 1 hour

Begin at the 1 **Old Exchange & Provost Dungeon**, where costumed guides lead tours of the dungeon where Stede Bonnet, the Gentleman Pirate, and Revolutionary War prisoners were once held.

Walk south to the pastel beauty of 2 **Rainbow Row**, a block of redone 1730s merchant stores that inspired the birth of the Preservation Society of Charleston in the 1920s.

Follow Tradd St to Church St and turn right. The 3 **Heyward-Washington House**, where the first president slumbered in 1791, is on your left.

Head south to East Battery and the 4 **Edmondston-Alston House**, where tours pass intricate woodwork and family artifacts.

Continue south to approach the 5 **Battery & White Point Garden**, named for the fortifications that lined the seafront and for the mounds of oyster shells once piled over the point.

Cut through the park and walk north along Meeting St to the 6 **Williams Mansion**, formerly known as the Calhoun Mansion. Famed for its opulent decor, this Gilded Age manor is Charleston's largest single-family residence.

Continuing north, the 7 **Nathaniel Russell House** appears on the left. You can see its free-flying spiral staircase on a tour.

At the 8 **Four Corners of Law**, notice St Michael's Church, representing God's law, on the southeastern corner.

Sweetgrass baskets are often for sale along Meeting St near the Four Corners of Law.

In the backyard at Nathaniel Russell House, the 16ft joggling board was used in the 1800s to help with rheumatoid arthritis.

The country's oldest liquor store, the Tavern at Rainbow Row has been selling spirits since 1686! Check its Facebook page for details about special tastings.

DEFINING THE LOWCOUNTRY

Much of South Carolina's south-eastern coastline, dubbed the Lowcountry, is a patchwork of barrier islands marked by small inlets and salt marshes as well as stretches of shimmery, oyster-gray sand and wild, moss-shrouded maritime forests. Bridges link to some of these islands, but many can be reached only by boat or ferry. Descendants of West African enslaved have long called the region home. Known as the Gullah-Geechee, these people have maintained strong cultural and culinary traditions over centuries, but their communities continue to shrink as resorts and commercial developments gobble up land.

EATING
1 Edmund's Oast
2 Hannibal's Kitchen
3 Leon's Oyster Shop

DRINKING & NIGHTLIFE
4 Little Jack's Tavern
5 Palmetto Brewing Company
6 Revelry Brewery

ENTERTAINMENT
7 Royal American

Panoramic bars and creative hubs

Several great rooftop lounges can be found in the French Quarter. With an infinity pool, illuminated umbrellas and stunning city views, the chic **Pavilion Bar** *(marketpavilion.com)* attracts a well-heeled set, but people sometimes end up barefoot when the staff throws plexiglass over the pool and converts it into a dance floor. **Rooftop at the Vendue** *(rooftopcharleston.com)* also has sweet views of downtown. **Henry's on the Market** *(henrysonthemarket.com)* is not the swankiest of the lot, but it sits atop Henry's, the oldest restaurant in the state, dating to 1932.

Further north, a bright neon orange overlooks the bar at the ever-stylish **Citrus Club** *(thedewberrycharleston.com),* which has impressive views of Holy City Church's steeples, Marion Sq

DRINKING IN CHARLESTON: COCKTAILS & WINE

MAP P138

Palmetto Lobby Bar: Foam-topped cocktails give a kick – the foam is infused with alcohol – at this stylish hotel bar. *4-11pm Mon-Thu, 11am-midnight Fri & Sat, 11am-11pm Sun*

Prohibition: Jazz Age gastropub serving excellent craft cocktails (from $16) that pair well with the lip-smackin' Southern grub. *4pm-2am Mon-Thu, from 11am Fri-Sun*

Ordinary (p140)**:** Yes, there are oysters, but the cocktails shine too inside this former bank building that has an appealing join-the-party vibe. *5-10pm Wed-Mon*

Bin 152: Pair adventurous wine selections with imported cheese, freshly baked bread and charcuterie at this elegant downtown wine bar. *2pm-midnight Mon-Thu, from noon Fri-Sun*

and the Ravenel Bridge from its perch atop the Dewberry. Around the corner, admire the artwork in the Hotel Bennett's lobby before gliding up to **Fiat Lux** *(hotelbennett.com)*, where you'll enjoy views of **Marion Square** with your cocktails.

A few miles further north, the **Refinery** *(therefinerychs.com)* is a special place to watch live music. Check for upcoming shows at this 2000-person outdoor venue beside the railroad tracks in North Charleston. Other tenants in this creativity hub include the **Whale**, a bar with a lengthy craft-beer list, and the sports bar **Cleats**.

An infamous fort

Grab a seat on the upper deck for the boat ride across Charleston Harbor to **Fort Sumter** *(nps.gov/fosu; free)*, where the first shots of the Civil War were fired. Upon arrival you'll disembark the ferry and walk to the fort. Travelers on the first ferry of the day may be asked to help raise the US flag, while those on the last may be asked to lower it. National park rangers and docents are available to answer questions and share information about the history of the site and its role in the Civil War. Buy tickets *(fortsumtertours.com; adult/child $40/26)* ahead of your visit to avoid missing out. Expect to spend about 2¼ hours total on your trip, including the ferry rides. Boats depart from both Liberty Square (in downtown Charleston) and Patriots Point.

Before hopping on the ferry, stop by the **Fort Sumter Visitor Education Center at Liberty Square** *(free)* to see exhibits about the roots of the conflict that led to South Carolina's secession, the Civil War and the war's aftermath.

Reachable by car, **Fort Moultrie** *(nps.gov/fosu; adult/child $10/free)* offers a deeper dive into the region's coastal defense systems, as its exhibits and structures span nearly 200 years. Across the street from the fort, the visitor center has an information desk staffed by park rangers, along with a theater, a museum and a bookstore.

Kayaking the coast

Numerous companies lead tours and boat trips through the marshes and along the coasts of Charleston County's sea islands. **Adventure Harbor Tours** *(adventureharbourtours.com)* runs harbor cruises, sunset excursions and fun trips to uninhabited Morris Island – great for shelling. Trips leave from the marina at Ashley Point in Charleston. Well-established **Coastal Expeditions** *(coastalexpeditions.com; kayak tour*

CHARLESTON'S LIVE-MUSIC VENUES

Liv Brownstein, Charleston musician and College of Charleston student, shares her favorite music venues.

At Folly Beach, **Chico Feo** is a relaxed kind of place. The tacos are really good. On Monday it has an open-mic night where lots of bands or solo people go and play all original music. It's super cute, outdoors and right off the beach.

Every single night there's something happening at **Pour House**. The farmers market on Sunday has live music.

On the way to North Charleston at the top of the peninsula, **Royal American** is an indoor-outdoor venue. It has food and a sit-down area. Lots of different kinds of bands come here and there's a lot of rock music.

DRINKING IN CHARLESTON: BREWERIES & PUBS

MAPS P138 & P142

Palmetto Brewing Company: The city's first microbrewery (since Prohibition, anyway) produces an amber ale, a pilsner and a couple of IPAs. *4-10pm Mon-Thu, noon-10pm Sat, noon-7pm Sun*

Revelry Brewery: Knock back artfully crafted cold ones on the fairy-lit and fire-pit-heated rooftop with Ravenel Bridge views. *noon-10pm Mon-Thu, to 11pm Fri & Sat, to 8pm Sun*

Blind Tiger: This atmospheric bar seduces with stamped-tin ceilings and good pub grub. Enjoy your cocktail in the expansive courtyard. *4-11pm Mon-Thu, 11am-midnight Fri & Sat, 11am-11pm Sun*

Little Jack's Tavern: A classy neighborhood cocktail bar and restaurant, with one helluva hamburger. *noon-10pm*

BEST SEA ISLANDS NEAR CHARLESTON

Isle of Palms: The 7-mile stretch at Isle of Palms is well suited to families, and there's a playground steps from the beach.

Sullivan's Island: A broad commercial-free swath of sand south of Mount Pleasant. Come here to decompress and avoid the crowds.

Folly Beach: A favorite of locals, this festive spot with good surfing feels most like a beach town (particularly around Center St).

Kiawah: A mostly private island, but visitors can enjoy a family-friendly beach day at **Kiawah Beachwater Park**.

Edisto Beach State Park: A gorgeous, uncrowded beach with oak-shaded hiking trails. Stop for gossip and fried seafood baskets at Whaley's Store

adult/child from $48/38) leads kayak tours through the salt marshes at Shem Creek and along the Kiawah River, where full-moon trips are on the schedule. They also rent kayaks.

Sunsets and nature walks in Mount Pleasant

Mount Pleasant, originally a summer retreat for Charlestonians, sits just north of the Cooper River from Charleston. It has a historic downtown, and some great spots for catching the sunset, including along Shem Creek, where folks drink beer on restaurant patios and soak up views of the creek and Charleston Harbor. You can also stretch your legs and scan for dolphins along the dock-lined **Shem Creek Boardwalk**, which overlooks the marsh. For an easygoing vibe after your walk, settle in with a beer on the deck at **Red's Ice House** *(redsicehouse.com)*.

Beaufort

Learn Reconstruction Era history

The southern half of the South Carolina coast is a tangle of islands cut off from the mainland by inlets and tidal marshes. From 1861 to 1900, Beaufort and the surrounding sea islands became a hub for organization, education and self-determination for the formerly enslaved, who comprised 80% of the local population. Established by Congress in 2019, the **Reconstruction Era National Historical Park** *(nps.gov/reer)* covers the history of this era at three separate sites – all free – near Beaufort. Start at the **Old Beaufort Firehouse Visitor Center** downtown where you'll find a few exhibits as well as details about the other locations and scheduled park programs.

The best way to experience this evolving park is by listening to the stories and history shared by rangers. Check the online calendar for program times.

St Helena & Hunting Islands

Gullah culture and history

St Helena Island, east of Beaufort, has the highest concentration of Gullah people in the state and is the best place to learn about their culture. The **Penn Center** *(penncenter.com; tours $15-20)* has a museum that's a great starting point. Exhibits cover Gullah culture and trace the history of the center.

South Carolina's best seaside state park

The lush and inviting **Hunting Island State Park** *(south carolinaparks.com/hunting-island; adult/child $8/4)* impresses

EATING IN BEAUFORT: OUR PICKS

Lowcountry Produce: A fantastic market for picnic supplies with an equally appealing cafe. Try an Oooey Gooey, a grilled pimento-cheese sandwich with bacon and garlic-pepper jelly. *11am-2:30pm* $

Blacksheep x Sabbatical: This small wine shop and restaurant serves an eclectic selection of toasts, sips and sandwiches downtown. *11am-6pm Tue-Sat* $

Old Bull Tavern: Delicious food and cocktails amid a low-lit, worldly aesthetic. Menu changes daily but always features playful American and European comfort dishes. *5-9pm Tue-Sat* $$

Ribaut Social Club: Celebrate a special occasion inside a refurbished mansion a short walk from downtown. Seafood dishes shine. *5-7:45pm Tue-Sat* $$$

4KCLIPS/SHUTTERSTOCK

SkyWheel, Myrtle Beach

with its acres of spooky maritime forest and tidal lagoons. The bone-white beach is littered with seashells and the occasional shark tooth. The Vietnam War scenes from *Forrest Gump* were filmed in the marsh, a nature-lover's dream. Climb the lighthouse *($2)* for coastal views.

Myrtle Beach

Sand and boardwalk fun

Stretching for 60 miles along South Carolina's north coast, Myrtle Beach is famously overdeveloped, but there's plenty of fun to be had if you're willing to embrace the kitsch. Get the lay of the land by taking a spin on the **SkyWheel** *(skywheelmb.com; adult/child $20/16)*, which overlooks the 1.2-mile coastal boardwalk. Get your fill of mini-golf, T-shirt shops and arcade games along the **boardwalk**. When you need a break, enjoy a nature fix at **Myrtle Beach State Park** *(southcarolinaparks /myrtle-beach.com; adult/child $8/4)*. Unfurling along an undeveloped mile of coastline 3 miles south of central Myrtle Beach, this park is a pretty destination for walking the two short (half-mile) nature trails through maritime forest. There's also a long pier that's ideal for fishing *(fishing pass for adults/children $8/3)* and rods are available for rental *($25 for the day)*.

A day at Brookgreen Gardens

A true storybook setting, **Brookgreen Gardens** *(brookgreen.org; adult/child $22/12)* in Pawleys Island has the largest collection of American figurative statuary in the United States. Botanical gardens, art galleries, Gullah-Geechee sites and a Lowcountry Zoo are also highlights on the 9100-acre property, founded by Archer and Anna Hyatt Huntington in 1931. Lowcountry classics, including salt marshes, live oaks and longleaf pines, provide the outer-garden backdrop.

FAMILY FUN IN MYRTLE BEACH

Family Kingdom: Old-fashioned amusement-and-water-park combo overlooking the ocean.

Market Common: Vast retail and entertainment hub with disc golf and the wonderful, all-abilities Savannah's Playground for the toddler set.

Broadway at the Beach: Outdoor mall with shops, restaurants, rides, a Ripley's aquarium, a Wonderworks funhouse and a movie theater.

Myrtle Beach Boardwalk & Promenade: Go old school: walk the piers, play arcade games, ride the SkyWheel and eat some ice cream on the 1.2-mile promenade.

Topgolf: Yep, it's a national chain, but this multilevel golf-game outpost offers bays that are cooled or heated year-round.

GULLAH CULTURE

Starting in the 16th century, African people were transported from the so-called Rice Coast (Sierra Leone, Senegal, Gambia and Angola) to a remarkably similar landscape of swampy coastlines and tropical vegetation. These new African Americans were able to retain many of their homeland traditions after the fall of slavery and well into the 20th century. The resulting culture of Gullah (also known as Geechee in Georgia) has its own language, an English-based Creole with many African words and sentence structures, and traditions including storytelling, art, music and crafts. Gullah culture is celebrated during the Original Gullah Festival in Beaufort, while **Gullah-N-Geechie Mahn Tours** *(gullahngeechietours.com)* stop at sites on St Helena Island.

KEVIN RUCK/SHUTTERSTOCK

Columbia

River adventures

The Saluda and Broad Rivers merge just northwest of state capital Columbia, joining forces to create the Congaree River. June through August you can inner tube down the Lower Saluda to the Congaree, floating past Riverbanks Zoo. **Palmetto Outdoor** *(palmettooutdoor.com; tube & shuttle $20)* will rent you a tube and shuttle you upriver from the West Columbia Riverwalk & Amphitheater beside the Gervais Bridge. After your float, which runs about three hours, walk to **Savage Craft Ale Works** for a pint and river views from its rooftop.

Greenville

South Carolina's prettiest town center

In photogenic Greenville, the Reedy River twists through the city center, and its dramatic falls tumble beneath the sleek Liberty Bridge at Falls Park. Downtown Main St rolls past a lively array of indie shops, great restaurants and craft-beer pubs. Public art on Main honors town founders and features a whimsical collection of objects, from suitcases to mice. Good bets for shopping are **Mast General Store** *(mastgeneral store.com)*, a regional outdoor shop and old-fashioned candy

EATING & DRINKING IN MYRTLE BEACH: OUR PICKS

Earth Cafe: Tuck into the salads, wraps and smoothies at this hip and healthy place. *8:30am-4pm Mon & Tue, to 10pm Wed-Sun* $$

Hook & Barrel: Join the fun at this natty central bar where seafood is the showstopper. *4-9pm Mon-Thu, to 9:30pm Fri & Sat* $$$

New South Brewing: Try the bestselling Dirty Myrtle DIPA at this hyperlocal craft brewery – at it since 1998. *4:30-7pm Mon-Fri, 1-5pm Sat & Sun*

Atlas Tap House: Scruffy but friendly, with numerous craft beers on tap, near the boardwalk. Top-notch happy-hour tacos (from $1). *4pm-2am*

Greenville

emporium, and nearby **Poppington's** *(poppingtons.com)*, known for its imaginatively flavored gourmet popcorn. **M Judson Booksellers** *(mjudsonbooks.com)* is a sunny woman-owned bookshop (with cafe) in the old courthouse, while the patio at **Soby's** *(sobys.com)* is the place to see, be seen and savor Southern favorites like shrimp and grits. The chocolate-chunk cookies are a delicious complement to your latte at **Coffee Underground** *(coffeeunderground.info)*. Main St downtown closes to cars every Saturday morning May through October for the **Saturday Market** *(saturdaymarketlive.com)*.

Cycle the Swamp Rabbit Trail

You can walk it, jog it or skate it, but the most popular way to experience the fabulous **Swamp Rabbit Trail** – a former railway corridor – is on two wheels. The best section of the paved, tree-shaded greenway stretches 22 miles along the Reedy River, linking downtown Greenville with Furman University and the town of Travelers Rest. Pretty bridges, cafes and breweries dot the path. Expect the round-trip ride to take half a day. You can rent bikes in downtown Greenville from **Reedy Rides** *(reedyrides.com)* or a city bikeshare with **Greenville B Cycle** *(greenville.bcycle.com)*.

SWEETGRASS BASKETS

Sweetgrass baskets are for sale across the Lowcountry. These eye-catching coiled baskets have been made by hand by the Gullah-Geechee since the 18th century, when they were used by the enslaved on the region's rice plantations, and the craft of sweetgrass weaving was passed down through the generations. Today the baskets are often intricately patterned and are considered pieces of decorative art. Designs may vary by family. Learn more about the history behind sweetgrass baskets at the Sweetgrass Basket Pavilion – where they are also for sale – beside the Mount Pleasant Visitor Center and Memorial Waterfront Park. The park also hosts the annual Sweetgrass Festival in late July.

EATING IN GREENVILLE: OUR PICKS

Soby's: Book yourself one of the intimate brick-walled banquettes at this bastion of New Southern cuisine. *5-9pm, plus weekend brunch* **$$**

Trappe Door: Descend beneath E Washington St for rib-sticking Belgian food and an extensive beer list. *5-10pm Sun-Thu, to 11pm Fri & Sat* **$$**

Jianna: Savor rustic Italian cuisine and oysters galore in this cheerful 2nd-floor restaurant near Falls Park. *5-9pm Tue-Fri, from 11am Sat & Sun* **$$**

Anchorage: Local food and booze reign supreme in West Greenville – particularly true at the Anchorage. Look for its bright, enormous mural depicting produce. *5-9:30pm* **$$**

ZACK FRANK/SHUTTERSTOCK

Boardwalk Trail

TOP EXPERIENCE

Congaree National Park

Thick with knobby bald cypress trees, moss-covered tupelos and tangled Spanish moss, the swampy interior of Congaree National Park is a Southern Gothic setting at its most elemental. Home to the largest old-growth forest in the Southeastern USA, the park is on a plain fed by the floodwaters of the Congaree and Wateree Rivers. This eerie wonderland is 20 miles southeast of Columbia.

DON'T MISS

- Boardwalk Trail
- Dorovan muck
- Weston Lake
- Cedar Creek paddling
- Champion Trees
- Wildlife watching
- Skeeter Meter

Boardwalk Trail

The most efficient way to explore the floodplain here is to walk the 2.6-mile **Boardwalk trail**, an elevated walkway that loops through the park's old-growth bottomland forest. This easy trail passes beneath loblolly pines, water tupelos and bald cypresses, and it provides up-close views of the dark Dorovan muck, an 8ft-deep mix of clay and dead leaves. The trail also swings past boggy Weston Lake. Due to the lack of sunlight, few plants grow at the base of the trees, but you might see

PRACTICALITIES

- nps.gov/cong
- park 24hr; visitor center 9am-5pm
- admission free

turtles and snakes or hear a pileated woodpecker pecking away for insects at the base of a dead tree, known as a snag.

The trail begins and ends at the Harry Hampton Visitor Center and is open to wheelchairs, strollers and pets.

Paddling Through a Primeval Landscape

For an even more interactive experience, join a half-day guided paddling trip on the Cedar Creek Canoe Trail. This 15-mile water trail meanders through the park's old-growth forest, which provides thick shade. Look for otters, deer, snakes and even alligators while kayaking or canoeing along the marked path. The soundtrack may be the ratatatat of pileated woodpeckers doing their thing and the spooky calls of barred owls. Guided trips take about three hours and cost around $100 per person. Palmetto Outdoor (p146) among other approved outfitters lead trips. It's a relatively easy excursion, but some paddling experience is helpful and will keep you from holding up the group. Outings depart from the South Cedar Creek Canoe Landing, which is a seven-minute drive from the park visitor center.

See Synchronous Fireflies

For two weeks sometime between mid-May and mid-June, synchronous fireflies light up at night while searching for a mate within the park. Visitors can view this annual mating ritual along the Firefly Trail. Synchronous firefly displays occur in very few places in the US, and viewing events have become extremely popular. To view them in Congaree you will need to enter a park-sponsored lottery and hope you score a ticket. (Check nps.gov/cong/fireflies.htm for complete details.) The lottery typically opens in late March/early April. Synchronous fireflies can also be seen in early June in the Elkmont area of Great Smoky Mountains National Park.

Spot Champion Trees

The park harbors 25 so-called champion trees, meaning they are record-holders for their species based on their immense size. The champion loblolly pine here soars nearly 17 stories and boasts a circumference of more than 15ft. A champion sweet gum tree in the park reaches a height of 160ft. A park naturalist leads a three-hour hike to some of the park's biggest trees during a monthly Big Tree Hike, which occurs the second Saturday of the month. Space is limited and online registration is required.

CAMPING IN CONGAREE

Congaree has two front-country campgrounds. Longleaf Campground (individual/group site $15/25) is located near the park entrance. There are vault toilets here but no running water. Water is available at the visitor center, however. Bluff Campground ($10) has six hike-in sites. There are no restrooms or water sources here. A reservation is required for both campgrounds. Backcountry camping is allowed with a free permit.

TOP TIPS

- Look up along the entranceway to the visitor center to see the daily rating on the Skeeter Meter (from 'all clear' to 'war zone'), which will let you know if you need to apply bug spray before hitting the Boardwalk Trail. To be safe, bring some spray with you.
- Pack a picnic or snacks before your visit. There are no restaurants in the park and few options nearby. The park visitor center sells water, nuts and granola bars.
- Some ranger-led tours require a reservation and have limited availability. Check the park website to see if you need to sign up ahead of time.

Georgia

ARTS & CULTURE | CAPTIVATING NEIGHBORHOODS | ISLAND ESCAPES

Places

TOP TIP

A good Southern meal needs to be washed down with iced tea, and the default here is always sweet (ask for unsweetened if you have a lower sugar tolerance). Most soul food spots will likely send you home with another one to go.

When it comes to the Peach State, Atlanta hogs headlines (a film industry upstart, Fortune 500 epicenter and sporting powerhouse) while everything else seems to fly bewilderingly under the radar (Georgia has beaches?). That's just fine by natives, who'd love nothing more than to keep Georgia's other gems, including the northern mountains – and their surrounding foothills and upcountry – to themselves. Other lesser-known attractions pockmark the hinterlands, including the wildlife-rich landscape of the Okefenokee Swamp and the astonishing Native American legacy of Ocmulgeee Mounds.

Along the coast, Savannah has long captivated out-of-towners with its mix of history, creativity and culinary prowess, not to mention a heavy dollop of Southern charm. Nightlife thrives year-round and there are bustling watering holes aplenty. Savannah is also the gateway to picturesque sea islands lapped by salt tides and peppered with marshes, estuaries and beaches. These islands have a lost-in-time, almost Gothic, beauty; every corner seems to drip with sweat and Spanish moss.

GETTING AROUND

In Atlanta the four-line **MARTA** train system is generally a plus-sign shape, with two north-south lines (red and gold) and two east-west ones (blue and green). The Atlanta Streetcar line circles between Centennial Olympic Park and King Historic District, and there's an extensive bus system. You can explore Savannah's historic core by foot or the free DOT shuttle. A car is also your best bet for getting around coastline. Bus service is fairly limited though Greyhound and Megabus connect Atlanta to both Athens and Savannah, among other places.

Atlanta

MAPS P152, P154, P155

Exploring downtown

Some of Atlanta's biggest attractions all fall within a peach's throw of each other in the downtown area.

The city was a key focal point during th Civil Rights movement, and the **National Center for Civil & Human Rights** *(civilandhumanrights.org; adult/child $20/16)* shines a light on the past. One of the most powerful (and popular) installations is the interactive Lunch Counter Sit-In Simulation, inviting visitors to sit and gain an idea of the patience necessary to be part of nonviolent protests.

EATING IN DOWNTOWN ATLANTA: OUR PICKS

MAP P152

Food Shoppe: Creole specialties like shrimp and grits in easy-to-transport Walk & Eat bowls. Try Angie's bread pudding. *8:30am-8pm* $

Aviva by Kameel Downtown: Organic Mediterranean dishes in a corner of the Hub at Peachtree Center. *11am-3pm Mon-Fri* $$

Alma Cocina: Modern Mexican cuisine; guacamole and salsa samplers, and street tacos including chicken tinga. *11:30am-3pm & 5-10pm Mon-Fri, 5-10pm Sat, to 9pm Sun* $$$

Kwan's Deli & Korean Kitchen: Bustling deli with everything from bibimbap and katsu to Italian sandwiches and chicken wings. *10:30am-3pm Mon-Thu, to 8pm Fri & Sat* $

ATLANTA'S FOOD TRUCKS

Chase Davis, an Atlanta chef who launched King Kabob in 2015, shares his insight on the city's food trucks *@thekingkabob*

The Atlanta food-truck scene is special for its rich diversity, offering cuisines from around the world, often fused with Southern flavors reflecting the city's cultural melting pot. It thrives in vibrant, community-centered spaces like food-truck parks and festivals, creating a lively social atmosphere. Apart from **King Kabob**, one must-visit food truck is the **Kitchen**, which serves Asian-soul fusion delights such as Korean barbecue tacos. For dessert, don't miss the **Experience**, offering decadent Southern-style sweets including peach-cobbler milkshakes.

HIGHLIGHTS
1 National Center for Civil & Human Rights

SIGHTS
2 Centennial Olympic Park
3 Georgia Aquarium
4 SkyView
5 World of Coca-Cola

SLEEPING
6 Glenn Hotel

EATING
7 Alma Cocina
8 Aviva by Kameel Downtown
9 Food Shoppe
10 Kwan's Deli & Korean Kitchen
11 Sun Dial Restaurant & View

DRINKING & NIGHTLIFE
12 Atlantucky Brewing
13 Der Biergarten
14 RT60
see 6 SkyLounge

Next door, the **World of Coca-Cola** *(worldofcoca-cola.com; adult/child from $23/19)* is an ode to the beloved beverage – some 1.9 billion servings are enjoyed across 200-plus nations daily. Start by entering The Loft, packed with more than 200 relics of the brand's history, before watching a six-minute film about its global impact, and then entering the museum for exhibits on its formula, history and pop culture impact.

Nearby, the **Georgia Aquarium** *(georgiaaquarium.org; from $43)* is packed with wonders from the sea, including one of the world's largest single aquatic exhibits (a tank holding

DRINKING IN DOWNTOWN ATLANTA: OUR PICKS

MAP P152

Atlantucky Brewing: Craft-brew bar in Castleberry Hill opened by rapper Nappy Roots; affordable beers on tap in a beer hall–like space. *3-10pm Wed-Sun*

SkyLounge: Covered rooftop in the Glenn Hotel; cocktails on weeknights and small plates on weekends. *4-9pm Mon-Thu, 6pm-midnight Fri & Sat*

RT60: Hard Rock Hotel's 34th-floor bar rocks, well, hard. DJs and drinks including a mini martini flight and sangria tower. *4pm-midnight Mon-Wed, to 2am Thu-Sat, to 11pm Sun*

Der Biergarten: Ascending the staircase feels like walking into Germany: lagers, wine and cocktails alongside Wiener schnitzel and wurst. *4-9pm Wed-Fri, from noon Sat & Sun*

TOP EXPERIENCE

Martin Luther King Jr National Historical Park

America's Civil Rights movement was powered by the fearless leadership of Martin Luther King Jr, who believed in peaceful protest as a means to action. Long before he gave his most famous 'I Have a Dream' speech in Washington, DC, he was a boy spending his formative years in the neighborhood along Atlanta's Auburn Ave that is now the Martin Luther King Jr National Historical Park preserved as a time capsule to his legacy.

Ebenezer Baptist Church

Understand the Context of King's Life

Since the park site is spread out over a few blocks, make the **visitor center** your starting point to get oriented. The information desk will also provide the times for that day's programs, including must-hear talks inside the Ebenezer Baptist Church. The main exhibit, 'Courage to Lead,' outlines King's life and the growth of the Civil Rights movement, culminating in a life-size rendition of the Freedom Road walkway with marchers of every age.

Walk in King's Footsteps

On the next block, at 501 Auburn Ave, is a brown-and-beige **Queen Anne Victorian house** built in 1895. This is where King's mother grew up and where King himself was born. Birth Home tours are available on a first-come, first-served basis on the day of the tour. On the corner, peek in at Fire Station No 6, which served the segregated neighborhood.

One of the most moving experiences at the historical park is sitting in the pews of the **Ebenezer Baptist Church**, where King was baptized and also where he was ordained as a minister when he was 19, eventually becoming co-pastor with his father.

TOP TIPS

- On the way to the visitor center, stop and smell the roses. They're one of five major World Peace Rose Gardens in the world.
- Find the side-by-side tombs of Dr and Mrs King amid the fountains at the King Center for Nonviolent Social Change.

PRACTICALITIES

- nps.gov/malu
- 9am-5pm
- free

TINY DOORS ATL

Atlanta has its own brand of geocaching in the form of **Tiny Doors ATL** *(tinydoorsatl.com)*. Launched by artist Karen Singer in 2014, the project consists of more than 30 colorful little art pieces in the shape of doors hidden throughout the city. Her three main criteria are to make them all accessible, public and free. For instance, a trio of doors is hidden in one art piece in Centennial Olympic Park. (Hint: search for colorful scenery and don't forget to look up.) Also keep your eyes open at the Krog Street Tunnel, the Trap Music Museum and State Farm Arena.

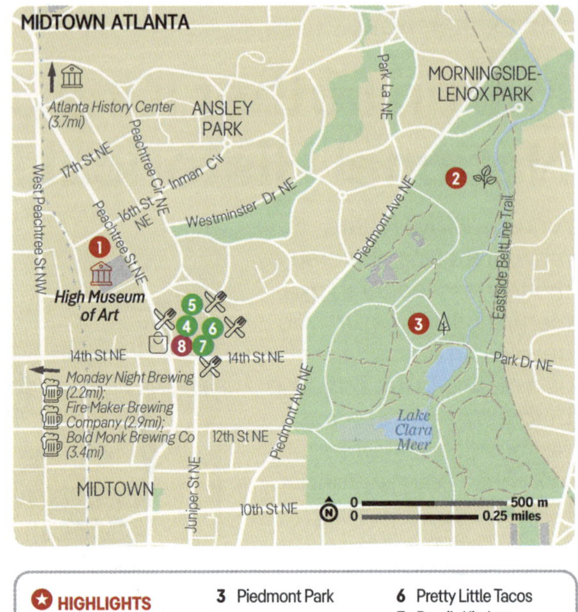

HIGHLIGHTS
1 High Museum of Art

SIGHTS
2 Atlanta Botanical Garden
3 Piedmont Park

EATING
4 Delilah's Everyday Soul
5 Holeman & Finch
6 Pretty Little Tacos
7 Rumi's Kitchen

SHOPPING
8 Colony Square

6.3 million gallons of water). Highlights include standing in the shadows of the beluga whales in Cold Water Quest, eyeballing great hammerhead sharks in Sharks! Predators of the Deep and climbing through a tunnel to come face-to-face with African penguins.

Anchoring these attractions is 22-acre **Centennial Olympic Park** *(gwcca.org/centennial-olympic-park)*, which commemorates the 1996 Games and serves as the city's central plaza.

On the southeast corner of the park, you can enjoy dazzling views over the city by taking a spin on the **SkyView Ferris wheel** *(skyviewatlanta.com; adult/child $19.50/14.45)*. It rises 20 stories high in 42 sealed, climate-controlled gondolas with floor-to-ceiling windows.

For dining (or not) with a view, there's the Westin Peachtree Plaza, home to the upscale **Sun Dial Restaurant & View**

EATING IN MIDTOWN ATLANTA: BEST COLONY SQUARE EATS

MAP P154

Pretty Little Tacos: Started as a food truck and quickly known for juicy birria tacos. *11am-9:30pm Mon-Thu, to 10:30pm Fri & Sat, to 8:30pm Sun* $

Delilah's Everyday Soul: Oprah Winfrey called the mac 'n' cheese here the best in the country. *11am-10pm Mon-Thu, to 11pm Fri & Sat, to 9pm Sun* $$

Rumi's Kitchen: Bustling Persian favorite; kebabs and labne are among popular picks. *11:30am-10pm Mon-Thu, to 11pm Fri, 11am-11pm Sat, to 10pm Sun* $$$

Holeman & Finch: Cozy lounge with elevated pub food, in chic digs with a dress code. *11am-10pm Sun-Wed, to midnight Thu-Sat* $$

HIGHLIGHTS
1 Martin Luther King Jr National Historic Park

SIGHTS
2 Historic Fourth Ward Park
3 Jimmy Carter Presidential Library & Museum
4 Krog Street Tunnel

EATING
5 Krog Street Market
6 Ponce City Market
7 Vortex

DRINKING & NIGHTLIFE
8 Euclid Avenue Yacht Club
9 Nine Mile Station
10 Porter
11 Star Community Bar
12 Village Coffee House

ENTERTAINMENT
13 Skyline Park

SHOPPING
14 Little Five Points

(sundialrestaurant.com; adult/child $10/5), which rotates on the 72nd floor. Between 11am and 9pm daily, visitors can take in the panorama.

Art and greenery in Midtown

Hailed as the Southeast's most renowned art destination, the **High Museum of Art** *(high.org; $23.50)* boasts a vast collection ranging from classic European paintings to contemporary works, with an emphasis on artists of the South. Of particular note is the folk and self-taught gallery, as well as its many rotating exhibitions showcasing the work of Black artists. For a personalized (and fun) experience, the museum's site *heartmatch.org* lets you swipe on art you like (much like a dating site) and generates a custom map.

A short walk south of the museum, **Colony Square** *(colony square.com)* feels like Midtown's living room, with its beauty spas, yoga, Pilates and a robust calendar of events. Step into the buzzy 20,000-sq-ft **Politan Row** food hall, where each of the dozen or so options is chef-driven with a local twist. There are also lively sit-down restaurants and bars. Top off the day by catching a flick at IPIC Theaters, which serves food and cocktails at your seat.

HIPPIE HAVEN

Bart Pond is a musician and a Little Five Points resident since 2010.

Little Five is Haight-Ashbury with Southern charm and hospitality. The murals here are constantly changing. This isn't graffiti; it's art. You learn who the artists are through their tags – this one is the Junkyard Chef and this is Paul Athol. Even the sidewalks have them. I can't give away all my secrets, but they have messages and if you follow them they'll lead you to two secret venues. There's other kinds of art too, like this sticker on the back of the street sign. A guy just puts free stories up. This one starts, 'My child was possessed by a demon who injured him through his rotting baby teeth....'

A few blocks east of there, the nearly 200-acre **Piedmont Park** *(piedmontpark.org)* has woods, wetlands and walking paths, plus a race track and the 11.5-acre Lake Clara Meer. Along the park's northwestern side is the 30-acre **Atlanta Botanical Garden** *(atlantabg.org; adult/child $29/26)*. There, the Cascades Garden is anchored by a topiary goddess sculpture, while the Kendeda Canopy Walk allows visitors to walk 40ft up among the trees. Piedmont Park is a popular site for events such as the Atlanta Dogwood Festival *(dogwood.org)* in April.

Experience the cutting edge at Little Five Points

At **Little Five Points**, a skeleton head with psychedelic eyes welcomes customers into the **Vortex** *(thevortexatl.com)* bar and grill, while the **Village Coffee House** *(instagram.com/villagecoffeehouselittle5)* has a retro photo booth outside and a rack of vintage clothes for sale inside. Tattoo parlors and smoke shops are interspersed among a metaphysical crystal store and a record shop, while in between there are vintage boutiques for every kind of shopper, imaginative bars and some dazzling street art.

DRINKING IN ATLANTA'S LITTLE FIVE POINTS: OUR PICKS

MAP P155

Euclid Avenue Yacht Club: Standard dive-bar fare in an eclectic environment. *noon-3am Mon-Sat, to midnight Sun*

Star Community Bar: All about its characters, with events from honky-tonk dance lessons to drag competitions. *5pm-2:30am Mon-Thu, 1pm-2:30am Fri & Sat, to midnight Sun*

Vortex: Featuring an eclectic booze menu and quirky vibe, this eatery and bar delivers on memorable clientele. *11am-midnight Sun-Thu, to 2am Fri & Sat*

Porter: Relatively clean-cut Porter has 60 craft brews on draft and a massive beer cellar. *5pm-midnight Wed-Fri, from 11am Sat & Sun*

NICHOLAS LAMONTANARO/SHUTTERSTOCK

Skyline Park mini golf

Explore Atlanta BeltLine's Eastside Trail

Any time of day along the **Atlanta BeltLine's Eastside Trail** *(beltline.org)* there will be folks running, biking, walking their dogs and riding scooters. In essence, this 3-mile section of what will eventually be part of a 22-mile loop around the entire city is proof of what all of Atlanta could soon become. A colorful starting point is the mural-covered **Krog Street Tunnel** connecting Cabbagetown and Inman Park. Heading north, just to the left the paved trail soon comes into view. You'll walk past **Krog Street Market** *(thekrogdistrict.com)*, an enticing food hall in an 1889 building. Let your instincts guide you, whether it's stopping off at a brewery for a pint or taking a break to watch the daredevils in the skatepark. You'll soon arrive near **Historic Fourth Ward Park** *(h4wpc.org)* and the vast **Ponce City Market** *(poncecitymarket.com)*, one of the biggest and best food halls in the South. Don't miss the rooftop, where you'll find **Skyline Park** *(poncecityroof.com/skyline-park; from $7)*, with boardwalk games, mini golf, a three-story slide and Heege Tower for even higher views. Also up top is the **Nine Mile Station** *(9milestation.com)* beer garden, which has private igloos in the cooler months.

The city's past through living history

Set on 33 acres, the **Atlanta History Center** *(atlantahistory center.com; adult/child $27/15)* is unlike other city historical society museums. With a rare in-the-round painting, a mansion made famous by a movie franchise, blooming gardens, sunken woods, historic buildings and a farm – with sheep and goats. – this Buckhead neighborhood museum is creating its own history as much as it's preserving the city's. Follow the events that shaped Atlanta through exhibits on how railroads set the city's foundation (even climb aboard a restored Texas

THE BEER BUS

Hopping from brewery to brewery is a great way to get to know the city, with each brewery offering its own unique atmosphere. The Upper Westside has emerged as the newest favorite concentration for breweries in the city. A cluster of them have established an Ale Trail and offer rides on the **Atlanta Beer Bus** *(atlantabeerbus.com; free)*, which runs alternating routes on Sunday. From 1pm to 7pm riders can start from any one of the area breweries and pick up a passport and get a beer at each spot. The stops include **Fire Maker Brewing Company** *(firemakerbeer.com)*, **Bold Monk Brewing Co** *(boldmonk brewingco.com)* and **Monday Night Brewing** *(monday nightbrewing.com)*.

BEST OUTDOOR FUN IN NORTHERN GEORGIA

Tallulah Gorge State Park: Both easygoing and challenging hikes amid forests and waterfalls, plus a dramatic suspension bridge.

Unicoi State Park & Lodge: See sublime cascades, including Anna Ruby Falls in the Chattahoochee-Oconee National Forest.

Brasstown Bald: Ascend Georgia's highest point (elevation 4784ft); it's a paved, 0.6-mile hike uphill walk from the parking lot.

Blood Mountain: Get a taste of the Appalachian Trail on this iconic, moderately difficult 4.4-mile (round-trip) day hike from Neel Gap to the 4452ft mountaintop.

Vogel State Park: One of Georgia's oldest parks sits at the base of Blood Mountain and has many trails, including an easy 1-mile (round-trip) walk to Trahlyta Waterfall.

locomotive) and another on Atlanta 1996 (meet the fuzzy blue Olympic mascot, Izzy).

Explore the Jimmy Carter Presidential Library

Set in the midst of 30 acres of landscaped greenery between a pair of lakes, the **Jimmy Carter Presidential Library & Museum** *(jimmycarterlibrary.gov; adult/child $12/free)* feels like a peaceful sanctuary in the center of Atlanta. Inside, interactive exhibits trace Carter's path from his modest roots to the Oval Office, including a replica of the White House space as it was during his tenure. Also fascinating is the exhibit on the Camp David meetings: the secret negotiations between Israel and Egypt. Don't miss the chance to pose behind the presidential podium on the way out.

Athens

Visit Georgia's finest college town

One of the USA's quintessential college towns, beery, artsy and laid-back Athens is home to the **University of Georgia** and its fiercely followed football team. If you don't manage a ticket for a game at **Dooley Field at Sanford Stadium** (look on *seatgeek.com*), head downtown and pick a bar – they'll all be packed. You can freely wander the 760-acre campus. The **Athens Welcome Center** *(athenswelcomecenter.com)* produces a self-guided walking tour.

For a different take on the Athens' experience, head to the excellent **Georgia Museum of Art** *(georgiamuseum.org; free)*. Here you can gawk at modern sculpture in the courtyard garden as well as the tremendous collection from American realists of the 1930s.

At the 323-acre **State Botanical Garden of Georgia** *(botgarden.uga.edu; free)* at the University of Georgia, 3 miles south of town, gorgeous winding outdoor paths lead to an amazing collection of plants, including rare and threatened species, across eight specialty gardens. There are nearly 5 miles of top-notch woodland walking trails, too. If you're toting little ones, the interactive children's garden features a treehouse, a fossil wall, a granite map of Georgia and more.

Macon

Walking the Ocmulgee Mounds

Poised to become the country's newest national park, **Ocmulgee Mounds** *(nps.gov/ocmu; free)* has Indigenous ceremonial

EATING & DRINKING IN & AROUND ATHENS: OUR PICKS

Mama's Boy: Fluffy, buttery biscuit sandwiches are the calling card of this detour-worthy Southern breakfast bastion off the North Oconee Greenway. *7am-2.30pm* $

Last Resort Grill: Southwestern-inspired plates satiating Athens for 30 years. Fantastic patio. *hours vary* $$$

Hendershots: Quintessential Athens coffeehouse; also a great bar and live-music venue. *hours vary*

Creature Comforts Brewing Co: In a former tire shop, the three-bar, 54-tap brewery is the epitome of everything great about Athens. *hours vary*

JOANNE DALE/SHUTTERSTOCK

Okefenokee National Wildlife Refuge

mounds dating back thousands of years with special ties to the Muscogee (Creek) people who lived here before their removal on the Trail of Tears. The park has a museum with artifacts recovered from a 1930s archaeological dig that was the largest in US history. You can also climb the stairs to the top of the Great Temple Mound Complex, which offers views of the Ocmulgee River and beyond. Try to time your visit to catch a ranger-led tour, held on alternating weekends throughout the year. Better yet, plan your trip around Ocmulgee's cornerstone annual events, such as the **Lantern Light tours** (March) and the **Ocmulgee Indigenous Celebration** (September).

Okefenokee National Wildlife Refuge

Primeval wetlands

The **Okefenokee National Wildlife Refuge** *(fws.gov/refuge/okefenokee; $5)* is the nation's largest blackwater swamp – 'blackwater' refers to the tea-like hue created by the ancient peat at the bottom. Spanning 354,000 acres of rivers, lakes and islands, the swamp's name comes from the Indigenous word for 'land of the trembling earth.' Several creatures call the area home, including thousands of alligators and more than 200 species of bird, plus endangered indigo snakes and wood storks. There are a few short trails here (all less than a mile), but the best way to experience this watery landscape is by boat. Guided 90-minute boat tours are operated by **Okefenokee Adventures** *(okeswamp.org; adult/child $35/30)* and you can also rent canoes *($50)* and kayaks *($30 to $50)*.

For a driving tour, pick up a brochure at the **Bolt Visitor Center** to make the scenic 7-mile Swamp Island Drive by car or bicycle. Along the way, signs indicate several trails including the 1.5-mile (round-trip) boardwalk to the old Chesser Island Homestead. There are also markers pointing out the habitats of alligators, black bears and woodpeckers.

MOTHER OF THE BLUES

If there's one artist to add to your Georgia soundtrack, it's **Gertrude 'Ma' Rainey**, who was born in Columbus in 1886. She started singing at a young age, following in the footsteps of her parents, performing at a talent show at the famed Springer Opera House at age 14. She joined the touring circuit, performing around the country in her unique style, a mix of jazz and blues with her signature raspy voice. Rainey returned to her hometown in 1933, where she retired and is now buried. Her former home still stands, and tours *(parks.columbusga.gov/parks/ma-rainey-home)* are offered on an appointment basis. Don't miss the award-winning 2020 film *Ma Rainey's Black Bottom*, set in 1920s Chicago.

BEST HISTORIC HOUSE TOURS

Mercer-Williams House: Tour the 1st floor of Savannah's most notorious house.

Flannery O'Connor Childhood Home: This stone row house on Lafayette Sq is where the literary great was born in 1925 and lived until she was 13.

Juliette Gordon Low Birthplace Museum: Childhood home of the founder of the Girl Scouts of the USA, which runs the museum.

Sorrel Weed House: Fans of the paranormal can get their thrills at one of Savannah's spookiest mansions.

Owens-Thomas House & Slave Quarters: Completed in 1819 by British architect William Jay, this gorgeous villa exemplifies English Regency-style architecture, known for its symmetry.

Savannah

Step back in time in the Historic District

Savannah's Historic District is home to 18th- and 19th-century homes, fascinating museums and monuments, and world-class restaurants, all enveloped by a canopy of Spanish-moss-laden live oaks. After taking a stroll around the neighborhood, head to the **Telfair Academy** *(telfair.org; adult/child $30/10)*, considered Savannah's top art museum. Ensconced in the historic and captivating Telfair family mansion, the gallery is filled with 19th-century American works and a smattering of European pieces. Admission includes unlimited entries to the **Jepson Center** (which focuses on 20th- and 21st-century art) and the early-19th-century **Owens-Thomas House** for a week.

Visit the Plant Riverside District

Stepping into the generator hall at this former power station (now a JW Marriott hotel) in the **Plant Riverside District** *(plantriverside.com)* is a big 'Whoa!,' especially if you're walking in from the riverfront or the leafy Historic District. Throngs of people flow past as they explore the vast space, and there's an enormous chrome-dipped dinosaur hanging overhead. Glittering geodes and minerals beckon in every direction.

Galleries, boutiques and exuberant works of art fill the cavernous lobby, which exudes steampunk cool with its mix of modern amenities and original power-plant fixtures. After checking out whimsical creations at art-minded shops like **18Loves Art** *(18loves.com)*, head skyward to the **Myrtle & Rose Rooftop Bar** or the nearby **Electric Moon Skytop Lounge** for drinks overlooking the river. For something more structured, check out the indoor music venue here, **District Live**, which hosts touring acts with regional and national followings.

Georgian Coast

Beachcombing on Tybee Island

Savannah's favorite getaway is **Tybee Island**, with its eclectic art shops, laid-back cafes and pretty beaches. For sheer beauty, set your sights on **North Beach**, a beautiful swath of white sand. With fewer services and a vibe that feels more remote, this stretch of shoreline is a great place to relax – though you can also get active, climbing the 178-step staircase that corkscrews to the top of the **Tybee Island Light Station**

EATING IN SAVANNAH: OUR PICKS

Treylor Park: Amid a retro-chic aesthetic, enjoy fried chicken on a biscuit paired with an excellent cocktail. *11am-1am Mon-Fri, from 10am Sat & Sun* $

Mrs Wilkes Dining Room: Once you're seated family-style, the kitchen unloads the likes of fried chicken, beef stew and black-eyed peas. *11am-2pm Mon-Fri* $$

Grey: A wonderfully retro makeover of a 1930s Greyhound bus terminal, serving up deliciously inventive 'Port City Southern' cuisine. *5-9pm Tue-Sun, also 11am-3pm Sun* $$$

Starland Yard: For alfresco dining and drinking, stop in this lively food-truck park, which offers plenty of variety, plus events (live music, line dancing). *5-10pm Mon-Wed, noon-9pm Thu-Sun* $

WALKING SAVANNAH'S SQUARES

One of the joys of visiting Savannah is walking around the Historic District amid some of the most beautiful residential architecture in the country.

START	END	LENGTH
Forsyth Park	Johnson Square	1¾ miles; 2 hours

Begin at the iconic fountain in ❶ **Forsyth Park**. Continue north on Bull St toward the intersection with Wayne St, where a statue of General Casimir Pulaski soars above ❷ **Monterey Square**. Walk north and turn right on cobblestoned Jones St, flanked by Greek Revival homes and live oaks. Turn left on Abercorn to see the spectacular ❸ **Cathedral Basilica of St John the Baptist**. Head north to Colonial Park Cemetery. Wander past Gothic tombs and monuments, then turn west on E Perry St. A bronze statue of Savannah founder James Oglethorpe oversees the action from ❹ **Chippewa Square**. The park-bench scenes in *Forrest Gump* (1994) were shot on the north side along Hull St (the actual bench was a prop). Keep truckin' north on Bull St to ❺ **Wright Square**, burial site of Tomochichi, the Yamacraw tribe leader who befriended Oglethorpe and helped him establish the colony. Head west to ❻ **Telfair Square**, where the Telfair Academy and the Jepson Center border Barnard St. Continue north, cross busy Broughton St and continue to ❼ **Ellis Square**, a hub of commerce from the 1730s through the 1950s. In the 1850s it housed a market for the sale of enslaved human beings. Head east down St Julian St toward Bull St and end at ❽ **Johnson Square**, Savannah's first and largest square.

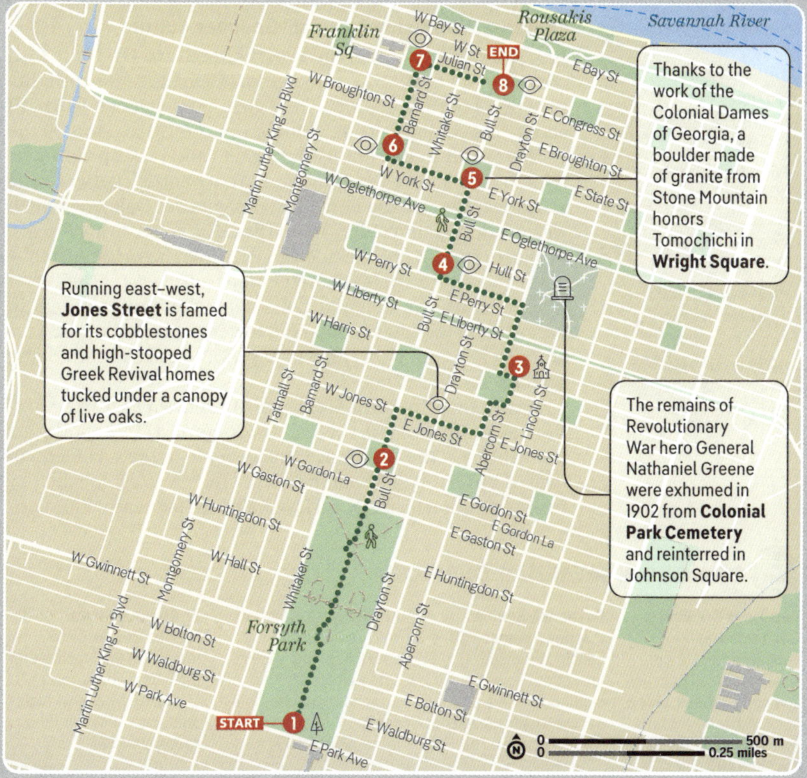

Thanks to the work of the Colonial Dames of Georgia, a boulder made of granite from Stone Mountain honors Tomochichi in **Wright Square**.

Running east-west, **Jones Street** is famed for its cobblestones and high-stooped Greek Revival homes tucked under a canopy of live oaks.

The remains of Revolutionary War hero General Nathaniel Greene were exhumed in 1902 from **Colonial Park Cemetery** and reinterred in Johnson Square.

BEST ANNUAL EVENTS ON TYBEE ISLAND

SCAD Sand Arts Festival: Students from the Savannah College of Arts & Design create magical sand sculptures on South Beach in August.

Tybee Island Beach Bum Parade: Come prepared with a water gun – no one's safe at this giant traveling water fight – which is oh so welcome on hot days. Held mid-May.

Tybee Turtle Trot: Coinciding with sea-turtle nesting season in late April, this 5km beach run is a fundraiser for turtle-preservation efforts.

Fourth of July: Catch the spectacular fireworks show, with views anywhere along the eastern beaches.

Pirate Fest: Dress up like your favorite buccaneer and party like it's 1699 at this four-day fest in mid-October.

DENNIS MACDONALD/SHUTTERSTOCK

(tybeelighthouse.org; adult/child $12/10; closed Tue), where even more glorious views await. Tickets include admission to the adjacent lighthouse keeper's cottage and museum.

Exploring Wormsloe & Gullah-Geechee culture

Just south of Savannah, the **Wormsloe State Historic Site** *(gastateparks.org/Wormsloe; adult/child $12/6)* spotlights the state's earliest history. On a visit here, you can learn all about this colonial estate, founded in the 1730s. Stop by the visitor center to buy admission tickets and pick up a property map. You'll also board the tram that shuttles between the visitor center and the park museum via Live Oak Ave, which was originally flanked by more than 400 moss-draped oaks. Property highlights include the ruins of the original tabby house (tabby is a crude concrete composed of oyster shells and lime mortar), the Colonial Life Area, where interpreters in period costumes may be on hand to demonstrate Colonial-era crafting and tool work, and an observation deck overlooking a pretty stretch of marsh.

Nearby, the **Pin Point Heritage Museum** *(chsgeorgia.org/pin-point-heritage-museum; adult/child $15/7)* spotlights the culture of the Gullah-Geechee people in the secluded village of Pin Point. The community, which was established by first-generation formerly enslaved, thrived for nearly 100 years.

DRINKING IN SAVANNAH: OUR PICKS

Two Tides Brewing Co: A small quirky brewery and cafe with an adventurous beer list and good coffees, plus a cocktail bar downstairs. *7am-10pm Sun-Thu, to midnight Fri & Sat*

Savannah Smiles Dueling Pianos: It's a deliciously kitschy good time at this sing-along nightspot, where patrons decide what's played on stage. *7pm-2am Thu-Sat*

Artillery: Mixologists craft novel, quality cocktails in this opulent space where 19th-century eclecticism meets modern design. *4-11pm Mon-Thu, to midnight Fri & Sat*

El-Rocko Lounge: You'll feel the '70s-inspired swank but then realize that the vibe is absolutely chill. DJs keep the energy high. *5pm-midnight Mon-Wed, to 3am Thu-Sat*

Wormsloe State Historic Site

Vibrant arts-loving Brunswick

Some 80 miles south of Savannah, the town of Brunswick dates from 1771, and has a multicultural vibe with West Indian flavors and a rich local art scene. Check out the new restaurants, bars and tasting rooms that have opened on the main drag, Newcastle St, and if you're sticking around for the night, catch a performance at the **Historic Ritz Theatre** *(goldenislesarts.org),* which hosts plays, concerts and films.

Captivating Jekyll Island

An easy 20-minute drive from Brunswick, Jekyll Island has miles of beaches, wilderness and historic buildings. Get the lay of the land at **Mosaic Jekyll Island Museum** *(jekyllisland.com; $10),* which shares the history of the island across a half dozen or so historic time periods, with evocative exhibits - sweetgrass baskets, a miniature portrait and a Red Bug flyer - highlighting the varied stories. Trolley and historic tours *(from adult/child $20/15)* depart the museum throughout the day, including the new Millionaire Motorcar Tour *(up to four people $125)* in a 1930s Model T replica.

Beaches & wild horses of Cumberland Island

More remote, Cumberland Island is the southernmost barrier island in Georgia, and was once an exclusive playground for the elite. Visitors can access it via daily ferries *(cumberlandislandferry.com; adult/child round trip $40/30)* from tiny St Marys and explore the ancient 17-mile-long stretch of moss-covered oak forests, salt marshes and untouched beach. Wild horses roam, sea turtles hatch, and the ruins of a once-grand mansion still stand, begging to be discovered. Reserve well ahead for the ferry.

JEKYLL ISLAND: NEED TO KNOW

An exclusive refuge for millionaires in the late 19th and early 20th centuries, Jekyll Island is a 4000-year-old barrier island with 10 miles of beaches. These include photo darling Driftwood Beach, famed for its fallen skeleton trees. Today the island is an unusual clash of wilderness, preserved historic buildings, modern hotels and a massive campground. And, oddly, it's all part of **Jekyll Island State Park** *(jekyllisland.com),* complete with a $10 per day parking fee payable upon entry. It's also an easily navigable place - you can get around by car, horse or bicycle.

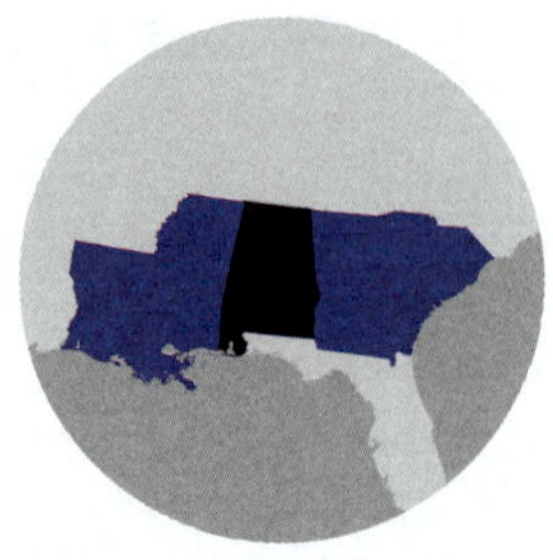

Alabama

CIVIL RIGHTS | OUTER SPACE | OFFBEAT ADVENTURES

Places

TOP TIP

Several regions in Alabama (including Muscle Shoals, Huntsville, Montgomery and Birmingham) offer an All-in-One Ticket, allowing you to visit multiple attractions over a set time period at a substantial saving. Purchase it online *(alabama.travel/attraction-tickets)*.

The land of red soil and lilting accents, Alabama is a complicated and oft misunderstood place. Follow a meandering road trip across the state and you'll see cotton fields and vast forests, peaceful riverside towns and booming cities (Huntsville) fueled by burgeoning aerospace and tech industries. And Alabama's nature reserves encompass both sandy Gulf beaches and wooded canyons dotted with waterfalls.

As elsewhere in the South, locals' love for the state runs deep – and not just when it comes to college football. Alabamans take pride as being the birthplace of the Civil Rights movement, where pioneers like Martin Luther King Jr, Rosa Parks and John Lewis inspired people around the globe to fight for a more just and inclusive society. The state is also home to an incredible musical heritage (visit Muscle Shoals for the inside scoop), and the oldest Mardi Gras celebrations in the country – with colorful parades rolling through the Franco-Caribbean streetscape of Mobile.

Huntsville

Culture and green spaces downtown

The birthplace of Huntsville was the gushing **Big Spring**, which produces some 7 million gallons of fresh water each day. A scenic **park** surrounds the meandering waterway, which also anchors downtown Huntsville. You can go for a pleasant stroll here, or feed the ducks, geese and koi fish (strategically placed dispensers dole out pellets for 25 cents).

GETTING AROUND

Decent intercity transportation is lacking across Alabama, though it is possible to reach some urban areas (including Birmingham, Mobile and Montgomery) by slow Greyhound bus. You'll find walkable centers in some cities, though you'll need a car to reach many sites. Huntsville and Montgomery also have a bikeshare network, Blue Bikes (find details on *tandem-mobility.com*). In 2025, Amtrak re-established train service between Mobile and New Orleans, with two daily departures (morning and evening) in each direction.

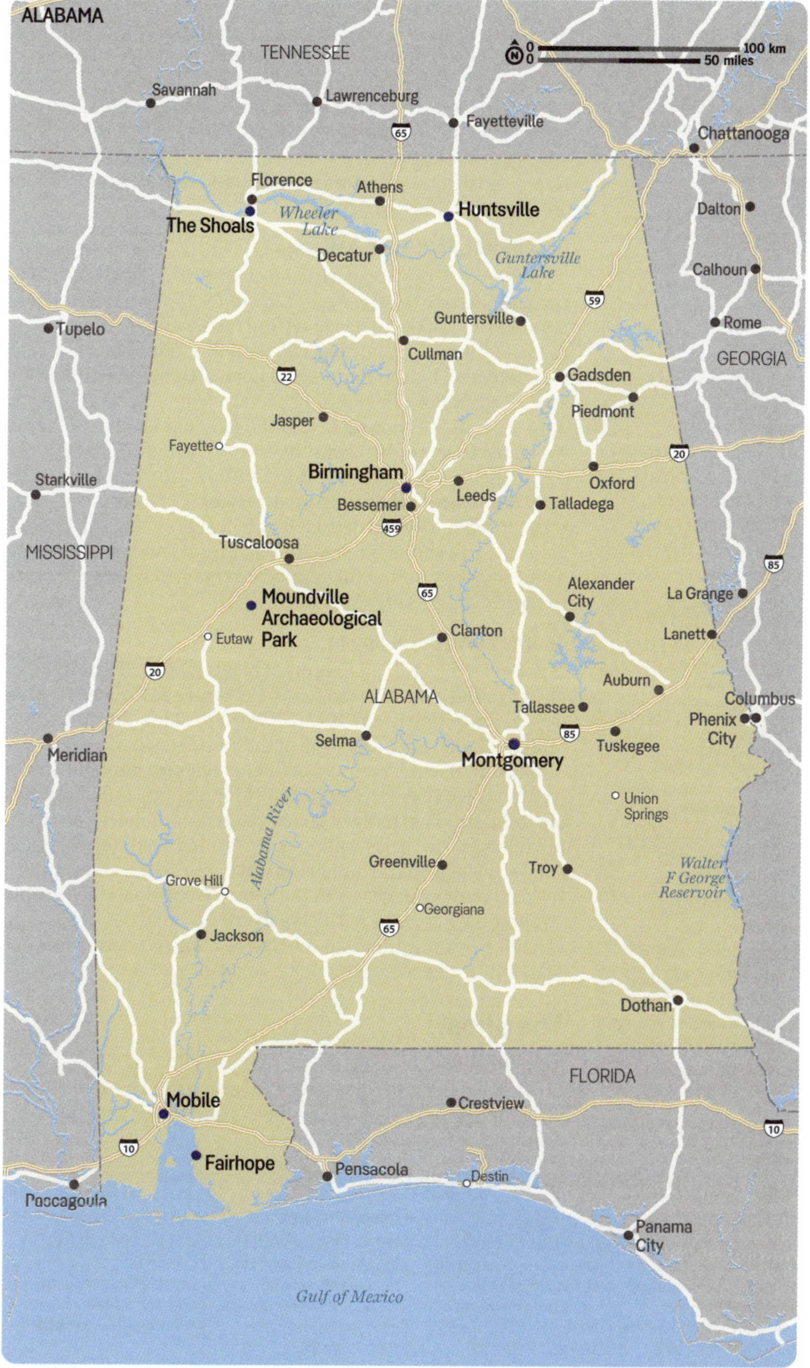
ALABAMA
TENNESSEE
0 100 km
0 50 miles
Savannah
Lawrenceburg
Fayetteville
Chattanooga
Florence
Athens
The Shoals
Wheeler Lake
Huntsville
Dalton
Decatur
Guntersville Lake
Calhoun
Guntersville
Rome
Tupelo
Cullman
GEORGIA
Gadsden
Piedmont
Jasper
Fayette
Birmingham
Oxford
Starkville
Leeds
Bessemer
Talladega
MISSISSIPPI
Tuscaloosa
Moundville Archaeological Park
Alexander City
La Grange
Eutaw
Clanton
Lanett
Auburn
ALABAMA
Columbus
Tallassee
Phenix City
Selma
Tuskegee
Meridian
Montgomery
Union Springs
Alabama River
Greenville
Troy
Walter F George Reservoir
Grove Hill
Georgiana
Jackson
Dothan
FLORIDA
Mobile
Crestview
Fairhope
Pensacola
Destin
Pascagoula
Panama City
Gulf of Mexico
65
59
22
20
459
85
10

BEST NATURE ATTRACTIONS IN NORTHERN ALABAMA

Monte Sano State Park: The forested upland just east of Huntsville boasts some 20 miles of paths across 2000 lovely acres.

Cane Creek Canyon: Open weekends only (7am to 5pm), this private nature reserve has some rewarding hikes, including a 6.5-mile loop.

Little River Canyon: Dramatic rock formations and river-smoothed bluffs form the backdrop to one of the deepest, most intricate gorge systems in the Eastern USA.

Dismals Canyon: Walk amid ferns, giant trees and cascades through a stunning sandstone gorge. Return by night to see 'Dismalites' (glowworms).

Lake Guntersville State Park: Hiking, fishing, boating and other activities across 6000 acres of forests and waterways.

Overlooking the park, the beautifully designed **Huntsville Museum of Art** *(hsvmuseum.org; adult/child $12/5)* houses regional pieces from across the Southeast United States, as well as collections from Asia, Africa and Europe.

The best time to visit the city is in late April, when it hosts its big arts weekend. **Panoply** *(artshuntsville.org/event/panoply; adult/child $15/free)* features over 100 artists, some 30 different musical performances, plus food trucks and loads of creative activities for kids.

Botanical beauty and galleries

Less than a 10-minute drive from downtown, **Huntsville Botanical Garden** *(hsvbg.org; adult/child $20/13)* stretches across 118 acres and makes a lovely setting for a wander. Aquatic gardens, a fern glade, a butterfly house and a giant Mother Earth troll (created by Danish artist Thomas Dambo) are favorite spots. Check the calendar for special events: live music, yoga, Shakespeare in the garden, and the fabulous Galaxy of Lights (when the trees and walkways boast colorful light installations).

A little over a mile southwest of downtown, **Lowe Mill ARTS & Entertainment** *(lowemill.art)* is a former textile mill turned into a vast arts facility. There are scores of studios, galleries and shops, along with restaurants and performance venues. Check online for regular events, from free concerts to Saturday markets (May to October).

Journey into outer space

If you ever entertained dreams of playing Major Tom to someone's ground control, head to the **US Space & Rocket Center** *(rocketcenter.com; adult/child $30/20)*. This Smithsonian-affiliated museum boasts one of the world's largest collections of space artifacts. There are simulator rides for kids and adults (try the G Force accelerator or the Moon Shot), and play areas for toddlers. The array of space-related paraphernalia, from lunar landers to rocket components, is mind-boggling. Daytime shows at the planetarium bring you closer to the stars thanks to spectacular images from the James Webb Space Telescope.

If you have a child with a space or aeronautics obsession, consider signing them up for **Space Camp**, a weeklong immersion in science, technology, robotics and more.

The Shoals

Reliving music history

Stretching along the Tennessee River 70 miles west of Huntsville, the Shoals is a conglomeration of four towns with nebulous

EATING & DRINKING IN HUNTSVILLE: OUR PICKS

Blue Plate Cafe: Down-home cooking, with hearty breakfasts (berry pancakes, country-fried steak) and lunchtime specials of Southern hits. *6am-8pm Mon-Sat* $

Pane e Vino: Tuck into perfectly cooked Neapolitan-style pizzas, while enjoying the views from the terrace overlooking Big Spring Park. *11am-9pm* $$

Campus No 805: This former high school has breweries and convivial restaurants serving Mexican dishes, pub fare and wood-fired pizzas. *11am-10pm* $$

Cotton Row: One of Huntsville's most celebrated restaurants, with highlights like foie gras and lobster risotto. *4-9:30pm Tue-Sat* $$$

DANITA DELIMONT/SHUTTERSTOCK

US Space & Rocket Center

boundaries and little-known but captivating attractions. Beginning in the 1960s, this lightly populated region became ground zero for some of the most important music production of an era. At **Muscle Shoals Sound Studios** *(muscleshoals soundstudio.org)*, you can learn all about the legends that recorded here, including the Rolling Stones, Bobby Womack, Paul Simon and countless others. On a small, intimate guided tour *(adult/child $25/12)*, you'll hear some wild stories from the recording days and listen to iconic songs made right in the studio. Hour-long tours typically run throughout the day, Tuesday through Saturday.

A couple miles south, you can take a similar guided tour through **Fame Studios** *(famestudios.com; adult/child $20/15)*, where Wilson Pickett recorded 'Mustang Sally' and Aretha Franklin cut 'Do Right Woman' – among many, many other tracks.

Complete the musical journey with a visit to the **Alabama Music Hall of Fame** *(alamhof.org; adult/child $15/8)*, which has instruments, attire and even an over-the-top golden convertible belonging to some of the musical stars that emerged from the state.

Learn about a sightless pioneer

Helen Keller – to this day perhaps the most beloved native of Alabama – was blind and deaf from the age of 19 months. With the aid of companion Anne Sullivan, Keller would go on to attend Radcliffe College, earn a degree and become a noted writer, lecturer and activist for pacifist and socialist causes. The **Helen Keller Birthplace** *(helenkellerbirthplace.org; adult/child $10/5)*, her childhood home, is maintained with personal mementos, and guides on hand are happy to share pivotal episodes from Helen's life. *The Miracle Worker,* a play based on Keller's autobiography, is performed here at select dates in June and July.

THE MUSCLE SHOALS SOUND

Chase Brandon, sound engineer at Muscle Shoals Sound Studio, describes the versatile musicians that everyone wanted to record with back in the '60s and '70s *@muscleshoals soundstudio*

The Swampers have been described as very soulful musicians. They confused a lot of people because they looked kind of nerdy. You might see them and think country music, but they were totally into soul and R&B. In the '60s they worked almost exclusively with Black artists doing R&B records: Aretha Franklin, Wilson Pickett, Percy Sledge, the Staple Singers. In the '70s, the Swampers evolved from this one-genre rhythm section, and they recorded with a huge variety of artists: Boz Scaggs, Lulu, Duane Allman, Bob Seger and Paul Simon among many others.

BIRMINGHAM'S BEST OUTDOOR ATTRACTIONS

Sloss: Wander past soaring, iron-producing blast furnaces that powered Birmingham's economy from 1882 to 1971.

Vulcan: On a hill above Birmingham, a cast-iron statue of the Roman god of metal-working celebrates the city's industrial past. Head up the observation tower for wide views.

Railroad Park: A much-loved downtown green space where all are welcome to regular events (zumba, yoga, line dancing, outdoor concerts).

Red Mountain Park: Some 16 miles of trails including overlooks along forested ridge lines, 8 miles southwest of downtown.

Oak Mountain State Park: Hiking and mountain-biking on over 100 miles of trails in Alabama's largest state park *(adult/child $5/2)*. It's 18 miles south of downtown.

Birmingham

Civil Rights history

One sight not to miss in Alabama is the **Birmingham Civil Rights Institute** *(bcri.org; adult/child $15/13)*, which takes you on a journey through one of the country's most tumultuous periods. A maze of moving audio, video and photography exhibits tells the story of racial segregation and the Civil Rights movement, with a focus on the activities in and around Birmingham.

Nearby, you can learn about the horrifying bombing of the **16th Street Baptist Church** *(16thstreetbaptist.org; adult/child $10/5)*, when four Black children were killed in 1963. Visits are by hourly tour (10am to 3pm Tuesday to Saturday). Today the rebuilt church is a memorial and house of worship (services 11am Sunday).

Across the street, in **Kelly Ingram Park**, walk in the footsteps of those who risked it all to bring an end to segregation. Various sculptures and monuments depict a moment in the Civil Rights struggle. In one space, the path becomes a gauntlet of snarling police dogs, while further along, a water cannon is aimed at visitors.

Around the corner from the park, the **AG Gaston Motel** was where Civil Rights leaders, including Martin Luther King Jr, stayed while in town. It's now run by the National Park Service, with exhibits about the dynamic entrepreneur AG Gaston, a pillar of the Black community.

Showtime!

Going strong since 1927, the **Alabama Theatre** *(alabama theatre.com)* is one of the anchors of cultural life in downtown Birmingham. Built as a 2000-seat movie palace, the architectural landmark hosts plays, concerts, big-name comedians and classic films – often followed by audience sing-alongs with the Mighty Wurlitzer (a red-and-gold pipe organ). Across the street, the **Lyric** *(lyricbham.com)* is a former vaudeville theater that offers a similar line-up of concerts, comedy and dance.

Up the road, the **Sidewalk Film Center** *(sidewalkfest.com)* is an artfully designed space set beneath the Pizitz Building. Its two theaters screen independent films, and you can while away the evening in the bar and comfy lounge areas before or after catching a film.

Two miles east of downtown, **Saturn** *(saturnbirmingham.com)* is a sleek live-music venue with a '70s-meets-outer-space aesthetic. There's a fine roster of talent featuring up-and-coming indie rock stars (shows are ages 18 and up). Music aside, there are pinball machines, video consoles and board

EATING & DRINKING IN BIRMINGHAM: OUR PICKS

Fish Market: Casual spot for fresh-off-the-boat seafood, including crab legs and red snapper. *11am-8:30pm Mon-Sat* $$

Essential: Trendy spot with a creative menu and popular weekend brunches. *11am-9pm Mon-Fri, 9am-2pm & 5-9pm Sat & Sun* $$

Collins Bar: A beautiful space for sipping handmade cocktails under a Birmingham-centric periodic table of the elements. *4pm-midnight Mon-Sat*

House of Found Objects: Bubble machines, a video booth, costumes (ask about cookie monster) and a backroom, entered via a birth canal. *4pm-midnight Tue-Sat*

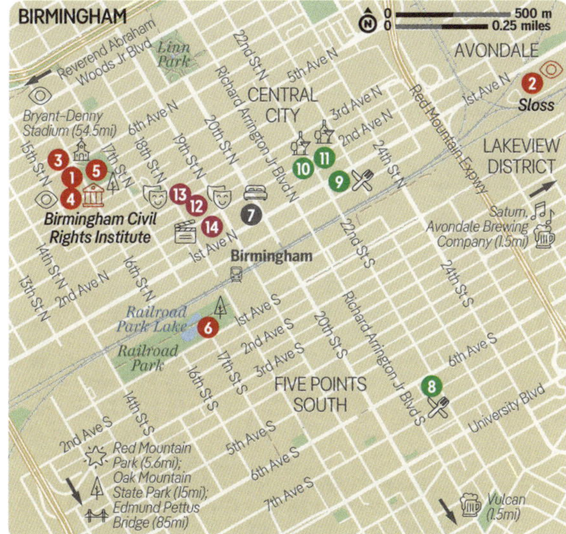

HIGHLIGHTS
1 Birmingham Civil Rights Institute
2 Sloss

SIGHTS
3 16th Street Baptist Church
4 AG Gaston Motel
5 Kelly Ingram Park
6 Railroad Park

SLEEPING
7 Elyton Hotel

EATING
8 Fish Market
9 The Essential

DRINKING & NIGHTLIFE
10 Collins Bar
11 House of Found Objects

ENTERTAINMENT
12 Alabama Theatre
13 Lyric
14 Sidewalk Film Center

games. You can even stop in early (from 8am) if you're after coffee and warm pastries.

Across the road from Saturn, **Avondale Brewing Company** *(avondalebrewing.com)* pours out the good times courtesy of hazy IPAs, farmhouse ales and easy-drinking lagers. It also has a large outdoor concert venue, where all ages can catch rock, indie and country bands.

Montgomery

In the footsteps of Martin Luther King Jr and Rosa Parks

Martin Luther King Jr had other job offers, but he and his wife Coretta Scott were drawn to Montgomery, and he served as pastor to a dynamic church – with a long history of progressivism – from 1954 to 1960. Now known as the **Dexter Avenue King Memorial Church** *(dexterkingmemorial.org)*, this beautifully designed house of worship draws visitors who want to feel close to an inspiring man – and a congregation – that changed history. Call ahead for a guided tour *($10)*, which touches on King's leadership during the Civil Rights movement. All are welcome at Sunday services, which begin at 10:30am.

ROLL TIDE!

In the fall, the battle cry of 'Roll Tide' is ubiquitous across Alabama. The 'Tide,' in this case, is the Alabama Crimson Tide, the name of the University of Alabama's football team in Tuscaloosa (an hour's drive from Birmingham), which supposedly derives from a celebrated game of yesteryear. During the 1907 Iron Bowl against Auburn University (still one of the most fiercely contested college-sports rivalries in the country), the Alabama players, dressed in white jerseys, held off their much-favored opponents to a tie while playing in a slurry of red mud.

Seeing Alabama take the field in 100,000-seat **Bryant-Denny Stadium** is a near spiritual experience for avid football fans. Games usually sell out, but you can find resale tickets on StubHub and other sites.

TOP EXPERIENCE

Legacy Sites of Montgomery

Three different sites in Montgomery explore one of the most important topics in US history: the legacy of slavery. Through powerful exhibitions, memorials and monuments, visitors come face to face with 400 years of racial injustice, extending from the first people kidnapped in Africa, through the Jim Crow laws of the post-Civil War era to the rise of mass incarceration today.

JNIX/SHUTTERSTOCK

The Legacy Museum

TOP TIPS

- You needn't visit all three sites on one day. Your ticket grants admission on subsequent days.
- Free shuttles connect the three sites and the boat launch. A good plan is to park at the Legacy Museum and take the shuttle from there.

PRACTICALITIES

- legacysites.eji.org
- $5
- 9am-6pm Wed-Sun

The Legacy Museum

Allow at least two hours to wander amid evocative **exhibitions** that bring the horrors of enslavement to life: a wall of waves crashing over the heads of the captured and drowned, jars containing dirt gathered at sites where innocents were lynched, and dramatizations of families being split apart. There are film clips, sound recordings, screenings in small theaters and lots of interactivity – including simulated one-on-one encounters with incarcerated people.

National Memorial for Peace & Justice

On a 6-acre site, a grassy courtyard frames 800 steel **monuments**, each suspended from a metal pole and bearing the names of lynching victims from a particular county. In all, these sculptures memorialize 4400 Black people violently killed across the south and beyond between 1877 and 1950.

Freedom Monument Sculpture Park

Though you can drive there, it's more memorable to take the boat ride (included with admission) to reach the **Freedom Monument Sculpture Park**. The journey alludes to the (involuntary) voyage taken by over 12 million enslaved Africans, nearly two million of whom would die along the way. Once at the park, a path winds past brilliantly conceived sculptures that touch on the traumas of everyday life for those without freedom.

For deeper insight into Martin Luther King's life in Montgomery, visit the **Dexter Parsonage Museum** *($10),* open Friday and Saturday from 10am to 4pm. You'll watch a short introductory film, then take a docent-led tour through the house where King and his family lived. There's an intimacy to the well-preserved 1950s-era spaces, and it's hard not to feel the great man's presence in rooms like his office, with some of his books on theology, philosophy and activism.

King would make history thanks in large part to Rosa Parks. In 1955, activist Parks refused to give up her seat in the whites-only section of a public bus. The **Rosa Parks Museum** *(facebook.com/TroyUniversityRosaParksMuseum; adult/child $7.50/5.50),* set in front of the bus stop where Parks took her stand, delves into the story behind her courageous stand. Parks, along with King, helped launch the Montgomery bus boycott, which inspired countless communities across the South to stand up to injustice during the Civil Rights movement.

Moundville Archaeological Park

Traces of an ancient civilization

One of the largest and best-preserved sites of the pre-Columbian Mississippian civilization, the 326-acre **Moundville Archaeological Park** *(moundville.museums.ua.edu; adult/child $8/6)* preserves the grassy remains of a mound city. Within the complex you find 29 mounds of varying sizes, arranged in a manner that suggests a highly stratified social structure. The excellent on-site museum is filled with pre-Columbian art, including pottery and disks inscribed with underwater panthers, feathered serpents and skulls. The site is about an hour's drive southwest of Birmingham.

Mobile

Exploring downtown Mobile and the waterfront

The only sizable coastal city in Alabama, Mobile (moh-*beel*) was founded in 1702 – 16 years before New Orleans – and its walkable downtown is awash in history. Speaking of New Orleans, Mobile throws some impressive Mardi Gras parades itself, with bead-tossing, marching bands and abundant merrymaking over several weekends leading up to the big day in February (or early March).

Get your bearings by taking a stroll through the old streets. Conti and Dauphin are dotted with restaurants and pubs, with live music spilling out of doors come sundown. Along the way, stop in scenic green spaces like Bienville Sq and Cathedral Sq, and take in the grandeur of the

REMEMBERING MARTIN LUTHER KING JR

Nikki Tucker Davis, Deacon at Dexter Avenue King Memorial Baptist Church *dexterkingmemorial.org*

For our church in those days, Dr King was just our pastor. He was very approachable. The kids loved him, the members loved him. When he announced that he was resigning in order to go do more work, he was tearful and emotional, just as our membership was tearful and emotional. He was a funny, caring, charismatic man, who brought forth these big ideas. My uncle, who is 101 years old, was at that first meeting when Mrs Rosa Parks was arrested. He talked about how dynamic Dr King was when he spoke. He moved a whole community, and that spread. That inspiration went throughout this state, and then it spread throughout the world.

EATING & DRINKING IN MONTGOMERY: OUR PICKS

Martin's Restaurant: Casual spot in a strip mall that's famed for its fried chicken. *11am-7pm Mon-Fri, 10:45am-2:30pm Sun* $

Central: Fine dining on wood-fired dishes with international accents, served in an atmospheric 19th-century setting. *5:30-9pm Tue-Sat* $$$

Red Bluff Bar: Family-friendly outdoor spot with pub fare, live music and sweeping river views. *4-10pm Tue-Fri, from 1pm Sat & Sun* $

Tower Taproom: Lively spot downtown with pour-your-own craft beers, juicy burgers, wings and salads. *11am-9pm Mon-Fri, 2-10pm Sat* $

BEST OUTDOOR SITES ON THE GULF COAST

Audubon Bird Sanctuary: On Dauphin Island, a 3-mile trail wends through maritime forest, sand dunes and wetlands – a prime bird habitat.

Gulf State Park: A lovely spot to enjoy the seaside, with beaches, a small nature center (open weekdays) and 28 miles of hiking and cycling trails.

Fort Morgan State Historic Site: Explore this fascinating relic from the past – built during the War of 1812 to protect against potential British invasion of Mobile Bay.

Bon Secour National Wildlife Refuge: Ospreys, alligators and sea turtles can all be found here, along with four trails and a lovely beachfront.

Graham Creek Nature Preserve: Some 10 miles of trails (including accessible boardwalks), plus kayaks for rent.

Cathedral Basilica of the Immaculate Conception *(mobilecathedral.org)*.

A good place to learn about the city is the **History Museum of Mobile** *(historymuseumofmobile.com; adult/child $14/11)*, with interactive exhibits covering Indigenous people, colonial times, slavery, Civil War days, shipbuilding during WWII and the Civil Rights era. Admission also gives you access to the nearby colonial **Fort Condé**, with both reconstructed and original rooms dating back to the early 18th century.

Nearby, the **National Maritime Museum of the Gulf** *(nmmog.org; adult/child $14/11)* has interactive exhibits on nautical topics like sailing, piloting big vessels, shipwreck exploration and navigation skills. It's a hit with kids.

Three miles east of downtown, the **USS Alabama** *(ussalabama.com; adult/child $18/6)* is a 690ft behemoth famous for escaping nine major WWII battles unscathed. It's worth taking the self-guided tour just to experience the awesome size and might of the 'Lucky A.'

Fairhope

Small-town charm

On the eastern shore of Mobile Bay, the small town of Fairhope has a quaint and pedestrian-friendly center where the order of the day is browsing independent shops, gallery-hopping and enjoying a fine array of food and drinks. You can park at the (free) lot on Oak Ave, then head into the **Eastern Shore Art Center** *(esartcenter.org; free)* for a look at painting, photography and sculpture by local and regional artists. From there, it's a five-minute walk south to the **Fairhope Museum of History** *(free)*, where you can peer at a vintage 1935 fire engine, learn about the founders' utopian ideals and see photos of important figures from the Civil Rights era.

Half a block further along, you'll reach the heart of Fairhope (Section St and Fairhope Ave). There's prime shopping within one block in any direction. Staff at the beloved bookstore **Page & Palette** *(pageandpalette.com)* can help you find some new reading material, or head to the back for coffee, cocktails or (later in the day) live music. Music fans should stop in **Dr Music Records** *(drmusic123.com)*, which is packed with new and used vinyl. If you have kids in mind, **Fantasy Island Toys** *(fantasyislandtoys.com)* stocks puzzles, board games, dolls and lots of other eye-catching items for children of all ages.

The big event of the month is the **First Friday Art Walk**, when you can catch art openings, live music and special store events (6pm to 8pm).

EATING IN MOBILE & FAIRHOPE: OUR PICKS

Wintzell's: A Mobile classic since 1938, there's no better spot for fresh or grilled oysters and other Gulf seafood. *11am-9pm Tue-Sun* **$$**

Loda Bier Garten: Landmark on Mobile's lively Dauphin St, with comfort food, outdoor tables and over 100 draft beer choices. *11am-midnight* **$**

Panini Pete's: Follow the brick walkway under Fairhope's 'French Quarter' sign to this charming back courtyard, with fabulous beignets and panini. *8am-2:30pm* **$**

Tamara's: Fairhope's favorite restaurant boasts a wide-ranging menu for brunch, lunch and dinner, and unrivaled happy hour deals (3pm to 5:15pm). *10am-9pm Wed-Mon* **$$**

Mississippi

THE BLUES | SOUL FOOD | HISTORY

Flanked by the mighty Mississippi River along its entire western border, the Magnolia State encompasses many identities. You'll find palatial mansions and rural poverty; haunting cotton flats and verdant hill country; sandy beaches on the coast and serene farmland in the north. Often mythologized and misunderstood, this is the land with some of the rawest history in the country – evidenced in the powerful Civil Rights sites in Jackson.

Mississippi is also a place of exceptional artistry. You can see it for yourself in the one-room juke joints of the Delta (especially Clarksdale), where blues players sing heartfelt ballads of love and sorrow that echo the creative spirit that reaches back to the earliest forms of American music. There's folk art on display in shops and galleries across the state, and a rich literary heritage. Richard Wright, Tennessee Williams and Eudora Welty were all born in Mississippi, as was William Faulkner, whose grand house in Oxford draws literary pilgrims from across the globe.

Places

TOP TIP

Clarksdale is the big draw for live music, with lots happening on Friday and Saturday nights (it's quieter other days). Check the Cathead store's website *(cathead.biz/music-calendar)* for blues performances in Clarksdale. Find out what's happening elsewhere in Mississippi at *visitmississippi.org/events*.

GETTING AROUND

Most visitors explore the state by car, but there is an Amtrak train (the *City of New Orleans* line) that passes through Mississippi on its run from the Big Easy to Memphis on to Chicago. The train stops in downtown Jackson, and as well as Marks, which is 18 miles east of Clarksdale – reach out to **CDRY Touring and Cab Services** *(facebook.com/cdrytouringandcabservice)* for a ride. Drivers who want to get off the beaten path can plan their route around scenic byways like Hwy 61 (aka the Blues Highway) or the Natchez Trace Pkwy.

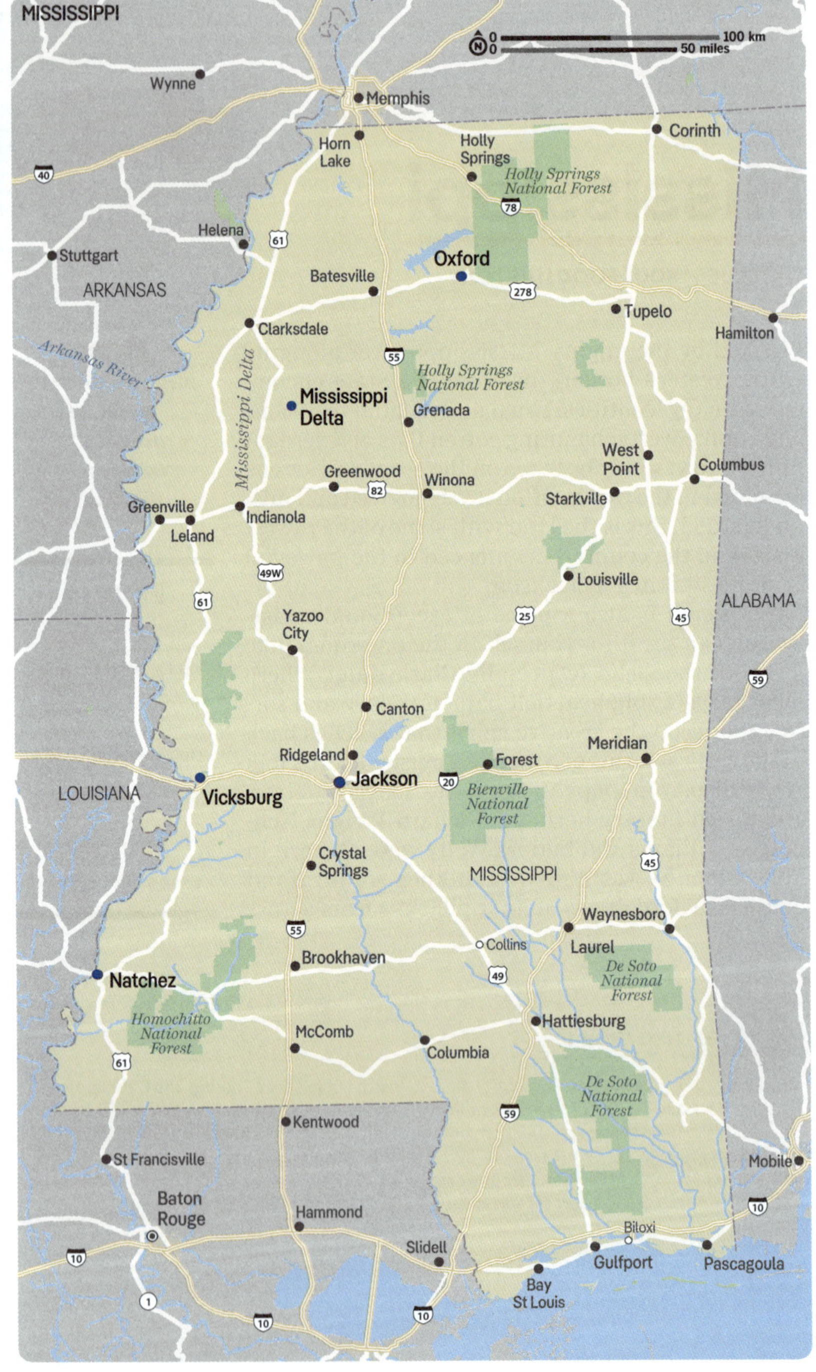
MISSISSIPPI
0 100 km
0 50 miles
Wynne
Memphis
Horn Lake
Holly Springs
Corinth
Holly Springs National Forest
Helena
Stuttgart
ARKANSAS
Oxford
Batesville
Tupelo
Hamilton
Clarksdale
Arkansas River
Mississippi Delta
Holly Springs National Forest
Mississippi Delta
Grenada
West Point
Columbus
Greenwood
Winona
Starkville
Greenville
Leland
Indianola
Louisville
ALABAMA
Yazoo City
Canton
Ridgeland
Meridian
Forest
LOUISIANA
Vicksburg
Jackson
Bienville National Forest
Crystal Springs
MISSISSIPPI
Waynesboro
Collins
Laurel
De Soto National Forest
Brookhaven
Natchez
Hattiesburg
Homochitto National Forest
McComb
Columbia
De Soto National Forest
Kentwood
St Francisville
Mobile
Baton Rouge
Hammond
Biloxi
Slidell
Gulfport
Pascagoula
Bay St Louis

Mississippi Delta

Tracing the Blues Highway

Hwy 61, which follows along the course of the Mississippi River, is often called the Blues Highway for its connection to the USA's rich musical heritage. If you're driving down from Memphis, the **Gateway to the Blues Museum** *(tunicatravel.com; admission $10)* provides a fine introduction to the Delta. Stepping inside the weathered building (modeled after an old-fashioned juke joint), you'll find musical instruments and artwork that reference Muddy Waters, WC Handy and other blues greats. There's also a mini recording studio, where you can record your own song.

Leave ample time for Clarksdale, then continue the journey south to Leland. Take a stroll through the tiny downtown, checking out the various trail markers describing some of the talent (Johnny Winter, James 'Son' Thomas, Charley Booker) connected to the town. Afterwards, visit the **Highway 61 Blues Museum** *(adult/child $7/free)*, which has a collection of photos, memorabilia and folk art affiliated with Delta blues singers. The folks who run the place are usually willing to regale you with local stories and blues lore.

Before leaving Leland, check out the **Birthplace of Kermit the Frog** *(free)*. Local luminary Jim Henson, the creator of the Muppets, spent the first 12 years of his life in Leland, and his creative work is celebrated at this small exhibit on the bank of Deer Creek. Head onto the deck overlooking the slow waters and bottomland forest, and it's easy to imagine the inspiration for a certain green felt frog.

Take a 15-mile detour east off Hwy 61 to reach Indianola, another sleepy town with deep blues roots. Music fans come here to visit the **BB King Museum** *(bbkingmuseum.org; adult/child $15/10)*, which charts the life of the pioneering musician through photographs, film footage, interviews and, of course, music. There are lots of guitars to gawk at (he even gave one to the pope) as well as vehicles (a Rolls Royce, El Camino, and his sleek touring bus). On the grounds attached to the museum, you can see King's final resting place, surrounded by the lyrics of his songs.

Catching live blues in Clarksdale

The scrappy epicenter of the Delta blues scene, Clarksdale is also the region's most useful base. You'll want to spend the night so you can hit the music scene (cover charges range from $10 to $20). Get an overview at the **Delta Blues Museum** *(deltabluesmuseum.org; adult/child $15/10)*, which has a small but

SONGS OF THE DELTA

Wilsherie Hopson is a pianist, singer and author of *Recluse: Neglect, Survival, Recovery* *@starjukezeta2k1112*

Gospel and blues intertwine in Clarksdale. Most blues singers start off in the church. People begin at a young age – often in the choir. It's the foundation for the music scene in Clarksdale, which then becomes our own expression of life, celebration and heartache. The blues are a form of storytelling. There are a lot of great artists here – people like Edna Nicole. We call her 'the sweetheart of the Delta.' Her recent single 'Delta Dirt' basically describes the Delta in one song. You've got to listen to it.

EATING IN CLARKSDALE: OUR PICKS

Our Grandma's House of Pancakes: Start your day off with a hearty breakfast made with care at this old-fashioned charmer. *7am-1pm* $

Hooker Grocer & Eatery: Named after bluesman John Lee Hooker, this inviting place serves up brisket sliders, catfish platters and other comfort classics. *5-9pm Wed-Sun* $$

Abe's Bar-B-Q: Facing the crossroads, Abe's fires up Clarksdale's best pulled pork, plus nicely spiced tamales. *10am-8pm Mon-Sat, 11am-1:30pm Sun* $$

Meraki: The convivial community coffeehouse makes a fine place to recharge over cappuccinos, breakfast sandwiches and occasional live music. *7am-2pm Sun-Thu, to 8pm Fri & Sat* $

BIRTHPLACE OF THE BLUES

The alluvial plains that stretch across the low-lying stretch of Mississippi are a patchwork of cotton fields, lush bayous and lonely roads. American music took root in this place, evolving from the simple but soul-stirring songs developed by Black sharecroppers on cotton fields in the early 1900s. Musician and promoter WC Handy, dubbed the 'Father of the Blues,' helped popularize the 12-bar sound after hearing a sharecropper pluck his guitar with a knife and sing a repetitive tune while the two waited for a train in 1903. Across the Delta today, blues pilgrims can dig deep into the music's genesis and development. Historic interpretive markers pepper the region, noting key sites on the Mississippi Blues Trail *(msbluestrail.org)*.

JAMES KIRKIKIS/SHUTTERSTOCK

Square Books

well-presented collection of memorabilia (including guitars from John Lee Hooker and BB King). The shrine to Delta legend Muddy Waters includes the actual cabin where he grew up.

Clarksdale is home to half a dozen atmospheric places to catch live blues. Co-owned by actor Morgan Freeman, **Ground Zero** *(groundzerobluesclub.com)* is a huge and friendly hall with a dance floor surrounded by tables. Bands take to the stage Wednesday to Saturday, and there's good food available. Going strong since the 1980s, the famous **Red's** *(facebook.com/RedsBluesLounge)* has neon-red lighting, which makes a moody backdrop for watching the blues players howl. Another battered juke joint not to miss is **Bad Apple Blues Club** *(facebook.com/badapplebluesclub)*, with memorable afternoon sessions (3pm to 6pm Wednesday to Saturday).

Another requisite stop in Clarksdale is **Cat Head** *(cat head.biz)*, a colorful, all-purpose, blues emporium. Shelves are jammed with books, face jugs, local folk art and blues records. Owner Roger Stolle seems to be connected to everyone in the Delta, and knows when and where the bands will play. Stop here for his weekly 'Sounds Around Town!' music calendar, also posted on the website.

In mid-April, the **Juke Joint Festival** *(jukejointfestival.com)* draws blues lovers to four days of live music from an array of talented musicians. Saturday is the big day, with some 17 outdoor stages scattered around an eight-block stretch of Clarksdale. Daytime events are free, but it's worth buying a wristband *($60)* to get access to nighttime performances at over two dozen venues.

Oxford

Faulkner and Ole Miss

Mississippi's most famous college town has a attractive town center, with restaurants, bars and shops encircling the main square (aka **Courthouse Square**). Start the day with a cafe latte among the collegiate at **Heartbreak Coffee Roasters** (two blocks north of the square), then pick up some new reading material at the excellent **Square Books** *(squarebooks.com)*, one of several booksellers facing the old courthouse.

From here, you can drive or stroll into the campus of the University of Mississippi, better known as Ole Miss. It's about a half mile from Courthouse Sq to the **University of Mississippi Museum** *(museum.olemiss.edu; free)*, where you'll find an intriguing collection of Southern folk art, American luminaries (like Georgia O'Keeffe) and some surprising ancient Greek and Roman works. It's another half mile from here to the Grove, the park-like epicenter of the pretty campus. Alternatively, the museum is also the starting point for a pretty 0.6-mile walk along the easy-going **Bailey Woods Trail**. The path ends at the edge of **Rowan Oak** *(rowanoak.com; adult/child $5/free)*, the grand manor home of William Faulkner, one of America's most lauded 20th-century writers. On a self-guided tour, you can peer in beautifully preserved rooms (some with original furnishings) and learn curious episodes from the author's life – like angrily writing drafts for *A Fable* on the walls of his office after the fan kept blowing his pages around.

Jackson

History and the fight for Civil Rights

You could easily spend half a day exploring the powerful **Mississippi Civil Rights Museum** *(mcrm.mdah.ms.gov; adult/child $15/8, Sun free)* located just a few blocks from the old domed capitol building. Whether it's a voice from overhead yelling at you to 'keep on moving,' graphic photos of lynchings hitting you with a gut punch, or the towering wall of mugshots of Freedom Riders stopping you in your tracks, the exhibits at this compelling museum keep you on high alert. The national Civil Rights movement is explored through the lens of the fight for racial equality in Mississippi, with eight exhibit halls tackling the key eras through photos, film footage, news clippings and interactive screens.

Your ticket also gives you admission to the adjoining **Museum of Mississippi History** *(mmh.mdah.ms.gov)*. For a broader context on the state's history, start here – watch the 10-minute film narrated by Mississippi's favorite native son Morgan Freeman, then wander through the thoughtfully presented galleries. Noteworthy displays, which are often supplemented by informative videos, cover prehistoric mound builders, the Chickasaw and Choctaw tribes and their legends,

BEST MISSISSIPPI MUSIC FESTS

Bentonia Blues Festival: Going strong for over 50 years, this admission-free fest draws blues fans to Bentonia (34 miles north of Jackson) over three days in late June.

Juke Joint Festival: Clarksdale's big mid-April gathering features dozens of bands playing at outdoor stages by day, and packing into the clubs by night.

King Biscuit Blues Festival: The huge October jam happens across the river in Helena, Arkansas, though everyone stays in nearby Clarksdale, and top blues performers play here afterwards.

Bright Lights: In September, several venues in Jackson's Belhaven district host this music and arts fest, featuring jazz, soul, indie-rock and blues.

Double Decker Arts Festival: Catch over a dozen bands playing over one fun weekend in Oxford in late April.

EATING & DRINKING IN JACKSON: OUR PICKS

Brent's Drugs: By day, enjoy burgers and milkshakes at a '50s-style diner. By night visit the hidden bar (Apothecary) for well-made cocktails. *hours vary* $

Elvie's: In a restaurant-packed corner of upscale Belhaven, this stylish gastropub showcases imaginative cooking from Gulf and pasture. *8am-2pm & 4:30-9pm Tue-Sat* $$$

Saltine: A spacious indoor-outdoor spot for seafood, especially oysters, which you can enjoy raw or wood-fired with creative toppings. *11am-10pm* $$

Bean: A delightful coffeeshop with breakfast bowls, avocado toast and sweet pastries, plus a bigger Saturday brunch menu. *7am-6pm* $

THE SIEGE OF VICKSBURG

In 1863 General Grant set his sights on Vicksburg, a city deemed vital to the Civil War's success. The challenge: Vicksburg sat high on bluffs over the Mississippi and was heavily fortified by the Confederates. After several unsuccessful attacks, the Union army laid siege, aiming to starve the city into submission. Under constant shelling, civilians dug shelters underground, making Vicksburg – as one resident described it, 'so honeycombed with caves that the streets look like avenues in a cemetery.' With provisions scarce, mules were eaten, dogs and cats went missing, and even rats were skinned and sold at the market. After 47 days, the Confederates surrendered, and the Union army took control of Vicksburg, which proved a turning point in the war.

the cotton industry, the barbaric practice of slavery, the Civil War and Mississippi's rich cultural heritage.

About a mile west of Mississippi Civil Rights Museum, the **Smith Robertson Museum** *(jacksonms.gov/smith-robertson-museum adult/child $7/4)* is housed in the state's first public school for African American children. The alma mater of the famed novelist Richard Wright, the former school offers insight and explanation into the pain and perseverance of the African American legacy in Mississippi.

Around 3½ miles northwest of there, the **Medgar and Myrlie Evers Home** *(nps.gov/memy; free)* is the ranch-style house where Civil Rights activist Medgar Evers lived with his young family from 1956 until 1963. You can freely wander through the home (don't forget to peek in the fridge), and learn about one of the rising stars in the fight for Civil Rights who was murdered here – shot in the back by a sniper while standing in the carport in 1963. It's run by the National Park Service, with tours hourly from 9am to 4pm (except noon).

Vicksburg

Strolling Mississippi's prettiest town center

Washington St (aka Hwy 61) between Clay and Main Sts is lined with historic buildings that today house galleries, cafes and tiny museums – the fine backdrop to a few hours of exploring. Parking is free on the street.

Get a dose of history at the **Vicksburg Civil War Museum** *(vicksburgcivilwarmuseum.org; adult/child $10/3.50)*. One of the region's only African American–owned Civil War museums gives insight into the conflict, with a special focus on Black soldiers, freedmen and abolitionists.

Just up on the right, **Lorelei Books** *(loreleibooks.com)* is an atmospheric little shop, where you can discover new titles – and there's a good selection from regional authors. Next door, **Highway 61 Coffeehouse** (open 7am to noon) is a cozy spot to curl up with your new book. Upstairs, you'll find one of the best folk art galleries in the state. The **Attic Gallery** *(atticgalleryvicksburg.com)* is packed from floor to ceiling with extraordinary works (paintings, sculptures, mixed media) created by self-taught artists.

One block up, the **Lower Mississippi River Museum** *(free)* explores the region's deep ties to the famous waterway, from the ancient peoples that hunted and fished here to the devastating floods of the 20th century. Head through the galleries to reach the MV *Mississippi IV*, a dry-docked research vessel that you can wander through (a favorite of young visitors).

EATING & DRINKING IN VICKSBURG: OUR PICKS

Walnut Hills: Savor rib-sticking, down-home Southern food, served family-style (solo diners enjoy the round table). *11am-9pm Mon & Wed-Sat, to 2pm Sun* $$

10 South: Take in the views while munching salads, shrimp and grits or hearty sandwiches from this rooftop spot. *5-9pm Tue-Sun, plus 11am-2pm Sat* $$

Key City Brewery: Satisfying house-brewed beers, plus creatively topped pizzas, swordfish and perfectly crispy fries. *4-10pm Mon-Thu, from 11am Fri-Sun* $$

Sun Izakaya: Buzzing new addition, with good sushi, soba and Japanese snacks like *takoyaki* (fried octopus balls). *11am-2:30pm & 4-9:30pm Mon-Sat* $$

USS Cairo Museum

Across the street, visit the small **Catfish Row Museum** *(catfishrowmuseum.org; free)*, which touches on Vicksburg history – including the fight for Civil Rights. Don't miss the drumset of the Red Tops, a group symbolizing the unifying force of the era. More recent is the evocative *Faces* mural painted by Vicksburg artist Kennith Humphrey.

Speaking of murals, it's well worth heading downhill to Levee St, for a look at the **Vicksburg Riverfront Murals** *(riverfront murals.com)*. Created to beautify the city's flood wall in the early 2000s, the 32 works spotlight key people and events in Vicksburg's past: Civil War, natural disasters (like the tornado of 1953) and cultural luminaries (famed Bluesman Willie Dixon).

Driving into the past

Vicksburg controlled access to the Mississippi River, and its seizure was one of the turning points of the Civil War. At the **Vicksburg National Military Park** *(nps.gov/vick; car $20)*, you can follow a 16-mile driving tour that passes artfully carved memorials and historic markers explaining battle scenarios and key events from the city's long siege. Get an overview at the visitor center, where you can watch a 20-minute film and peruse displays about the siege. Afterwards, follow the road to some 15 numbered stops. Don't miss the **USS Cairo Museum**, which covers the ironclad gunboats used by Union forces, including the salvaged USS *Cairo*. For audio commentary along the way, download the free NPS app and follow the Vicksburg self-guided park tour.

Natchez

Centuries of history in a riverside city

Sprawled across a bluff overlooking the Mississippi, the old city of Natchez (settled in 1716) is packed tight with historic buildings – some transformed into museums, restaurants and shops.

NATCHEZ' COMPLICATED PAST

Before the Civil War, the cotton plantations on the eastern banks of the Mississippi River produced the most millionaires in the US – all on the backs of enslaved Africans. In Natchez, plantation owners built over-the-top estates. By the time the Civil War came to Natchez, the town surrendered to Union forces without a fight (interestingly, locals voted against secession in 1861). Abolition stripped plantation owners of their income, but their estates remain frozen in time. Some plantations have been transformed into B&Bs, although it's far more enlightening to visit the federally managed sites (including Melrose) that are part of the Natchez National Historical Park *(nps .gov/natc)*.

DIETMAR RAUSCHER/SHUTTERSTOCK

THE NATCHEZ TRACE

If you're driving through Mississippi, it's worth planning at least part of your trip around one of the oldest roads in North America: the **Natchez Trace Parkway** *(nps.gov/natr)*. This 444-mile road, today administered by the National Park Service, traces a route once used by Native American tribes and runs from the edge of Natchez, Mississippi, to just outside of Nashville, Tennessee. It's a lovely, scenic drive that traverses a wide array of Southern landscapes: thick forests, soggy wetlands, gentle hill country and long swaths of farmland. There are more than 50 access points to the parkway and a helpful visitor center outside Tupelo. There are no stoplights or stop signs to ruin your ride.

DENNIS MACDONALD/SHUTTERSTOCK

Swamp along the Natchez Trace Parkway

Before delving into the town center, stop at the **Grand Village of the Natchez Indians** *(mdah.ms.gov; free)*. A visitor center displays pottery, tools and fragments of baskets while shedding light on the Mississippian people that lived here for over a thousand years (roughly CE 700 to 1730). Afterwards, take a stroll across the grassy expanse (once a plaza) to see the bare mounds that were previously topped with a temple and a chief's residence.

Fast forward through the years to the 19th century, with a visit to the **Melrose Estate** *(nps.gov/places/melrose.htm; free)*, a sprawling Greek Revival mansion and former plantation. You can freely wander the grounds, but to see inside the house, you'll need to book a guided tour *(recreation.gov; adult/child $11/1)*. Rangers do a decent job describing life for both the plantation-owning McCurran family as well as the enslaved.

Next head into central Natchez and continue your visit on foot. The **Natchez Museum of African American Culture and History** *(visitnapac.net; free)* highlights Black Mississippians who helped shape the state's history, including the writer Richard Wright and musician Clarence 'Bud' Scott. There are also exhibits on slavery, the cotton industry and Civil Rights.

A few blocks away, the displays inside the **William Johnson House** *(free)* show what life was like for free African Americans in the pre–Civil War South. When you need a break from the heavy weight of the past, head down to the river and admire the views along the half-mile **Natchez Bluff River Trail**.

EATING & DRINKING IN NATCHEZ: OUR PICKS

Camp Restaurant: Fun atmosphere, good pub grub (pork belly tacos, catfish) and craft beer on tap with Mississippi River views. *11am-8pm* **$$**

Frankie's on Main: Tuck in to high-end southern cooking inside a grand Greek Revival dining room (and former 1826 bank). *11am-10pm Tue-Sat* **$$$**

Pig Out Inn: Barbecue fans can't leave Natchez without trying smoky pork or brisket at this casual spot. *11am-9pm Mon-Sat, to 7pm Sun* **$**

Smoot's Grocery: Listen to blues while sipping tall bloody Marys at this river-facing bar. *6-10pm Thu & Fri, 1pm-late Sat, noon-6pm Sun*

New Orleans

CREOLE COOKING | FIERY JAZZ | EUROPEAN ARCHITECTURE

No matter how many cities on this planet you visit, you'll never find one quite like New Orleans. When it comes to food, live music and celebration, New Orleanians have perfected the art of living large. Creole chefs have honed recipes for gumbo, jambalaya, char-grilled oysters, crawfish and decadent seafood combinations from the bountiful Gulf Coast. The city is famed for Mardi Gras and its weeks of parades, bands and costuming, but there's revelry throughout the year – from the myriad performances at Jazz Fest to the merriment of Halloween. The birthplace of jazz is also a great place to enjoy the vibrant, ever-evolving soundtrack that defines the Big Easy.

The starting point for the New Orleans experience is undoubtedly the French Quarter, with its centuries-old architecture, historic restaurants and cobblestone streets both elegant (Royal) and louche (Bourbon). Outside the Quarter, you'll find fascinating, largely local-centric neighborhoods, including the bohemian-loving Bywater, the grand Garden District and the Marigny – the epicenter of NOLA's live music scene.

GETTING AROUND

New Orleans has a flat, fairly compact center. Streetcars, buses, bikeshares and rideshares connect different parts of the city. Within neighborhoods, walking is one of the best ways to get around. Riding one of New Orleans' historic streetcar lines is a must. The most scenic is the St Charles Ave line, which runs from the the edge of the French Quarter, passing through the Garden District, Uptown and lovely Audubon Park. Two slightly different lines follow Canal St to Mid-City, including the City Park line, which takes you to the entrance of New Orleans' biggest green space.

Celebrating New Orleans' Style

Fun times during Mardi Gras and Jazz Fest

Mardi Gras *(mardigrasneworleans.com)* is about many things: massive floats rolling through packed streets, hilariously costumed krewes shimmying in unison to vintage disco and vast marching bands blasting out heart-pounding rhythms. There are also walking parades open to all (with a costume), and joining in is the best way to experience New Orleans' biggest celebration.

The parade season is a 12-day period beginning two Fridays before Fat Tuesday (in February). Early parades are charming, neighborly processions that whet your appetite for later events, which increase in size and grandeur until the spectacles of the

HIGHLIGHTS
1 Cabildo
2 Presbytère
3 Royal Street
4 St Louis Cemetery No 1

SIGHTS
5 Bourbon Street
6 Congo Square
7 Gallier House Museum
8 Historic New Orleans Collection
9 Louis Armstrong Park

ACTIVITIES & TOURS
10 Cemetery Tours NOLA
11 New Orleans Pharmacy Museum
12 Steamboat Natchez

SLEEPING
13 Olivier House

EATING
14 Bayona
15 Brennan's
16 Central Grocery
17 Deanie's Seafood Restaurant
18 Jewel of the South
19 Namaste Nola
20 Napoleon House
21 Sylvain
22 Tableau

DRINKING & NIGHTLIFE
23 Bar Tonique
24 Carousel Bar
25 Fritzel's European Jazz Pub
26 Latitude 29

ENTERTAINMENT
27 21st Amendment Bar
28 Balcony Music Club
29 Davenport Lounge
30 House of Blues
31 Mahogany Jazz Hall
32 Preservation Hall

TRANSPORT
33 Canal Streetcar

superkrewes emerge during the final weekend. Download the WDSU Parade Tracker app to see what's on when.

Held in late April and early May, the New Orleans **Jazz & Heritage Festival** *(nojazzfest.com)* features a fabled lineup of bands and soloists from a wide range of genres. Local talent adds to the national and international superstars, and there's also outstanding food, a folklife village and kids' activities. In January, the musical acts are announced and tickets go on sale. Get info and buy tickets on the website. It all happens in Mid-City at the Fair Grounds Race Course.

Delve into New Orleans' History & Culture

MAP P182

A quartet of thought-provoking museums

A combination of preserved buildings, museums and research centers all rolled into one, the **Historic New Orleans Collection** *(hnoc.org; free)* presents a series of regularly rotating exhibits – among the most insightful in the city. Don't miss the French Quarter Galleries, with multimedia displays ranging from Native American settlement to 18th-century French colony to buzzing modern cultural hub.

The former seat of power in colonial Louisiana, the **Cabildo** *(louisianastatemuseum.org; adult/child $11/9)* gives a fine overview of the past with its collection that covers everything from Native American tools (1st floor) to 'Wanted' posters for escaped enslaved people (3rd floor).

Next door to the Cabildo, the 1791 **Presbytère** *(louisianastatemuseum.org; adult/child $11/9)* focuses on both the positive and negative aspects of life in New Orleans, namely Mardi Gras revelry and devastating hurricanes – in particular Hurricane Katrina.

Set in one of the country's oldest apothecaries, the **New Orleans Pharmacy Museum** *(pharmacymuseum.org; adult/child $10/7)* has cabinets full of assorted elixirs once thought to be therapeutic, along with frightening-looking hypodermic needles and bone saws. Book ahead for 45-minute guided tours *(adult/child $20/17)* that shed light on the epidemics, nefarious 'cure-alls' and primitive medical treatments (opium, leeches, mercury injections) of centuries past.

THE CARIBBEAN CONNECTION

Following a 1791 revolt led by enslaved people, thousands of slaveholders fled St Domingue (now Haiti) with their 'property' (enslaved human beings) to Louisiana, which bolstered French-speaking Creole traditions. At the same time, thousands of the formerly enslaved also relocated from St Domingue to New Orleans as free people of color. By 1810, some 10,000 of these islanders had come to the city, doubling the total population and tripling the population for the free people of color. This influx from St Domingue also injected an indelible trace of Caribbean culture that remains in evidence to this day. Their most obvious contribution was the practice of voodoo, which became popular in New Orleans during the 19th century.

EATING IN THE QUARTER: CASUAL DINING

MAP P182

Napoleon House: A 1797 building packed with history; its atmospheric courtyard is a magical spot for classic Creole cooking. *11am-10pm* **$$**

Sylvain: In a stylish carriage house, Sylvain is a convivial spot for well-executed comfort fare. *10:30am-3pm Fri-Sun, plus 4-11pm daily* **$$**

Central Grocery: Famed for its muffuletta, a massive sandwich stuffed with meat, cheese and olive salad. Get it to go and eat by the river. *9am-5pm* **$**

Deanie's Seafood Restaurant: Temptations run from BBQ shrimp to charbroiled oysters. *11am-9:30pm Thu-Mon, from 4pm Tue & Wed* **$$**

A PROMENADE IN THE FRENCH QUARTER

Explore the historic heart of New Orleans, taking in eclectic architecture, iconic monuments and a grand sweep of riverside.

START	END	LENGTH
Jackson Square	Riverfront	1 mile; 1½ hours

Start on Chartres St on the edge of 1 **Jackson Square**, which is quiet in the morning but later in the day bubbles with activity (buskers, tarot readers, tour groups). From here, you can take in some of the Quarter's grand architecture, including 2 **St Louis Cathedral**. Though the current building dates from the 1850s, previous iterations of the church date as far back as 1718.

At 3 **632 1/2 St Peter Street**, you can peer up at the 2nd-floor balcony of the house, where Tennessee Williams lived in 1946 and 1947. It was here that he wrote his famed *A Streetcar Named Desire*. Head around the corner and continue along elegant 4 **Royal St**, which has plenty of architectural eye candy, before making your way to the 5 **French Market**, which has numerous food and craft stalls. A trading post for centuries, the present 19th-century structure was designed by Joseph Abeilard, one of the USA's first African American architects.

New Orleanians have an abiding affection for Joan of Arc, manifest in the gilded 14ft, 2700-pound 6 **statue** that was gifted to the city by the people of France in 1964. Cross Decatur and head up to the 7 **riverfront**. From here you can amble along the muddy Mississippi enjoying fine views across the water.

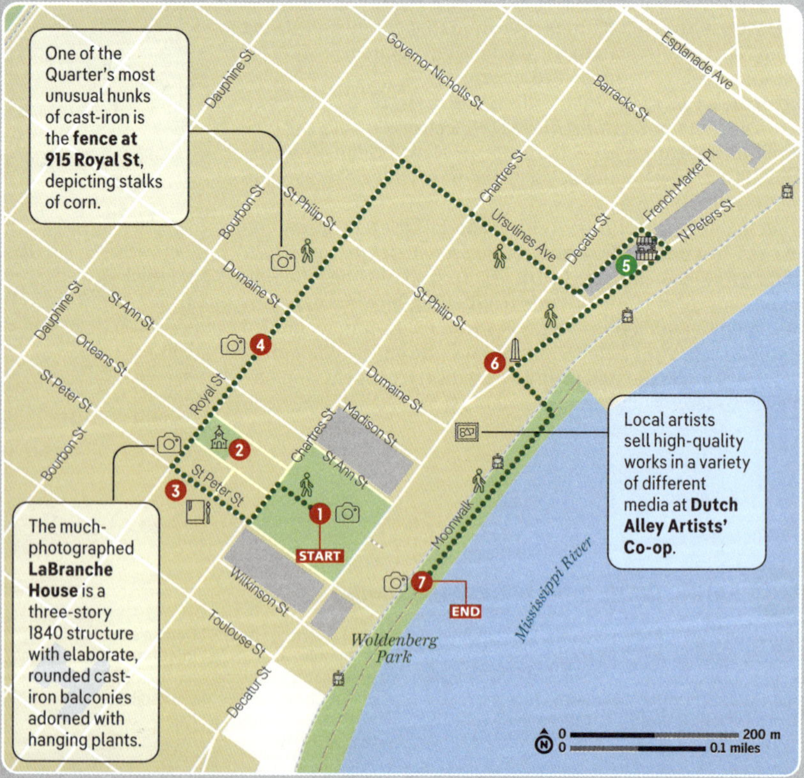

One of the Quarter's most unusual hunks of cast-iron is the **fence at 915 Royal St**, depicting stalks of corn.

The much-photographed **LaBranche House** is a three-story 1840 structure with elaborate, rounded cast-iron balconies adorned with hanging plants.

Local artists sell high-quality works in a variety of different media at **Dutch Alley Artists' Co-op**.

Strolling Royal Street

MAP P182

Architecture and eye-catching shops

Royal Street, with its handsome storefronts stretching beneath cast-iron balconies, is one of the Quarter's prettiest thoroughfares. Several blocks of the strip are dedicated to antiques stores and art galleries, making Royal a sort of elegant 19th-century outdoor shopping arcade. The stretch between Bienville and Orleans closes to traffic between 11am and 4pm (until 7pm weekends), when musicians, performers and other buskers set up shop (don't forget to tip).

Cruising the Mississippi

MAP P182

Fun times on a paddlewheeler riverboat

For an old-fashioned dose of slow travel, book a trip along the Mississippi in an old paddle wheeler. Two main boat companies offer similarly themed cruises, including history-themed tours *(adult/child $42/17)*, jazz brunches *(adult/child $69/35)* and dinner excursions with live music (adult/child $95/40). The **Steamboat Natchez** *(steamboatnatchez.com)* departs from a pier near the base of Toulouse St, while the **Creole Queen** *(creolequeen.com)* sails from the river end of Poydras St, behind the Four Seasons Hotel.

Portal into the Past

MAP P182

Take a historic house tour

Get a deeper understanding of New Orleans by taking a guided tour through one of its house museums (reserve these ahead). The **Gallier House Museum** *(hgghh.org; adult/child $17/14)* exemplifies a style unique to the French Quarter thanks to the innovations of famed architect James Gallier Jr, who designed the house in 1860. Guides point out unique features like double skylights and indoor plumbing with hot and cold running water – cutting-edge technology at the time. You'll also learn about the residents, including the four enslaved people – Laurette, Rose, Julienne and Francois – who occupied the quarters out back.

The Legendary Jazz Spot

MAP P182

An evening at Preservation Hall

Housed in a former art gallery dating from 1803, **Preservation Hall** *(preservationhall.com; $25)* is one of New Orleans' most storied live-music venues, but it's unlike other places in town. You must purchase tickets online before coming, shows

TOP LIVE MUSIC SPOTS IN THE QUARTER

21st Amendment Bar: A great jazz bar that rarely has a cover charge (one drink minimum) on Iberville.

House of Blues: Home to several different live music venues, this national chain stages some excellent bands – not just blues.

Davenport Lounge: The Davenport is inside the Ritz Carlton and offers quality jazz to a well-dressed crowd.

Balcony Music Club: This buzzing spot on Decatur St has live music daily with a wide range of acts – jazz, blues, rock and funk.

Mahogany Jazz Hall: This somewhat newish space has vintage vibes and outstanding performances from the likes of trumpeter Leroy Jones.

EATING IN THE QUARTER: FINE DINING

MAP P182

Jewel of the South: Tucked behind a cottage, the courtyardhere is as enchanting as the cuisine. *5-11pm Wed-Mon, from 11:30am Fri & Sat* $$$

Bayona: A slow-food pioneer, Bayona is classy but unpretentious. *6-8:30pm Tue-Sat, plus 11:30am-1:30pm Thu-Sat* $$$

Brennan's: One of the grandes dames of Creole dining, Brennan's has famous dishes (Gulf fish amandine) and decadent breakfasts. *9am-9pm* $$$

Tableau: Book a table on the balcony for memorable views while indulging in haute-Creole cuisine and crème brûlée. *11am-9pm Wed-Sun* $$$

THE BOURBON-POWERED ECONOMY

Locals love to hate on **Bourbon St** – which can indeed be crass and malodorous – and yet it plays a vital role in the city's economy. Each year New Orleans welcomes over 18 million visitors, who spend some $9 billion during their stay. An estimated 80% of those visitors come to Bourbon St, pumping tens of millions of dollars into the local economy. It also supports over 7000 jobs compressed into 20 square blocks straddling both sides of the street – a job density that is nearly 100 times more productive than the rest of New Orleans. The real estate value of the street is also no small matter, with estimates hovering around $500 million.

run just 45 minutes and happen several times nightly, and all ages are welcome.

Behaving Badly on Bourbon Street

MAP P182

Neon-lit debauchery

Like Vegas and Cancún, the main stretch of **Bourbon Street** is where the great id of the repressed American psyche is let loose into a seething mass of karaoke, strip clubs and bachelorette parties. It's one of the tackiest experiences in the world, but there's never a dull moment here, and you can't come to New Orleans and not visit the place.

At St Philip St, Bourbon shifts from a Dante's Inferno–style circle of neon-lit hell into an altogether more agreeable stretch of historical houses, diners and bars, many of which cater to the LGBTIQ+ community. Great spots here include Lafitte's, the oldest continuously operating gay bar in the country.

Tour St Louis Cemetery No 1

MAP P182

City of the dead

New Orleans is famed for large above-ground necropolises. The most impressive is **St Louis Cemetery No 1**, with its artfully designed tombs and burial sites of famed residents (like Voodoo practitioner Marie Laveau). Access is by guided tour only. Book with **Cemetery Tours NOLA** *(cemeterytourneworleans.com; adult/child $25/18)*. The 45-minute tour departs from across the street at Basin St Station *(basinststation.com)*, which also has exhibits on city history.

The Heart of the Backstreet

MAP P187

Explore the culture of the Tremé

The Tremé sits at the heart of New Orleans Black culture, and is a great place to learn about the city's deep-rooted traditions. Start your visit at the small **Backstreet Cultural Museum** *(backstreetmuseum.org; adult/child $25/10)* on St Philip St. Mardi Gras Indian suits grab the spotlight with dazzling flair – and finely crafted detail – in this informative space, which examines many of the distinctive elements of African American culture in New Orleans.

Everyone Is a Star

MAP P187

A DIY music experience

Created by a group of local artists and tinkerers, **Music Box Village** *(musicboxvillage.com, adult/child$15/7)* is not just

DRINKING IN THE QUARTER: OUR PICKS

MAP P182

Carousel Bar: Go early to snag a seat at the spinning carousel, a 1949 landmark inside the Hotel Monteleone. *11am-midnight*

Fritzel's European Jazz Pub: A Bourbon St original, this atmospheric spot often has live music. *4pm-midnight Mon, noon-2am Tue-Sun*

Bar Tonique: Walking a fine line between lounge and dive bar, this place shakes excellent cocktails in a low-lit setting. *noon-2am*

Latitude 29: Hallowed ground for Tiki lovers, Latitude 29 serves delicious rum cocktails. *3-9pm Sun-Thu, noon-11pm Fri & Sat*

THE MARIGNY, BYWATER & THE TREMÉ

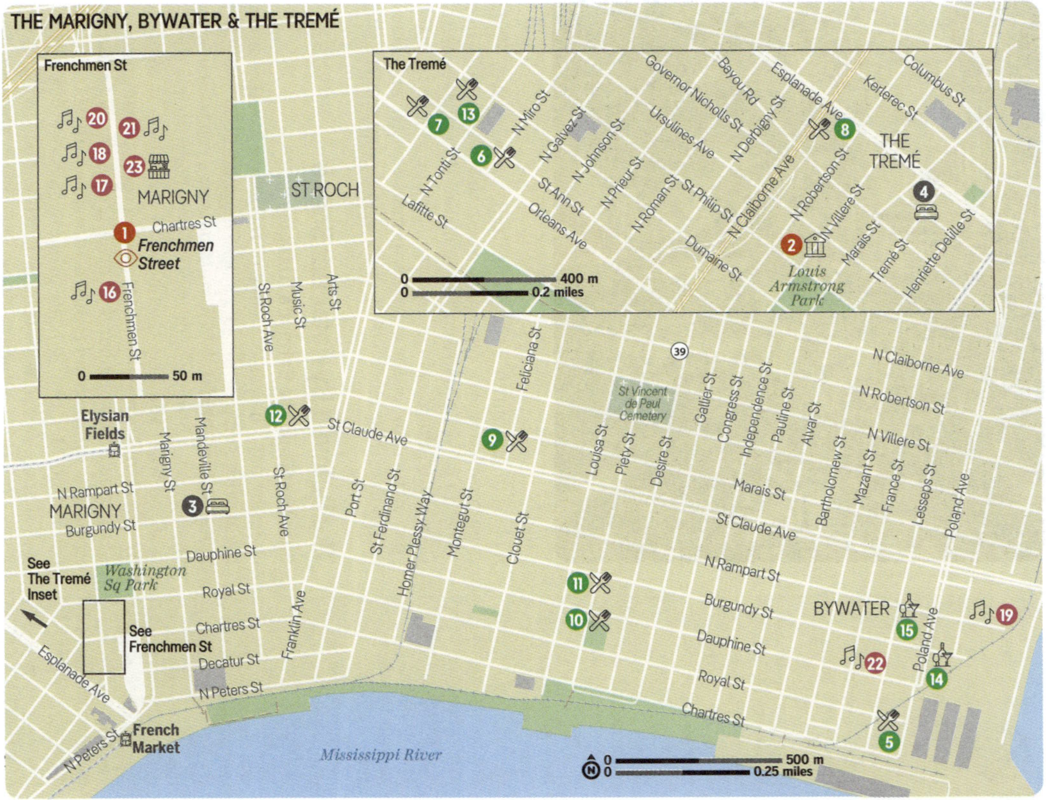

TOP TIPS

From March through early May, you can catch free concerts in Lafayette Sq in downtown. These happen Wednesdays from 5pm to 8pm (*ylcwats.com*). Bring an appetite – food vendors serve up all sorts of decadence.

BIRTHPLACE OF JAZZ

Bridging the French Quarter and Tremé, leafy **Louis Armstrong Park** hosts small festivals throughout the year. Near the south end of the park, a small inconspicuous plaza known as **Congo Square** played a vital role in the musical heritage of New Orleans – and the world beyond. During colonial days, enslaved people were permitted to gather here on Sundays, their only day of rest. Their gatherings were a celebration of West African rituals, and largely revolved around song and dance. Though the practice was shut down when US settlers took over the city, the memory remained, and by the late 19th century, brass bands were blending African rhythms with classical music. The innovative sounds eventually evolved into the well-known music of jazz.

MICHAEL SERNA/500PX/GETTY IMAGES

a place to play music – the venue itself can be played. Made from recycled metal, pipes and wood, the village looks like something from a Mad Max film and everything makes noise. Come ding, dong, spin, whizz and slap the village to make your own music, or see a live performance where musicians collaborate to produce a truly unforgettable sonic experience.

The Beloved Bywater Bar Scene

MAP P187

Bacchanal and the Barmuda Triangle

Quiet by day, the eastern edge of the Bywater wakes up at night with some of the city's best neighborhood watering holes. At **Bacchanal** *(bacchanalwine.com)*, you walk into an unassuming entrance to discover a wine bar with fine cheeses. Grab what you like, then head to the backyard where a live jazz band is playing. There's also a cocktail bar upstairs.

Other beloved neighborhood dives are nearby. **Vaughan's** *(@vaughansloungenola)*, has a fun vibe with Mardi Gras colors and Mexican *papeles picados* flags overhead. **BJ's** *(@bjslounge)* fashions itself as the neighborhood living room; it has a full calendar of live music. Enter below the neon 'Bar' sign to **Bar Redux** *(@barreduxnola)*, another dive bar with performers in the garden along with finger-lickin-good Creole fried wings and gumbo.

EATING IN TREMÉ: OUR PICKS

MAP P187

Gabrielle: This little cottage doles out rich Cajun plates of braised rabbit, slow-roasted duck and other favorites. *5-10pm Wed-Sat* **$$$**

Lil' Dizzy's: Join the crowds at this legendary lunchtime Creole buffet on the corner of Claiborne. *11am-3pm Mon-Sat* **$**

Willie Mae's Scotch House: Serves up signature fried chicken – among the world's best! *hours vary* **$**

Dooky Chase: New Orleans' most famous destination for Creole cooking has been dazzling diners (President Obama included) since 1941. *11am-3pm Tue-Fri, plus 5:30-9pm Fri & Sat* **$$**

Frenchmen Street

Go Bar-Hopping on Frenchmen Street MAP P187

Join the jazz-fueled street party

Lined with music venues, street jazz and perhaps a piano on wheels, **Frenchmen Street** is a chaotic cacophony and loads of fun. A who's who of legendary jazz musicians frequently play here, including Kermit Ruffins and John Boutté. Top events are usually held at **Snug Harbor** *(snugjazz.com)*, **d.b.a.** *(dbaneworleans.com)*, the **Spotted Cat** *(spottedcatmusic club.com)*, **Blue Nile** *(bluenilelive.com)* and **Cafe Negril** *(cafenegrilnola.com)*.

Take a break from the music to browse the arts and crafts for sale at the **Art Garden** night market *(artgardennola.com; 7pm-midnight Thu-Sun)*.

Art Gazing Downtown MAP P190

A top museum and gallery district

The **Ogden Museum of Southern Art** *(ogdenmuseum.org; adult/child $11/6)* illuminates unique facets of the South in all its complexity. Rotating exhibitions showcase lots of intriguing subjects, from photography on the streets of New Orleans to the overlooked communities of Appalachia. The permanent collection (3rd floor) has 18th-century portraits

SECOND LINES!

Second Line refers to New Orleans' neighborhood parades, especially those put on by the city's African American Social Aid and Pleasure (S&P) clubs. The S&P members deck themselves out in flash suits, hats and shoes, and carry decorated umbrellas and fans. This snazzy crowd, accompanied by a hired band, dances through the city. This is the First Line. Marching behind it is the Second Line: the crowds that gather to celebrate the music. Hundreds, sometimes thousands, of people dance in the Second Line, stopping for drinks and food along the parade route. All are welcome to join. Second Lines occur every Sunday from September through May. To find the parade route, check out WWOZ's Takin' It to the Streets section *(wwoz.org)*.

EATING IN THE MARIGNY & BYWATER: OUR PICKS MAP P187

Sneaky Pickle: Mostly vegan pub with excellent mac 'n' cheese, smoked tempeh Reubens and carrot juice Micheladas. *11am-9:30pm Wed-Mon* **$$**

St Roch Market: Food court in an 1875 market with cuisine from Cuba, Italy, Malaysia and elsewhere. *7am-9pm Sun-Thu, to 10pm Fri & Sat* **$$**

Satsuma: Bohemian, exposed-brick cafe with a shaded garden and sandwiches for breakfast and lunch. *8am-2pm* **$**

N7: Memorable French, Japanese and fish tapas served in a romantic, twinkly-lit garden. *5-9pm Mon-Thu, 11:30am-2:30pm & 5-10pm Fri-Sun* **$$$**

GARDEN DISTRICT, LOWER GARDEN & CENTRAL CITY

Among the most photogenic corners of the city, the **Garden District** exudes Old Southern excess with its historic mansions, lush greenery, chichi bistros and upscale boutiques (namely along Magazine St). Between the Central Business District (CBD) and the Garden District, the **Lower Garden District** is somewhat like its upriver neighbor but not quite as posh. There's a slightly more bohemian vibe, and plenty of bars and restaurants. Up above St Charles Ave, **Central City** is very much in transition. While there are large stretches of urban blight, there is also a dynamic concentration of community activist organizations rebuilding what was once one of the city's most important African American neighborhoods (Oretha Castle Haley is the main thoroughfare).

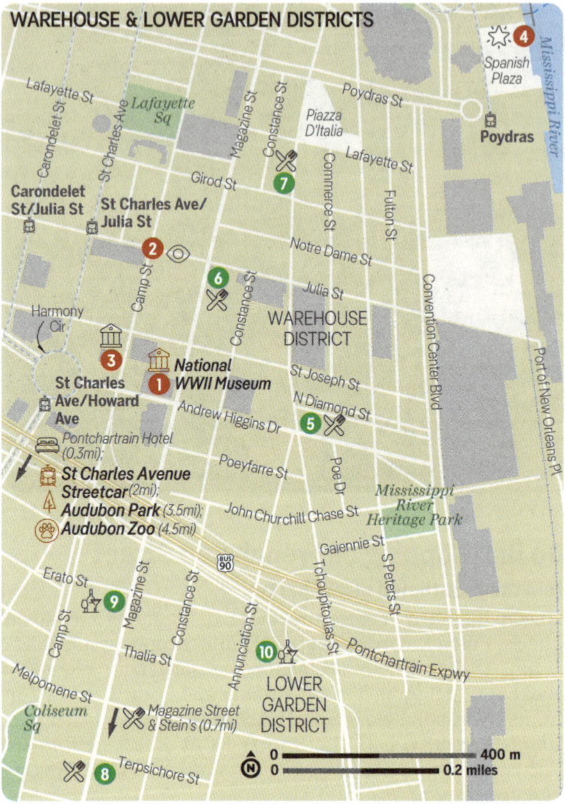

WAREHOUSE & LOWER GARDEN DISTRICTS

HIGHLIGHTS
1 National WWII Museum

SIGHTS
2 Julia Street
3 Ogden Museum of Southern Art

ACTIVITES
4 Creole Queen

EATING
5 Cochon
6 Pêche
7 St James Cheese Company
8 Surrey's Cafe & Juice Bar

DRINKING & NIGHTLIFE
9 Barrel Proof
10 Tell Me Bar

by French artists, lush Louisiana landscapes of the 1800s and socialist-realist artists of the 1930s.

Sometimes referred to as Gallery Row, **Julia Street** (between St Charles and Tchoupitoulas) is the heart of the Warehouse Arts District *(artsdistrictneworleans.com)*, with a smattering of galleries dotting the old buildings along this one-way thoroughfare. Things are liveliest on the first Saturday of the month *(6pm to 9pm)*, when there are special exhibitions and free wine.

See WWII in all its complexity

MAP P190

A sprawling, immersive museum

The **National WWII Museum** *(nationalww2museum.org; adult/child $36/26)* drops you straight into the action. Wall-sized photographs capture the confusion of D-Day. Riveting oral histories tell remarkable stories of survival. A walk through the snowy woods feels eerily cold. Exhibits like these make this grand facility engaging; artifacts, battles and war strategies are humanized through personal recollections and heat-of-the-moment displays. You could easily spend a full day (or more) here, so plan your visit carefully.

The must-see film of the museum is *Beyond All Boundaries,* which takes a 4D look at the USA's involvement in the war on a panoramic 120ft-wide screen. Get ready for rumbling seats and a dusting of snowflakes. Oscar-winning actor Tom Hanks narrates this evocative 48-minute experience, which runs on the hour from 10am to 4pm daily.

HIGHLIGHTS
1 City Park

SIGHTS
2 Botanical Gardens
3 New Orleans Museum of Art
4 Sydney & Walda Besthoff Sculpture Garden

ACTIVITIES
5 City Putt
6 Louisiana Children's Museum

DRINKING & NIGHTLIFE
7 Cafe du Monde

ENTERTAINMENT
8 Carousel Gardens
9 Jazz & Heritage Festival
10 Storyland

EATING IN THE CBD & WAREHOUSE DISTRICT: OUR PICKS

MAPS P182, P190

Namaste Nola: Despite the hotel setting, this place fires up beautiful Indian fare, including a rich paneer tikka masala. *11am-3pm & 5-10pm Thu-Tue* **$$**

Cochon: Donald Link pays homage to his Cajun culinary roots, serving meats smoked and wood-fired to perfection. *11am-10pm* **$$**

Pêche: One of New Orleans' best seafood restaurants lets the high-quality ingredients speak for themselves. *11am-10pm* **$$$**

St James Cheese Company: Heavenly cheesy sandwiches like Gruyère with caramelized onions. *11am-6pm Mon-Sat, to 4pm Sun* **$**

BEST KID-FRIENDLY SPOTS IN CITY PARK

Louisiana Children's Museum: Interactive exhibits, huge grounds and an enormous outdoor play area. Take your kids here on a hot day.

Storyland: Chase small children past life-size replicas of storybook characters at what might be the gentlest tourist attraction around.

City Putt: Home to two separate courses, this 36-hole putt-putt is the only minigolf attraction in the city.

Couturie Forest: A spaghetti tangle of pleasant trails wind past waterways and the 'highest point in New Orleans.'

Carousel Gardens: There are rides, a merry-go-round, a mini-roller coaster and plenty of fun to be had.

JTUCKER/SHUTTERSTOCK

St Charles Avenue Streetcar

Strolling & Shopping on Magazine

MAP P190

Indie boutiques, cafes and restaurants

Magazine Street is by far Orleans' best shopping strip. As a center for commercial activity it begins in the Lower Garden District, near the intersection with Felicity St. From here, you can follow Magazine west all the way to Audubon Park and shop or window browse in antiques stores and boutiques almost the entire way. The densest concentration of shops and restaurants lies around these intersections: Jackson, Washington, Louisiana and Napoleon.

Ride the St Charles Avenue Streetcar

MAP P190

Vintage DIY adventure

Some of the grandest homes in the US line St Charles Ave, shaded by enormous oak trees. Clanging through this bucolic corridor comes the iconic **St Charles Avenue Streetcar**, running since 1835. It's a delightfully nostalgic way to get across town. Hop on at Canal – or anywhere along the line (there are stops every few blocks) and ride it to Audubon Park. Pay the $1.25 fare in cash ($3 for an all-day pass), or via the city's Le Pass app.

EATING & DRINKING IN THE GARDEN DISTRICT: OUR PICKS

MAP P190

Surrey's Cafe & Juice Bar: Colorful neighborhood charmer offering outstanding breakfasts like shrimp and grits. *8am-3pm Thu-Mon* $

Stein's: The famed deli is an unrivaled spot for bacon, egg and cheese bagels and pastrami on rye. *8am-5pm Tue-Fri, from 9am Sat & Sun* $

Barrel Proof: A festive bourbon-centric option with corrugated iron walls, a long dark wood bar and fine cocktails with a creative edge. *4pm-1am*

Tell Me Bar: This well-hidden natural wine bar has a beautiful indoor and outdoor design and unusual wines from around the globe. *4-11pm*

Walk Amid Leafy Audubon Park

MAP P190

Verdant oasis and zoo

Audubon Park is a grand green space, run through with live oak trees, walking and cycling paths and a picturesque little lake, all framed by some lovely houses. Students lounge on the grass under Spanish moss while joggers lope by, dog owners play with their pets, golfers tee off and friends share an outdoor sundowner.

Appropriately enough, the **Audubon Zoo** *(audubonnature institute.org; adult/child $30/25)* is inside Audubon Park. It's a large place with sections including African, Asian and South American landscapes and fauna, and kids will find some of the world's most popular animals here, from elephants to giraffes. During the summer months, part of the zoo becomes a dedicated water park for youngsters. Don't miss the Louisiana Swamp section: a wet wonderland of bald cypresses and Spanish moss, carefully landscaped to reflect the natural wonders of southern Louisiana bayou country.

A Day at City Park

MAP P191

Art, sculpture and hands-on hijinks

City Park is so big that it includes two of the city's most wonderful museums, plus a sculpture garden, botanical garden and lots of walking paths. You can get there on the streetcar – take the **Canal Street line** (board the No 48 'City Park/ Muse' route).

A good place to begin at **Cafe Du Monde** *(shop.cafe dumonde.com)*. Order beignets and coffee with chicory, while listening to birdsong. Afterwards, take a stroll along the narrow bayou, which is lined with huge centuries-old live oak trees.

A short hop from there, the elegant **New Orleans Museum of Art** *(NOMA; noma.org; adult/child $20/free)* was opened in 1911 and is well worth a visit for its special exhibitions, gorgeous marble atrium and galleries of African, Asian, Flemish, Italian and American Southern art.

The **Sydney & Walda Besthoff Sculpture Garden** *(free)* is just outside NOMA, amid a wooded quilt of streams, pathways, lovers' benches and, of course, sculpture – mainly of the contemporary sort. For even more greenery – and countless flower species – head to the **Botanical Garden** *(adult/child $12/6)*.

LEGENDARY GUMBO

Candi Vanardo, sous-chef at Deelightful Roux School of Cooking, gives insight into New Orleans' quintessential dish. *chefdeelavigne.com*

The secret to gumbo is your roux and filé. If there is no filé – ground sassafras leaves – then it is not gumbo. The filé gives it a certain taste, texture and color. They say gumbo should look like the Mississippi River, and filé has that ability that makes it kind of dredgy. What you put in it depends on where you grew up. People put different things in their gumbo. For me, there's going to be filé, seafood, smoked sausage, hot sausage – this is a 9th Ward gumbo we're talking about. For seafood, I use shrimp, blue crab or even snow crab.

Louisiana

BLACK HISTORY | CAJUN CULTURE | WETLANDS & WILDLIFE

Places

French and Spanish explorers alike were drawn to the magnificent Mississippi River, and both countries would lay claim to the region, which was ultimately named after French king Louis XIV in the 17th century. Even after Louisiana was purchased from France by the fledgling United States in 1803, it retained its francophone roots thanks to the generations of Europeans living here, along with the influx of French-speaking Acadians (later known as Cajuns) and Haitians in the years following the St Domingue Revolution.

Not surprisingly, Louisiana feels completely different from other parts of the country. Cajun and Creole music still spills out of dance halls along the bayou, and you may feel like you're entering another realm while boating through fertile wetlands of alligators, birdsong and soaring bald cypress trees. There are also ample opportunities to explore the past, whether visiting a Native American mound-building settlement (and present-day World Heritage Site) or learning about the enslaved people who helped build this nation.

TOP TIP

The best time to visit Lafayette is during **Festival International de Louisiane** *(festivalinternational.org)*. Held on the last weekend in April, the free music event (simply called 'Festival' in these parts) brings incredible talent from far-flung corners of the world to the multiple stages set up around town.

GETTING AROUND

Most travelers explore Louisiana by car as it's quite difficult to get around without your own wheels. If you're flying in, New Orleans is the best place to arrange affordable rentals. If you don't plan on doing much traveling within the state, rail fans can take one of three weekly departures aboard Amtrak's *Sunset Limited*, which connects New Orleans with Los Angeles. The train makes several stops in Louisiana, including in New Iberia and Lafayette, though once there you'll still need a vehicle to get around (Uber and Lyft both operate in Lafayette, however).

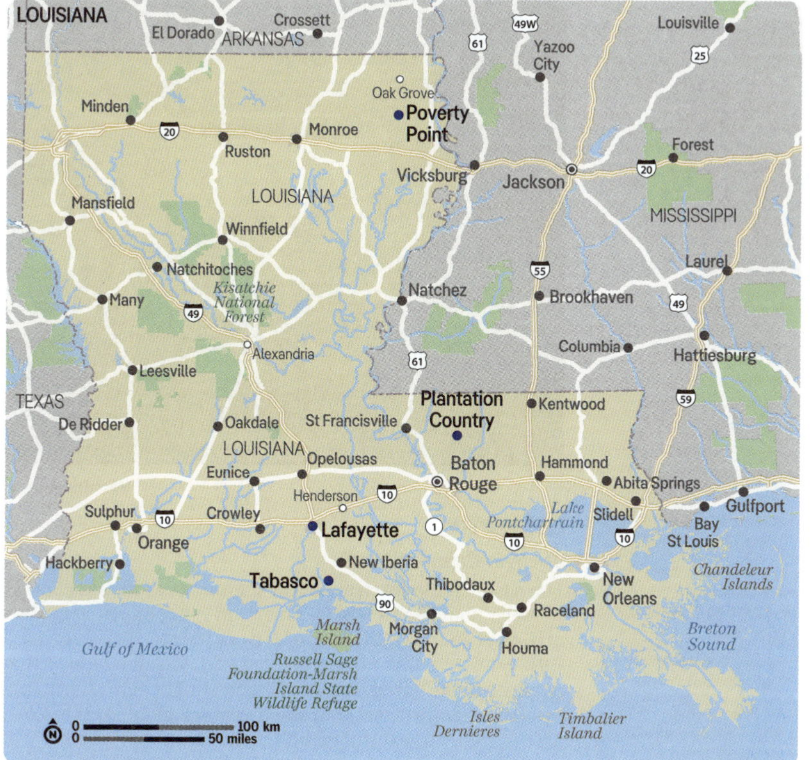

Plantation Country

See the other side of plantation life

The excellent **Whitney Plantation** *(whitneyplantation.org; adult/child guided tour $32/18, self-guided tour $25/11)* rewrites the script with 1½- to two-hour guided tours that focus on the lives of the enslaved. It isn't easy history to hear, but the guides do a wonderful job – many of them locals whose ancestors may have worked on the plantation. Guided tours are offered Wednesday to Monday at 10:45am, 12:45pm and 2:15pm. Self-guided tours with an audio device or app are available from 9:30am to 3pm.

Another 10-minutes' drive up the road, the **Laura Plantation** *(lauraplantation.com; adult/teen/child $28/20/15)* also does a remarkable job of contextualizing the life of both the free and enslaved on the Duparc Sugar Plantation. Guides rely on historical records and the first-hand accounts of Laura Locoul, a Creole woman who grew up here. Guided tours, available in English and French, last about 75 minutes and run every 20 to 40 minutes from 10am to 3:20pm.

LAKE PONTCHARTRAIN

The 630-sq-mile waterbody north of New Orleans is not really a lake, but an estuary connected to the Gulf of Mexico. Whatever you call it, it's huge, and the 23.8-mile Lake Pontchartrain Causeway that crosses it is the world's longest continuous bridge over water. The first lane of the twin bridge, going southbound, was constructed in just 14 months and opened in 1956. The northbound bridge was added in 1969, and both have survived major storms with minimal damage.

It takes about 25 minutes to drive across the bridge. Unsurprisingly, you won't see land for most of the journey. Driving northbound is free, but you'll have to pay a $6 toll on the drive back.

PHILIP GOULD/GETTY IMAGES

Vermilionville

Lafayette

Uncover Cajun culture

The best place to learn about the Cajuns, in addition to Southwestern Louisiana's Native American inhabitants, is at **Vermilionville** *(adult/child $10/6)* in Lafayette. This recreated 19th-century Cajun village is filled with wooden houses that wind along the bayou. Knowledgeable staff in period garb spin wool and hammer metal to teach visitors about local history. An especially impactful exhibit is the classroom where 'I will not speak French' is written dozens of times on the chalkboard – for decades, French was banned in public schools. There's plenty to read and an excellent restaurant if you're hungry. Check the calendar for live music on weekends.

Dance to Cajun & Creole rhythms

If you overnight in Lafayette, be sure to check out the town's renowned music scene. At the **Blue Moon Saloon** *(bluemoonpresents.com)*, you can catch one of the best backyard jam sessions in town (it's also a guesthouse). For something a little different, head to **Pat's Fisherman's Wharf** *(patsfishermanswharf.com)* in Henderson (a 25-minute drive east of Lafayette), where Cajun bands draw dance-loving crowds on Saturdays *(8:30pm)* and Sundays *(4:30pm)* at the **Atchafalaya Club**.

Some 10 miles east of Lafayette, tiny Breaux Bridge is famous for its Saturday morning zydeco breakfasts at **Buck & Johnny's** *(buckandjohnnys.com; $10)*. The Cajun-meets-Italian restaurant has a dining hall that vibrates with zippy zydeco (a genre that blends Creole, R&B and blues) from 8:30am to 11:30am. It's an uproarious time as young and old bob and spin on the dance floor – the $20 for bottomless mimosas certainly helps. If you can't make it on Saturday, Buck & Johnny's also has live music from around 6pm to 9pm on Thursdays, Fridays and Saturdays.

Go boating in the swamp

Touring the swamps and bayous ('streams' in the Choctaw language), on the lookout for alligators and bald eagles, is a bucket-list experience. Recommended outfitters such as **Cajun Country Swamp Tours** *(cajuncountryswamptours.com; $25)* will take you on a two-hour boat excursion to see alligators, yellow-crowned herons and other wetland wildlife on **Lake Martin**, some 15 miles east of Lafayette. If you prefer to get a bit of a workout while you sightsee, **Champagne's Swamp Tours** *(champagnesswamptours.com)* rents kayaks *($20 per person per hour)*. You can paddle your way across mirror-like waters and stop in secluded spots where you'll hear nothing but the sound of the birds.

Tabasco

Birds & Hot Sauce

Near the town of New Iberia, you can visit Avery Island, home to one of the country's most famous hot sauces, **Tabasco** *(tabasco.com; adult/child $16/13)*. Avery is not really an island but rather a salt dome that extends 8 miles below the surface. The salt mined here goes into Tabasco sauce, as do locally grown peppers. You'll learn all this on a self-guided tour that takes you from seed to sauce, with tastings at the end. Afterwards, you can walk or drive through **Jungle Gardens** (included with Tabasco admission), with its 250 acres of moss-covered live oaks and subtropical jungle flora. There's an amazing array of waterbirds (especially snowy egrets, which nest here in astounding numbers) as well as turtles and alligators.

Poverty Point

Engineers of the ancient world

Louisiana has just one UNESCO World Heritage Site, and it remains little known, even to many state residents. Near the Mississippi border, some four hours north of New Orleans (and just an hour northwest of Vicksburg, p178), **Poverty Point** *(povertypoint.us; admission $4)* preserves the monumental earthworks built by a highly organized society some 3400 years ago. In the visitor center, you can browse exhibits and pick up a map for a self-guided tour of the site. A 2.6-mile walking trail takes you past 20 points of interest and through various landscapes (including a stretch of forest and a view over the Bayou Macon), and up a 72ft mound built by hand from some 15 million bushels of earth brought from elsewhere. If you're not up for the walk, you can instead do a more condensed 2-mile driving tour of the site passing 11 points of interest – ask rangers for this separate driving tour guide.

CAJUNS & CREOLES

You may be excused if you're confused by the terms Cajun and Creole – they are confusing indeed. The initial definition of a Creole was someone born in the European colonies who spoke a Romance language and practiced Catholicism, though it later became associated with people of mixed European, African and Native American ancestry. Cajun derives from Acadian, the French-speaking people who settled in Louisiana after the British exiled them from what's now eastern Canada in Le Grand Dérangement (The Great Displacement; 1755–64). In the present day, most people identifying as Cajuns are white, while Creoles are Black or of mixed race, though the two cultures have historical and genealogical connections that are often overlooked.

Places We Love to Stay

$ Budget $$ Midrange $$$ Top End

South Carolina

MAPS P138, P142

Starlight Motor Inn (Charleston) $ Spare but snazzy, this revamped motor court in North Charleston has a pool and an on-site pub.

Andrew Pinkney Inn (Charleston) $$ Two restored historic buildings hold bright, comfy rooms. Complimentary wine social and breakfast in upper-level atrium. Great value.

Old Village Post House (Mt Pleasant) $$ This pale-yellow-and-blue clapboard house is a down-home, relaxing option tucked into a historic fishing community.

Swamp Rabbit Inn (Greenville) $$ Fun six-room inn in a '50s-era former boarding house downtown. Feels like a hostel but features colorfully decked-out private rooms.

Georgia

Thunderbird Inn (Savannah) $ A vintage-chic 1964 motel offering complimentary popcorn and frosted breakfast donuts in the lobby, and RC Colas and Moon Pies in every room.

Glenn Hotel (Atlanta) $$ This 1920s neoclassical revival building boasts a cozy boutique feel and one of Downtown's best rooftop bars, SkyLounge.

River Street Inn (Savannah) $$ Historical-chic rooms with hardwood floors and four-poster beds – the best ones have balconies. The building dates to 1817.

Rivet House (Athens) $$$ In the repurposed Mill District, this 50-room newcomer turned a former denim factory into Athens' hippest hotel. Great Italian restaurant, cool bar, no breakfast.

CASTLE LIGHT IMAGES/ALAMY

Thunderbird Inn

Alabama

106 Jefferson (Huntsville) $$ Stylish, newish boutique hotel in a great downtown location, with mid-century modern-style rooms and a rooftop bar.

Elyton Hotel (Birmingham) $$ In a grand 1909 building, this boutique beauty has crisp white rooms with pops of color and contemporary art. Great downtown location.

SpringHill Suites (Montgomery) $$ Though part of the Marriott chain, this historic property is no cookie-cutter, with industrial chic style in a walkable downtown setting.

Malaga Inn (Mobile) $$ Tastefully designed rooms with a Victorian-era vibe are set in two converted townhouses from the 1860s. Lovely courtyard and a central location.

Mississippi

Auberge Clarksdale Hostel (Clarksdale) $ Perfect downtown setting and a convivial traveler vibe (the lounge has a turntable and guitars) with simple dorms and private rooms.

Shack Up Inn (Clarksdale) $ Stay outside of town in refurbished sharecropper cabins or the creatively renovated cotton gin. There are loaner guitars and a barnlike bar.

Natchez Grand Hotel (Natchez) $ Contemporary design with 119 rooms in a great central location. Book a room with views of the Mississippi River.

Corners Mansion Inn (Vicksburg) **$$** Delightful B&B with a welcoming host, atmospheric rooms, homemade breakfasts and river views from the front porch swing.

New Orleans

MAPS P182, P187, P190

Rathbone Mansions (Tremé) **$** These pre-Civil War mansions have hardwood floors, four-poster beds and an art-deco-meets-the-19th-century vibe at a very forgiving price point.

Olivier House (French Quarter) **$$** 1838 gem offering wide-ranging options, from the economical to the elaborate, with balconies, exposed brick and antique furnishings.

Peter & Paul (Marigny) **$$** Like a page from an architecture magazine, with 71 antique-filled rooms spread across several buildings: a 19th-century Catholic schoolhouse, rectory, convent and church.

Pontchartrain Hotel (Garden District) **$$** On St Charles, this grande dame has handsomely furnished rooms with old-fashioned charm. There's great dining, live music and a rooftop bar.

Louisiana

Blue Moon Saloon (p196; Lafayette) **$** A draw for music lovers with fun (but loud) backyard jam sessions; boasts a friendly backpacker vibe, with dorms and private rooms.

Bayou Cabins (Breaux Bridge) **$** Quintessential Cajun spot on a bayou with 14 historic cabins boasting retro furnishings (ranging from 1949 wallpaper to century-old cypress flooring).

Maison Mouton (Lafayette) **$$** An oasis amid flower-filled gardens and live oaks with 12 rooms spread over historic cottages dating back to 1820.

Pontchartrain Hotel

Researched and curated by Jesse Scott

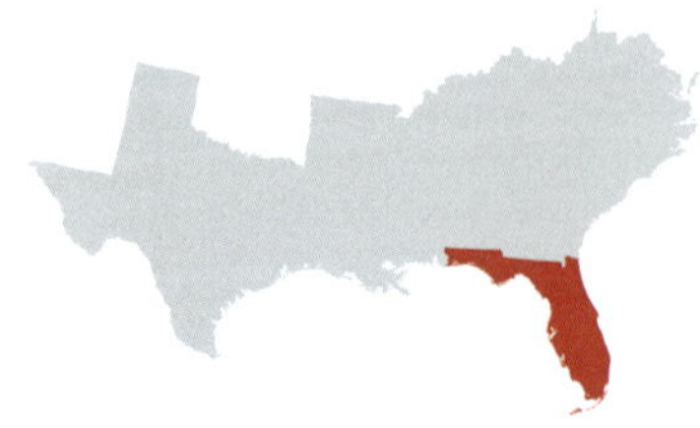

Florida

BEACHES, CULTURE AND SUN-SOAKED TROPICS

Shoreline rhythms, lively cities and wild backwaters shape a state of contrasts – electric, eccentric and steeped in stories old and new.

Florida refuses to be just one thing. At first glance, it's all sunshine and shoreline – a long, lanky canvas brushed with pastel lifeguard towers, sea oats swaying in Atlantic winds, and sunsets that melt into the Gulf. But scratch below the sunburn and you'll find a land of contrasts: cosmopolitan and kitschy, wild and refined, proudly weird and endlessly welcoming.

Start in Miami, where art-deco façades glitter against Latin beats, Wynwood murals blaze bold, and Cuban cafes fuel locals and night owls alike. Glide south into the Everglades, where the modern world disappears in a sweep of sawgrass, cypress domes and prehistoric silence pierced by the bellow of a gator. Keep going and you hit the Keys – a coral-capped chain where time slows, the water glows and sundowners are a ritual.

In Southeast Florida, high-rises kiss the sea while retirees, creatives and snowbirds mingle in brunch lines. Central Florida is another universe altogether – especially in Orlando, where theme parks aren't just attractions, but their own gravity. Along the Space Coast, rockets streak skyward, reviving dreams of the cosmos. Tampa blends Gulf Coast breezes with cigar-rolling heritage, and in the northeast, moss-draped oaks line brick streets in cities like St Augustine and Jacksonville, where history lingers in the humid air. Florida dazzles, defies and demands a closer look.

DENNIS W DONOHUE/SHUTTERSTOCK

THE MAIN AREAS

For places to stay in Florida, see p262

FOKKEBOK/GETTY IMAGES

Left: Alligator in Everglades National Park (p218); Above: South Beach (p206), Miami

Find Your Way

Stretching more than 500 miles from the Gulf Panhandle to the Keys, Florida fans out into beaches, swamps and cities – with distinct regions spanning coasts, wetlands, islands and inland theme-park country.

Orlando & Walt Disney World®, p238

Theme parks reign, but Orlando surprises with a vibrant LGBTIQ+ scene, cultural events and international flair beyond the thrill rides.

Tampa Bay & Southwest, p256

Tampa buzzes with nightlife, while St Pete shines with arts, beaches, and offshore islands for a laid-back Gulf escape.

Everglades & Biscayne National Park, p218

These wild wetlands teem with gators, birds and beauty. A rare pocket of primordial nature tucked between Florida's cities and suburbs.

Gulf of Mexico

BUSES

Although cars are recommended for getting around Florida, **Greyhound** (*greyhound.com*) runs intercity buses between 40 cities. They might move at the pace of a sea turtle, but they're more economical and eco-friendly. **Megabus** (*megabus.com*) also serves Miami, Orlando and Jacksonville.

TRAINS

Amtrak offers limited service within Florida, but other rail services pick up the slack. **Tri-Rail** (*tri-rail.com*) connects cities in the south, while **SunRail** (*sunrail.com*) serves 16 stops in Central Florida. **Brightline** (*gobrightline.com*) offers economical high-speed service connecting Miami and Orlando.

PLANES

Florida has many international and regional airports, so there's always a fast way to get around. **Southwest Airlines** (*southwest.com*) is a popular go-to for quick city hops. Otherwise, save the airport hassle and drive or use commuter rail services instead.

Northeast Florida, p250
St Augustine oozes charm. Jacksonville brings barbecue and beach vibes. Amelia Island blends historic grace and Southern serenity on the Atlantic.
Space Coast, p245
Rockets roar over quiet shores. The Space Coast mixes NASA wonder with surfing, kayaking and beaches perfect for space buffs and nature lovers alike.
Southeast Florida, p230
Fort Lauderdale and beyond blend yacht culture, mansions, malls and beach-town cool. Expect surf, sun and anything-goes energy with a luxe twist.
Miami, p206
Latin-meets-Caribbean spirit with glitz to match. Miami pulses with glamour, global flavor, neighborhood pride and vibrant culture from Little Havana to Wynwood.
Florida Keys & Key West, p224
A quirky island chain brimming with bars, fishing and charm, Key West dazzles with creativity, character and come-as-you-are energy.
0 100 km
0 50 miles
GEORGIA
ATLANTIC OCEAN
Fernandina Beach
Amelia Island
Talbot Islands State Parks
Jacksonville
Northeast Florida
St Augustine
Steinhatchee
Gainesville
Silver Springs
De Leon Springs State Parks
Ocala
Daytona Beach
Deland
Crystal River
Homosassa Springs
Titusville
Space Coast
Walt Disney World®
Orlando
Cocoa
Cocoa Beach
Melbourne
Clearwater
Tampa
Winter Haven
St Petersburg
Tampa Bay
St Pete Beach
Tampa Bay & Southwest
Sarasota
Sebastian Inlet
Vero Beach
Fort Pierce
Hobe Sound
Lake Okeechobee
Punta Gorda
West Palm Beach
Palm Beach
Fort Myers
Captiva Island
Sanibel Island
Southeast Florida
Boca Raton
Coral Springs
Lauderdale-by-the-Sea
Naples
Alligator Alley
Big Cypress National Preserve
Fort Lauderdale
Hollywood
Everglades City
Miami Beach
Chokoloskee
Miami
Everglades & Biscayne National Park
Florida City
Flamingo
Key Largo
Florida Bay
Islamorada
Florida Keys
Marathon
Grassy Key
Big Pine Key
Key West

Plan Your Days

With everything from untamed wilderness to world-renowned theme parks, planning a Florida trip means first choosing your vibe – beachy, wild, cultural, whimsical or a little of it all – and letting the Sunshine State do the rest.

CONNECT IMAGES/GETTY IMAGES

Christ of the Abyss (p226), John Pennekamp Coral Reef State Park

Iconic South Florida

Start in **Fort Lauderdale** (p230) and cruise its scenic waterways via water taxi, stopping at Bonnet House or the Riverwalk for breezy bites and people-watching. Next, dive into Miami's color-splashed culture: admire the murals of **Wynwood Walls** (p211), dig into Cuban flavors in **Little Havana** (p213), and dance the night away in **South Beach** (p206). Then head west for a day with the gators in **Everglades National Park** (p218) – get on the water in a canoe or kayak to view wildlife. Finally, cruise the Overseas Highway to the Florida Keys. Start in **Key Largo** (p224) for snorkeling or a slice of key lime pie, then roll south to **Islamorada** (p226) or funky **Key West** (p228), where sunsets, street performers and rum punches make for a perfect finale.

Seasonal Highlights

Florida's subtropical climate means year-round adventures – from turtle hatchings and rocket launches to food fests and art fairs.

JANUARY

Art Deco Weekend transforms Miami's Ocean Dr, manatees gather near Tampa, and dry weather is ideal for Everglades hikes and stone crab feasts.

FEBRUARY

Dry, crisp days for patio dining on Gulf oysters or spotting roseate spoonbills and nesting bald eagles in wetlands.

MARCH

Spring break fills beaches, citrus is at its peak – sip fresh OJ or try key lime pie.

Gulf Coast Swing

Start in **Tampa** (p256) with riverfront walks, Cuban sandwiches in **Ybor City** (p258) and a nightcap at a rooftop bar. Then hop to **St Petersburg** (p261) to admire Dalí's surreal genius, hunt murals downtown and sip small-batch beers at breweries aplenty. Afterward, it's off to the sands: unwind on the family-friendly beaches of **St Pete Beach** (p261). From here, you're at the epicenter of some of the Gulf's most prized beaches – head south to **Pass-a-Grille Beach** (p261) and take a ferry out to the unspoiled Shell Key. Make sure to spend an evening at nearby **Clearwater Beach** (p261), where its Pier 60 nightly sunset celebrations – with entertainers galore – rival those in Key West.

Theme Park Parade

Kick things off with two days at **Walt Disney World®** (p241), diving into the world's most beloved theme-park empire. Zoom through space, soar on banshees and sing along with animatronic dolls (you know the ones). Next, give the grown-ups their due: take in downtown Orlando's **Leu Gardens** (p242) or cool off at **Wekiwa Springs State Park** (p240). **Universal Orlando Resort** (p243) is next – where Diagon Alley, Marvel heroes and Jurassic coasters collide. Cap things off with a day at **SeaWorld Orlando** (p244) or **LEGOLAND Florida** (p242) in Winter Haven – ideal for kids and anyone still clinging to their inner child. End your trip with a breezy evening at **Disney Springs** (p241), where souvenirs and chef-driven fare await.

MAY

Sunrise beach walks are magical, mangoes ripen in South Florida and rising heat calls for mid day breaks indoors or by water.

JULY

Fireworks light up St Augustine's bayfront and Tampa's **Riverwalk**. Expect daily afternoon thunderstorms and steamy heat.

OCTOBER

Universal's haunted houses and costumed crowds fill Orlando for Halloween, while migrating butterflies flutter over wildflower patches and coastal dunes statewide.

DECEMBER

Boat parades in the Keys, Miami's **Art Basel** draws global crowds, and cool, dry weather is ideal for beach strolls and spiny lobster dinners.

Miami

FIRE, FLAIR, FLAVOR – MORE THAN BEACHES

GETTING AROUND

South Beach is best explored on foot – it's compact, vibrant and packed with visual treats. The free Miami Beach Trolley is a breezy option for hopping between SoBe, Mid-Beach and North Beach. To explore the broader city, rideshares, the Metrorail and the free Metromover in downtown Miami make it easy to zip between neighborhoods.

TOP TIP

From college reunions and spring break to foodie, music and art festivals, Miami is ground zero for large-scale gatherings in every season. Check the calendar before you arrive – the vibe is often dictated by the theme of whatever event is on, and Miami tends to go all-in on whatever it's celebrating.

Miami is a city of many moods – a place where Caribbean heat, Latin flair and coastal cool collide. Yes, Miami Beach still shines with its signature art-deco glow, oceanfront energy and ever-buzzing nightlife. But cross the causeways and you'll find a wider city with just as much pulse. Wynwood's street art and indie galleries rival any major art capital, Little Havana hums with café cubano culture and domino games, and Coconut Grove offers breezy bayside calm beneath lush tropical canopies. Whether it's sunrise yoga in South Beach, a foodie crawl through Calle Ocho or sunset cocktails in Brickell's glassy high-rises, the typical Miami experience isn't one-size-fits-all. It really is a choose-your-own-adventure city, where beach mornings, museum afternoons and all-night dance floors coexist with jungle gardens, historic districts and family-run bakeries. Don't just stay put in Miami – explore. Miami rewards the curious with culture, rhythm and sunshine around every colorful corner.

Lay of the Sandy Land

Beaches beyond South Beach

When it comes to sun, sand and surf, Miami Beach covers all the bases – and with a different vibe to look forward to depending on the stretch where you choose to unfurl your beach towel.

South Beach is without a doubt the section of sand most people think of when they hear the words 'Miami Beach,' but there's far more coast to saunter along out here. Unless otherwise noted, the numbered streets here all extend off Collins Ave (A1A), which runs north and south parallel to the beach itself.

Mid-Beach spans the sands from 23rd to 63rd Sts. It's not like the crowds out here stop preening and showing off – this is still model/influencer territory – but many have shifted from posting TikToks of their nights at the club to boosting reels of their growing families. The Mid-Beach area is attached to

(continues on p209)

HIGHLIGHTS
1 Faena Hotel Miami Beach
2 Fontainebleau
3 Freehand Miami
4 Miami Beach Boardwalk
5 South Beach

SIGHTS
6 Art Deco Museum and Welcome Center
7 Bass Museum
8 Jewish Museum of Florida-FIU
9 Mid-Beach
10 Romero Britto Fine Art Gallery
11 Wolfsonian-FIU

SLEEPING
12 Kimpton Surfcomber

EATING
13 Abbalé Telavivian Kitchen
14 Baires Grill
15 Forte dei Marmi
16 Lilikoi
17 Macchialina
18 MILA
19 RAO's
20 Stubborn Seed

ART-DECO AMBLE

Spend a morning walking around South Beach to admire the world's largest collection of 1920s and 1930s art-deco buildings.

START	END	LENGTH
Art Deco Museum	Wolfsonian-FIU	1 mile; 1 hour

Some 800 art-deco buildings here are listed on the National Register of Historic Places, and you'll encounter many of them whether you set out on a purposeful stroll past bold facades and whimsical tropical motifs or not.

Start at the 1 **Art Deco Museum** for background and exhibits on art-deco style. Stroll north along Ocean Dr between 12th and 14th Sts to spot some of the area's most famous art-deco hotels. 2 **The Leslie** is known for its boxy shape and 'eyebrows' (cantilevered sunshades) that wrap around the building; 3 **The Carlyle** has modernist styling; and the graceful 4 **Cardozo South Beach**, built by Henry Hohauser and now owned by Gloria and Emilio Estefan, is recognized for its sleek, rounded edges.

When you arrive at 14th St, peek inside the 5 **Winter Haven Hotel** to admire its fabulous terrazzo floors, made of stone chips set in mortar and polished to a shine. Then turn left down 14th St to Washington Ave and the 6 **US Post Office**, located at 13th St, known for its curvy block of white art-deco and stripped classical style.

Finish your amble nearby at the 7 **Wolfsonian-FIU**, an excellent design museum in the former Washington Storage Company, where wealthy snowbirds of the '30s stashed their pricey belongings before heading back north.

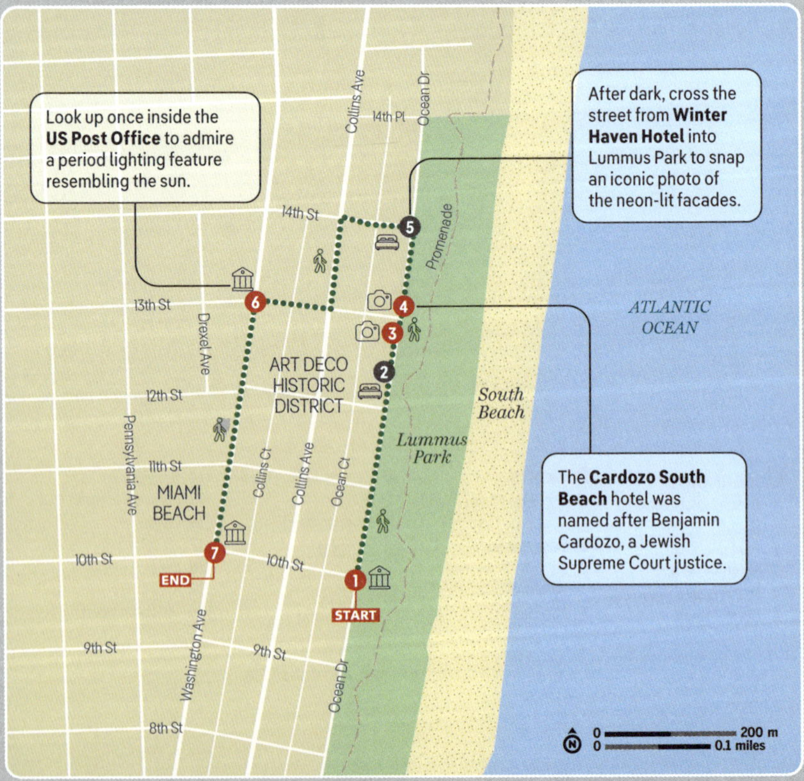

Look up once inside the **US Post Office** to admire a period lighting feature resembling the sun.

After dark, cross the street from **Winter Haven Hotel** into Lummus Park to snap an iconic photo of the neon-lit facades.

The **Cardozo South Beach** hotel was named after Benjamin Cardozo, a Jewish Supreme Court justice.

(continued from p206)
a lot of the area's big luxury hotels, such as the **Fontainebleau** and **Faena Hotel Miami Beach**. On the bay side of the beach is North Bay Rd, where you can see (well, glimpse over the walls) some of the area's largest mansions. This area includes the official **Miami Beach Boardwalk** *(miamibeachboardwalk.com; free)*. It runs between 21st and 46th Sts, where Orthodox Jews often mix with social media mavens.

North Beach extends from 63rd St to 87th Tce. The beaches here are smaller and more family-friendly, although this is also where you'll find **Haulover Beach** (4.5 miles north of 71st St); the northern section of this beach park is clothing-optional and has been popular with naturists since the 1990s.

Free Downtown Tour up High

MAP P210

Metromover groovin'

What's that train whirring overhead through some of Miami's densest real estate? The answer is the **Metromover** *(miamidade.gov/global/transportation/metromover.page; free)*, an elevated, electric monorail meant to alleviate the traffic woes of Downtown and Brickell. The Metromover did not succeed in doing this, as anyone who has driven in South Florida can attest. But it's a beloved, complete rail line that moves thousands of passengers each month – for free! It also happens to be a pretty cool way to see central Miami from above, which is a nice thing, given the city's 'skyscraper canyon' landscape.

The Metromover opened in 1986 and sports that distinctive, so-modern-it-looks-dated appearance of public works from that period. Its three lines – the Omni Loop, Inner Loop and Brickell Loop – span 4.4 miles and connect major Downtown spots like **Bayfront Park**, the **Kaseya Center** (where the Miami Heat play) and the **Adrienne Arsht Center for the Performing Arts**, among others. The mover is a particularly good way of seeing the full architectural span and beauty of the **Freedom Tower** (p212), modeled after the Giralda bell tower in Seville.

MIAMI BEACH'S BEST MUSEUMS & GALLERIES

The Bass: Founded in 1964, this contemporary art museum sits in a 1930s art-deco building *(thebass.org)*.

Jewish Museum of Florida-FIU: Florida Jewish history is celebrated within two art-deco buildings, one a former synagogue *(jmof.fiu.edu)*.

Wolfsonian-FIU: A museum, library and research center devoted to art and design *(wolfsonian.org)*.

Romero Britto Fine Art Gallery: This gallery of the eponymous visual artist from Brazil bursts with color, inside and out *(shopbritto.com)*.

Art Deco Museum: Dive into the major design styles that influenced Miami Beach: Mediterranean revival, art-deco and Miami Modern *(mdpl.org)*.

EATING IN MIAMI: MIAMI BEACH

MAP P207

Lilikoi: Laid-back, indoor-outdoor spot for healthy, mostly organic, veg-friendly dishes. *8am-3pm* $$

Macchialina: Rustic-chic Italian trattoria with all the ingredients for a terrific night out. *6-11pm Mon-Thu, from 5pm Fri-Sun* $$

Abbalé Telavivian Kitchen: Mediterranean-inspired weekend brunch and shared mezze plates. *11am-10pm Mon-Thu, to 11pm Fri, 10am-11pm Sat, to 10pm Sun* $$

Baires Grill: Argentinean *parrillada* (barbecue) alongside *milanesas* just like in Buenos Aires. *noon-11pm Sun-Thu, to 11:30pm Fri & Sat* $$

MILA: Omakase-style rooftop bar, this swanky restaurant takes guests on a culinary odyssey. *hours vary* $$$

Stubborn Seed: Michelin starred and James Beard awarded for its adventurous haute-American cuisine. Reserve. *6-10pm Sun-Thu, to 11pm Fri & Sat* $$$

RAO's: Italian restaurant in Loews Miami Beach Hotel. Raw bar, antipasti and southern Neapolitan cuisine. *5:30-10pm Sun-Thu, to 11pm Fri & Sat* $$$

Forte dei Marmi: Led by a two-Michelin-starred chef, this coastal Italian spot evokes a Tuscan villa in a Mediterranean revival building. *hours vary* $$$

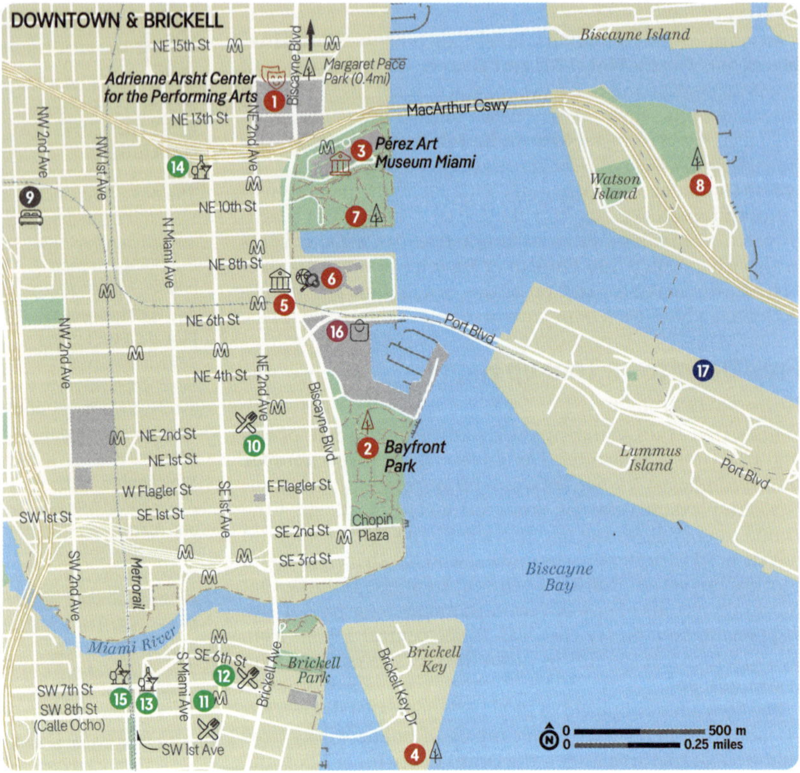

DOWNTOWN & BRICKELL

HIGHLIGHTS
1 Adrienne Arsht Center for the Performing Arts
2 Bayfront Park
3 Pérez Art Museum Miami

SIGHTS
4 Brickell Key Park
5 Freedom Tower
6 Kaseya Center
7 Maurice A. Ferré Park
see 5 Museum of Art & Design
8 Watson Island Park

SLEEPING
9 Dunns Josephine

EATING
10 NIU Kitchen
11 Quinto
12 River Oyster Bar
see 3 Verde

DRINKING & NIGHTLIFE
13 Blackbird Ordinary
14 Elleven Miami
15 Rosa Sky
see 11 Sugar

SHOPPING
16 Bayside Marketplace

TRANSPORT
17 Port of Miami

EATING IN MIAMI: DOWNTOWN

MAP P210

Quinto: Sexy rooftop in the EAST Miami hotel with tropical greenery, incredible cocktails and fusion fare. *hours vary* **$$**

Niu Kitchen: Stylish, living room–sized restaurant serving Catalan cuisine and a killer wine list. *6-10pm Tue-Thu & Sun, to 10:30pm Fri & Sat* **$$**

Verde: Inside the Pérez Art Museum Miami is a local favorite for tasty market-fresh dishes in an atmospheric setting. *11am-4pm Fri-Mon, to 8pm Thu* **$$**

River Oyster Bar: A few paces from the Miami River, this buzzing little spot whips up excellent plates of seafood. *noon-10:30pm* **$$**

The high-rises of Brickell make for a shiny sight from the Metromover, and the Omni Loop offers great views of Biscayne Bay, the Miami River and the **Pérez Art Museum Miami**. Trains run from 5am to midnight every day, arriving roughly every three minutes (more frequently during rush hour).

The Metromover isn't the only elevated rail line in town. Miami's **Metrorail** links Downtown with residential neighborhoods like Coral Gables and Coconut Grove. Beneath it runs the **Underline** – a planned $146 million, 10-mile-long linear park to be completed in 2026. The section from Brickell to Vizcaya Station was unveiled in 2024. You'll find weekly community yoga classes staged on the Underline, an outdoor gym, a meditation garden, and a walking and biking path to explore.

Get Out on the Water

MAP P210

Cruise on Biscayne Bay

The Atlantic Ocean might be a causeway away from Downtown Miami, but you can still get out on the area's sparkling waterways from Downtown's shoreline when you head out on a boat tour with one of the companies operating from **Bayside Marketplace**.

For a serious rush, **Thriller Miami Speedboat Adventures** *(thrillermiami.com; $45)* offers 45-minute 'Miami Vice–style' tours (Don Johnson sightings not guaranteed) aboard its fleet of three catamarans that take you across Biscayne Bay and past the mansions of Fisher Island and Star Island.

Island Queen Cruises *(islandqueencruises.com; $35, child 4-12 $25, child under 4 $5)* offers a slower-paced, 90-minute sightseeing jaunt on a private ship with an open upper deck and air-conditioned salon during which you'll cruise pass sites like **Millionaire's Row**, Miami Beach and the **Port of Miami**.

On both tours, it's impressive to catch sight of Downtown Miami's shoreline and skyscrapers from the turquoise waters, showcasing just how truly tropical the city is.

Color Pop & Shop

MAP P212

Walk the Wynwood Walls

One of the most photographed locations in Miami (if social media hashtags are anything to go by), **Wynwood Walls** *(thewynwoodwalls.com; adult/child $12/5)* is a collection of murals and paintings laid out over an open courtyard that bowls people over with its exuberant colors and commanding

DOWNTOWN MIAMI'S BEST PARKS

Bayfront Park (p209): Downtown Miami's green heart spans 32 acres fronting Biscayne Bay. It has two performance venues, playgrounds and picnic areas.

Watson Island Park: Follow the MacArthur Causeway to this small park with grand views of Downtown Miami's spectacular skyline.

Brickell Key Park: Beautifully landscaped, waterfront park with picnic areas, palms and walking trails.

Maurice A Ferré Park: A 21-acre urban park featuring the longest waterfront bay walk in Miami, a jogging and strolling favorite.

Margaret Pace Park: Waterfront park on Biscayne Bay with basketball courts, picnic tables, outdoor gym equipment, playground and walking trails.

DRINKING IN MIAMI: PARTYING PICKS

MAP P210

Rosa Sky: Rooftop cocktail bar in Brickell with jaw-dropping views of the Downtown Miami skyline. *4:30pm-2am Tue-Sat, 2pm-1am Sun*

Blackbird Ordinary: Late-night drinking spot in Brickell with excellent cocktails that draw a neighborhood crowd. *3pm-5am*

Elleven: Multi-level club and social playground spread over 20,000 sq ft. Great cocktails and huge party vibes. *hours vary*

Sugar: Come for creative cocktails and Biscayne Bay views on the tropical rooftop deck of the EAST Miami hotel. *hours vary*

IMMIGRATION ICON AMID SKYSCRAPERS

Impossible to miss along Biscayne Blvd, the richly ornamented **Freedom Tower**, completed in 2025, is one of two surviving towers modeled after the Giralda bell tower in Spain's Cathedral of Seville. As the 'Ellis Island of the South,' it served as an immigration processing center for almost half a million Cuban refugees in the 1960s. Placed on the National Register of Historic Places in 1979, the tower houses the **Miami Museum of Art & Design** *(MOAD; moadmdc.org)*, with exhibits ranging from contemporary sculpture to historical photography. The tower and MOAD are scheduled to reopen to the public in late 2025 with a re-imagined visitor experience celebrating the tower's 100th anniversary.

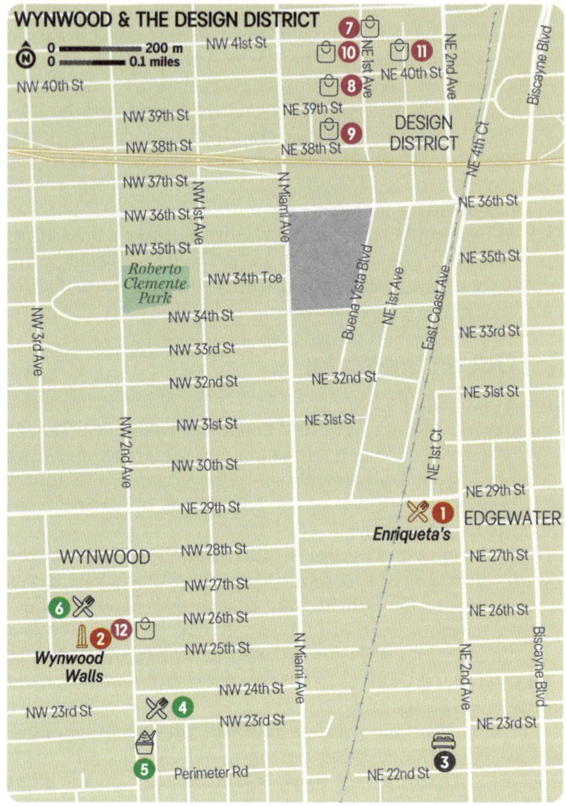

HIGHLIGHTS
1 Enriqueta's
2 Wynwood Walls

SLEEPING
3 Arlo

EATING
4 1-800-Lucky
5 Dasher & Crank
6 Zak the Baker

SHOPPING
7 Acne Studios
8 Alice + Olivia
9 GANNI
10 Golden Goose
11 Maison Francis Kurkdjian
12 Wynwood Walls Shop

EATING IN MIAMI: WYNWOOD

MAP P212

Enriqueta's: No-frills Cuban diner with daily specials, great Cuban sandwiches and coffee. *7am-3pm Mon-Fri, to 2pm Sat* $

1-800-Lucky: Miami's take on an Asian hawker market, with tons of street food and Wynwood neon to boot. *noon-1am Mon-Thu, to 3am Fri-Sun* $

Zak the Baker: Artisan and kosher bakery helmed by a Miami native, known for its pastries and BLTs on croissants. *7am-5pm Sun-Fri* $

Dasher & Crank: Quite literally churns out ice cream, ranging from passion fruit sorbet to (of course) mojito. *noon-11pm Mon-Thu, to midnight Fri-Sun* $

presence. What's on offer tends to change with the coming and going of major arts events, such as Art Basel, but it's always eye-catching, interesting stuff, and the energy that congregates around the Walls is buzzy and exciting. Depending on your worldview, the Walls are either a triumph of Wynwood's unwritten mission of bringing street-generated contemporary art to the masses...or a triumph of the commercial forces that have taken the creative energy of the street and repackaged it for conspicuous consumption. Are we thinking too hard about it? Maybe, but that's the point of art, right? In any case, if you want to take a little piece of the Walls home, pop into the on-site shop. You can also learn the spray paint basics and create your own piece of graffiti here with the **Wynwood Graffiti Experience** (*wynwoodartwalk.com; adult/child $42/34*).

The Soundtrack Goes Clickety-Clack

MAP P214

Doing Domino Park

Perhaps Little Havana's most evocative reminder of street life from Cuba is **Máximo Gómez Park** (*miami.gov; free*). More commonly called Domino Park, it's a tree-shaded, gated oasis on Calle Ocho. The big iron gates are open between 9am and 6pm daily. Regulars file in from around the neighborhood and across Miami, and the competitive banter and strategizing get going as cups of Cuban coffee are sipped. The sound of seasoned players trash-talking over games of dominoes is harmonized with the quick clack-clack of slapping tiles – though photo-taking tourists do give an odd spin to the experience, not that the players pay them any heed. In fact, they don't seem to mind people watching them at all – if anything, they feed off the crowd's energy.

The heavy cigar smell and a sunrise-bright mural of the 1994 **Summit of the Americas** add to the atmosphere. You might spend a few minutes here passing through or get sucked into watching a game for longer. The walkways around the park are decorated with domino-inspired tiles and there are benches where you can sit for a spell to soak up the ambience of it all in the shade. The neighborhood's cult ice creamery, **Azucar** (*azucaricecream.com*), is right across the street if all the spectating makes you peckish.

THE DESIGN DISTRICT'S BEST SHOPS

Acne: Italian leather and Japanese denim are among the elite raw ingredients in this cult Swedish atelier's stable.

Alice+Olivia: Women's clothing boutique known for designer denim and beautiful print dresses.

Golden Goose: There are sneakers, and then there is this beloved high-fashion Italian brand known for its emblematic star.

Maison Francis Kurkdjian: Pop in for a signature scent from this luxury French perfumery. Candles and scented body lotions round out the offerings.

GANNI: If it's cool enough for Copenhagen's cool girls, you'll find the Scandinavian fashion favorite here.

EATING IN MIAMI: LITTLE HAVANA

MAP P214

Sanguich de Miami: Gourmet takes on Cuban sandwiches have 'em lining up at this cult neighborhood spot owned by first-gen Cuban Americans. *10am-6pm* $

Old's Havana Cuban Bar & Cocina: Snag a table in the tropical garden of this Calle Ocho *cocina* to feast on *picadillo, ropa vieja* and *vaca frita*. *11am-11pm Sun-Thu, to midnight Fri & Sat* $$

Sala'o Cuban Restaurant & Bar: With live music every night, this Calle Ocho eatery does specialties like *rabo encendido* (oxtail). *noon-midnight Sun-Wed, to 2am Thu, to 3am Fri & Sat* $$

Versailles: Miami's not-to-miss Cuban restaurant on Calle Ocho, famed for sit-down feasts and walk-up window *cafecitos*. *hours vary* $$

VIERNES CULTURALES

Every third Friday of the month, from noon until late, **Viernes Culturales** (Cultural Fridays) turns Little Havana into a street festival celebrating art, music and culture. Expect live music on stage, and galleries open until 11pm to celebrate the neighborhood's creativity and *joie de vivre*. The action plays out in the **Little Havana Historic District** along Calle Ocho, between SW 15th and 17th Aves, and features cigar rollers, local arts and crafts for sale, *mucho* music and dancing under the stars. The event draws thousands of revelers – come ready for a good time, and you'll fit right in the mix.

HIGHLIGHTS
1 Máximo Gómez Park

EATING
2 Azucar Ice Cream
3 Old's Havana Cuban Bar & Cocina
4 Sala'o Cuban Restaurant & Bar
5 Sanguich de Miami

ENTERTAINMENT
6 Viernes Culturales

SHOPPING
7 Little Havana Visitors Center

Beauty at the Biltmore

MAP P215

Take a free tour of a grande dame

In the most opulent neighborhood of one of the showiest cities in the world, Coral Gables' **Biltmore Hotel** *(biltmorehotel.com)* has a classic beauty that seems impervious to the passage of time. Sure, you could book a room to fully bask in its beauty – or save some pennies and reserve a spot on one of the free tours of this National Landmark Hotel. Led by guides from the **Dade Heritage Trust** *(dadeheritagetrust.org; free)*, tours take place every Sunday at 2pm.

This elaborate hotel spans 150 acres, encompassing tropical grounds, tennis courts, a massive swimming pool, and a restored 18-hole golf course. Inside, you could spend a few days occupied by the many activities on offer. One example:

EATING IN MIAMI: CORAL GABLES & COCONUT GROVE

MAP P215

Coral Bagels: They are bagels, and they are cheap, and they are also very, very good at this family-owned shop. *7am-3pm* $

PLANTA Queen: This bright, beautiful queen is a vegan's dream, serving plant-based Asian-inspired fare. *hours vary* $$

Matsuri: Miami doesn't want for trendy sushi spots, but this strip-mall hideaway trades in the real deal. *hours vary* $$

Threefold Cafe: Cheerful cafe with Down Under vibes, espresso drinks, divine eggs Benedict and a memorable salmon salad. *7:30am-3pm Mon-Thu, to 4pm Fri-Sun* $$

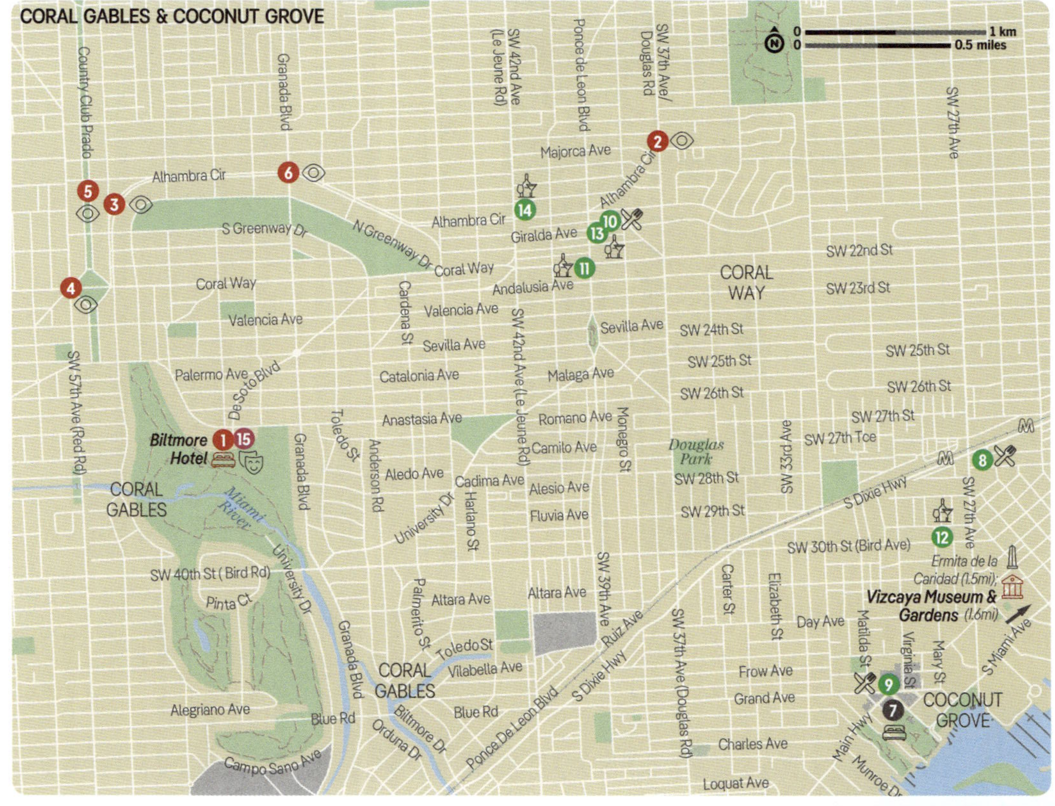

HIGHLIGHTS
1 Biltmore Hotel

SIGHTS
2 Alhambra Entrance
3 Alhambra Water Tower
4 Coral Way Entrance
5 Country Club Prado
6 Granada Entrance

SLEEPING
7 Mr C

EATING
8 Coral Bagels
9 PLANTA Queen
10 Threefold Cafe

DRINKING & NIGHTLIFE
11 Copper 29
12 Happy Wine in the Grove
13 The Bar
14 The Globe

ENTERTAINMENT
15 GableStage

GATES TO THE CITY BEAUTIFUL

Designer George Merrick planned a series of elaborate entry gates to Coral Gables, but a real-estate bust left many unfinished. It's a shame, as the gorgeous Gables deserve over-the-top entrances. Then again, the unfinished nature adds a timeless atmosphere... or maybe speaks to humanity's hubris? Either way, they look cool.

Among the completed gates worth seeing – many resembling and named after entrance pavilions to grand Andalusian estates – are the **Country Club Prado**, the **Alhambra Entrance**, the **Granada Entrance** and the **Coral Way Entrance**. Also notable is the **Alhambra Water Tower**, where Greenway Ct and Ferdinand St meet Alhambra Circle, which resembles a Moorish lighthouse.

FELIX MIZIOZNIKOV/SHUTTERSTOCK

GableStage *(gablestage.org)*, a local theater company, puts on thought-provoking contemporary works in an intimate venue at one end of the Biltmore – there's not a bad seat in the house.

Design-wise, there's nothing subtle about the grande dame's soaring central tower, modeled after Seville's 12th-century La Giralda. The showy grandeur continues inside, starting in the colonnaded lobby with its hand-painted ceiling, antique chandeliers, and Corinthian columns, and flowing into the landscaped courtyard set around a central fountain. Back in the day, gondolas transported celebrity guests like Judy Garland and the Vanderbilts around via a private canal system. Though the waterways are gone, the lavish pool remains.

Are there ghosts? The mobster Thomas 'Fatty' Walsh was gunned down by another gangster on the 13th floor, and some say his spirit still roams the hallways.

DRINKING IN MIAMI: CORAL GABLES & COCONUT GROVE

MAP P215

The Bar: Count on this spot to be divey, laid-back and big on cold brews and burgers. Very affordable, too. *3pm-3am*

Copper 29: Retro gastropub on the Miracle Mile with DJs, craft cocktails and bottle service for those who wouldn't have it any other way. *hours vary*

The Globe: A lively bar, Euro cafe undertones and Saturday-night live jazz make it a perennial pick. *hours vary*

Happy Wine in the Grove: Happy-hour tapas at this neighborhood spot go down even better when you have hundreds of wine labels on offer. *hours vary*

Biltmore Hotel (p214)

The Magic City's Magic Mansion

MAP P215

Go full golden age at Vizcaya

Back in 1916, industrialist James Deering started a Miami tradition of making a ton of money and building ridiculously grandiose digs. He employed 1000 people (then 10% of the local population) and stuffed his home with Renaissance furniture, tapestries, paintings and decorative arts.

You'll want a few hours to see all there is to see at **Vizcaya Museum & Gardens** (*vizcaya.org; adult/child $25/10*). The Coconut Grove mansion fronts Biscayne Bay and is a classic of Miami's Mediterranean-revival style. The largest room is the informal living room, sometimes dubbed 'Renaissance Hall' for its works dating from the 14th to 17th centuries. The music room is intriguing for its beautiful wall canvases from northern Italy, while the banquet hall's regal furnishings evoke the grandeur of European imperial dining rooms. On the south side of the house, a series of gardens, modeled after the formal Italian gardens of the 17th and 18th centuries, form a counterpoint to the wild mangroves beyond. Sculptures, fountains and vine-draped surfaces give an antiquarian look to the grounds, and an elevated **Garden Mound** terrace provides a fine vantage point over the greenery. You can access a free, informative audio tour by downloading the Vizcaya app.

A CHURCH WITH TIES TO THE ISLA

The Catholic diocese purchased some bayfront land from Deering's Villa Vizcaya estate and built a shrine here for its displaced Cuban parishioners. Built in 1967, **Ermita de la Caridad** is a beacon, facing the homeland, 290 miles due south, as well as a lighthouse for those Miamians who long for a land they may never have visited. This isn't the only way this church, Santuario Nacional de Nuestra Señora de la Caridad, engages with Cuba. A mural depicts the island's history, and a Spanish-language presence is the norm for the congregation. Outside the church is a grassy stretch of waterfront that makes a fine picnic spot.

Everglades & Biscayne National Park

WILD WETLANDS | GATORS GALORE | WATER ADVENTURES

GETTING AROUND

A car is essential for exploring Everglades National Park, with its far-flung entrances and sprawling terrain. From Shark Valley to Flamingo, most sites require driving, but once inside, you can explore by tram, bike, foot, canoe, or kayak – with rentals through park-approved vendors. Over at Biscayne National Park, it's all about the water – you'll need to book a guided boat tour to truly experience it. Most departures leave from the Dante Fascell Visitor Center, located near Homestead.

Stretching across South Florida, Everglades National Park is a vast, otherworldly wilderness of marshes, mangroves and slow-moving sawgrass sloughs. Whether by tram, bike, kayak or on foot, there's no wrong way to explore it. Shark Valley, about 40 miles west of Miami, offers a 15-mile paved loop perfect for tram rides, cycling and wildlife-watching. The Gulf Coast Visitor Center in Everglades City launches boat tours through the bird-rich Ten Thousand Islands. Near Homestead, Royal Palm provides easy-access trails and alligator sightings, while Flamingo, farther south, is a launchpad for paddling Florida Bay and camping under the stars. Just east of Homestead lies another natural marvel: Biscayne National Park. Though 95% underwater, it's a snorkeler and paddler's paradise, with coral reefs, shipwrecks and uninhabited keys offering a watery contrast to the Everglades' swampy sprawl. Together, these two parks show off South Florida's wild side – above the waterline and below.

Primordial Wilderness Vistas

Cycle or tram Shark Valley

A major destination for many visitors to the Everglades, **Shark Valley** *(nps.gov; pedestrian/motorcycle/car $20/30/35)* is named not for its marine life but rather its location at the headwaters of the little-known Shark River, which drains into the Gulf of Mexico. The big draw is the 15-mile paved loop trail that leads into Shark River Slough. You'll pass small creeks, tropical forest and 'borrow pits' (human-made holes now used as basking spots for gators, turtles and birdlife). Herons stalk prey along the water, and clouds shimmer like mirror images on the vast expanse of the River of Grass.

Closed to cars, the pancake-flat trail is perfect for bicycles. The halfway point is the spiraling 45-ft-high **Shark Valley Observation Tower**, a brutalist concrete structure with dramatic 360-degree views of the landscape. If you don't feel

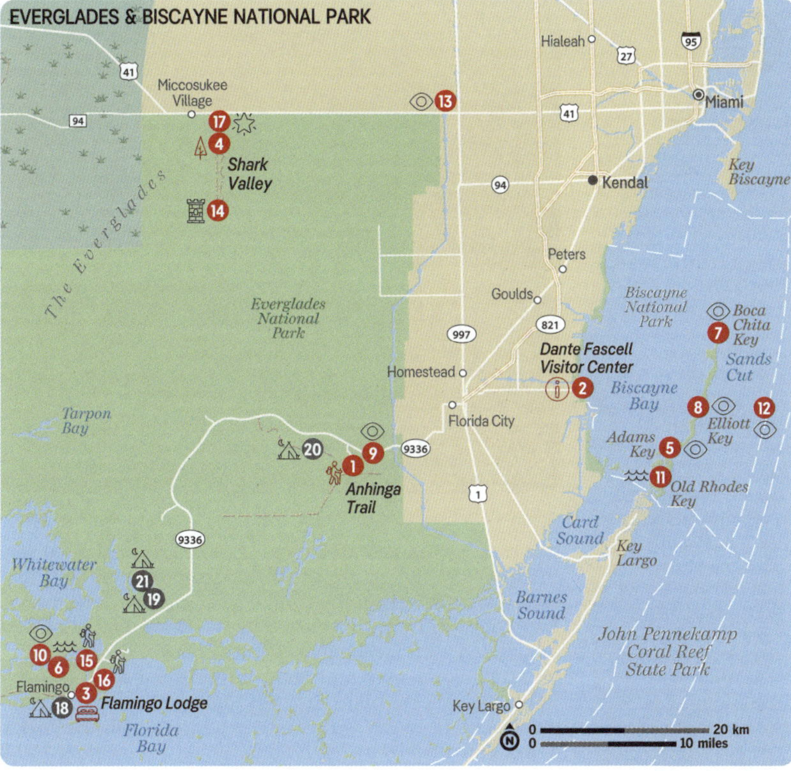

HIGHLIGHTS
1 Anhinga Trail
2 Dante Fascell Visitor Center
3 Flamingo Lodge
4 Shark Valley

SIGHTS
5 Adams Key
6 Bear Lake
7 Boca Chita Key
8 Elliott Key
9 Ernest F Coe Visitor Center
10 Homestead Canal
11 Jones Lagoon
12 Mandalay Shipwreck
13 Miccosukee Casino & Resort
14 Shark Valley Observation Tower

ACTIVITIES
15 Bear Lake Trail
16 Christian Point Trail
see 1 Gumbo Limbo Trail
17 Shark Valley Tram Tours

SLEEPING
see 7 Boca Chita Key Campground
see 8 Elliott Key Campground
18 Flamingo Campground
19 Lard Can Campsite
20 Long Pine Key Campground
21 Pearl Bay Chickee

INFORMATION
see 3 Flamingo Visitor Center
see 1 Royal Palm Visitor Center

TOP TIP

The culinary landscape is sparse in Everglades National Park. Snacks and drinks are available at visitor centers, but the restaurant at the Flamingo Lodge (p262) is the sole sit-down option. Your best bet is to stock up and pack a cooler in nearby Homestead, Florida City, Miami or near the Miccosukee Casino & Resort.

GUARDIAN OF THE GLADES

One of Florida's most beloved iconoclasts, Marjory Stoneman Douglas (1890–1998), fought to save the Everglades decades before conservation was mainstream. In 1947, the year Everglades National Park was established, she published her beautifully written classic *The Everglades: River of Grass,* a commercial success that helped shift public perception from 'infernal swamp' to 'national treasure.'

She continued writing and speaking about the threats posed by development and agriculture, and in 1969 (at the age of 79), founded Friends of the Everglades – a nonprofit that still plays a pivotal role in garnering political and financial support for restoration.

BLUEBARRONPHOTO/SHUTTERSTOCK

Anhinga Trail

like exerting yourself, the most popular (and painless) way to experience the Everglades is the two-hour tram tour that runs along the entire loop trail. If you only have time for one Everglades activity, this should be it – the guides are informative and witty, and you may spot alligators sunning themselves along the road.

You can reserve bikes or tram tours in advance (recommended in the busier winter months) through **Shark Valley Tram Tours** *(sharkvalleytramtours.com; adult/child $33/18)* at the visitor center. Plan to go early in the day to beat both the heat and the crowds.

An Overnight Serenade

Camp on an above-water chickee

Everglades National Park has two drive-in campgrounds, accessible via the Homestead entrance: the 274-site **Flamingo Campground** *(flamingoeverglades.com/campgrounds; per night $33-60)* and the 108-site **Long Pine Key Campground** *(flamingoeverglades.com/campgrounds; per night $33-60).*

And then there are chickees. What's a chickee, you ask? In Everglades-speak, it's a wooden platform built above the water where you can set up a tent. It's like having your own little island with seemingly endless horizon – sunrises and sunsets are unobstructed, and depending on the day, you may see gators coasting by, wading birds galore and frogs crooning you to sleep.

Most chickee sites are found near the **Flamingo Visitor Center** *(nps.gov/ever/planyourvisit/gbvc; per night $20-35).* You'll need a few things in addition to your camping gear: a backcountry camping permit (available at any park visitor center), bug repellent for the inevitable mosquitoes, and a canoe, since the platforms are only reachable by water. Canoes and kayaks can be rented from several spots around the park. Off the Hell's Bay Trail, a handful of chickee sites sit within a 5-mile paddle, including **Lard Can** and **Pearl Bay Chickee** *(nps.gov; $21, plus per person per night $2).*

Beaches, Boardwalks & Prairies

Check off quick hikes aplenty

You'll find fewer than three dozen trails in the entirety of Everglades National Park, many of which are short interpretive trails less than a mile long. Yet the trails you'll find are ones you won't soon forget. Regardless of where your Everglades hiking adventure takes you, you can be sure the route will be flat. Just make sure to pack sun-protective clothing, sunscreen and bug repellent for any Everglades hike to mitigate sun- or mosquito-related headaches.

For a moderate hike with a little history, **Bear Lake Trail**, located 2 miles north of the Flamingo Visitor Center in Homestead, is the top choice. Trickling alongside the trail, you'll see the **Homestead Canal**, which was constructed in 1922 to funnel freshwater from the marshland out to sea. The project's (dubious) goal? To create a drier piece of land for future development. The result? Just the opposite, as saltwater entered what had been a freshwater ecosystem, forever making a hybrid habitat in that portion of the park. The 3.3-mile trail features more than 50 different tree species, with hardwood hammocks towering above, culminating in a sweeping vista of **Bear Lake**, dotted with mangrove islands. Wear sturdy hiking shoes to navigate the thick grass patches and downed branches.

Christian Point Trail is for experienced hikers with its multifaceted terrain and takes upwards of three hours for the 3.2-mile experience. You'll find the trailhead 1 mile north of the Flamingo Visitor Center – and once you set out, you'll discover that the trail's difficulty stems from its jagged terrain, including thick mangrove patches and sporadic debris from hurricanes of yesteryear. A stretch of open prairie offers a welcome respite on dry days. If rain is in the forecast or the area has seen recent downpours, prepare for a muddy experience. Even the flattest prairies are a slushy mudfest, so bring the right pants and boots.

For families and a gentle saunter, the **Anhinga Trail** is 0.8 miles. This pristinely paved trail, with portions of well-kept and railed wooden boardwalks hovering over the marshland, is perhaps your easiest and best chance to see turtles and a hearty selection of the Everglades' bird species. To access the Anhinga Trail trailhead, venture to the **Ernest F Coe Visitor Center** *(nps.gov/ever/planyourvisit/coedirections)* in Homestead and head approximately 4 miles south to the **Royal Palm Visitor Center** *(nps.gov/ever/planyourvisit/royal-palm).* The trailhead is about 50ft behind the building. If you're itching for a bonus hike, the 0.4-mile **Gumbo Limbo Trail**, draped in massive hammock trees, is a stone's throw from the visitor center.

ALLIGATORS & CROCS COEXISTING

While Florida and the Everglades receive a lot of hype around the number of American alligators lurking below the surface of freshwater ecosystems, it's not so well known that American crocodiles are also native to the Sunshine State. In fact, this is the only place in the world where alligators and crocodiles coexist. Though it's less common to spot a crocodile due to their lower population and elusive habits, the lucky few who do differentiate the two by their color and snout. Alligators tend to be darker with broad snouts and only live in freshwater, while crocodiles are lighter with narrow snouts and can thrive in both fresh and saltwater environments.

LORE AMID THE LUSHNESS

There's no shortage of lore surrounding Everglades National Park. Its history and remoteness are the perfect backdrop to stories of mystery and paranormal activity. Al Capone was rumored to have made moonshine in the desolate Lost City. Hauntings have been reported on aircraft built with scraps from the Eastern Airlines Flight 401 crash. Several murders were allegedly committed by Ed Watson, an Everglades farmer, and townsfolk took justice into their own hands and killed him – his farm is said to be haunted. Today, you can backcountry camp at Watson Place, view memorials for plane crashes, and visit the now-abandoned, hard-to-find Lost City.

FRANCISCO BLANCO/SHUTTERSTOCK

Gliding Above & Below the Surface

Boating, kayaking and making a splash

Most travelers come for a day's adventure in **Biscayne National Park**, which could entail kayaking, snorkeling or island exploring. The Biscayne National Park Institute, located at the **Dante Fascell Visitor Center** *(nps.gov/bisc)*, offers a variety of excursions, all of which are best reserved in advance. Wherever you go in Biscayne, you're likely to see plenty of seabirds, from cormorants perched on mooring posts and flocks of brown pelicans flying in formation to steely-eyed osprey gliding just above the water. Pods of bottlenose dolphins zip across the horizon, while crabs and lizards scuttle among the roots of red mangroves along the water's edge.

The **Heritage of Biscayne cruise** *(biscaynenationalpark institute.org; adult/child $83/49)* takes you across the bay and past **Adams**, **Elliott** and **Boca Chita Keys**. Aboard this half-day tour, guides bring the islands' past to life, sharing stories of some of the people who lived here over the years. There was Israel Jones, an African American man who settled on Porgy Key in the 1850s and transformed it into one of South Florida's most prosperous key-lime and pineapple farms. His descendants were instrumental in helping preserve the islands for future generations (instead of taking a hefty payout from developers).

Industrialist Mark Honeywell, on the other hand, left his mark on Boca Chita Key. After founding his eponymous

Kayaking through mangroves

thermostat and home-heating company, he purchased the key as a holiday retreat, constructing an ornamental lighthouse and a chapel, and polishing up old Spanish cannons that were fired to welcome guests to the lavish parties he loved to host. The cruise typically stops at Boca Chita, where you can admire the views from atop the lighthouse, walk a short nature trail amid the mangroves and relax on the island's tiny beach.

For a closer look at the park's natural beauty, you can sign up for one of several **paddling tours** *(1½hr $39)*. Hidden between Totten Key and Old Rhodes Key, **Jones Lagoon** has calm, clear waters fringed by mangroves. After a 30-minute motorboat ride from the mainland, you'll hop onto a stand-up paddleboard (which offers better visibility of marine life than a kayak) and look for great blue herons, great egrets and roseate spoonbills as you glide silently along. In the aquamarine waters below, you might spy sea turtles, baby sharks, rays, upside-down jellyfish or sea stars.

Snorkeling trips *(3½hr $115)* offer you immersion in Biscayne's most biologically diverse ecosystem. On a half-day trip, you'll visit two different sites, exploring coral reefs, a shipwreck or a bayside mangrove, where you can see soft coral and sea sponges. Scuba-certified divers can opt for a six-hour trip with two **dives** *($298)*. There's also the option to explore half a dozen sunken ships on the park's Maritime Heritage Trail. Three of the vessels are suited for scuba divers, while the others, especially the **Mandalay**, a two-masted schooner that sank in 1966, can be accessed by snorkelers.

A PARTY ON STILTS

Stiltsville's history is shrouded in mystery, but it was once a hot spot for parties and socializing. The collection of wooden shacks on stilts, only accessible by boat, hovers above the water of Biscayne Bay. Stiltsville began when its original core shack was built in the 1930s, and in its heyday, it was home to as many as 27 buildings. Some were social clubs or fisheries, others weekend getaways. Only a handful remain due to the exposed location and havoc-wreaking storms. In 1985, the area became a part of Biscayne National Park. Use of the houses is by permit only, but the structures are preserved to highlight the park's marine resources and remain a reminder of the area's history.

Florida Keys & Key West

ISLAND-HOPPING | SUNSET CELEBRATIONS | QUIRKY CHARM

GETTING AROUND

Getting around the Florida Keys is best done by car, especially if you're exploring the full stretch from Key Largo to Key West. From Miami, Miami-Dade Transit's bus 301 reaches Key Largo in about 90 minutes, but beyond that, public transport options thin out. Most towns are compact and walkable, but a car or bike is best for reaching beaches, state parks and waterfront eateries. Rideshare services like Uber and Lyft operate throughout the Keys, though availability can dip late at night or during low season. Boat rentals and charters are also widely available.

TOP TIP

For a quieter sunset than Mallory Square, head to the pier at Fort Zachary Taylor Historic State Park. Bring a blanket and snacks to watch the sun dip into the Gulf with fewer crowds.

The Florida Keys stretch like a lazy smile across the southern tip of Florida, offering an island-hopping escape packed with natural wonders, fresh seafood and offbeat charm. While Key Largo greets you with mangroves and the coral treasures of John Pennekamp Coral Reef State Park, the journey only entices further as you follow the Overseas Highway south. Islamorada reels in anglers with world-class sportfishing and breezy waterfront bars, while Marathon has family-friendly beaches and dolphin encounters. Big Pine Key slows the pace with quiet nature trails and glimpses of the elusive Key deer. Then there's Key West – the irreverent, free-spirited finale where pastel streets, live music and historic homes channel tropical nostalgia and sunset celebration. Just 70 miles farther west, accessible only by boat or seaplane, lies Dry Tortugas National Park, home to 19th-century Fort Jefferson and pristine snorkeling waters. Together, the Keys deliver a sun-soaked, sea-sprayed adventure unlike anywhere else in the US.

Soaking up Scenery & Sun

Diving into the John Pennekamp Coral Reef State Park

John Pennekamp *(floridastateparks.org; vehicle $8, plus per person 50¢)* holds the distinction of being the USA's first underwater park. It includes 170 acres of dry parkland here and more than 48,000 acres (75 sq miles) of water – the vast majority of the protected area is ocean. Before heading out onto or into the water, be sure to enjoy the pleasant beaches and stroll the park's nature trails.

Three trails are short, flat and more educational than strenuous. The **Mangrove Trail** is a good boardwalk introduction to this ecologically awesome species (the trees, often submerged in water, breathe via long roots that act as snorkels). At a whopping 0.6 miles long, the **Grove Trail** is the longest and winds through tropical fruit groves that occasionally attract butterflies. If you're curious about the trees of the Keys, have

FLORIDA KEYS & KEY WEST

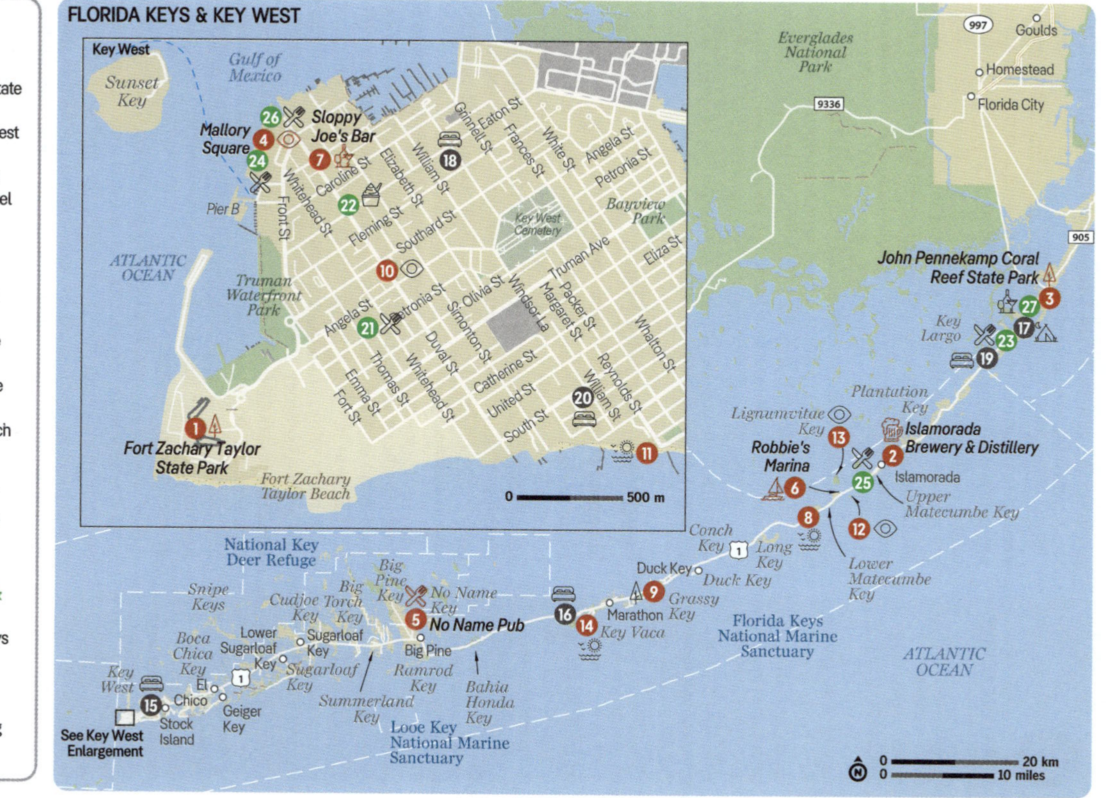

HIGHLIGHTS

1 Fort Zachary Taylor State Park
2 Islamorada Brewery & Distillery
3 John Pennekamp Coral Reef State Park
4 Mallory Square
5 No Name Pub
6 Robbie's Marina
7 Sloppy Joe's Bar

SIGHTS

8 Anne's Beach
9 Curry Hammock State Park
10 Duval Street
11 Higgs Beach
12 Indian Key Historic State Park
13 Lignumvitae Key Botanical State Park
see 13 Matheson House
14 Sombrero Beach

SLEEPING

15 Havana Cabana
16 Isla Bella
17 John Pennekamp Coral Reef State Park
18 NYAH Key West
19 Playa Largo Resort & Spa
20 Seashell Motel & Key West Hostel

EATING

21 Blue Heaven
22 Kermit's Key Lime Shoppe
23 Key Largo Conch House
24 Key West Original Conch Fritters
25 Lazy Days
see 2 Lorelei
see 19 Sol by the Sea
26 Sunset Pier

DRINKING & NIGHTLIFE

see 2 Florida Keys Brewing Company
27 Jimmy Johnson's Big Chill

CORAL BLEACHING

Coral reefs develop over thousands of years, with tiny reef-building coral polyps coming together and growing many layers of hard exoskeleton. Their color comes from the symbiotic relationship with zooxanthellae, a microscopic algae that live in coral tissue and produce food and oxygen for the coral. When water temperatures become too hot or coral gets stressed, it loses its zooxanthellae and appears white or bleached. If the coral goes too long without its main energy source, they can starve and die. Coral bleaching leads to larger issues, like loss of biodiversity and increased risks of coastal flooding. Widespread restoration efforts in the Keys continue to focus on preventing and repairing one of Florida's important natural resources.

a saunter around the **Wild Tamarind Trail,** where many of the hardwoods are labeled.

Stick around for nightly campfire programs. The **visitor center** is informative and well run, with a small saltwater aquarium and nature films providing a glimpse of what's below those waters. To really get beneath the surface, take a 2.5-hour, glass-bottom-boat tour aboard a catamaran to **Molasses Reef**, where you'll see filigreed flaps of soft coral, technicolor schools of fish, dangerous-looking barracuda and massive yet graceful sea turtles.

The park's most famous attraction is the **Christ of the Abyss**, a coral-fringed, 8.5ft, 4000-pound bronze sculpture of Jesus – a replica of one off Italy's Portofino Peninsula. On calm days, the park offers snorkeling trips to the statue, 6 miles offshore. You can also arrange diving excursions, which are obviously a big draw, or paddle through several miles of 'blue' trails among the mangroves.

Feed Very, Very Big Fish

Shopping at Robbie's and exploring beyond

Islamorada's scruffy jewel, **Robbie's Marina** *(robbies.com)*, covers all bases: it's a local flea market, tacky tourist shop, sea pen for tarpons (massive fish), waterfront restaurant and jumping-off point for fishing expeditions – all wrapped into one driftwood-laced compound. Boat rentals and tours are also available.

When you park, you'll first encounter the market section of Robbie's, showcasing crafts and art from around the islands. It's a good spot for picking up a unique piece of memorabilia. If folks aren't perusing paintings, they might be knocking back beers while enjoying the waterfront view. If it all feels like a bit of sensory overload, you can escape the bustle by renting a kayak *(kayakthefloridakeys.com; per day $50-60)* for a peaceful paddle through nearby mangroves, hammocks and lagoons. In fact, this is a major launch point for paddlers heading to Indian Key and Lignumvitae Key, two state parks accessible only by boat.

Now lonely and eerie, **Indian Key** was once a thriving town with a warehouse, docks, streets, a hotel and about 40 to 50 permanent residents. It was even the first seat of Dade County – now dominated by metro Miami, which is just a wee bit larger on the population scale. **Lignumvitae Key Botanical State Park** is a 280-acre island of virgin tropical forest ringed by alluring waters. The official attraction is the

EATING IN THE KEYS: OUR PICKS

Key Largo Conch House: Fresh seafood abounds at this waterfront restaurant. For an authentic Keys taste, start with conch fritters. *8am-9pm* **$$$**

Sol by the Sea: Opt for the 'water table' experience for sunset dining around a table in the water. *11am-10pm Mon-Fri, from 10am Sat & Sun* **$$$**

Lorelei: Relax and enjoy drinks, bites and live music on the Islamorada waterfront. Try the key lime peppercorn snapper. *7am-10pm* **$$**

Lazy Days: Take your pick of award-winning seafood and ocean-view dining: tables in the Islamorada sand, on the patio or indoors. *11am-10pm* **$$$**

HERITAGE TRAIL ROAD TRIP

Cruise the Upper Keys on the Overseas Highway. Pull off the road for biker bars, seafood grills and blissful beaches along the way.

START	END	LENGTH
Dagny Johnson Key Largo Hammock Botanical State Park	Long Key State Park	45 miles; 8 hours

How many of the 84 protected species of plants and animals – including the elusive American crocodile – can you count at 1 **Dagny Johnson Key Largo Hammock Botanical State Park**? Drive south next along the Overseas Highway to 2 **John Pennekamp Coral Reef State Park**. Stroll along the Mangrove Trail, a short loop adjacent to the park's paddling trail. After, whet your whistle at the 3 **Caribbean Club**, the oldest bar in the Upper Keys, just a six-minute drive from the state park.

As you make your way further south, satisfy your sweet tooth with a slice of authentic key lime pie at 4 **Blond Giraffe Key Lime Pie Factory**.

Down the road in Islamorada, pause to snap a photo with the 30-ft-high sculpture of Betsy the Lobster at 5 **Rain Barrell Village** and explore art by local artisans.

Following the highway further south brings you to the 6 **History of Diving Museum** where you can nerd out on the history of underwater exploration. After working up an appetite learning about diving, fuel up with craft bites and brews at 7 **Islamorada Brewery**. Keep it classic with a draft of the subtly citrus Sandbar Sunday or taste the Keys with the key lime and coconut-y No Wake Zone. Wrap up your road trip at 8 **Long Key State Park** with a geocaching session.

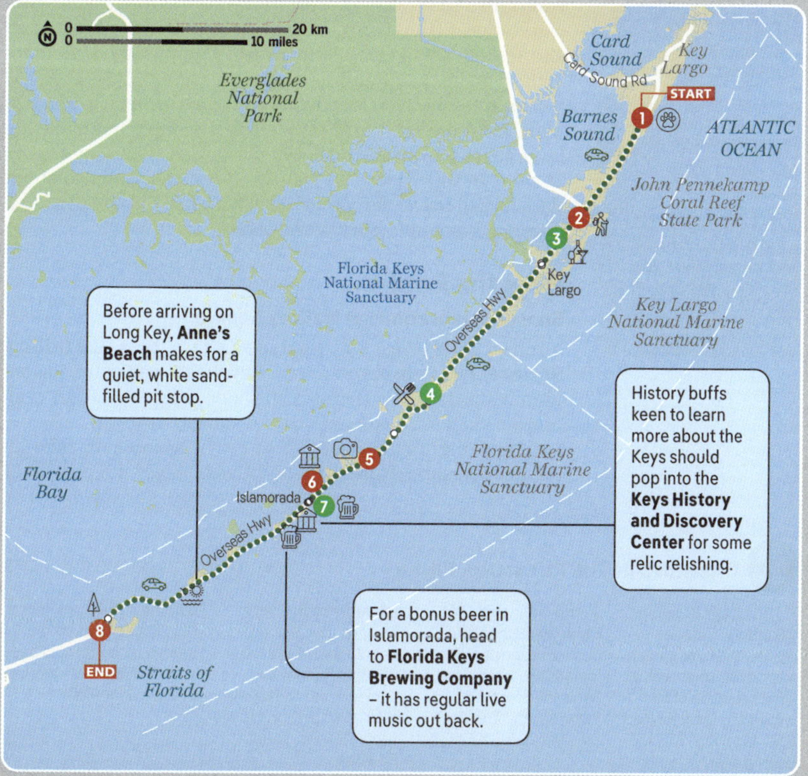

Before arriving on Long Key, **Anne's Beach** makes for a quiet, white sand-filled pit stop.

History buffs keen to learn more about the Keys should pop into the **Keys History and Discovery Center** for some relic relishing.

For a bonus beer in Islamorada, head to **Florida Keys Brewing Company** – it has regular live music out back.

BEST BEACHES IN THE KEYS

Anne's Beach: Family-friendly Islamorada beach with calm shallow waters, pavilions, a boardwalk and restrooms.

Sombrero Beach: This tranquil Marathon beach has shaded picnic spots, barbecue pits, a playground, volleyball courts and plenty of space to unwind.

Curry Hammock: Between Duck Key and Marathon, this park sports 1000 lush acres for outdoor adventures.

Higgs Beach: If Fido tagged along for your Keys adventure, this beach has one of Key West's best dog parks.

Fort Zachary Taylor Park: Beyond its historical allure, the park is a stellar spot for a swim in shallow, serene waters.

ERIKA CRISTINA MANNO/SHUTTERSTOCK

1919 **Matheson House** *(floridastateparks.org; $2.50)*, with a windmill and cistern; the real draw is the shipwrecked sense of isolation. Strangler figs, mastic, gumbo-limbo, poisonwood and lignum vitae trees form a dark canopy that feels more South Pacific than South Florida.

Back at Robbie's, you can also book a snorkeling trip and bob amid coral reefs. If you'd rather stay dry, feed the freakishly large tarpon from the dock ($3 per bucket, $2.25 to watch). 'Watch,' in this case, isn't just about the fish, but also about the shocked reactions of tourists when a fish the size of a large dog comes snapping out of the water.

Rays the Roof

Sunset celebrations at Mallory Square

A sunset in Key West is a visual spectacle in itself. At **Mallory Square** *(mallorysquare.com)* – Key West's epicenter, loaded with restaurants, museums and shops – nightly sunset celebrations kick off two hours before sunset.

No two nights are ever the same. In a nutshell, take all the energy, subcultures and oddities of Key's life and focus

DRINKING IN THE KEYS: OUR PICKS

Florida Keys Brewing Company: Colorful Islamorada beer garden and tasting room with a large selection of beer inspired by local flavors. *11am-10pm Sun-Thu, to 11pm Fri & Sat*

Jimmy Johnson's Big Chill: Sunsets and drinks don't disappoint at this famous Key Largo tiki bar named for the Hall of Fame coach. *11am-9pm Sun-Thu, to 10pm Fri & Sat*

Islamorada Brewery: Neon-yellow icon with popular brews like OG Sandbar Sunday and cocktails on tap featuring their own spirits. *10:30am-10pm Sun-Thu, to 11pm Fri & Sat*

No Name Pub: Legendary Big Pine Key pub off the beaten path with cold beer and a fish dip that can't be missed. *11am-10pm*

Mallory Square

them into one torchlit, family-friendly (but playfully edgy), sunset-infused street party. The result of all these raucous forces is cinematic and a bit tourist-clogged. The waterfront setting is magnificent, and food vendors often gather here. Among the oft-kitschy activities, you can watch a dog walk a tightrope, a man swallow fire, and British acrobats tumble and sass each other. The showmanship and camaraderie of the performers are matched by the crowd's energy and the fading light of day.

Then – lucky you – you'll find yourself right at the top of **Duval Street**, ready for the **Duval Crawl**. Duval is Old Town Key West's main drag, a conglomeration of neon and historic buildings. Its upper reaches are packed with bars and restaurants, while the southern end has more galleries and gift shops – though it certainly doesn't lack for bars and restaurants either. From Mallory Square, you'll want to pace yourself as two of Duval's biggest dive bars, **Hog's Breath Saloon** *(hogsbreath.com)* and **Sloppy Joe's Bar** *(sloppyjoes.com)*, are right there.

WHY I LOVE THE FLORIDA KEYS

Jesse Scott, Lonely Planet writer

I've called Fort Lauderdale home for nearly a decade. We have pristine beaches and stretches of world-class resorts. Honestly, a beach is the last place I want to vacation. But the Keys hit differently. Key West has a bohemian-historic vibe that is seldom found in South Florida and worth the jaunt. Talking to the story-filled locals fuels my soul. As do the ever-orange sunsets – a memorable one being a recent dinner with my wife at the Playa Largo resort. We sat at a 'water table' – literally a table anchored in shallow waters, noshing fresh ceviche and watching kids frolic on floating cabanas nearby. The Keys are a true escape, even if you're a local.

EATING IN KEY WEST: ICONIC SPOTS

Sunset Pier: The views from this spot, poised for best sunset dining, are undeniable. *11:30am-8:30pm* **$$$**

Key West Original Conch Fritters: Skip the sit-down meal and snag a classic Key West snack from this stand at the heart of Mallory Square. *10:30am-6pm* **$**

Kermit's Key Lime Shoppe: A popular place to relish all things key-lime flavored. The frozen, chocolate-dipped key-lime-pie bar is a hit. *10am-9:30pm* **$**

Blue Heaven: Customers (and free-ranging fowl) flock to dine on Caribbean fare in a ramshackle tropical garden. *8am-2:30pm & 5-10pm* **$$**

Southeast Florida

SUNNY BEACHES | LGBTIQ+ HOT SPOTS | WATER EXCURSIONS

GETTING AROUND

Getting around Southeast Florida is easiest by car, but alternatives abound – especially in urban areas. In Fort Lauderdale, skip pricey parking and hop on LauderGO! shuttles or the free electric Micro Mover to reach spots like Las Olas, downtown and the beach. In West Palm Beach, the free downtown trolley connects the waterfront with key districts. Brightline, a sleek high-speed rail, links Fort Lauderdale, West Palm Beach and beyond, making coastal travel a breeze. In Vero Beach, consider biking waterfront trails or strolling its walkable downtown.

Southeast Florida, stretching from Vero Beach to Fort Lauderdale, blends laid-back beach towns, vibrant cultural hubs and sun-soaked luxury into a scenic coastal corridor like few others. Once known as the raucous spring-break capital, Fort Lauderdale has gracefully outgrown its party-hard past. Today, it's a polished, palm-fringed city of yachts, waterfront dining and stylish hotels lining the A1A and well inland. With 300 miles of inland waterways and more than 50,000 registered yachts, it's earned nicknames like the 'Yachting Capital of the World' and the 'Venice of America.' But Southeast Florida doesn't stop here. Head north and you'll find West Palm Beach, where historic charm meets a buzzing arts and dining scene, particularly along Clematis St and in the Warehouse District. Further up, Vero Beach offers a quieter coastal retreat with white-sand beaches, elegant resorts and a small-town vibe that's long attracted artists and snowbirds alike. From glossy marinas to turtle-tracked shores, Southeast Florida delivers sun, style and evolving appeal.

Catch Some Rays

Enjoy the largest beach in Lauderdale

Fort Lauderdale's sandy shoreline, stretching for miles along the Atlantic, is conveniently sectioned into smaller portions, each radiating its own unique personality and flavor. The largest and most popular of the bunch is **Fort Lauderdale Beach**. It's swank and chic, targeted by Instagrammers. At its heart is **Fort Lauderdale Beach Park**, sporting volleyball and basketball courts, a playground, restrooms and showers. The promenade's always hopping with rollerbladers and joggers, while yoga groups stretch on the beach. Luxury hotels, surf-inspired stores and oceanfront restaurants abound, with plenty of parking *($6/hr)* nearby.

HIGHLIGHTS
1 Bonnet House

SIGHTS
2 Fort Lauderdale Beach & Promenade
3 Fort Lauderdale Beach Park
4 Hugh Taylor Birch State Park
5 Riverwalk

ACTIVITIES
6 Jungle Queen Riverboat

SLEEPING
7 Conrad Fort Lauderdale Beach
8 Snooze Hotel
9 The Grand Resort & Spa

EATING
10 Bohemian Latin Grill
11 Café Seville
see 8 Casablanca Cafe
12 Coyo Taco
13 Greek Islands Taverna
14 Heritage
15 MAASS
16 Mykonos
17 Southport Raw Bar
see 7 Takato
see 7 Vitolo

DRINKING & NIGHTLIFE
see 10 4:30 Boardroom Bar
18 Ann's Florist & Coffee Bar
19 Elbo Room
20 Georgie's Alibi Monkey Bar
21 Ramrod
see 16 Swizzle Rum Bar
22 The Manor
23 Wreck Bar

SHOPPING
24 Out of the Closet
25 Pride Factory

INFORMATION
26 Pride Center

TRANSPORT
27 LauderGO! Water Trolley

THE STINGING PORTUGUESE MAN O' WAR

Fort Lauderdale's beaches are generally considered safe, with lifeguards patrolling the most popular stretches. One thing to watch out for, though, is the Portuguese man o' war. This jellyfish-like creature is actually a species of siphonophore, and while usually not deadly, it delivers a painful sting. It resembles a small, blue-tinted plastic bag or balloon and can be found floating in the water or washed up on shore. If you see one, stay a few feet away: its long tentacles can still sting even after it's dead.

BRIAN LOGAN PHOTOGRAPHY/SHUTTERSTOCK

Bonnet House Museum & Gardens

Biking & Beaching

MAP P231

The hidden Hugh Taylor Birch State Park

One of the best-kept secrets in all of Southeast Florida, **Hugh Taylor Birch State Park** *(floridastateparks.org/hughtaylorbirch; vehicle $6)* is great for all things outdoors. Tucked between the ocean and intracoastal waters, it provides the best of both worlds. Bike the 2-mile Perimeter Trail, kayak through mangroves or sunbathe on hidden shorelines. The park is also accessible by the city's **Water Taxi** *(watertaxi.com; per day adult/child $38/18, after 5pm $25/18)*, departing from 11 stops in Fort Lauderdale and another 15 in nearby Pompano Beach and Hollywood Beach.

A Waterfront Stroll

MAP P231

Admire the Intracoastal Waterway

The Atlantic might steal most of the attention, but Fort Lauderdale is endowed with over 300 miles of inland waterways, too. Take in views of the New River with a stroll along the **Riverwalk** footpath, spotting historical homes, luxury condos and art sculptures en route. Allow a couple of hours to stroll the circular route or, if you succumb to the heat, hop aboard the free **LauderGO! Water Trolley**, which makes

EATING IN SOUTHEAST FLORIDA: FORT LAUDERDALE BEACH

MAP P231

MAASS: Fort Lauderdale's first Michelin-starred restaurant wows with contemporary American fare. *5-10pm Mon-Thu, from 11:30am Fri-Sun* $$$

Takato: Ocean views and pan-Asian dishes at Conrad Fort Lauderdale Beach. Pair duck bao buns with a lychee martini. *8-10:30am & noon-10pm Sun-Thu, to 11pm Fri & Sat* $$$

Vitolo: This high-end Italian restaurant has all of the classics. Don't miss 4pm to 6pm happy hour. *noon-10pm Sun-Thu, to 11pm Fri & Sat* $$$

Casablanca Cafe: Perfect date-night spot where the architecture and ocean views are as charming as the Mediterranean food is delicious. *hours vary* $$$

eight stops. Bicycle and Segway rentals are also available, but narrow paths and sharp turns present a challenge when it's crowded.

Water Taxis to Luxury Boats

MAP P231

Cruise the waterfront

Swap your walk for a cruise along Fort Lauderdale's inland waterways. The **Jungle Queen Riverboat** *(junglequeen.com; adult/child $31.50/21, parking $13)* offers 90-minute, fully narrated cruises showcasing homes of the rich and famous – an area dubbed 'Millionaire's Row.' For something more intimate, the locally owned **Rent a Boat Fort Lauderdale** *(rentaboat fortlauderdale.com; 4hr for up to 10 people from $400)* offers private deck boat and pontoon rentals, with or without a captain. The most affordable option is the **Water Taxi** *(watertaxi.com; per day adult/child $38/18, after 5pm $25/18)*, which provides lighthearted, narrated cruises around town between 10am and 10pm. Hop on and off at 10 different stops.

History & Nature Unite

MAP P231

An orchid oasis at Bonnet House

Bonnet House Museum & Gardens *(bonnethouse.org; adult/child $25/8)* is a plantation-style, oceanfront homestead. Its 35 acres of subtropical gardens feature one of America's most esteemed orchid collections. The buildings were designed by professional artist and self-taught architect Frederic Bartlett in the early 1920s. Frederic's second wife, Evelyn, deeded the property to a historical trust before her death in 1997 to secure it against greedy developers. Thanks to her, you can enjoy nature trails winding through five distinct ecosystems on the area's last bastion of undeveloped shoreland. (Watch for spider monkeys in the treetop canopies.)

LGBTIQ+ Hot Spot

MAP P231

Explore Wilton Drive

Wilton Drive (sometimes called 'The Drive') is abundant with queer-friendly restaurants, shops and watering holes. LGBTIQ+ nightclub **Georgie's Alibi Monkey Bar** *(alibiwiltonmanors.com)* is perpetually packed, while **The Manor** *(themanor complex.com)* is a glamorous club featuring flashy chandeliers and more bars than you can shake a stick at. Younger crowds often spill onto its second level.

If leather's your thing, you'll enjoy the raunchy cowboy vibe at **Ramrod** *(ramrodbar.com)*, a popular hangout since 1994, where patrons rock to edgy tunes in a medieval dungeon-style setting.

Eager to shop? Neighborhood thrift shop **Out of the Closet** *(outofthecloset.org)* sells size 12 stilettos and offers free HIV testing while you browse. You'll also find quite a selection of gay clientele-geared clothing around the corner at **Pride Factory** *(pridefactory.com)*.

CELEBRATE FLORIDA'S LGBTIQ+ CAPITAL

Despite the state government's push for anti-LGBTIQ+ legislation in 2023 and 2024, Fort Lauderdale remains a thriving LGBTIQ+ community and a popular queer holiday destination. LGBTIQ+ retirees and remote workers flock to Wilton Manors and neighboring Victoria Park, cementing its status as the hub for LGBTIQ+ nightclubs, bars, restaurants and social clubs. A rainbow-painted 'Love Wins' bridge welcomes visitors to Wilton Manors, where street lamps glow with artistic wire sculptures. The local **Pride Center** *(pridecenterflorida.org)* distributes information on area highlights.

But the LGBTIQ+ pride really comes to life during the **Greater Florida Pride Parade and Festival** *(pridefort lauderdale.org)*, with floats, costumes and a celebration of diversity and love.

GREAT LOCAL HANGOUTS

Captain Danny Grant, owner of Floridian Coastal Charters *(floridiancoastal charters.com)*, shares his favorite spots to eat and drink.

4:30 Boardroom Bar: Awesome saloon in the north entertainment district with strong drinks and a surf-skate-hot-rod-inspired setting. Free vintage car show Saturdays.

Bohemian Latin Grill: A friendly couple serving up the tastiest Latin food in town. They'll even deliver to your bar stool next door at the Boardroom Bar.

Southport Raw Bar: Locals love grabbing fresh oysters and a pitcher at this casual waterfront restaurant with tasty seafood.

Café Seville: Every dish is a winner, with traditional Spanish cuisine and great wine. Start with *gambas as ajillo* (garlic seafood dish) and *ensalada maite* (palm hearts). Reserve.

IAN G DAGNALL/ALAMY

A Fort Lauderdale Tradition

MAP P231

Elbo Room

Hopping since 1938, this famed two-level beach bar is the ultimate throwback. Immortalized in the 1960 film *Where the Boys Are,* it became a magnet for spring breakers and a rite of passage for an entire generation of college students. Today, the legendary **Elbo Room** *(elboroom.com)* – often called the world's best beach bar – might feel lonely and forgotten by day, but by night, it morphs into a loud, brash party zone. The crowds pack so tightly it's nearly impossible to reach the bar (cash only). Elbo Room may be showing some wrinkles, but it's unlikely this old-school favorite will ride into the sunset anytime soon.

Brunch with Swimming Mermaids

MAP P231

Showtime at the Wreck Bar

Frank Sinatra strutted the hallways at the historic **Wreck Bar** *(boceanresort.com/dining/the-wreck-bar)* when it opened in the 1950s at B Ocean Resort. The bar's nautical theme,

EATING & DRINKING: DOWNTOWN FORT LAUDERDALE

MAP P231

Mykonos: A Greek island-inspired riverwalk spot serving seafood and small plates. *5-10pm Sun-Thu, to 11pm Sat & Sun* **$$$**

Coyo Taco: Enjoy 50% off select tacos on Taco Tuesdays! Don't miss the incredible smoky cauliflower tacos. *11am-9pm Sun-Thu, to 11pm Fri & Sat* **$**

Swizzle Rum Bar: Feel the speakeasy vibes when you cozy up in a booth with the best craft cocktails in town. *6pm-2am Mon-Thu, to 3am Sat & Sun*

Ann's Florist & Coffee Bar: Grab lunch and flowers, plus floral-inspired drinks and snacks from the back bar. *8am-11pm Mon-Sat, 9am-9pm Sun* **$$**

Clematis Street

with its chiseled wood bar and briny decor, suggests you're in a 1600s Spanish galleon. But it's the aquarium portholes behind the bar that reveal some extraordinary sights: on Saturday and Sunday mornings, mermaids and mermen put on a magical, family-friendly show ($15 excluding food and drinks). Enjoy standard American brunch fare as they swim past. The mermaids also make brief appearances during Thursday and Friday dinners. For an adults-only (ages 21+) mermaid show, reserve a Saturday dinner show ($40 excluding food and drinks).

The Heart of West Palm Beach

MAP P236

A night out on Clematis Street

Stroll over to **Clematis Street** *(clematisstreet.org)*, a vibrant entertainment strip dripping in history. Henry Flagler, the founder of West Palm Beach, was florally obsessed, naming downtown streets after plants and flowers – in this case, a bright purple buttercup. During the day, the street isn't all that busy, with shops and midday restaurants being the primary draw. But when night falls, things turn up a notch.

TOP TIP

Avoid extra driving and parking fees by selecting accommodations based on what matters most. For beach access, stay at a hotel along AIA. For restaurants, nightlife and shopping, opt for a place near main corridors like Las Olas Blvd in Fort Lauderdale.

EATING IN SOUTHEAST FLORIDA: GREATER FORT LAUDERDALE

MAP P231

Heritage: Innovative takes on Italian favorites: think sweet-and-sour calamari and short rib masala pizza. *11:30am-3pm & 5-11pm Wed-Sun* $$

YOT Bar & Kitchen: Watch yachts sail by as you enjoy cinnamon buns and lobster rolls at this riverfront brunch hot spot. *hours vary* $$

Larb Thai-Isan: This casual Thai restaurant between Fort Lauderdale and Pompano Beach is beloved by visitors and locals alike. *11:30am-10pm Wed-Mon* $

Greek Islands Taverna: You can't go wrong at this family-owned restaurant, which offers perhaps the best Greek food in town. *11am-10pm Mon-Sat, from noon Sun* $$

MEET THE JAEGA PEOPLE

Prior to colonization, the Native American tribe known as the Jaega called West Palm Beach – and the rest of modern-day Palm Beach County – their home. They were hunter-gatherers who relied heavily on marine resources such as fish, shellfish and sea turtles, as well as skilled canoeists and traders.

Unfortunately, the Jaega people were decimated by European diseases and warfare in the 18th century, and there are no known descendants of the Jaega people today. However, their legacy lives on via the archaeological sites and artifacts found in Palm Beach County.

HIGHLIGHTS
1 Blind Monk

SIGHTS
2 Centennial Square
3 Clematis Street

SLEEPING
4 Hilton West Palm Beach
5 The Ben

EATING
6 Galley
7 Hullabaloo
8 Kapow Noodle Bar
9 Proper Grit
10 Spruzzo

DRINKING & NIGHTLIFE
11 Clematis Social
12 Juicy
13 Spazio

ENTERTAINMENT
14 Respectable Street

Clematis' trendy dining and drinking options have exploded, stealing attention from their flashy nightclub neighbors. The manga-themed **Kapow Noodle Bar** *(kapownoodlebar.com)* pairs artfully crafted drinks with contemporary pan-Asian bites. Next door at **Hullabaloo** *(sub-culture.org/locations/hullabaloo)*, musician-inspired cocktails are always a blast. Nearby, **Juicy** *(juicywpb.com)* is a popular spot known for using the highest-quality ingredients in its internationally inspired drinks, while rooftop bar **Spruzzo** *(spruzzowest palm.com)* offers panoramic views to go with its top-notch drinks and Mediterranean plates.

EATING IN SOUTHEAST FLORIDA: WEST PALM BEACH

MAP P236

Blind Monk: A classy, romantically lit tapas and wine bar. Pop in during happy hour for a chill and affordable night out. *5-10pm Mon-Sat* **$$**

Okeechobee Steakhouse: Florida's oldest steakhouse perfects Kansas City strip steak and key lime pie. *11:30am-10pm Mon-Fri, 4-10pm Sat, to 9pm Sun* **$$$**

Galley: Enjoy trendy bistro fare on an outdoor patio with an aromatic fire pit. Best smoky Old Fashioned cocktails around. *5-10pm* **$$$**

Proper Grit: Cozy and intimate. Try the hanging bacon and sticky citrus boar rib appetizers before your pick of flavor-bomb mains. *7am-10pm* **$$$**

Looking for live music? **Clematis Social** *(clematissocial wpb.com)* has long been the go-to spot, with its Billboard Hot 100 songs and large dance floor. Then, there's **Respectable Street** *(sub-culture.org/locations/respectable-street)*, known for its punk rock vibes, and **Spazio** *(lynoras.com/spazio)*, where EDM fans find their home. Last but not least, the free live-concert series **Clematis by Night** takes the stage at **Centennial Square** on Thursday evenings from 6pm to 9pm.

Spot Gentle Giants

MAP P236

Learn about magical manatees

After discovering that warm-water outflows from their Riviera Beach generating station attracted manatees in winter, Florida Power & Light opened an eco-discovery center to honor these gentle giants. **Manatee Lagoon** *(visitmanateelagoon.com; free)* provides educational exhibits and two levels of observation decks for visitors to view these docile sea cows – along with nurse sharks, sea turtles and other colorful marine life – as they swim freely through the Intracoastal Waterway. The best viewing is from November to March.

Stroll Through the First US National Wildlife Refuge

MAP P236

Explore the Pelican Island National Wildlife Refuge

Established in 1903 in Vero Beach to protect pelicans from feather hunters, **Pelican Island National Wildlife Refuge** *(fws.gov/refuge/pelican-island; free)* encompasses 5445 acres of protected water and land. With more than 218 species of birds, the area's a huge hit with bird-watchers. Almost 8 miles of nature trails lead walkers through multiple habitats packed with greenery and wildlife. Even better, the Centennial Trail is ADA-accessible, ending at an observation tower.

All of that said, bird-spotting can be difficult for newbie ornithologists, so consider a free guided tour. Taking place each Wednesday from January to April, these tram tours come with an expert local guide and a pair of binoculars. Call 772-581-5557 to reserve.

FLORIDA CITRUS PRODUCTION

It is widely believed that Spanish explorer Ponce de Léon introduced orange trees to Florida near St Augustine in the mid-16th century. It wasn't until 1763, however, that a man named Jesse Fish started the first commercial orange grove in the same area. For about 100 years, this grove – and many more – continued to thrive in the warm north Florida sun. But in the late 1800s, northern Florida was hit with devastating freezes, decimating most of the state's citrus crops. Some farmers left, while others migrated further south to the warm and soil-rich Indian River, where many of the world's best oranges are grown today.

EATING IN SOUTHEAST FLORIDA: VERO BEACH

Tres Hermanos: Hole-in-the-wall eatery in the back of a Mexican grocery store with incredible, authentic tacos. *7am-7pm Mon-Sat* $

Citron Bistro: Innovative American fare with a breezy patio and can't-miss weekend brunch. *11am-3pm & 5-8pm Mon-Sat, from 9am Sun* $$

Mama Hue: Unassuming strip-mall spot serving pan-Asian food. Must-try pad thai and tapioca dumplings. *10am-8pm Mon-Wed & Fri, from noon Sat & Sun* $$

Pepper & Salt BBQ: Under-the-radar BBQ restaurant known for tender, flavorful brisket – with a side of creamy mac and cheese, of course. *10:30am-3pm Wed-Sat* $$

Orlando & Walt Disney World®

STUNNING GARDENS | IMMERSIVE MUSEUMS | THEME PARK UTOPIA

GETTING AROUND

For the most part, you'll need a car to get around Orlando. There are some exceptions to the rule, like the adorable I-Ride Trolley on International Dr and the LYMMO bus in downtown Orlando. Rideshares are widely available in Greater Orlando and can be more economical. For a more sustainable option, Orlando has electric bikes and scooters (from $1 per ride) through Lime, Bird and Veo.

TOP TIP

Prepare for Orlando's heat, humidity and daily summer thunderstorms. Dress is typically casual in this Theme Park Capital of the World, so pack lightweight, breathable clothing, comfortable shoes, a rain poncho and a wide-brimmed hat to keep the sun off your face.

Most visitors to Orlando rarely venture beyond the fabricated worlds of Disney and Universal Orlando. Yet beyond the theme park thrills, the city of Orlando is home to several fantastic gardens and nature preserves, plus a delightfully slower pace.

Prior to 1965, when Walt Disney announced plans to build Walt Disney World®, Orlando had been a sleepy city. Its historic core, Old Orlando, is located along Church St between Orange and Garland Aves. Wetlands make up much of Greater Orlando, its landscape dotted with lakes, including the largest, Lake Apopka. The rainy season lasts from May to late October, and northern sunseekers flock during its delightful warm and dry season, from November through April. While the average visitor to Orlando spends their vacation indulging in theme-park food, locals know that just a few miles outside of these tourist attractions is a gateway to true Central Florida charm.

Black History & Culture

African American heritage at Wells'Built Museum

In the center of Orlando's historic Parramore district, the small **Wells'Built Museum** *(wellsbuilt.org; $5)* is dedicated to the city's African American history and culture. It's housed in the former Wells'Built Hotel, opened in 1926 by Dr William Monroe Wells to host African American performers forbidden from staying in the city's segregated accommodations. Count Basie, Cab Calloway, Billie Holliday, Ella Fitzgerald and Duke Ellington all spent a night under its roof. On the top floor, a hotel room remains frozen in time, complete with furniture and decor that would have greeted guests in the 1930s.

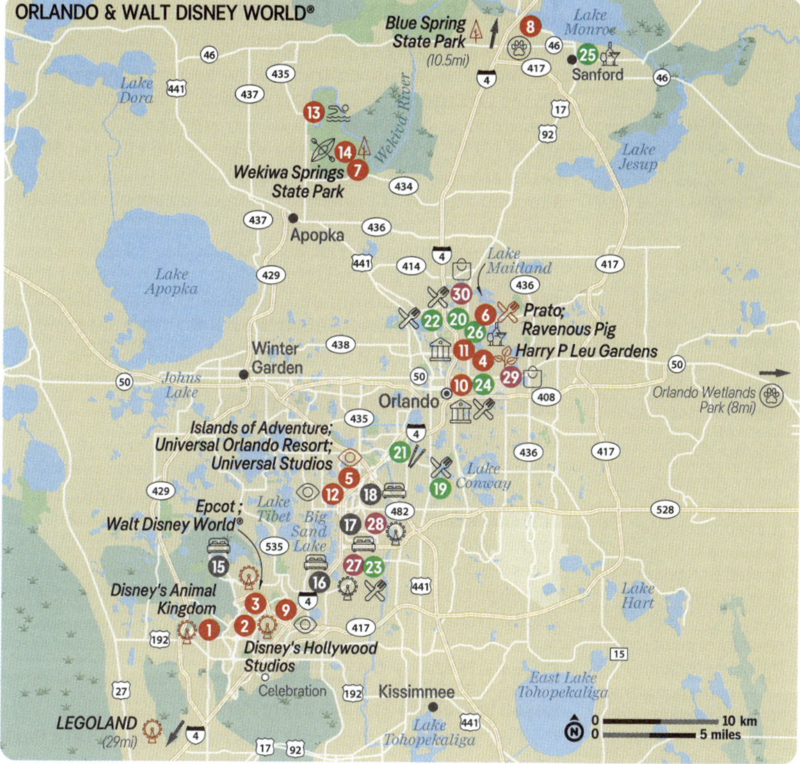

HIGHLIGHTS

1 Disney's Animal Kingdom
2 Disney's Hollywood Studios
3 Epcot
4 Harry P Leu Gardens
5 Islands of Adventure
6 Prato
see 6 Ravenous Pig
see 5 Universal Orlando Resort
see 5 Universal Studios
see 3 Walt Disney World®
7 Wekiwa Springs State Park

SIGHTS

8 Central Florida Zoo & Botanic Gardens
9 Disney Springs
10 Orange County Regional History Center
11 Orlando Science Center
see 5 Universal CityWalk
12 Volcano Bay
see 10 Wells' Built Museum

ACTIVITIES

13 Kelly Park
14 Nature Adventures

SLEEPING

see 6 Alfond Inn
see 12 Cabana Bay Beach Resort
15 Disney's Polynesian Village Resort
see 10 Grand Bohemian Hotel
16 Hilton Garden Inn Lake Buena Vista
17 Rosen Inn at Pointe Orlando
18 Villatel Orlando Resort

EATING

19 Bombay Street Kitchen
see 17 Gordon Ramsay Fish & Chips
20 Hunger Street Tacos
21 Isan Zaap
22 Mediterranean Deli
see 17 Ole Red
23 Selam Ethiopian & Eritrean Cuisine
24 Swine & Sons

DRINKING & NIGHTLIFE

see 17 Icebar
see 24 Otto's High Dive
25 Suffering Bastard
26 The Courtesy

ENTERTAINMENT

see 15 Magic Kingdom
27 SeaWorld
see 17 Orlando Eye
28 Universal Epic Universe

SHOPPING

29 Atomic Horror
30 Bossa N' Roll Records
see 6 Frank
see 6 Gasp
see 6 Winter Park Farmers' Market

WHY I LOVE BLUE SPRINGS STATE PARK

Sarah Etinas, Lonely Planet writer

Don't get me wrong – I love the Orlando theme parks as much as the next person, but there's something special about Florida's springs. Sitting pretty at around 72°F year-round, these crystal-clear, turquoise springs, framed by Spanish moss–laden cypress trees, are natural masters of color and composition. Of all of the publicly accessible springs in the Greater Orlando area, Blue Springs State Park is my personal favorite. Each winter, it's easy enough to check the park's Facebook page for an update on the daily manatee count – the number occasionally reaches 400 – and drive on over for an afternoon watching the manatees float on by.

Take a Spin above Orlando

Board the Orlando Eye at ICON Park

The most eye-catching attraction on the famed International Dr, the **Orlando Eye** *(iconparkorlando.com/attractions/the-orlando-eye-at-icon-park; adult/child $30/25)* rises 400ft above ICON Park, from where views of the city and theme parks are spectacular. The massive Ferris wheel rotates in about 20 minutes. Connect to the free, in-capsule Bluetooth, and open any music player on your device for an insightful narrative on the history of Central Florida.

Back on the ground, take some time to roam around ICON Park's shopping, dining and nightlife options – including famous chef **Gordon Ramsay's Fish & Chips** spot and the Blake Shelton–owned country-music venue **Ole Red**.

Say Hello to Wild Manatees

Welcome to Blue Spring State Park

Blue Spring State Park *(floridastateparks.org; vehicle $6)* has incredible opportunities for swimming, kayaking, tubing and snorkeling. But what sets this spring apart is manatees. In the colder months of the year (November to March), manatees flock to the 72°F waters of Blue Spring State Park for warmth. On some days, you might see over 500 manatees lazing around in its turquoise waters.

Dust off Your Paddling Skills

Kayak in Wekiwa Springs State Park

Cool off in emerald springs at **Wekiwa Springs State Park** *(floridastateparks.org/parks-and-trails/wekiwa-springs-state-park; vehicle $6),* about 20 miles northwest of downtown Orlando in Apopka. Spot some of the 190 species of birds recorded here while hiking miles of trails meandering through woods, swamplands and along the banks of the Wekiva River.

You can rent a kayak or canoe from **Wekiwa Springs Adventures** *(wekiwaspringsadventures.com; 2hr from $40)* to paddle the scenic, still waters. It's actually possible to kayak 8.5 miles from the state park, through neighboring **Rock Springs Run State Reserve** *(floridastateparks.org; vehicle $3),* into **Kelly Park** *(ocfl.net; vehicle $3).* Along the way, enjoy the beauty of the turquoise waters and the fairytale-like, Spanish moss–laden trees, all while keeping an eye out for birds, fish, turtles, and the occasional alligator. Be sure to arrive early, as parking regularly reaches maximum capacity.

EATING IN ORLANDO: CHEAP EATS

Bombay Street Kitchen: Casual Indian spot known for great food and value. Don't miss the kale chaat and street special dosa. *11:30am-3pm & 5-10pm* $

Swine & Sons: Fill up on Southern comfort classics like breakfast biscuits, fried pickles and spicy fried chicken sandwiches in Winter Park. *hours vary* $

Mediterranean Deli: Greek sandwiches here are affordable and flavor-packed. *10:30am-5:30pm Mon-Sat* $

Isan Zaap: Delicious northeastern Thai cuisine, with dishes like *som tum* (Thai papaya salad) and *laab* (minced pork). *11:30am-10pm* $$

TOP EXPERIENCE

Walt Disney World®

Where else can you dine in a castle, race through space and shake hands with a mouse in one day? Walt Disney World® is a storytelling spectacle with four theme parks, two water parks and a slew of hotels, restaurants and entertainment all working to make magic. From nostalgic rides to cutting-edge attractions, it's a choose-your-own-adventure playground for kids, grown-ups and superfans.

Fireworks at Disney's Magic Kingdom

Themed Lands, Legendary Rides

Start with Cinderella Castle at **Disney's Magic Kingdom®**, where fairy tales come to life and fireworks dazzle nightly. Over at **EPCOT®**, it's a race through the cosmos on *Guardians of the Galaxy: Cosmic Rewind* or a stroll through 11 countries in World Showcase. **Disney's Hollywood Studios®** delivers *Star Wars* drama and *Toy Story* whimsy, while **Disney's Animal Kingdom®** pairs thrills with wildlife encounters, from Everest coasters to jungle safaris.

Getting Around

Spanning 47 sq miles, Walt Disney World Resort is a city unto itself. Hop between parks by Monorail, Disney Skyliner, water taxi or bus. Rideshares and Minnie Vans offer extra convenience, but driving remains popular – just factor in time to transfer from parking areas to park gates.

Beyond the Parks

Shopping and dining districts like **Disney Springs®** tempt with Cirque du Soleil shows, chef-driven restaurants and one-of-a-kind shops. At resort hotels, you'll find everything from African savannas with roaming giraffes to poolside Polynesian luaus.

TOP TIPS

- Arrive early or stay late to enjoy cooler temps and lighter crowds.
- Lightning Lane passes save major time on high-demand rides.
- For the best castle fireworks view, claim a Main Street spot at least 30 minutes early.

PRACTICALITIES

- disneyworld.disney.go.com
- 9am-10pm
- prices vary

BEST BOUTIQUES & SHOPPING IN ORLANDO

Winter Park Farmers' Market: Shop for local goods like cheeses, flowers, baked goods and produce at this Saturday morning market.

Gasp: Winter Park boutique selling stationery, accessories and home decor from artists and creators. Girly-pop core at its finest.

Frank: Gift shop in Winter Park showcasing curated goods like precious-stone jewelry and coconut wax candles.

Bossa N' Roll Records: Leaning into old-school Orlando, this Maitland store boasts a well-curated vinyl selection.

Atomic Horror: A haven for horror enthusiasts in Baldwin Park with memorabilia and merch from horror film franchises.

Stroll a Flora-Filled Oasis

Take in Harry P Leu Gardens

Stroll the 50-acre **Harry P Leu Gardens** *(leugardens.org; adult/child $15/10),* an impressive botanical oasis just minutes from downtown Orlando. The plant collection includes primitive cycads, bright red hibiscus and almost 400 species of palm trees. The citrus grove's 50 different kinds of citrus trees highlight Florida's agricultural bounty, while a native wetland garden attracts wading birds and other wildlife. Tours of the 18th-century **Leu House** run every 30 minutes: former owner Mary Jane Leu loved roses, and her collection of old garden roses (those existing before 1867) forms the most extensive formal rose garden in Florida. Bring provisions for a lakeside picnic.

Say Hello to Wildlife in the Wild

Birding in the Orlando Wetlands

The artificial **Orlando Wetlands Park** in Christmas, about 30 miles east of downtown Orlando, was designed to provide advanced treatment for reclaimed water. An education center houses seasonal exhibits that include live animals and interactive displays. From the center, set off on the 2-mile **Birding Loop**, one of many trails that wind through the park. Not all trails are open to cyclists, but many are accessible for horseback riders. Be cautious of alligators on the trails – they're especially attracted to the sun-warmed, lime-rock surfaces that line many trails.

A Colorful World Built with Iconic Bricks

LEGO's relaxed theme-park experience

Manageable crowds and lines, interactive and educational exhibits, a fun, colorful backdrop and a water park make **LEGOLAND** *(legoland.com/florida; adult/child under 2 from $74/free)* a fantastic destination for families looking for a more stress-free vacation.

Located in Winter Haven, about 50 miles southwest of downtown Orlando, LEGOLAND has attractions geared toward children aged two to 12. At **Ford Driving School**, kids can drive cars through a pretend town, while **Miniland** is a grand LEGO-made model of iconic American landmarks and cities. Don't miss the **Imagination Zone**, an interactive learning

DRINKING IN ORLANDO: OUR PICKS

The Courtesy: Speakeasy vibes and crafted drinks at Greater Orlando's first cocktail bar. *4pm-midnight Tue-Thu, to 1am Fri & Sat, to 10pm Sun*

Suffering Bastard: Savor tropical cocktails at this tiki bar in the Sanford suburb. *5-10pm Wed, Thu & Sun, to midnight Fri & Sat*

Otto's High Dive: Known more for its rum than cuisine, the guava pastelito and coquito cocktails are incredible. *4pm-midnight Tue-Sat, 11am-10pm Sun*

Icebar: Sit on an ice-cold seat and sip icy drinks at this out-of-the-ordinary ice bar. *5pm-midnight Mon-Thu, to 2am Fri & Sat, to 1am Sun*

TOP EXPERIENCE

Universal Orlando Resort™

Welcome to the ultimate movie-lovers' playground, where rides, lands and shows bring blockbusters to life. Universal Orlando Resort features three epic theme parks – Universal Studios Florida™, Islands of Adventure™ and Epic Universe™ – plus splash-filled Volcano Bay™ and Universal CityWalk™. From dodging dinosaurs to casting spells or racing Mario, it's nonstop action and storytelling at every turn.

How to Train Your Dragon, Isle of Berk

Movie Magic in Every Direction

Universal Studios is where the silver screen springs to life. Race alongside Harry Potter through Gringotts, laugh with the Minions and blast aliens with Men in Black. Grab a Butterbeer in Diagon Alley or spot the fire-breathing dragon atop the wizarding bank. Over at Islands of Adventure, ride the Jurassic World VelociCoaster, soar with Spider-Man or brave Hagrid's Magical Creatures Motorbike Adventure. Don't skip E.T. Adventure – a charming classic still loved today.

Brand-New Worlds Await

The 2025 debut of Epic Universe introduced five new lands. Highlights include Super Nintendo World, complete with Mario Kart races, and Dark Universe, a moody realm of reimagined monsters. The Isle of Berk invites *How to Train Your Dragon* fans to soar through the sky, while the Wizarding World's Ministry of Magic blends 1920s Paris with wizard-filled London. Celestial Park, the park's radiant hub, offers intergalactic rides and a futuristic promenade.

Soak, Stroll & Snack

Cool down at Volcano Bay, a tropical water park with slides, splash pads and the Krakatau Aqua Coaster – all accessed with wristbands that hold your place in line. Come evening, unwind at CityWalk with mini golf, global eats, cocktails and entertainment. It's also the easiest way to walk between parks.

TOP TIPS

- Stay at a Universal Premier Hotel to receive complimentary Express Passes (a serious time-saver).
- Catch the Hogwarts Express between parks – it's different each way, and you'll need a park-to-park ticket.
- Arrive 30 minutes before park opening and head straight to Hagrid's or Mario Kart.

PRACTICALITIES

- universalorlando.com
- tickets from $119
- generally 9am–9pm

ORLANDO FAMILY ATTRACTIONS

Jeff Stanford, Orlando local and VP of Marketing at Orlando Science Center (*osc.org*), shares his favorite family attractions.

Orlando Science Center: There's something for kids of all ages...exhibits for infants and toddlers, dinosaurs and live animals for young kids, a Maker's Space and a giant-screen theater for teens.

Central Florida Zoo & Botanic Gardens: Besides animals, they've got a train, ziplines and merry-go-rounds. It's big enough to spend the day, but small enough to feel like an intimate experience.

Orange County Regional History Center: There's more to Orlando than theme parks. The OCRHC is a nice spot to learn about Orlando's history.

DOUBLE2A/SHUTTERSTOCK

LEGOLAND (p242)

center where skilled LEGO builders are on hand to help children of all ages build their next block masterpiece.

An Emphasis on Conservation & Sustainability

Consider the new SeaWorld Orlando

SeaWorld *(seaworld.com/orlando; adult/child under 2 from $143/free)* is one of the largest theme-park franchises in Orlando. When the 2013 documentary *Blackfish* was released, alleging SeaWorld's mistreatment of its captive orcas, things took a turn, both in visitor numbers and in SeaWorld's practices. Today, SeaWorld Orlando works hard on education and conservation, rehabilitating hundreds of marine animals and implementing sustainable practices across its Orlando parks.

Oddly enough, SeaWorld Orlando is also making a name for itself in the thrill-ride world with ocean-themed roller coasters like Mako and Pipeline. SeaWorld Orlando's water park **Aquatica** *(2-day combined ticket with SeaWorld adult/child under 2 $215/free)* holds its own, too.

EATING IN ORLANDO: OUR PICKS

Hunger Street Tacos: This spot is a contender for Greater Orlando's best tacos. The brisket or fried avocado tacos are top-notch. *11:30am-8pm Mon-Sat* **$$**

Selam Ethiopian & Eritrean Cuisine: From lentil samosa starters to the concluding coffee ceremony, Selam is a treat. *noon-9pm Mon, Wed & Thu, to 10pm Fri-Sun* **$$**

Ravenous Pig: Innovative takes on locally sourced American gastropub fare. The restaurant is a long-time local favorite. *hours vary* **$$**

Prato: Modern takes on Italian classics, celebrating local and sustainable ingredients. Don't miss the meatball appetizer. *hours vary* **$$$**

Space Coast

ASTRONAUTS | BEACHES | UNTAMED REFUGE

Florida's Space Coast is where cosmic dreams and coastal charm reign. Titusville and Kennedy Space Center form the epicenter of interstellar intrigue, a place where you don't just watch rockets launch, you feel them shake the earth. Since NASA planted its flag here in 1958, this stretch of Merritt Island has been launching missions, telescopes and imaginations skyward. But there's more to the region than space-age feats. Cape Canaveral is home to active launchpads, pristine beaches and the scenic Canaveral National Seashore. Just south, Cocoa Village adds a dose of vintage Florida with walkable streets, galleries, waterfront dining and a healthy dose of small-town soul. Nature and technology coexist here: one minute you're kayaking among manatees in the Indian River Lagoon, the next you're walking beneath a Saturn V rocket. Whether you're here for liftoffs, lattes or lagoons, the Space Coast delivers a down-to-earth adventure with out-of-this-world appeal (literally).

GETTING AROUND

There's considerable distance between the space attractions and the surrounding wildlife refuge and national seashore, so you'll definitely want your own car to explore. If you're coming over from Orlando for the day, **Gray Line Orlando** *(graylineorlando.com)* offers round-trip sightseeing excursions from Disney, Kissimmee and Orlando to Kennedy Space Center Visitor Complex aboard comfortable buses.

Secrets of Space Travel

Stratospheric fun at Kennedy Space Center

No visit to the Space Coast is complete without spending several hours – or a couple of days – at ground zero for America's space program, **Kennedy Space Center Visitor Complex** *(kennedyspacecenter.com; adult/child $75/65)*, where decades of interstellar history has been made. Part of a working launch facility, this popular attraction offers something for anyone who's ever stared at the sky and wondered.

Embark on the 90-minute bus tour (included with admission) for close-as-you-can-get views of launch facilities (unless you're an astronaut) and the massive Vehicle Assembly Building (the world's largest one-story building, its 465ft-high doors also the largest in the world). Tours stop at the Apollo/Saturn V Center, where you'll see the largest rocket ever flown (one of just three remaining), which transported astronauts to the moon, and many other Apollo mission artifacts.

TOP TIP

Looking for an epic spot to watch space launches? Head to **Scobie Park** in Titusville, a postage-stamp-sized park across from NASA's launching pads. Two Hi-Spy viewing machines are at your disposal for even closer views – free of charge! Download the Next Spaceflight *(nextspaceflight.com)* app for up-to-date launch schedules.

HIGHLIGHTS
1 Crydermans Barbecue
2 Dixie Crossroads
3 Fat Snook
4 Kennedy Space Center
5 Merritt Island National Wildlife Refuge
6 Pompano Grill

SIGHTS
7 Cocoa Riverfront Park
8 Jetty Park
9 Scobie Park

ACTIVITIES
10 Island Watercraft Beach Rentals

SLEEPING
11 Beachside Hotel & Suites
12 Courtyard Titusville Kennedy Space Center
see 12 Hyatt Place Titusville/Kennedy Space Center
see 8 Jetty Park Campground

EATING
13 Café Margaux
14 Fishlips Waterfront Bar & Grill
15 Flavour Kitchen & Wine Bar
16 Milpa Tacos y Tortillas
17 Orleans Bistro & Bar
18 Pier 220 Seafood & Grill
see 9 Tree of Life Cuban Bakery

DRINKING & NIGHTLIFE
19 Coconuts on the Beach
20 Ellie Mae's Tiki Bar
21 Rikki Tiki Tavern
22 Village Bier Garten
23 Wine Lady

SHOPPING
24 Antilles Trading Company
25 Antiques & Collectibles Too
26 Carolyn Seiler Studios

TRANSPORT
27 Port Canaveral

Or perhaps taking in a movie at the IMAX Theater and catching some thrills aboard one of four immersive rides at Gateway: The Deep Space Launch Complex – starring the awesome Red Planet ride that takes you to Mars – is more your speed.

Immerse yourself in deeply cerebral experiences, from the US Astronaut Hall of Fame's films and multimedia exhibits to touring the actual Space Shuttle Atlantis that's on display. For goosebumps and an adrenaline rush, board the immersive Shuttle Launch Experience or Spaceport KSC flight simulators. Kids (ages two to 12) enjoy space-themed activities at Planet Play, while exhausted parents enjoy a drink at its bar lounge. You can even meet NASA astronauts, hearing all about their training and experiences during daily scheduled Astronaut Encounters – just be sure to check the center's event calendar in advance if you've got your heart set on meeting a certain someone. Pet kennels are available on-site (with proof of vaccinations).

A Perfect Beach Day

Great surf and pristine sands in Jetty Park

More than your average park, fabulous **Jetty Park** *(shop.portcanaveral.com; day pass $15)* is a 35-acre oasis located on the water's edge right in **Port Canaveral**. While it's perfect for enjoying a beautiful day at the beach, watching cruise ships pass by, some extend their visit by camping in a tent or RV under star-filled skies at its excellent on-site campground.

Day passes must be bought online in advance, as no payment is accepted at the gate. Pets are only permitted with registered campers.

When there's a launch scheduled from Cape Canaveral – which happens regularly these days – views from the park's golden strip of beach and 1200ft-long fishing pier are as good as they get for watching rockets blast off over the Atlantic.

The sloping sandbar just offshore makes Jetty Park a popular surf break for consistent wave action, and you'll usually find a gaggle of surfers scanning the horizon, waiting for a behemoth to roll in. If you're tempted to paddle out, you can rent boards from **Island Watercraft Beach Rentals** *(islandwatercraftbeachrentals.com)*, which also offers umbrellas, chairs, kayaks and other beach-day essentials.

When the fishing pier isn't closed due to hurricane damage and refurbishments, you'll find throngs of anglers trying to hook red fish, jack, Spanish mackerel and more.

WHERE TO WATCH A LAUNCH

Chris Eckles, who works in the commercial space industry on Cape Canaveral, shares locations he loves for catching a launch.

Westgate Cocoa Beach Pier: It's hard to beat a perch over the ocean at the tiki bar at the end of the pier, something frosty in hand, while scoping the horizon.

Port St John Boat Ramp: Right on the Indian River in Port St John, the boat ramp at the end of Fay Blvd has great views across to the launch pads.

Harbor Heights Beach: Grab a spot on the sand at this Cape Canaveral beach or head out for a surf and look north to see the streak in the sky at launch time.

EATING IN THE SPACE COAST: TITUSVILLE

Dixie Crossroads: A local favorite for wild ocean-caught seafood and steaks. Don't miss their buttery, broiled rock shrimp. *11am-9pm* $$

Pier 220 Seafood & Grill: Historic spot on the Indian River Lagoon. Tasty grouper tacos and peel-and-eat shrimp. *10:30am-9pm Sun-Thu, to 10pm Fri & Sat* $$

Orleans Bistro & Bar: Shrimp and crawfish get the Cajun treatment at this fashionable New Orleans-style spot. Try the Nola Boil. *11am-midnight Sun-Thu, to 1am Fri & Sat* $$

Tree of Life Cuban Bakery: Enjoy authentic Cuban sandwiches, coffees and other treats in the spirit of Old Havana. *hours vary* $$

SPACE COAST STATE PARKS & REFUGES

Sebastian Inlet State Park: Pristine beaches, great waves, one of Florida's best fishing piers and a secluded snorkeling cove.

Archie Carr National Wildlife Refuge: Stretching more than 20 miles along the coast, an important habitat for nesting loggerhead sea turtles.

Merritt Island National Wildlife Refuge: Originally acquired for NASA's Space Program, 218 sq miles of hiking trails and a self-guided wildlife drive.

Indian River Lagoon State Park: Featuring lots of native plants, birds and sea life, it's popular with kayakers, boaters and water waders.

WIRESTOCK/GETTY IMAGES

Something particularly fun to do here is bidding adieu to skyscraping cruise ships bound for the Bahamas and other ports of call as they pass along the shoreline on their way out of Canaveral Barge Canal into the wide-open Atlantic.

Antiquing & Cafe-Hopping

Explore historic Cocoa Village

Lest you think the Space Coast is all rockets, surfers and wildlife, you can also find one of Florida's most atmospheric downtowns for cafe-hopping, boutique shopping and antiquing here. Drive roughly 8 miles inland (west) from Cocoa Beach – crossing the sparkling waters of the Banana River and Indian River Lagoon – to reach Cocoa Village, a former riverfront trading post turned eclectic, artsy town.

A leafy urban oasis by the lagoon's edge, it's lined with historic buildings housing independent restaurants and cafes, wine bars and shops. Start your explorations at **Cocoa Riverfront Park**, where an amphitheater overlooking the Indian River often hosts concerts and festivals. The surrounding park affords a scenic view of the river and is a nice spot to sit for a spell atop benches painted with images of flamingoes and octopuses by local artists, watching boats sail by.

DRINKING IN THE SPACE COAST: BEST TIKI BARS

Rikki Tiki Tavern: Cocktails in a colorful setting above rolling surf at the end of Westgate Cocoa Beach Pier. *11am-9pm Sun-Thu, to 10pm Fri & Sat*

Ellie Mae's Tiki Bar: Friendly neighborhood place in Cape Canaveral with tiki cocktail specials and smoked fish dip. *hours vary*

Coconuts on the Beach: Classic, lively oceanfront tiki bar, steps from the sand in Cocoa Beach. Killer piña coladas! *11am-10pm*

Fishlips Waterfront Bar & Grill: Watch passing cruise ships from this nautical rooftop tiki bar in Port Canaveral. Frosty drinks, pub grub. *hours vary*

Cocoa Riverfront Park

Then venture a few blocks inland to explore the village's cute shops and eateries.

Carolyn Seiler Studios *(carolynseiler.com)* is a wonderful artist co-op housed inside a colorful cottage where you can shop for things like glass jewelry, coasters, wind chimes and paintings created by more than 30 local artisans. **Antiques & Collectibles Too** *(facebook.com/actcocoavillage)* has a maze of rooms filled with things like estate jewelry, decades-old Disney snow globes, rare chess sets and vintage NASA mission patches. And don't miss **Antilles Trading Company** *(antillestradingcompany.com)*, a pirate oddities store featuring an adjoining museum with timeless artifacts and pirate-related interactive exhibits.

Favorite spots for a drink or meal include German-themed **Village Bier Garten** *(villagebier.com)*, **Milpa Tacos y Tortillas** *(milpataco.com)* for Oaxacan and Baja-style fare, and boutique wine store and tasting bar **Wine Lady** *(thewineladycocoa.com)*. If you love barbecue, don't miss **Crydermans** *(crydermansbarbecue.com)* for succulent meat that pairs wonderfully with local craft beers and ciders. Just look for the gigantic cow mural – sporting sunglasses, of course.

HOMETOWN SURFING LEGEND

Look for a statue of the Space Coast's most famous surfer on the median strip approaching downtown Cocoa Beach on the A1A heading south. It pays homage to Kelly Slater, who was born in Cocoa Beach and surfed the area's beach breaks from the age of five. In fact, the area's consistently imperfect-shaped waves are often attributed with Slater's prowess – as they were more challenging beasts to master than perfect ones! A Cocoa Beach legend, this record-holding, 11-time World Surfing League champion still occasionally visits the Space Coast, so you never know when or where you might spot him along a casual paddle out (especially if surf's up at Sebastian Inlet).

EATING IN SPACE COAST: COCOA BEACH

Pompano Grill: A tiny, sweet hideaway for steak, seafood and crème brûlée. Family-run and welcoming. *5:30-8:30pm Tue-Thu, 5-9pm Fri & Sat* $$

Flavour Kitchen & Wine Bar: Exquisite dishes by affable Chef Jason. The seafood paella rocks, but so does everything else! *hours vary* $$

Fat Snook: Gourmet seafood restaurant in south Cocoa Beach, with a scratch kitchen and Caribbean-inspired dishes. *4-9pm Tue-Sun* $$$

Café Margaux: Casual elegance in Cocoa Village, serving French and European-inspired cuisine with fab wine pairings. *11:30am-9pm Mon-Sat* $$$

Northeast Florida

STORIED STREETS | BEACH BREAKS | RIVERFRONT BUZZ

GETTING AROUND

You'll need a car to visit many of Jacksonville's attractions and beaches – rent wheels or get a taxi, Uber or Lyft. Local buses *(jtafla.com)* are reliable, but don't cover all areas. There's a free elevated monorail downtown with a few stops, and the St Johns River Taxi takes you to some riverfront parks, docks, hotels and the TIAA Bank Field. Historic neighborhoods like Riverside, San Marco and Avondale are great places to wander on foot, as is the entirety of St Augustine.

Northeast Florida blends historic intrigue, beachside energy, and just the right dose of Southern hospitality. Jacksonville, the state's most populous city, sprawls with surprising ease – a mix of towering downtown, walkable historic districts and vast stretches of sand. Despite its size, Jax still feels like a tight-knit town, where tailgating is a ritual, fishing poles are standard gear and beach days come with live music and cold drinks. Just 40 miles south lies St Augustine, the oldest continuously occupied city in the US, where cobblestone streets, centuries-old forts and Spanish colonial architecture set a storybook scene. You can stroll the Castillo de San Marcos, sip from the legendary Fountain of Youth or simply wander among boutiques and wine bars. From Atlantic Beach's relaxed surf scene to St Augustine's old-world allure, Northeast Florida is a region where the past meets the present and every day ends with an ocean breeze.

Beach-Hopping

MAP P251

Pick your Jacksonville beach experience

Jacksonville has lots of entertainment, dining and shopping opportunities, but when residents want to relax, they head to beaches 20 miles east. Smaller towns dot the white sandy shoreline, each offering different coastal vibes.

Jacksonville Beach is a popular weekend getaway for Jacksonvillians, with its wide range of indoor and outdoor activities. Kids love **Adventure Landing Jacksonville Beach** *(jacksonville-beach.adventurelanding.com)* with its Shipwreck Island Waterpark, go-karts, mini golf and arcade. Popular **South Beach Park** *(jacksonvillebeach.org)* boasts Sunshine Playground, a skate park, grills, volleyball courts, walking trails and a seasonal splash pad.

People in their 20s and 30s flock to Jacksonville Beach to dance, hit a bar or soak up live entertainment. All ages enjoy sunbathing, swimming and surfing. Colorful surfboards, boats and pelicans usually dot the Atlantic's blue-gray waves. Enjoy

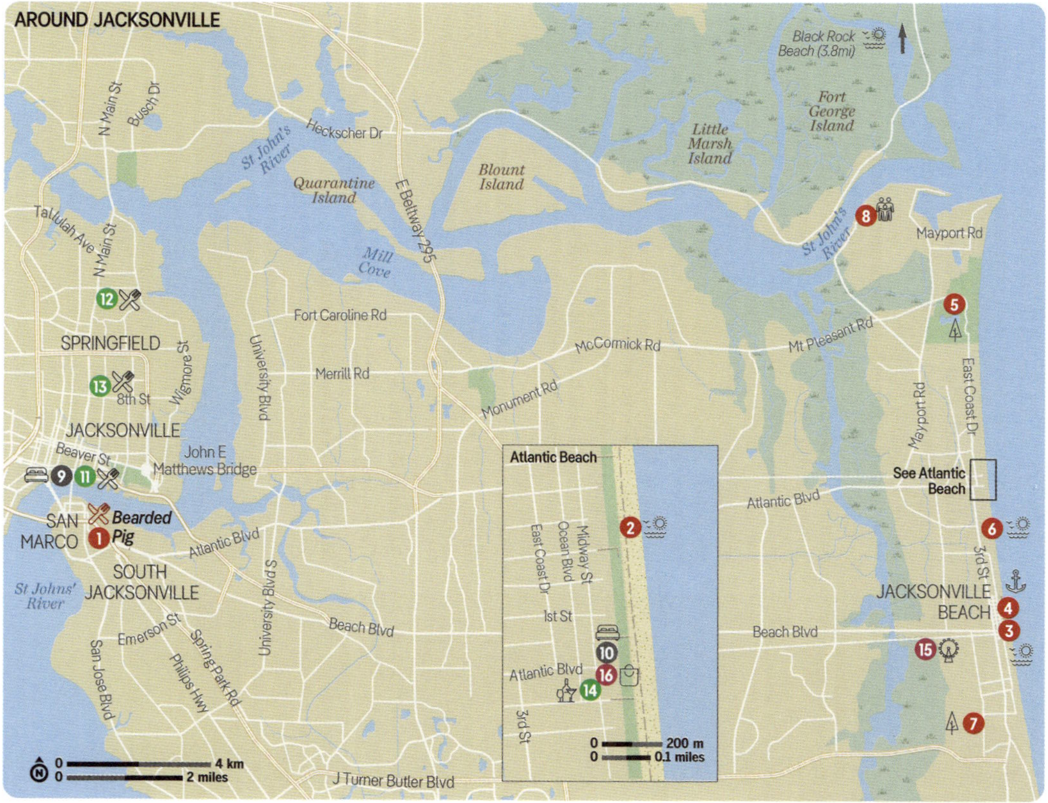

AROUND JACKSONVILLE

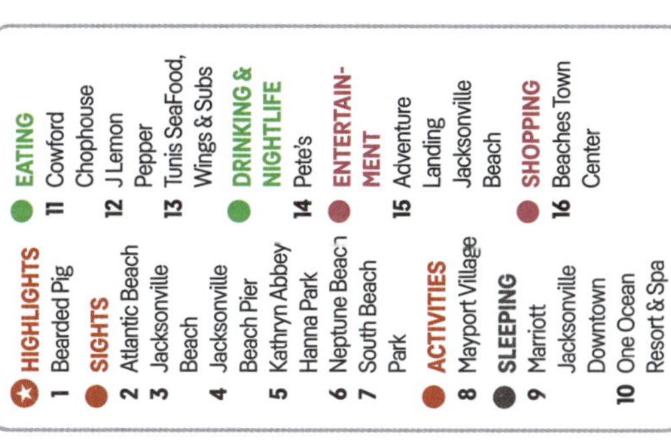

TOP TIP

Avoid interstates and major roads during weekday rush hours (7am to 9am and 4pm to 6pm), when accidents happen and delays can triple travel times. Jacksonville trouble spots include I-95 downtown; east-west routes like Butler, Southside and Blanding Blvds; and the Main St, Buckman and Acosta bridges.

BONEYARD BEACH

Radically different from hard-packed, golden-sand beaches, **Black Rock Beach** was formed at the end of the last ice age, some 10,000 years ago. Live oak and cedar tree skeletons carved by wind and water line the shore, comprised of geological soil formations that appear primordial. It's not so much a beach to sunbathe on as a place to connect with the region's prehistoric past. The beach is an official archaeological site today, so don't try taking anything. Nicknamed Boneyard Beach, it is at Big Talbot Island State Park, 20 minutes north from downtown Jacksonville, off State Rd A1A.

a stroll or bike ride along the scenic boardwalk, where there are plenty of restaurants, a beach-trolley shuttle, and free beach-buggy service in summer. Cast a line off 1300ft **Jacksonville Beach Pier** *(thejaxpier.com)* where anglers catch various saltwater fish, black drums to flounders, and the occasional stingray or shark.

Located off Atlantic Blvd, **Neptune Beach** is the first beach town north. It's a quiet, residential town born in the 1930s as a community of vacation rental cottages. It shares the **Beaches Town Center** *(beachestowncenter.com)* with **Atlantic Beach**, offering an assortment of tiny boutiques, a wine and cigar bar, a surf shop hawking boards and gear, restaurants with open-air seating, and a place to park your car and walk to the beach. Be sure to drop into **Pete's**, a legendary watering hole seemingly stuck in time, to enjoy some suds and wings or a game of pool.

Atlantic Beach is the northernmost of Jacksonville's beaches. **Kathryn Abbey Hanna Park** (known locally as 'Hanna Park') is a popular hangout and one of the best places to surf. It boasts a plaza, bike and walking trails, a splash park and picnic areas.

North of the beaches is **Mayport Village**, home to Naval Station Mayport. It's also famous for its fresh and plump shrimp, harvested here and sold regionwide.

St Augustine's Cobblestone Thoroughfare

MAP P254

Strolling pedestrian St George St

Founded in 1565, St Augustine – dubbed 'The Ancient City' – is the oldest city of European origin in the United States. Its narrow, cobblestone streets, wooden balconies, tabby walls and time-worn cemeteries breathe European heritage.

Cobblestoned **St George St** is the hub of St Augustine's historic district. Here, charming Spanish-Colonial shops peddle handmade sweets, tacky souvenirs, blown-glass confections and artisanal jewelry. Restaurants serve fragrant baked goods, glasses of Spanish red, aromatic espresso and tapas plates. Some taverns feature live entertainment on weekends, and the sound of violins, acoustic guitars or melodic voices mix with the sweet aroma of fudge from **Kilwins** *(kilwins.com)*. Stop for a vintage-style soft pretzel from **Ben's Soft Pretzels** *(order.benspretzels.com)* and devour it at a bistro table in the tranquil gardens hidden out back. If

EATING IN NORTHEAST FLORIDA: JACKSONVILLE

MAP P251

Bearded Pig: Casual local spot after sports games, serving smoked ribs, wings, pulled pork and tasty sides. *11am-9pm Tue-Sun* $$

J Lemon Pepper Fish & Chicken: Three locations cooking up ginormous portions at good-value prices. *hours vary* $$

Tunis Seafood, Wings & Subs: A Jax fave, serving the best fried shrimp in town – or try the lamb gyro or delish Cajun Ranch wings. *10am-10pm* $$

Cowford Chophouse: Timelessly romantic, this stylish downtown steakhouse boasts a rooftop lounge with views of the city's skyline. *4-10pm Tue-Sat* $$$

ANDRIY BLOKHIN/SHUTTERSTOCK

St George St

you're ready to imbibe, tip one back at **Prohibition Kitchen** *(pkstaug.com)*, a gastropub with rockin' live music and the longest bar in town.

Dating to the 1700s, you'll also find the **Oldest Wooden School House Museum & Gardens** *(oldestwoodenschoolhouse.com; adult/child $8/7)* here, steps from the **Colonial Quarter**. The street is only open to pedestrians. Cabs and trolleys stop at either end, bookended by city gates and the historic **Cathedral Basilica of St Augustine**. Built in 1797, the cathedral was remodelled under the guidance of renowned architect James Renwick Jr after a ravaging fire spared its coquina foundation in 1887.

A short walk from the southern end is **Plaza de la Constitución**, with giant oak-shaded eateries and galleries, and the small, open-air covered **Slave Market**, named for one of its unfortunate historical purposes. There's a ton of history here – each block packed with so many stories that it would take a weekend to stop and read all the memorial plaques.

Consider strolling across the majestic **Bridge of Lions**. Built in 1927 and restored in 2010, two marble lion statues still guard its crossing. The far side of the bridge affords a fantastic view of downtown, red Spanish tile roofs and quaint B&Bs lining the bayfront.

TROLLEY TOURS

Hands down, the easiest – and most fun – way to navigate the nation's oldest city, and score a lay of the land, is by old-fashioned trolley. Along the route, riders are regaled with interesting anecdotes and amusing tales about the businesses and historic sites they're passing.

The **Old Town Trolley** *(trolleytours.com/st-augustine; adult/child $37/18)* has 22 stops and offers 90-minute tours, as well as ghost tours. Tours include hop-on-and-off privileges, so passengers can stop to enjoy food and attractions along the way. **Ripley's Red Train Tours** *(ripleys.com/attractions/ripleys-red-train-tours-st-augustine; adult/child $24/13)* offers similar excursions, with 20 stops and an opportunity to visit Ripley's Believe-It-Or-Not Odditorium.

EATING IN NORTHEAST FLORIDA: ST AUGUSTINE

MAP P254

Floridian: Old Florida hipster vibes with courtyard dining, a cozy bar and an eclectic menu with gluten-free and vegan/veg options. *11am-late Wed-Mon* **$$**

St Augustine Fish Camp: Seafood so scrumptious there's usually a line, but it's worth the wait. Your taste buds will agree. *hours vary* **$$**

Lotus Noodle Bar: This Japanese-French styled hideaway is a foodie's paradise. Intimate dining. Reservations required. *5-9pm Tue-Thu, to 10pm Fri & Sat* **$$**

Chez L'Amour: Dimly lit restaurant/bar with live jazz, speakeasy charm, mouthwatering tapas-style cuisine and delectable desserts. *hours vary* **$$$**

HIGHLIGHTS
1 Castillo de San Marcos National Monument
2 St Augustine Eco Tours

SIGHTS
3 Bridge of Lions
4 Cathedral Basilica of St Augustine
5 Colonial Quarter
6 Fountain of Youth
7 Mission Nombre de Dios
8 Oldest Wooden School House
9 Plaza de la Constitución
10 St George St

ACTIVITIES
11 Old Town Trolley Tours
12 Red Train Tours
13 St Augustine Distillery

SLEEPING
14 St George Inn
15 Villa 1565

EATING
16 Ben's Soft Pretzels
17 Chez L'Amour
18 Floridian
19 Kilwins
20 Lotus Noodle Bar
21 St Augustine Fish Camp

DRINKING & NIGHTLIFE
22 Auggie's Draft Room
23 Dog Rose Brewing
24 Prohibition Kitchen
25 Rendezvous

Old Fort, Older Mission: Fountain of Youth?

MAP P254

Exploring 'The Ancient City's' rich history

Meander sacred grounds at **Mission Nombre de Dios** *(missionandshrine.org; free)*, once thought to be the original landing site of Ponce de Léon, the Spanish explorer who discovered 'La Florida.' Although that's been rebuked, there's no disputing the site's historical significance: it was here that Pedro Menéndez de Avilés founded St Augustine in 1565, 55 years before the Pilgrims arrived. The first parish mass was held upon their arrival, with a thanksgiving dinner attended by Indigenous Timucuans.

Nowadays, a **Great Cross**, erected to commemorate the mission's 400th anniversary, towers 208ft above trails, foot bridges and saltwater marshes. Perfect for peaceful reflection, the serene **Memorial Pathway** passes archaeological excavations, a bell tower, crumbling tombstones, rustic buildings, statues and cascading fountains.

Nearby, the dog-friendly **Fountain of Youth Archaeological Park** *(fountainofyouthflorida.com; adult/child $23/10)* attracts visitors curious about its mythical springs. Sadly, it's all historical folklore, but indulge in a free cup o'youth nevertheless. Navigate your way through free-roaming peacocks, exploring a recreated Native Timucua village, and catching reenactors firing cannons and muskets.

Plagued by pirate attacks, military onslaughts, disease, pillaging, raiding and burning, St Augustine has flown five flags during its existence. One British invasion in 1702 saw every building torched to the ground except the formidable **Castillo de San Marcos** *(nps.gov/casa; adult/child $15/free)*, known locally as 'the fort,' which once contained defensive moats.

Built between 1672 and 1695, the imposing fort is the only extant 17th-century military construction in the country. It's also one of two fortresses in the world to be built in coquina, a locally quarried porous rock composed of tiny seashells compressed into limestone and capable of withstanding cannon fire (the other fortress is nearby **Fort Matanzas**). While the fort has changed hands a few times, it's never fallen, even while housing upwards of 1500 people during the English siege.

Allow at least two hours to visit the mostly accessible grounds on a self-guided tour. Parking costs $2.50 per hour.

BOTTLENOSE DOLPHINS

Spotted year-round, those fins slicing through the surface of the Matanzas River likely aren't sharks but, rather, common bottlenose dolphins - popular residents of St Augustine's inshore waters. Highly social, these intelligent, naturally acrobatic and playful sea creatures can live into their fifties, reach 6-12ft and weigh up to 400lb. Living in groups known as pods, they emit clicking noises to navigate, source food and avoid predators. To see and 'hear' these fascinating ocean-dwellers within their natural habitat, join marine naturalists at **St Augustine ECO Tours** *(staugustineecotours.com; prices vary)* on a scenic tour aboard vessels equipped with underwater microphones.

DRINKING IN NORTHEAST FLORIDA: ST AUGUSTINE TAPROOMS

MAP P254

Dog Rose Brewing Co: Fun gathering spot with a huge selection of handcrafted ales. Live music too. *noon-10pm Sun-Thu, to midnight Fri & Sat*

Rendezvous: Globetrot your way around 350 international beers at the city's 'original beer pub.' Family-friendly. *hours vary*

Auggie's Draft Room: Sample and sip at your own pace with 24 self-serve taps to choose from. *11am-8pm Sun-Thu, to 11pm Fri & Sat*

St Augustine Distillery: If you're a fan of premium bourbons, gins, vodkas and wines, you'll love this tour with generous samplings. *10am-6pm*

Tampa Bay & Southwest

WATERFRONT PATHWAYS | GULF HISTORY | GLOBAL MUSEUMS

GETTING AROUND

The TECO Streetcar has downtown routes, including to Ybor City, it's free and runs daily. Rent electric scooters or e-bikes through the Lime and Spin apps downtown. The Hillsborough Area Regional Transit Authority (HART) has bus routes throughout downtown and surrounds, including to Tampa International Airport. Downtown's Marion Transit Center is a hub for services to the zoo, Busch Gardens and the Henry B Plant Museum.

Few places in Florida fuse historic grit, artistic verve and breezy beach life quite like the Tampa Bay region. Tampa, with its brick-paved Ybor City and cigar-chomping past, pulses with a blend of Latin flavor and modern swagger. Its Riverwalk winds past concert halls, museums and sleek towers, while old neighborhoods like Seminole Heights trade in mid-century bungalows and craft beer. Across the bay, St Petersburg feels sun-splashed and soul-fed – a city where glass art, indie cafes and massive Salvador Dalí paintings live steps from marinas and banyan trees. Then there's St Pete Beach, a stretch of pure, powdery bliss where vintage motels and tiki bars keep things delightfully unpolished. This is where Florida loosens its collar a bit, ditches pretense and shows off its depth. It's a region shaped by salt air, immigrant legacies and rebellious creativity. It's where the Gulf isn't just scenery, it's a region's lifeblood.

River Views & Parks Aplenty

All along the Tampa Riverwalk

Stretching along the Hillsborough River, Tampa's best-loved green space takes you past palm-fringed parks and shimmering skyscrapers, always within view of the waterway where dolphins and manatees can be seen frolicking in the shadow of high-rises. For the full experience, you can join the runners, cyclists and skateboarders who traverse the full 2.5 miles, starting in either **Water Works Park** *(tampa.gov; free)* in

DRINKING IN TAMPA & SOUTHWEST: YBOR CITY

Gaspar's Grotto: Pirate-themed bar in the heart of the historic district with live entertainment and outdoor dining. *7am-2am Mon-Sat, from 11am Sun*

Ybor City Tap House: Live music and TVs tuned to whatever game is on draw sports fans, with 65 craft brews on tap. *hours vary*

Dirty Shame: Classic dive bar with darts, billiards and a loyal local crowd. A huge range of beers on tap, plus bottles and cans. *hours vary*

Castle: Ybor City's most famous nightclub has multiple floors and DJs, and crowds from goth to fetish and everything in between. *10:30pm-3am, Fri & Sat*

HIGHLIGHTS
1 Florida Aquarium

SIGHTS
2 Centennial Park
3 Curtis Hixon Waterfront Park
4 Glazer Children's Museum
5 JC Newman
6 Old Steel Railroad Bridge
7 Tampa Bay History Center
8 Tampa Museum of Art
9 Tampa Riverwalk
10 Water Works Park
11 Ybor City Museum State Park

SLEEPING
12 Hotel Haya

EATING
13 Columbia Restaurant
14 Rocca
15 Ulele

DRINKING & NIGHTLIFE
16 Castle
17 Dirty Shame
18 Gaspar's Grotto
19 Ybor City Tap House

BEST SPOTS FOR KIDS IN TAMPA

Florida Aquarium: Among the top aquariums in the country, with fresh and saltwater habitats, mangrove tunnels and a free-flying aviary.

Glazer Children's Museum: Beloved rainy-day spot where kids can build giant forts, steer a tugboat and climb a two-story course.

Zoo Tampa at Lowry Park: Manatees, kangaroos, giant tortoises and giraffes are among the menagerie of animals at this nonprofit zoo.

Museum of Science & Industry: Optical illusions, brain puzzles, a VR simulator and a planetarium.

Water Works Park: Let the littles run loose on the playground and splash pad at this riverfront downtown park.

Tampa Heights or the greenway's southeastern terminus near the **Florida Aquarium** *(flaquarium.org; from $30)*. Keep an eye out for Tampa landmarks such as the **Old Steel Railroad Bridge**, built in 1915, and the silver-hued minarets of the former Tampa Bay Hotel glinting in the sunlight across the river.

Apart from providing a scenic backdrop to a bit of exercise in the fresh air, the **Tampa Riverwalk** *(thetampariverwalk.com)* is also a great way to travel between key attractions, with major museums (like the **Tampa Museum of Art** and the **Tampa Bay History Center**) perched just steps from the vehicle-free path.

Curtis Hixon Waterfront Park is a gorgeous riverfront green lung that hosts festivals and pop-up events, including a holiday-season ice-skating rink.

Nighttime provides an entirely different perspective of the city, with colorfully illuminated pathways and underpasses, and the lights of waterfront buildings flickering on the river like fireflies. Also accessed off the Tampa Riverwalk, the city's lively lifestyle neighborhood of Water Street Tampa is brimming with trendy restaurants and bars.

History, Roosters & Cigars

MAP P257

Ybor City a go-go

Ybor City is a short car or trolley ride northeast of downtown. Like the illicit love child of Key West and Miami's Little Havana, this 19th-century district is a multicultural neighborhood that hosts Tampa's liveliest party scene. It also preserves a strong Cuban, Spanish and Italian heritage from its days as the epicenter of Tampa's cigar industry. You'll quickly find out why the rooster is Ybor's symbol: the birds are wild and proudly strutting everywhere.

A good place to begin your visit is at the **Ybor City Museum State Park** *(ybormuseum.org; $4; Wed-Sun)*. Set in a former bakery, this small history museum preserves a bygone era, with exhibitions full of striking photos and audio narratives from prominent members of the community. You can also explore the quaint Mediterranean-style gardens and three cigar-worker houses *(casitas)* that were built in 1895.

Opposite the museum is leafy **Centennial Park**. You'll see plenty of chickens, roosters and possibly little chicks, living wild and free as descendants of the hens kept by Ybor City's working-class residents over a century ago.

Cigar making is mostly a thing of the past, though **JC Newman** *(jcnewman.com; free)* keeps the old traditions alive at

EATING IN TAMPA BAY & SOUTHWEST: TAMPA

MAP P257

Streetlight Taco: Passionfruit margaritas and fabulous carnitas and brisket tacos in South Tampa. *11:30am-9pm Sun-Thu, to 10pm Fri & Sat* $

Rocca: Known for its tableside mozzarella cart, this Michelin-starred Italian in Tampa Heights is perfect for date night. *5-9pm Tue-Thu & Sun, to 10pm Fri & Sat* $$$

Barcelona Wine Bar: Lively spot with a great weekend brunch, a huge range of Spanish tapas and sangria in the south of the city. *hours vary* $$

Ulele: This native Florida-inspired restaurant serves gator tail, Gulf Coast oysters and locally caught grouper. *11am-10pm Sun-Thu, to 11pm Fri & Sat* $$

St Pete Pier

its recently restored El Reloj building. You can peruse the museum or book a guided factory tour *(adult/child $15/12)* and see the art of hand-rolling cigars in action.

End your day with a meal at **Columbia Restaurant** *(columbia restaurant.com)*, a striking Spanish-Cuban restaurant that's been going strong since 1905. The Cuban sandwich is legendary.

Stroll, Eat & Splash

MAP P260

Chill out on St Pete Pier

Before it reopened during the summer of 2020 after being completely renovated, the **St Pete Pier** *(stpetepier.org)* was a beloved but eyesore-inducing landmark on downtown's horizon. The new version of the pier, however, is nothing short of spectacular – all Scandinavian-inspired clean and contemporary lines interjected with beautiful public spaces that include a splash pad, marine-themed playground, **Tampa Bay Watch Discovery Center** *(tbwdiscoverycenter.org; adult/child $8/3)* with interactive conservation exhibits, and a sandy beach with plenty of spots for lounging on Tampa Bay.

You can easily while away a half-day or longer here, pausing for lunch or at least a tiki-themed cocktail with views of the city at **Pier Teaki** *(teakstpete.com/pier-teaki)* rooftop restaurant, or tossing out a fishing line from a dedicated platform on the pier. It's free to stroll the pier, which sprawls across a 26-acre district that hosts things like pop-up pickleball clinics and roller-skating rinks throughout the year.

TOP TIP

Visitors are often surprised to learn that Tampa itself is not on the beach. Clearwater Beach, one of the closest Gulf of Mexico beaches to Tampa, lies roughly 25 miles due west, with more options to the north and south.

SPARRING OVER A SANDWICH

Miami and Tampa both claim to have invented the American version of the Cuban sandwich – and the 'right' way to make the meaty wonder. If you've sunk your teeth into one in each city, you might have noticed the differences. Tampa lore credits the sandwich's origins to Ybor City, where it was made to feed Cuban cigar factory workers. And Tampa's version uses crispier bread on the outside while still fluffy inside and also adds Genoa salami to the usual mix of roasted pork, ham, Swiss cheese, dill pickles and mustard (the salami is said to be a nod to Ybor City's Italian immigrants).

EATING IN SOUTHWEST: ST PETERSBURG

MAP P260

Hangar: Casual spot for burgers and wings with direct views over the bayfront runway of Albert Whitted Airport. *8am-9pm* $

Juno & the Peacock: Sceney corner spot near the Vinoy resort with an incredible raw bar and cocktails. *11am-10pm Mon-Fri, from 10am Sat & Sun* $$$

El Cap: St Pete's most iconic spot for a burger or hot dog has been grilling them up since 1964. *11am-9pm Sun-Thu, to 10pm Fri & Sat* $

Mullet's Fish Camp: Choose from 15 types of fish served with house-made sauces at this South St Pete go-to. *hours vary* $$

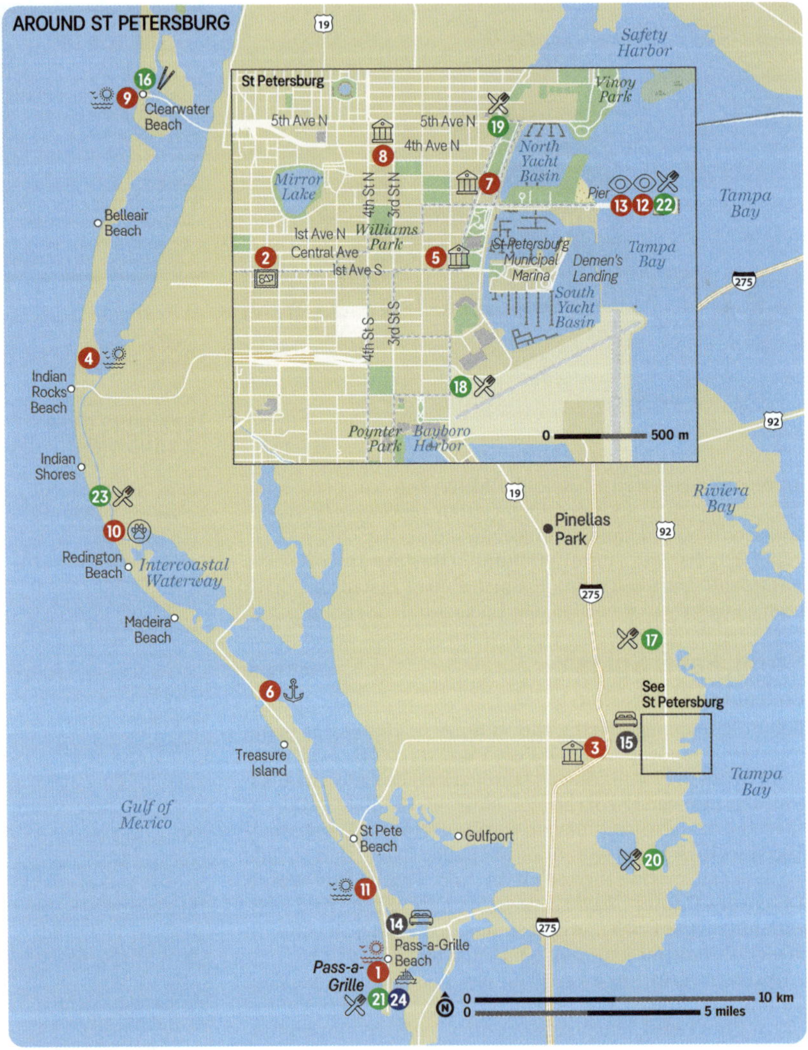

AROUND ST PETERSBURG

Safety Harbor
Clearwater Beach
Belleair Beach
Indian Rocks Beach
Indian Shores
Redington Beach
Intercoastal Waterway
Madeira Beach
Treasure Island
Gulf of Mexico
St Pete Beach
Gulfport
Pass-a-Grille Beach
Pass-a-Grille
Pinellas Park
Riviera Bay
Tampa Bay
See St Petersburg
0 10 km
0 5 miles

St Petersburg
5th Ave N
4th Ave N
Mirror Lake
4th St N
3rd St N
1st Ave N
Central Ave
1st Ave S
Williams Park
4th St S
3rd St S
Vinoy Park
North Yacht Basin
Pier
St Petersburg Municipal Marina
Demen's Landing
South Yacht Basin
Poynter Park
Bayboro Harbor
0 500 m

HIGHLIGHTS
1 Pass-a-Grille

SIGHTS
2 Chihuly Collection
3 Imagine Museum
4 Indian Rocks Beach Nature Preserve
5 James Museum of Western & Wildlife Art
6 John's Pass Village
7 Museum of Fine Arts
8 Museum of the American Arts & Crafts Movement
9 Pier 60
10 Seaside Seabird Sanctuary
11 St Pete Beach
12 St Pete Pier
13 Tampa Bay Watch Discovery Center

SLEEPING
14 Don CeSar
15 Moxy St Petersburg Downtown

EATING
16 Carreta on the Gulf
17 El Cap
see 16 Frenchy's Original Cafe
18 Hangar
19 Juno & the Peacock
20 Mullet's Fish Camp
21 Paradise Grille
22 Pier Teaki
23 Salt Rock Grill

TRANSPORT
24 Shell Key Shuttle

The Downtown Looper and Central Avenue Trolley make stops along the pier's length, in case you just want to view it as a drive-by.

White-Sand Beach Bliss

MAP P260

Clear waters and...Clearwater Beach, too

The closest Gulf of Mexico beachfront to the city is **St Pete Beach**, a mere 15-minute drive (on a good day) from bustling Central Ave in St Petersburg. The shoreline's key landmark is the towering Moorish Mediterranean **Don CeSar** hotel, a historic confection built in 1928 that's known to locals as the 'pink palace.'

The extra-wide beach itself ranks high for its natural beauty, and draws plenty of sunseekers who come for lounging by the waterside, long walks by the crashing waves and fiery sunsets. Proximity to the city has made this the most developed of the barrier-island beaches, with resorts, motels and restaurants just a few steps from the dune-backed sands.

Heading south from St Pete Beach, **Pass-a-Grille** anchors the southern end of Long Key. Here you'll find the most idyllic barrier-island beach, a narrow stretch of sand backed only by beach houses and metered public parking. You can watch boats coming through Pass-a-Grille Channel, hop aboard the **Shell Key Shuttle** *(shellkeyshuttle.com; round trip adult/child $30/15)*, which departs at 10am, noon and 2pm (2pm departure weekdays only) to unspoiled Shell Key, and retire for food and ice cream in the laid-back village center (essentially 8th Ave).

Slender barrier islands continue north of St Pete, harboring a handful of communities, from the tourist traps of **John's Pass Village** to the quieter, family-oriented Indian Rocks Beach. This is where you'll find the **Indian Rocks Beach Nature Preserve** *(indian-rocks-beach.com)*, which has a short boardwalk trail winding through mangroves out to a viewpoint of Boca Ciega Bay.

About a 15-minute drive north from there brings you to **Clearwater Beach**. It's hugely popular with tourists, particularly around **Pier 60** *(sunsetsatpier60.com)*, and hosts a nightly sunset celebration complete with buskers, and arts and crafts for sale.

Apart from beaches, the barrier-island chain is home to the largest wild-bird hospital in North America, the **Seaside Seabird Sanctuary** *(seasideseabirdsanctuary.org; free)*, which is home to over 100 sea and land birds for public viewing. You'll see a resident population of injured pelicans, owls, gulls, parrots and birds of prey, including a bald eagle. Several thousand birds are treated and released back to the wild annually. For a fine view over the beach, climb up the observation tower nestled in the back of the property.

BEST MUSEUMS & GALLERIES IN ST PETERSBURG

Museum of the American Arts & Crafts Movement: A local philanthropist founded the world's only museum that is dedicated to this historic movement.

James Museum of Western & Wildlife Art: Works by primarily living artists evoke the spirit of the West. The museum's façade is designed to resemble a sandstone mesa.

Museum of Fine Arts: Art representing ancient civilizations and modern masters makes up a world-class collection.

Chihuly Collection: Permanent collection of 18 installations by celebrated glass artist Dale Chihuly.

Imagine Museum: One-of-a-kind glass-art museum featuring works by American and international artists.

EATING IN SOUTHWEST: ST PETE BEACH

MAP P260

Paradise Grille: Casual walk-up spot on Pass-a-Grille Beach with tasty seafood, cold drinks and picnic tables overlooking the sand. *7am-8:30pm* **$**

Salt Rock Grill: Classy Indian Shores dinnertime spot renowned for local seafood and steaks. *4-10pm Mon-Fri, from noon Sat & Sun* **$$$**

Frenchy's Original Cafe: Famous grouper-sandwich spot at Clearwater Beach and other locations. *11am-10pm* **$$**

Carreta on the Gulf: Sandpearl Resort's signature restaurant serves divine sushi and seafood. *7am-midnight Sun-Thu, to 1am Fri & Sat* **$$$**

Places We Love to Stay

$ Budget $$ Midrange $$$ Top End

Miami

MAPS P207, P210, P212, P215

Freehand Miami $ Dorms and private rooms, two craft cocktail bars and an outdoor pool, about a mile north of the South Beach nightlife.

Kimpton Surfcomber $$ With a recently renovated pool, happening beach bar and poolside cabanas in Miami Beach.

Dunns Josephine $$ In historic Overtown, themed rooms celebrate the lives of notable Black figures like Ella Fitzgerland and Langston Hughes.

Arlo $$ With gorgeous murals inside and out, this high-rise hotel in Wynwood has beautiful common spaces that draw the neighborhood in.

Faena Hotel Miami Beach (p209) **$$$** Scenic, super-luxurious beachfront and art-centric hotel with restaurants, nightlife and entertainment on-site.

Mr C $$$ Rooms with European glamour wow at this Coconut Grove property. Its rooftop pool gazes out on Biscayne Bay.

Everglades & Biscayne National Park

MAP P219

Flamingo Campground (p220) **$** Drive-in campground in Everglades National Park with heated showers, grills, and access to fishing and hiking.

Elliott Key Campground $ A hiking trail and fishing on the island in Biscayne National Park. Restrooms and cold showers available. Access by boat only.

Boca Chita Key Campground $ Waterfront views, picnic tables, grills and toilets on-site in Biscayne. Access by boat only.

Flamingo Lodge $$ Comfortable accommodations deep in the Everglades. Waterfront rooms, dining on-site, rentals, glamping tents, and tours available.

Florida Keys & Key West

MAP P225

John Pennekamp Coral Reef State Park $ The park has campsites that can accommodate both tents and RVs. Restrooms, hot showers and coin laundry on-site.

Seashell Motel & Key West Hostel $ Basic dorm-style housing conveniently located near Old Town Key West.

NYAH Key West $$ Adult-only, elevated, dorm-esque lodging, plus a continental breakfast. Private rooms available.

Playa Largo $$$ This Key Largo oceanfront resort is the classic combination of luxury and seclusion.

Isla Bella $$$ Comfortable oasis where every room overlooks the water in Marathon. Relax with waterfront amenities or dabble in water sports at the marina.

Havana Cabana $$$ Adults-only hotel with vibrant influences of the art and culture of Cuba, plus Key West's largest pool.

Southeast Florida

MAPS P231, P236

Snooze Hotel $ Fort Lauderdale beachfront accommodation complete with a rooftop deck and complimentary beach gear.

Grand Resort & Spa $$ An LGBTIQ+-friendly resort, just steps from Fort Lauderdale Beach.

Historic Driftwood Resort $$ A fun, unique and nostalgic beachfront hotel in Vero, built in the 1920s using locally sourced driftwood.

Conrad Fort Lauderdale Beach $$$ Every room in this luxe, all-suite beach-front resort comes with an Italian marble bathroom, deep-soaking tub, and private balcony or terrace.

The Ben $$$ This luxury boutique hotel in West Palm Beach is part of the Marriott Autograph Collection. A block from Clematis St, many balconies overlook Palm Harbor Marina and the Intracoastal Waterway.

Hilton West Palm Beach $$$ This luxury property exudes style and grace: modern suites, resort-style pool, superb restaurants, full-service spa and complimentary valet parking.

Orlando & Walt Disney World®

MAP P239

Rosen Inn at Pointe Orlando $ A basic, affordable accommodation right in the middle of the action of I-Drive.

Hilton Garden Inn Lake Buena Vista $ An affordable resort, a 1-mile walk from Disney Springs® and the rest of the Walt Disney World® action.

Alfond Inn $$ Charming shops and restaurants

FELIX MIZIOZNIKOV/SHUTTERSTOCK

Faena Hotel Miami Beach (p209)

surround this artsy Winter Park boutique hotel.

Universal's Cabana Bay Beach Resort $$ An affordable Universal Orlando Resort hotel with retro-style single rooms and family suites.

Grand Bohemian Hotel $$$ In the heart of downtown Orlando, this AAA Four Diamond Resort combines luxury and a great location.

Disney's Polynesian Village Resort $$$ A volcano-inspired pool and lush grounds at this village resort transport guests to Fiji. Two monorail stops from the Magic Kingdom.

Villatel Orlando Resort $$$ Less hotel, more playful neighborhood, centrally located on I-Drive. Boredom never hits with amenities like water slides, pickleball courts, golf simulators and basketball.

Space Coast MAP P246

Jetty Park Campground $ Tent and full-service RV campsites at Port Canaveral with shuffleboard, playground and pier. Watch cruise ships passing by.

Hyatt Place Titusville/ Kennedy Space Center $$ Three-star hotel with a free daily breakfast buffet and outdoor pool.

Beachside Hotel & Suites $$ Retro surf vibes, balconies with ocean views in Cocoa Beach, and a water park with deck-side bar – oodles of family fun! On-site laundry; breakfast included.

Courtyard Titusville Kennedy Space Center $$$ Riverfront hotel with an outdoor pool and rooftop deck with launchpad views.

Northeast Florida MAPS P251, P254

Villa 1565 $ Classic Spanish architecture meets modern hospitality. Clean rooms surround a courtyard, home to a 650-year-old oak tree that pre-dates St Augustine.

Marriott Jacksonville Downtown $$ A four-star Water St hotel that's upscale and has a bar, bistro, pool and fitness area.

St George Inn $$ Centrally located, bodacious boutique inn offering apartment-style kitchenette suites with balconies overlooking St George St and the fort.

One Ocean Resort & Spa $$$ Atlantic Beach resort with oceanfront spa, swimming pool, pool bar and restaurant.

Tampa Bay & Southwest MAPS P257, P260

Gram's Place $ This small, welcoming hostel in Seminole Heights is for travelers who prefer personality over perfect linens.

Moxy St Petersburg Downtown $$ Right on Central Ave with a lively rooftop restaurant and bar, plus a podcast studio guests can use on the ground floor.

Hotel Haya $$$ Boutique hotel in Ybor City, offering art-filled rooms, a pool, and a great restaurant and cafe.

Don CeSar (p261) **$$$** Iconic 'pink palace' resort on St Pete Beach with a Gulf-front pool and bar.

Researched and curated by Regis St Louis

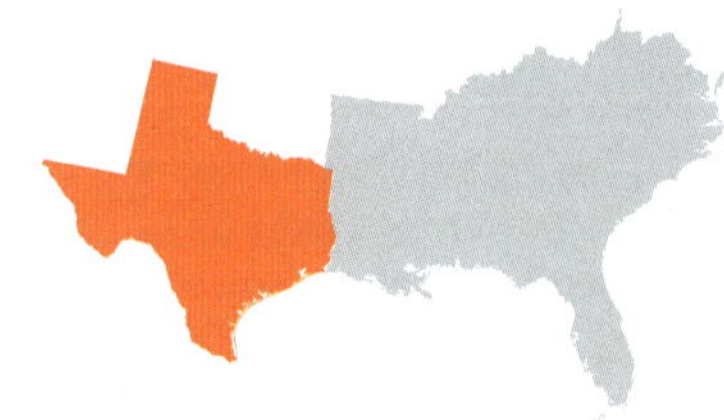

Texas

BIG SKIES AND OPEN ROADS

Dust off your boots and grab that cowboy hat: wide-ranging adventures in cities, mountains, deserts and beaches await in the Lone Star state.

Larger than many countries, Texas occupies a mammoth-sized footprint, both in terms of geography and the national psyche. Five of the country's 15 biggest cities are here in Texas. The state is home to the most valuable sports franchise in the world (Dallas Cowboys) and its cuisine (Tex-Mex) is known around the globe. Texas also has an astonishing diversity. Sure, there are sunny fields where the longhorn cattle roam, but this is also the land of craggy mountains and sunbaked deserts in the West, oasis-like springs in the Hill Country, and hundreds of miles of enticing Gulf Coast beaches.

Scenery aside, Texan cities and small towns alike offer a seemingly infinite array of attractions. You can explore cutting-edge art and culture, nightlife and cuisines from around the globe in Dallas, Fort Worth, Austin, San Antonio and Houston. There are atmospheric old music halls in tiny Hill Country settlements, and walkable neighborhoods bursting with creativity all across the state.

The Texas experience is about many things, from road trips across the windswept prairies to otherworldly art installations hidden on the edge of the wilderness. It's a place to create your own adventure, whether you're interested in hiking, rafting, stargazing, beach-hopping, birding, watching pro sports games or just immersing yourself in a place that's like nowhere else. Just don't try to pack in too much. You'd need a lifetime to experience it all.

ZORYANCHIK/SHUTTERSTOCK

THE MAIN AREAS

For places to stay in Texas, see p312

BILL KENNEDY/SHUTTERSTOCK

Big Bend National Park (p308)

Find Your Way

The bigger cities in Texas are found mostly on the eastern half of the state. Beaches and seaside towns stretch down the Gulf Coast, while deserts and mountains lie in the far west.

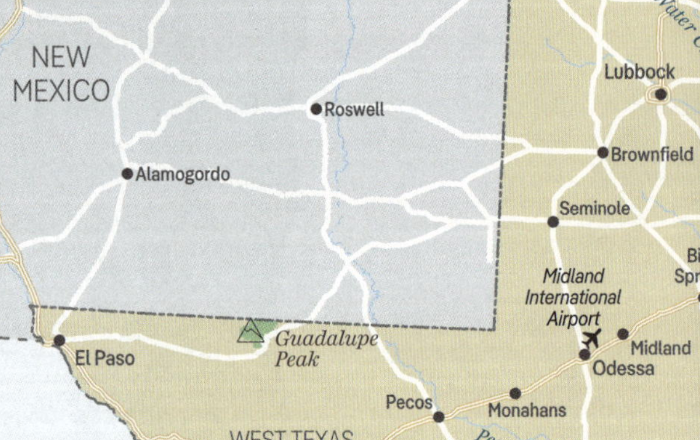

CAR

It's tough to get far without an automobile even in major cities. Be mindful of toll roads, which are most common in Houston and Dallas. Near the border, you may be stopped by the US Border Patrol, so make sure your ID is in order.

TRAIN

Texas has 19 Amtrak stations along three routes: Sunset Limited, Heartland Flyer and Texas Eagle. This can be a slow but scenic option for long-distance travel between major cities in Texas and to surrounding states.

BUS

Some Texans may doubt the notion, but you can travel by bus to reach some places in the state. Greyhound has the most extensive network, followed by FlixBus. There are even two luxury bus lines: Vonlane and RedCoach, which connect several cities in southeast Texas.

West Texas & Big Bend National Park, p306

Craggy mountains and desert landscapes form the backdrop to dramatic state and national parks, star-filled skies, and art-loving ranch towns.

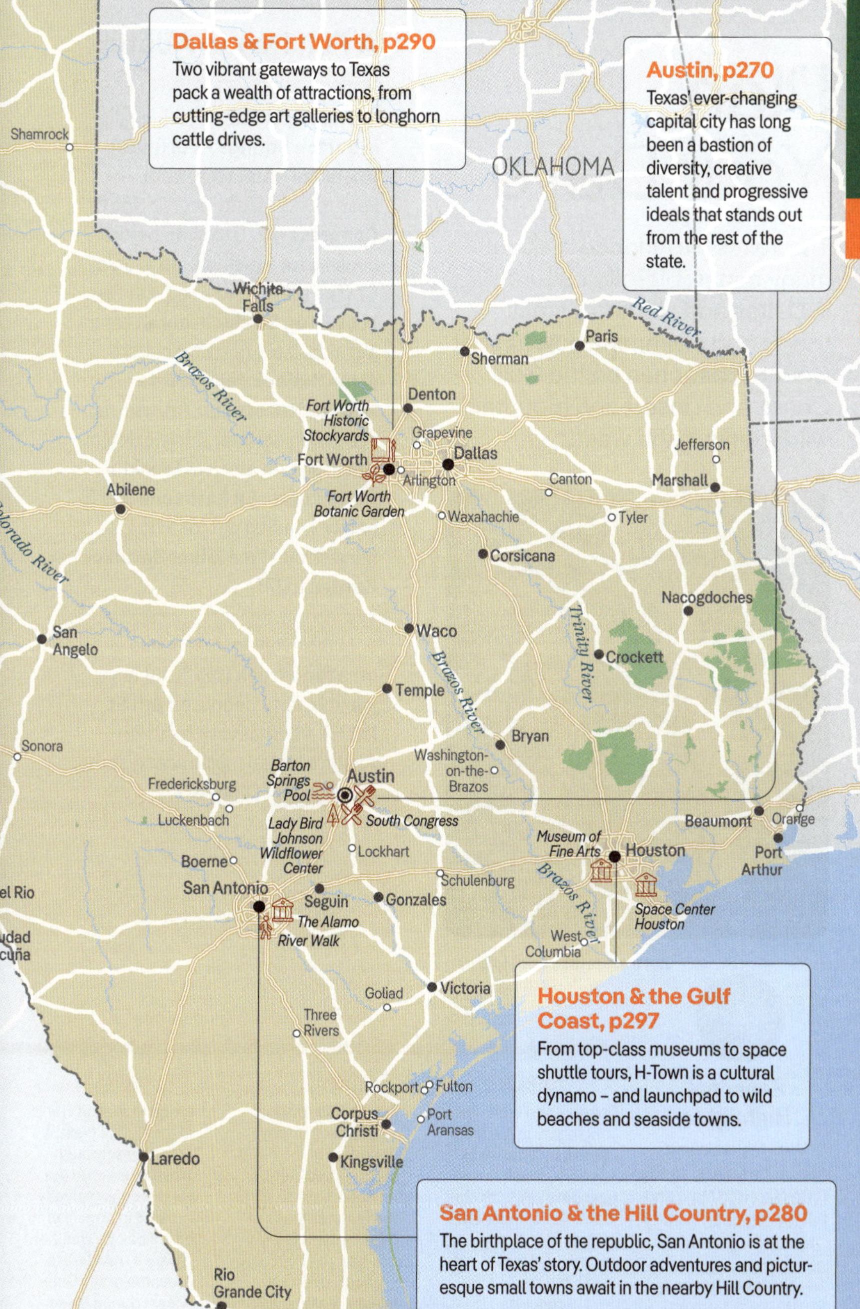

0 200 km
0 100 miles
Dallas & Fort Worth, p290
Two vibrant gateways to Texas pack a wealth of attractions, from cutting-edge art galleries to longhorn cattle drives.
Austin, p270
Texas' ever-changing capital city has long been a bastion of diversity, creative talent and progressive ideals that stands out from the rest of the state.
Houston & the Gulf Coast, p297
From top-class museums to space shuttle tours, H-Town is a cultural dynamo – and launchpad to wild beaches and seaside towns.
San Antonio & the Hill Country, p280
The birthplace of the republic, San Antonio is at the heart of Texas' story. Outdoor adventures and picturesque small towns await in the nearby Hill Country.
OKLAHOMA
Shamrock
Wichita Falls
Red River
Paris
Sherman
Brazos River
Denton
Fort Worth Historic Stockyards
Grapevine
Dallas
Fort Worth
Arlington
Jefferson
Canton
Marshall
Abilene
Fort Worth Botanic Garden
Waxahachie
Tyler
Colorado River
Corsicana
Nacogdoches
Waco
San Angelo
Trinity River
Crockett
Temple
Brazos River
Bryan
Sonora
Washington-on-the-Brazos
Barton Springs Pool
Austin
Fredericksburg
Luckenbach
South Congress
Lady Bird Johnson Wildflower Center
Lockhart
Beaumont
Orange
Museum of Fine Arts
Houston
Port Arthur
Boerne
Schulenburg
Brazos River
San Antonio
Seguin
Gonzales
Space Center Houston
The Alamo
River Walk
West Columbia
Goliad
Victoria
Three Rivers
Rockport
Fulton
Corpus Christi
Port Aransas
Laredo
Kingsville
Rio Grande City
Harlingen
McAllen
Weslaco
Port Isabel
Brownsville

Plan Your Days

The Texas experience is about many things: big-city culture in Dallas and Houston, small towns and swimming holes in Hill Country, beaches on the Gulf Coast, and desert and mountain wilderness in the west.

EMMA_GRIFFITHS/SHUTTERSTOCK

Barton Springs Pool (p275)

A Full Day in Austin

- Wake up with a refreshing dip in **Barton Springs Pool** (p275), where the water stays cool year-round. Mosey over to **South Congress** (p271) to shop before pausing for a pick-me-up at **Jo's Coffee** (p273) and a selfie at the **I Love You So Much mural**. Later get a dose of Lone Star culture at the **Bullock Texas State History Museum** (p270), with its eye-catching, interactive exhibits. Get in line for lunch at **Franklin Barbecue** or **La Barbecue** (p278) before heading out for a flower-filled stroll at the **Zilker Botanical Garden** (p273).

- In the evening, grab a bite off a **food truck** (p272), then join the party people on **6th St** (p278). Alternatively, focus on Austin's fabled music scene at the **Continental Club** (p277).

Seasonal Highlights

With festivals and pleasant weather, spring (late March to May) and fall (September to early November) are ideal times to visit. Summer swelters (cool off at the beach or an inland swimming spot).

MARCH

Creative and tech types congregate in Austin for **South by Southwest** (p277), which takes over downtown for nine days. Key components include film screenings, a comedy festival, art exhibitions and big concerts.

APRIL

Fiesta San Antonio (p284) is an 11-day celebration of the city's heritage and culture that dates back to 1891, and features loads of concerts, parades with costumes and marching bands, riverside events, feasting and merrymaking.

JUNE

Hurricane season starts in the Gulf of Mexico (and runs through November), with the worst storms typically arriving in August or September. Be weather aware if traveling to Houston or the Gulf Coast during these months.

Weekend in San Antonio & the Hill Country

- Start your day in San Antonio with breakfast at ultra-festive **Mi Tierra** (p284) then explore **Historic Market Square** (p284), where Mexican craft stores transport you south. Head to the **Alamo** (p280) to learn about Texas' most visited monument.

- Head up to the open-air restaurants at the **Pearl** (p284), a former brewery turned entertainment complex. Afterwards, stroll along the lovely **River Walk** (p283) and visit the impressive Latin American collections inside the **San Antonio Museum of Art** (p284).

- On your second day, hit the road for a scenic drive into Hill Country. Visit the charming town of **Boerne** (p287), followed by a hike and river swim in **Guadalupe River State Park** (p286).

Ten-Day Road Trip

- Start in Dallas at the **Sixth Floor Museum** (p290) to learn about Dallas' darkest day, then head over to **Bishop Arts District** (p292) for shopping, strolling and cafe-hopping. In neighboring Fort Worth, see cowboys in action during the daily cattle drive at **Fort Worth Stockyards** (p294), followed by boot-scootin' at **Billy Bob's Texas** (p294).

- Drive south to Houston, taking in the **Museum District** (p297) and exploring **Montrose** (p302). Admire NASA's **Space Center Houston** (p303), then head to the Gulf for beach time in **Port Aransas** (p304).

- Go northwest to San Antonio, stopping at the **missions** (p285) south of town, then veer west for experimental art in **Marfa** (p308), stargazing at the **McDonald Observatory** (p307) and exhilarating hikes in **Big Bend National Park** (p308).

SEPTEMBER

In Dallas, the **State Fair of Texas** (p294) brings ample amusement over 24 consecutive days. Carnival rides, livestock shows, concerts, fireworks and wondrous food stalls are a few draws for the 2 million-plus visitors each year.

OCTOBER

Make the journey to Marfa in West Texas to experience three days of creativity during the **Chinati Weekend** (p308). There's live music, artist talks and special exhibitions. Most events are free and open to the public.

NOVEMBER

Along the Gulf Coast, the colder months bring migrating birds passing through in huge flocks. November is a great month to see some of Texas' avian stars – endangered whooping cranes – at the **Aransas National Wildlife Refuge** (p305).

DECEMBER

Football season runs from September to January, but December is particularly exciting with NFL playoffs underway. You can also catch pro basketball. Houston is a great spot for seeing games live.

Austin

LIVE MUSIC | GREEN SPACES | BARBECUE

GETTING AROUND

The best way to get around Austin is to rent a car or use rideshare apps. Parking is expensive downtown.

Downtown Austin is laid out on a grid and best explored on foot. Bird, Lime and CapMetro rent scooters and bikes all over town, starting at $1. Download the apps to search pickup locations and to rent and return them.

It's fine to take the bus between the airport and downtown, but other routes can sometimes feel unsafe. CapMetro Rail has good service, but covers just nine stations between downtown and north Austin. Download the CapMetro app to purchase tickets.

Only a few decades ago, Austin was mostly known as a laid-back town full of slackers and no real industry besides the live music scene. Locals hopped about town in their flip-flops, cooling off at creeks under the blazing sun before emptying their pockets in dingy dive bars come dusk. Later, Austin became a safe space in the south for the queer community and for creatives honing their craft. Next came the Silicon Valley folk, lured in by tax incentives and a budding tech scene. The result has been an economic explosion and a city reimagined, which is usually what happens when a juicy secret gets out. Experience Austin's delights gastronomically through the city's blossoming food scene, during one of the capital's huge festivals like SXSW and Austin City Limits, or through the natural outdoor wonders that stretch from the outskirts right into the heart of downtown.

Capital Culture

MAPS P271, P274

Austin's top museums

Austin's museums might not have nationwide name recognition, but they'll surprise you. The mainstays clustered around Congress Ave satisfy an appetite for art, history and culture. The exterior walls at **The Contemporary Austin** routinely moonlight as canvases for national artists like Jenny Holzer – and outside means free viewing. Across the street, explore works by Mexican and Latino artists at the **Mexic-Arte Museum**, which also has a thoughtful gift shop. The **Bullock Texas State History Museum** takes visitors through

TOP TIP

From March until late October, the best free show in town happens beneath the Congress Avenue Bridge. Just after sunset, vast swarms of Mexican free-tailed bats emerge into the night in a feeding frenzy. Grab a spot on the sidewalk along the bridge or on the southeast corner, close to the Austin American-Statesman building.

the state's history by way of interactive exhibits and a 4D special-effects IMAX theater.

For retro discovery, the **Museum of the Weird** carries a collection of curiosities and oddities displayed in the tradition of PT Barnum. Speaking of weird, the **Cathedral of Junk** may not qualify as a museum, but the towering sculpture fills artist Vince Hannemann's backyard with everything from dolls and car bumpers to toilets and lawn-mower tires. Just call Hannemann *(512-299-7413)* ahead of time to make an appointment.

Get to Know South Congress

MAP P272

Austin's trendiest street

South Congress, or SoCo as it's often abbreviated, is equal parts authentic charm and commercialized cool, with plenty of food, shopping and entertainment options. Austin-born favorites like **Home Slice Pizza**, **Hopdoddy Burger Bar** and **Amy's Ice Cream** whet the appetites of a daytime crowd fresh from a dip in Lady Bird Lake, while sought-after reservations at **Otoko** and **June's** give people a good reason to change into fresh clothes.

Boutiques range from vintage to contemporary and keep all tastes satisfied for hours on end, including shops to pick

HIGHLIGHTS
1 Franklin Barbecue

SIGHTS
2 Bullock Texas State History Museum
3 Cathedral of Junk
4 Red Bud Isle

SLEEPING
5 ARRIVE Austin

EATING
6 Cuantos Tacos
7 La Barbecue
8 Leroy & Lewis Barbecue
9 Micklethwait Barbecue
10 The Vegan Nom

ENTERTAINMENT
11 AFS Cinema
12 Bullock Museum IMAX Theater

SOUTH AUSTIN

South Congress Avenue

See South Congress Avenue

EATING IN AUSTIN: FOOD TRUCKS

MAPS P271, P272, P274

Gordough's: Take their word for it when they say these are big, fat doughnuts. One is more than enough here. *10am-midnight Mon-Fri, from 8am Sat & Sun* $

The Vegan Nom: Vegan food truck serving up delicious tacos, nachos and burritos on the east side of town. *8am-2pm & 5-10pm Mon-Fri, 8am-10pm Sat & Sun* $

Kiin Di: Fantastic Thai food along South Lamar. The Killer Noodles are a must-try. *4:30-9pm Wed-Sun* $

Cuantos Tacos: Austin's must-visit yellow truck for Mexican-style street tacos. Make sure to try the suadero. *11am-10pm Tue-Sat* $

HIGHLIGHTS
1 Barton Springs Pool
2 South Congress
3 Zilker Park

SIGHTS
4 Broken Spoke
5 I Love You So Much Mural
6 Open Room Austin
7 Pfluger Pedestrian Bridge
8 Sand Beach Park
9 Willie Nelson Mural
10 Zilker Botanical Garden

SLEEPING
11 Austin Motel
12 Carpenter Hotel
13 Hotel San José
14 South Congress Hotel

EATING
15 Amy's Ice Creams
16 Better Half Coffee & Cocktails
17 Clark's Oyster Bar
18 Dovetail Pizza
19 El Alma
20 Fresa's
21 Gordough's
22 Home Slice Pizza
23 Hopdoddy Burger Bar
24 Jo's Coffee
25 June's
26 Kiin Di
27 Loro
28 Otoko
29 Perla's
30 Polvos
31 Terry Black's BBQ
32 Uchi

DRINKING & NIGHTLIFE
33 ABGB
34 Bouldin Acres
35 Continental Club
36 Courtyard Lounge at Hotel San José
37 Donn's Depot
38 Nightcap
39 Saxon Pub
40 Tiki Tatsu-Ya

ENTERTAINMENT
41 Alamo Drafthouse Cinema
42 Austin City Limits Music Festival
43 Austin Trail of Lights
44 Eeyore's Birthday Party
45 Food & Wine Festival
46 Reggae Festival

up some cowboy boots. Cafes are well staggered along the strip, with highlights like **Jo's Coffee** and its famous **I Love You So Much mural**. Another must see/photograph is the **Willie Nelson For President mural** on Elizabeth St a few blocks away.

Zilker Park & Barton Springs Pool

MAP P272

Bask under the Texan sun

The beloved 358-acre **Zilker Park** is a year-round haven for humans and dogs alike in Austin. Spring is when the flowers bloom at **Zilker Botanical Garden** and when the sky is colorfully decorated by the **ABC Kite Fest**. Summer brings sunbathers and revelers armed with giant coolers, as well as the free **Blues on the Green** concert series across multiple evenings in June and July. Fall provides cooler weather for Zilker's most famous event, the **Austin City Limits Music Festival** *(aclfestival.com)*. December's lack of white powder doesn't deter the park's festive efforts, as Zilker becomes the **Austin Trail of Lights** with 2 million bulbs, 90 Christmas trees, twinkling light tunnels and a merry sleigh of displays.

OTHER FAVORITE OUTDOOR SPOTS

Ky Harkey, founder of The Visitor Experience and former director of interpretation at Texas Parks & Wildlife, highlights his favorite outdoor spots in Austin. *(@kyharkey)*

Parking is really challenging at **Red Bud Isle**, but you can also access it by paddleboard or kayak for a super-unique experience. **McKinney Falls** is the only state park within Austin's city limits. People can camp and see live music on the same day. The **Pfluger Pedestrian Bridge** (p276) is one of my favorite spots in Austin at sunrise or sunset. **Sand Beach Park** has an art installation called **Open Room Austin** (p276). It's this grand, colorful picnic table that's 24ft long. You can't reserve it – it's meant to bring different groups of people together.

EATING IN DOWNTOWN AUSTIN: OUR PICKS

MAPS P272, P274

Better Half Coffee & Cocktails: A great spot for breakfast, brunch, lunch or dinner. *8am-3pm Mon, to 10pm Tue-Thu & Sun, to 11pm Fri & Sat* $$

Taqueria 10 de 10: A taco speakeasy. Enter through ReyRey bar in the alleyway between 2nd and 3rd Sts. *11:30am-10pm Sun-Wed, to 1am Thu-Sat* $

Clark's Oyster Bar: Oysters on the half shell and other seafood options inside a beautiful space in Old West Austin. *11am-10pm Sun-Thu, to 11pm Fri & Sat* $$

Arlo Grey: Fine-dining menu from Top Chef host (and winner) Kristen Kish and a prime spot to watch the South Congress bats. *5-10pm Wed-Sun* $$$

DOWNTOWN AUSTIN

Texas State Capitol
Red River Cultural District
6th Street
Warehouse District
See Warehouse District
Bullock Texas State History Museum (0.2mi); Bullock Museum IMAX Theater (0.2mi)
Cuantos Tacos (0.4mi)
Franklin Barbecue (0.2mi)
ARRIVE Austin (0.8mi)
Open Room Austin (0.25mi); Pfluger Pedestrian Bridge (0.25mi); Sand Beach Park (0.25mi)
The Vegan Nom (1mi); La Barbecue (1.1mi)

DRINKING IN DOWNTOWN AUSTIN: OUR PICKS

MAPS P272, P274

Donn's Depot: A former train depot turned dive bar and go-to hang-out for many in Austin. Live music most nights. *2pm-2am Mon-Fri, 6pm-2am Sat*

Elephant Room: An underground jazz bar that's exactly what you'd want in an underground jazz bar. *5pm-2am Mon-Fri, 8pm-2am Sat, 7pm-1am Sun*

Roosevelt Room: One of Austin's top cocktail bars with a jaw-dropping menu of drinks that spans different eras. *3pm-midnight Sun-Wed, to 2am Thu-Sat*

Nightcap: Old bungalow house turned bar-restaurant with a great outdoor view of the hustle and bustle along W 6th. *5-10pm Tue & Wed, to midnight Thu-Sat*

HIGHLIGHTS
1 6th Street
2 Red River Cultural District
3 Texas State Capitol

SIGHTS
4 Austin Public Library
5 Butterfly Bridge
6 Deep Roots Community Garden
7 Mexic-Arte Museum
8 Museum of the Weird
9 Shoal Creek Greenbelt
10 Tau Ceti
11 The Contemporary Austin
12 Waterloo Park
13 Willie Nelson Statue

ACTIVITIES
14 9th St BMX Park
15 Ann and Roy Butler Hike-and-Bike Trail

SLEEPING
16 Firehouse Hostel
17 Hotel Van Zandt
18 The Driskill

EATING
19 Arlo Grey
20 Stubb's Bar-B-Q
21 Taqueria 10 de 10
22 Walton's Fancy & Staple

DRINKING & NIGHTLIFE
23 Barbarella's
24 Blind Pig Pub
25 Cheer Up Charlies
26 Clive Bar
27 Coconut Club
28 Elephant Room
29 Highland Lounge
30 Iron Bear
31 Jackalope
32 Kung Fu Saloon
33 Lucille
34 Neon Grotto
35 Oilcan Harry's
36 Pete's Dueling Piano Bar
37 Rain
38 Rainey Street
39 Roosevelt Room
40 Rustic Tap
41 Star Bar

ENTERTAINMENT
42 Blue Starlite Urban Drive-In
43 Creek & The Cave
44 Esther's Follies
45 Mohawk
46 Paramount Theatre
47 Pecan Street Festival
48 South By Southwest
49 Violet Crown Cinema

BEST AUSTIN FESTIVALS & EVENTS

Austin knows how to party and is much more than just SXSW and ACL.

Reggae Festival: Two days of reggae for a cause every April, raising more than $1 million for the Central Texas Food Bank in 30-plus years.

Pecan Street Festival: A free downtown music and arts festival held twice a year.

Eeyore's Birthday Party: A day-long party in late April to raise money for nonprofits in honor of Eeyore, Winnie-the-Pooh's habitually sad buddy.

Trail of Lights: Annual celebration in Zilker Park each December to ring in the holiday season.

Food & Wine Festival: The absolute best of Austin's culinary scene gets together in Zilker Park each November.

Don't miss Zilker's summer savior, **Barton Springs Pool**, a 3-acre outdoor swimming spot fed by cold-water natural springs from deep underground. The water temperature averages between 68°F and 70°F (20-21°C) all year, particularly wonderful on those brutally hot summer days when the thermostat frequently hits triple digits. In the winter, admission fees are waived for those interested in a complimentary dose of cryotherapy.

A Hike-&-Bike Trail

MAP P274

Skip the gym

The **Ann and Roy Butler Hike-and-Bike Trail** is Austin's outdoor gym. Whether it's a walk, run, bike ride or quality time with your pup, this is where Austin congregates to get outside and burn calories – all while taking in stunning views of downtown. The 10-mile trail loops around Lady Bird Lake, using the Roberta Crenshaw Bridge under MoPac (to the west) and Longhorn Shores (to the east) to form a circle, and features public art exhibits and a live music series in the fall.

EATING IN SOUTH AUSTIN: OUR PICKS

MAP P272

Polvos: Delicious interior Mexican food. Now three locations, but visit the original on S 1st St for the atmosphere. *9:30am-10pm Sun-Thu, to 11pm Fri & Sat* $$

Fresa's: Another S 1st St favorite. The specialty here is wood-grilled chicken, but top it with the jalapeño crema. *11am-10pm Mon-Fri, 10am-10pm Sat & Sun* $

Dovetail Pizza: A little fancier than a normal, neighborhood pizza joint. Also located on S 1st. *11am-10pm Sun-Thu, to 11pm Fri & Sat* $$

Terry Black's BBQ: A long line on weekends, but it moves quickly. You might spend longer finding a place to park. *10:30am-9:30pm Sun-Thu, to 10pm Fri & Sat* $$

DOWNTOWN AUSTIN BIKE TOUR

Witness the best of downtown Austin on two wheels. An e-bike can be rented using the CapMetro Bikeshare app at Riverside/South Lamar Station.

START	END	LENGTH
Pfluger Pedestrian Bridge	Central Public Library	Roughly 5 miles; 50-60 minutes

Cross over the 1 **Pfluger Pedestrian Bridge**, and circle back through Sand Beach Park to turn left on the Lance Armstrong Bikeway. Ride past 2 **Open Room Austin**, a large picnic table slash public art installation. Turn left on West Ave and then right on 2nd St to go over the 3 **Butterfly Bridge**. At the corner of 2nd and Lavaca, stop at the 4 **Willie Nelson statue** at Austin City Limits Live. Keep heading east and pause for more pictures at the 5 **Tau Ceti rainbow mural** at 2nd and Brazos. In two more blocks, turn left on Trinity St, then right on the bike path on 4th St before turning left on Red River St. Two blocks down, cross 6 **6th Street** (p278), one of the country's most famous stretches of bars and clubs. Continue north through the 7 **Red River Cultural District** (p279), a hub for live music. At 12th and Red River, ride through 8 **Waterloo Park**, a new green space in downtown. Head back to 12th St and take a right up the hill toward the 9 **State Capitol**. Ride through the grounds and exit the west gate along 12th St. At 12th and Shoal Creek Boulevard, turn left to enter the 10 **Shoal Creek Greenbelt**. While approaching Duncan Neighborhood Park, take a slight left to avoid stairs before finding the 11 **9th St BMX Park**. Turn right on the trail and then a sharp left to cross the creek and pass the 12 **Deep Roots Community Garden**. Continue on Shoal Creek Trail until it hits the Lance Armstrong Bikeway at the 13 **Central Public Library**. There are stations nearby to dock your bike.

South by Southwest

MAP P274

Downtown Austin's March transformation

For Austin at its liveliest, visit in March during **SXSW**. Founded in 1987, the annual 10-day event features a celebration of technology, film, music, education and culture. Stop by for film premieres at the **Paramount Theatre** (p279), see hotshot new artists perform at **Mohawk** (p139), watch big-name comedians at **Esther's Follies**, and check out exhibits, panels and keynotes galore at the **Austin Convention Center**. Badge prices range from $700 to $1700, but there are also free shows for those without company budgets.

South Austin Entertainment

MAP P272

Where to let loose

South Austin continues to pull its weight in helping the city maintain its reputation as the Live Music Capital of the World. No visit is complete without a ticket to the **Continental Club**. Since 1955, the Continental has evolved from supper club to burlesque club to a legendary live-music stage.

Two of Austin's other most legendary live-music joints exist along a stretch of South Lamar. **Saxon Pub** is a cozy spot for happy hour or shows, and Austin mainstays like Bob Schneider and the Resentments still play regular gigs there. **Broken Spoke** is a dance hall famed for its country music and two-step lessons.

Lady Bird Johnson Wildflower Center

Bluebonnet heaven

The 284-acre **Lady Bird Johnson Wildflower Center** has been delighting generations since 1982. Every type of Texan native wildflower is represented on its grounds, with nearly 900 species of plants from the different regions of the state, which includes bluebonnets in the spring, of course. The center also offers bird-watching on the wildflower-rimmed trails, an interactive kids garden, a 1-mile tree arboretum and a quaint cafe with patio seating to rest your stems and refuel.

AUSTIN'S BEST MOVIE VENUES

Austin's film scene was born from Richard Linklater's 1990 flick *Slacker,* which acutely detailed the city's culture and vibe. Austin is now home to several film festivals and some of the best theaters in the country.

Alamo Drafthouse Cinema: Iconic Austin chain with beer and food delivery to your seat. Just don't talk or text during the movie.

Violet Crown Cinema: Small theater downtown with only a couple of rows for each screen.

AFS Cinema: Home theater of the Austin Film Society, founded by Linklater, on the city's north side.

Blue Starlite Urban Drive-In: Watch movies from your car on a downtown rooftop.

Bullock Museum IMAX Theater: The biggest screen inside the city's biggest history museum.

EATING IN SOUTH AUSTIN: DATE NIGHT SPOTS

MAP P272

Uchi: One of Austin's most popular high-end restaurants. Named one of the 20 most important restaurants in the country. *4-10pm Sun-Thu, to 11pm Fri & Sat* $$$

Loro: Asian-BBQ fusion from chefs Tyson Cole of Uchi and Aaron Franklin of Franklin Barbecue. *11am-10pm Sun-Thu, to 11pm Fri & Sat* $$

El Alma: Authentic Mexican food in a beautiful space at the Barton Springs location. *11am-10pm Mon-Thu, 11am-11pm Fri, 10am-11pm Sat, 10am-10pm Sun* $$

Perla's: Seafood and oysters while sitting underneath the trees on a massive patio along South Congress. *11:30am-10pm Sun-Thu, to 11pm Fri, 10:30am-11pm Sat* $$

TIPS FOR THE FRANKLIN LINE

Standing in line for Franklin Barbecue on a Saturday morning is a rite of passage for many Texans. **Aaron Franklin**, the pit master himself, helps you navigate the wait. *(@franklinbbq)*

Show up early. I would probably get here at about 8:30am. You won't be right up front, but you won't be out in full sun.

Wear comfortable shoes. You're going to be on your feet for a while. We do have a ton of chairs as loaners, though.

Stay hydrated. You're probably gonna drink some beers later.

Make new friends. People come from all over the world to hang out, and everybody's got a reason.

Be hungry. We'll crush you. It's gonna be a great nap afterwards, though.

ERIC LAUDONIEN/SHUTTERSTOCK

Neon Grotto

Austin's Barbecue Showdown

MAPS P271, P274

Top-notch smokers

Award-winning **Franklin Barbecue** *(franklinbbq.com)* has long been touted as the best barbecue in Austin and turned pit master Aaron Franklin into a national celebrity on the food scene. Spending a Saturday morning waiting for hours on a fold-out chair in front of the restaurant for a taste of that fatty brisket is as much an experience as the eating part.

But Franklin has plenty of legit competition for the barbecue crown these days. **La Barbecue** *(labarbecue.com)* has become one of Austin's favorite smokehouses since its opening in 2011.

Once known only for its famed food truck **Micklethwait Barbecue** *(craftmeatsaustin.com)* opened its first bricks-and-mortar location in Austin inside an old church in late 2024.

Further out, **Leroy & Lewis Barbecue** *(leroyandlewis bbq.com)* is a new-school barbecue joint that has gone from a small truck to its own, frequently sold-out store on Austin's south side.

Going Out on 6th Street

MAP P274

As wild or tame as you want

Any discussion of a night out in Austin likely starts with its famed **6th Street**. Locals call the portion from I-35 to roughly Congress Ave 'Dirty 6th,' and it's lined with bars and clubs that get rowdy after the sun goes down. Dirty 6th is primarily occupied by college students on the hunt for cheap-ish drinks, or bachelorette parties looking to let loose. This stretch has some fabled dive spots, including **The Jackalope**, **Blind Pig Pub** and **Pete's Dueling Piano Bar**.

The vibe changes somewhat dramatically as the party moves up to 'West 6th,' from San Antonio St to Lamar. Here, there's a slightly older crowd and establishments like **Star Bar**, **The Rustic Tap** and **Kung Fu Saloon**. Some of the city's trendiest restaurants can also be found on W 6th, such as **Walton's Fancy & Staple**, owned by Austin adoptee Sandra Bullock.

Another popular option for a night on the town is **Rainey Street**, a several-block stretch of old bungalow homes turned into bars like **Clive Bar** and **Lucille**. This area is under constant renovation with a new high-rise condo building seemingly going up every time someone turns around.

If you're looking for live performances, head to the **Red River Cultural District** along Red River St, which is home to **Mohawk**, a long-time favorite venue for smaller shows, and **The Creek & The Cave**, a stand-up comedy club. By day, **Stubb's** is a barbecue restaurant, but at night it becomes one of Austin's bigger outdoor concert stages. Street parking is easier to find here along the Red River side streets, and there are plenty of food trucks to keep your belly full.

LGBTIQ+ Nightlife

MAP P274

Party with a rainbow crew

The thriving queer community is what distinguishes Austin from the rest of Texas. Celebrate love and acceptance on and around the 4th St Warehouse District, where colorful gay bars stand loud and proud. **Rain**, **Coconut Club**, **Neon Grotto** and **Oilcan Harry's**, the oldest of them all, are must-visits near the rainbow pedestrian crossing.

In the Red River Cultural District, **Cheer Up Charlies** has a killer dance floor, a ton of live music and a vegan food truck out back. Also on Red River, **Barbarella's** hosts the TuezGayz dance parties.

After the bars close, keep going after hours at **Highland Lounge** – and make sure to do drag brunch the next morning at **The Iron Bear**.

Paramount Theatre

MAP P274

Glamorous entertainment

For more than 100 years, the **Paramount Theatre** on Congress Ave in the heart of downtown Austin has entertained people within its majestic, art deco walls. The likes of Miles Davis, Katharine Hepburn, Maya Angelou and Burt Bacharach have all taken to its prestigious stage. Today the restored auditorium continues to treat crowds with music, comedy and movies.

LGBTIQ+ AUSTIN

Colton Ashabranner is the marketing and communications manager at the Austin LGBT Chamber of Commerce. *(@coltonashh)*

Austin is very unique in that we don't actually have a gayborhood. We have 4th St, which is the unofficial LGBTIQ+ district, but we're everywhere – and I would say Austin is very welcoming to our community. There are so many LGBTIQ-owned and ally businesses in Austin. Check out the Chamber events calendar *(membership.austinlgbtchamber.com/events)* or **Gay Do 512** *(gay.do512.com)*. The *Austin Chronicle* also has a section called Qmmunity *(austinchronicle.com/events/qmmunity)* where they share upcoming events. There are so many options, and there's always something to do.

DRINKING IN SOUTH AUSTIN: MUST-TRY SPOTS

MAP P272

Courtyard Lounge at Hotel San José: Gorgeous outdoor bar at one of the premier boutique hotels in the city. *noon-10pm Mon-Thu, to midnight Fri & Sat*

ABGB: Award-winning local brewery with plenty of outdoor seating, great pizza and live music. *11:30am-11pm Tue-Fri, noon-midnight Sat, noon-10pm Sun*

Bouldin Acres: Outdoor playground for adults (and your canine companion) with pickleball courts and other games. *11am-midnight*

Tiki Tatsu-Ya: Tiki bar with a wild aesthetic inside meant to take you on an immersive journey to paradise. *4pm-midnight Mon-Fri, 1pm-midnight Sat, 4-10pm Sun*

San Antonio & the Hill Country

RIVERSIDE EXPLORING | SPANISH ARCHITECTURE | OUTDOOR ADVENTURES

GETTING AROUND

Around downtown, it's easy to walk, ride a bike or take the bus. Avoid the hassle and cost of parking and leave your car at the free lot at P+R Ellis Alley; it's a short bus ride from there to downtown (take No 25 or No 100).

Buses operated by VIA *(viainfo.net)* provide service around town. You can pay in cash ($1.30) or with the VIA goMobile+ app.

Various B-Cycle bike-share stations are scattered around downtown – as well as at the southern Missions.

You'll need a car when you're ready to head to the Hill Country.

One of Texas' most attractive major cities, San Antonio has long captivated visitors. The legendary Alamo, that iconic symbol of Texan independence, stands at the heart of the city, while the River Walk, a glorious network of waterside pathways that's tucked below street level and lined with bars and restaurants, offers leisurely strolling through downtown and beyond.

The San Antonio River has long been an integral part of life here. The headwaters were sacred to Indigenous tribes, and today the river flows past many of the city's must-see neighborhoods, including the trendy Pearl and historic King William, and reaches the edge of the historic missions south of town – part of a UNESCO World Heritage site.

San Antonio puts you in close proximity to the Hill Country, a beautiful region known for its charming small towns, refreshing swimming holes and rugged state parks. The wildflower-lined back roads are gateways to memorable scenic drives.

Exploring the Alamo

The famous battle site

The much-fabled **Alamo** *(thealamo.org)* is where Davy Crockett, James Bowie and 200 other revolutionaries died in 1836 during a battle against Mexican troops. There's much to see beyond the old church: reconstructed parts of the mission turned fort, various films that shed light on the past, and an impressive collection (admission $14) donated by Alamo enthusiast and '80s pop star Phil Collins. Admission to the church is free.

Continued on p284

TOP TIP

Don't leave San Antonio without trying a puffy taco, which is a corn tortilla fired up into a puffy, crispy form that's then filled with the usual taco accouterments. It originated in San Antonio in the 1950s. **Tito's Mexican Restaurant** serves some of the best near downtown.

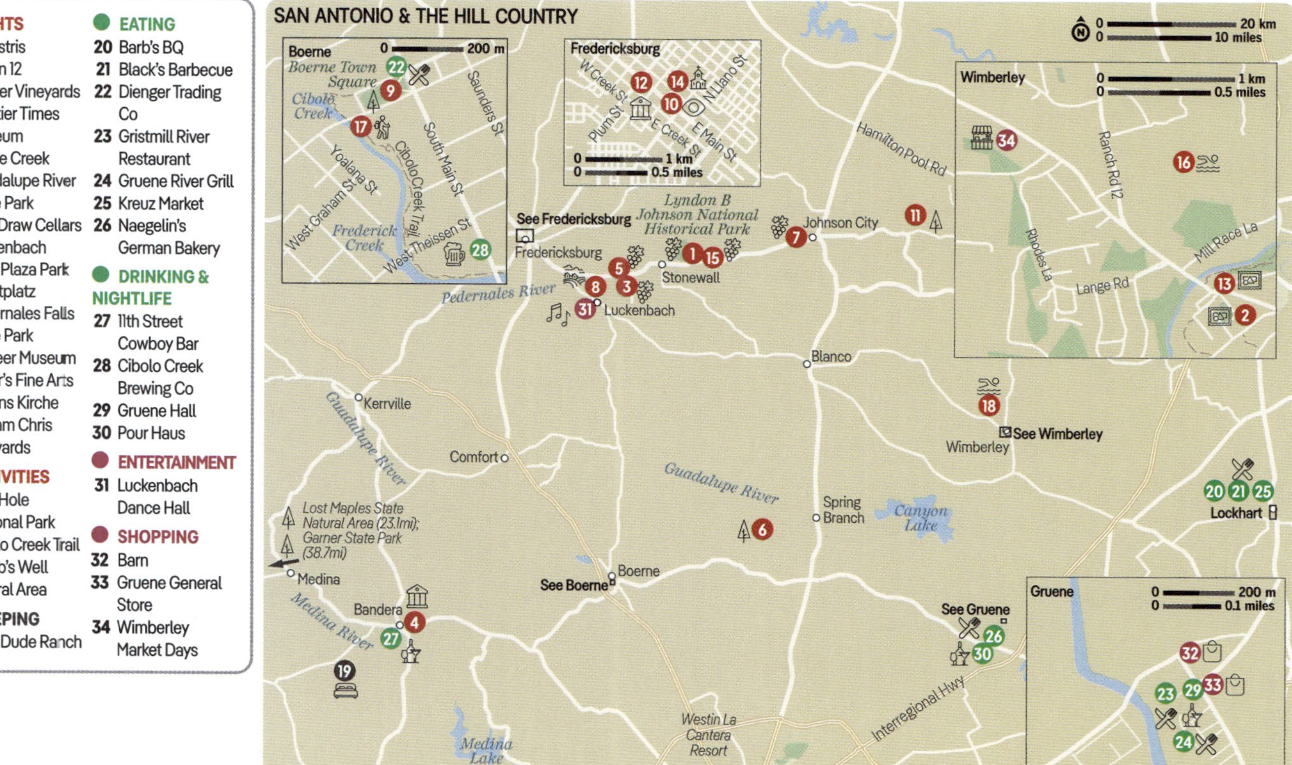

SIGHTS
1 Ab Astris
2 Art on 12
3 Becker Vineyards
4 Frontier Times Museum
5 Grape Creek
6 Guadalupe River State Park
7 Lost Draw Cellars
8 Luckenbach
9 Main Plaza Park
10 Marktplatz
11 Pedernales Falls State Park
12 Pioneer Museum
13 Pitzer's Fine Arts
14 Vereins Kirche
15 William Chris Vineyards

ACTIVITIES
16 Blue Hole Regional Park
17 Cibolo Creek Trail
18 Jacob's Well Natural Area

SLEEPING
19 Dixie Dude Ranch

EATING
20 Barb's BQ
21 Black's Barbecue
22 Dienger Trading Co
23 Gristmill River Restaurant
24 Gruene River Grill
25 Kreuz Market
26 Naegelin's German Bakery

DRINKING & NIGHTLIFE
27 11th Street Cowboy Bar
28 Cibolo Creek Brewing Co
29 Gruene Hall
30 Pour Haus

ENTERTAINMENT
31 Luckenbach Dance Hall

SHOPPING
32 Barn
33 Gruene General Store
34 Wimberley Market Days

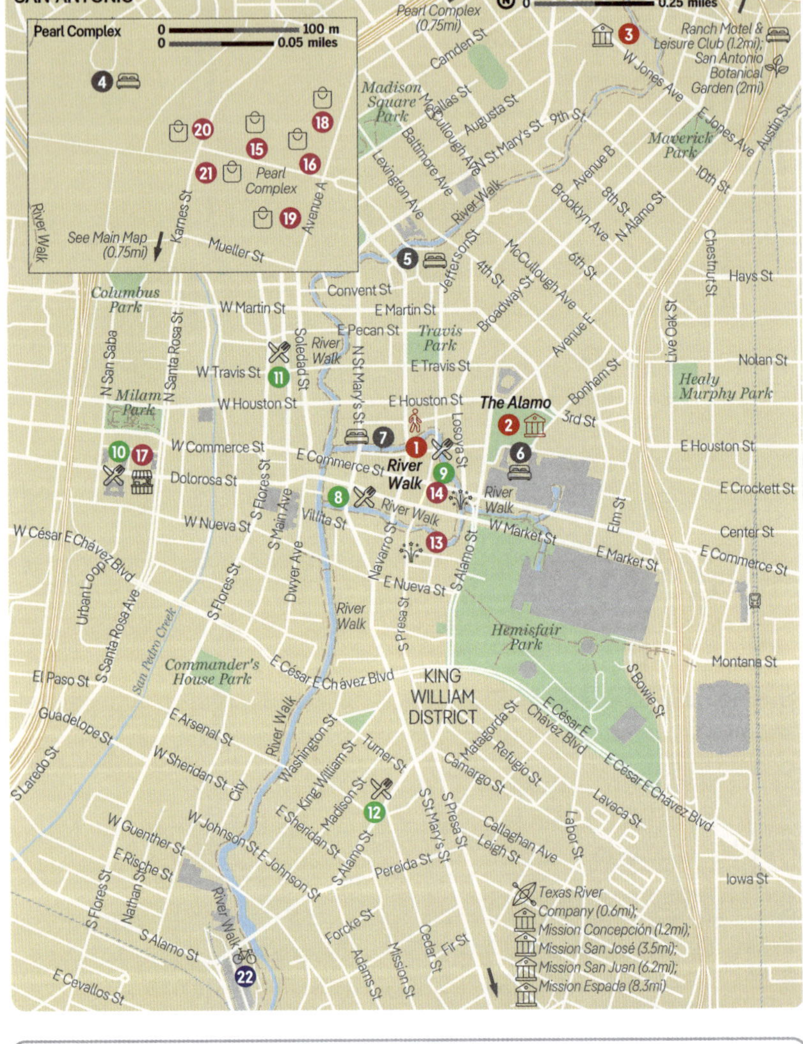

HIGHLIGHTS
1 River Walk
2 The Alamo

SIGHTS
3 San Antonio Museum of Art

SLEEPING
4 Hotel Emma
5 Hotel Havana
6 Menger Hotel
7 Omni La Mansión del Rio

EATING
8 Biga
9 Boudro's
10 Mi Tierra Cafe & Bakery
11 Pinkerton's Barbecue
12 Tito's Mexican Restaurant

ENTERTAINMENT
13 Fiesta Noche del Rio
14 Fiesta San Antonio

SHOPPING
15 Adelante
16 Dos Carolinas
17 Historic Market Square
18 King Ranch Saddle Shop
19 Niche at Pearl
20 The Pearl
21 The Twig Book Shop

TRANSPORT
22 Blue Star Bike Shop

TOP EXPERIENCE

The River Walk

A little slice of Europe in the heart of downtown, the 15-mile River Walk is an essential part of the San Antonio experience. Wandering this charming network of canals and pedestrian walkways, set just below the downtown streets, you can pass landscaped gardens and riverfront cafes, and linger on stone footbridges that arch gracefully across the water.

Dining & People Watching

The river makes a loop around one section of downtown, and this is the most commercial part of the River Walk. Here you'll find numerous restaurants and bars overlooking the water. It's lively day and night, with twinkling lights in the trees and music spilling out onto open terraces.

Peaceful Strolls

For a more peaceful experience, follow the river north or south of downtown. It's a memorable 1.7-mile walk from Houston St up to the Pearl District. Along the way, signposts point out unique river features – like the remains of the dam built by the visionary River Walk architect Robert Hugman in 1941. Look out for mosaics and other public artwork. Beneath the I-35 overpass, a school of larger-than-life fish floats overhead – an art installation by Donald Lipski. There's also an artificial grotto, complete with waterfall, near Newell Ave.

Boat Trips

On a fleet of of ecofriendly electric boats, **Go Rio** *(goriocruises .com)* operates narrated cruises ($16) that touch on San Antonio's history and culture. Boats depart from three different locations, including a dock below Commerce St near the Shops at Rivercenter mall. If you want to hop on and off, Go Rio runs a shuttle between downtown and the Museum Reach (north of downtown), with 15 different stops. Departures run roughly hourly between noon and 7pm (one-day pass $22).

TOP TIPS

- Rent kayaks from Texas River Company *(txrivercompany.com)*, which launches from Roosevelt Park, about 2 miles south of downtown.
- The southern River Walk is great for cycling. You can hire from Blue Star Bike Shop *(bluestarbikeshop.com)* and ride down to the missions (9 miles to the furthest).

PRACTICALITIES

- Check out *thesan antonioriverwalk.com* for info on exhibits and upcoming events.

SAN ANTONIO'S BIGGEST EVENTS

Fiesta San Antonio: Over 11 days in late April, this citywide party features river and flower-filled street parades, mariachi concerts and 100 other events.

Day of the Dead: In October, San Antonio hosts one of the biggest Day of the Day celebrations with traditional altars and parades.

Battle of the Alamo: History comes to life during the commemoration of the 13-day siege, held from late February to early March.

Holiday River Parade: Gear up for the holidays with a festive parade and dazzling lights along the River Walk. It happens in late November.

Fiesta Noche del Rio: On Friday and Saturday nights in June and July catch Latin music and dancing at the Arneson River Theater.

Continued from p280

Guided tours are available throughout the day for $45 (reserve ahead). For in-depth exploration at your own pace, book a self-guided audio tour for $20.

Little Mexico

Shops, food and entertainment

About half a mile west of the River Walk, **Historic Market Square** *(marketsquaresa.com)* is a little piece of Mexico in downtown San Antonio. It's a fair approximation of a trip south of the border, with Mexican food, mariachi bands and more than 100 locally owned shops filled with Mexican folk art, handmade goods and clothes. A big chunk of the square is taken up by **El Mercado**, the largest Mexican marketplace outside of Mexico.

Treasures from Latin America & Beyond

5000 years of art

The **San Antonio Museum of Art** *(samuseum.org; adult/child $22/free)* houses an impressive trove of Latin American art, including Spanish Colonial, Mexican and pre-Columbian – one of the most comprehensive collections in the US. Beyond Latin American works, the museum holds a little of everything, from Egyptian antiquities to contemporary abstracts, as well as an impressive Asian wing with a collection of Chinese ceramics, paintings and decorative items.

Fun at the Pearl

Shopping, dining and concerts

A former brewery turned urban playground, **The Pearl** *(atpearl.com)* is a large complex with restaurants, shops, a boutique hotel, green spaces, a splash pad for kids and a branch of the CIA – as in Culinary Institute of America. It sits near the River Walk, and there's even a shaded amphitheater overlooking the water. The best time to visit the Pearl is on weekend mornings, when you can catch one of its captivating markets *(atpearl.com/weekend-market)*.

Botanical Bounty

Flora from Texas and beyond

The **San Antonio Botanical Garden** *(sabot.org; adult/child $22/15)* is an immaculately tended, 38-acre complex with a variety of diverse environments. One area not to miss is the

EATING IN SAN ANTONIO: OUR PICKS

Boudro's: Ideal waterfront spot for indulging in blue crab tostadas, prickly pear margaritas and other creative temptations. *11am-10:30pm* $$$

Mi Tierra Cafe y Panaderia: This festive Mexican eatery and bakery in Market Sq is a San Antonio landmark, opened in 1941. *8am-10pm* $$

Biga: A welcoming outdoor patio on the River Walk and an acclaimed menu of New American cuisine. *5-9:30pm* $$$

Pinkerton's Barbecue: Fires up some of San Antonio's best barbecue, which you can enjoy at picnic tables overlooking a small park. *11am-9pm* $$

TOP EXPERIENCE

The Mission Trail

Spain's missionary presence can best be felt at the ruins of the four missions south of town, all overseen by the National Park Service as part of the San Antonio Missions National Historical Park. The San Antonio missions were constructed in the 18th century, and Catholic services are still held in the churches, which are supported by vibrant communities.

Mission Concepción

Mission Concepción

Heading south from San Antonio, **Mission Concepción** is first mission along the Mission Trail and the oldest unrestored stone church in the country.

Mission San José

Known in its time as the Queen of the Missions, **San José** is the largest and arguably the most beautiful of the four. Because it's a little more remote and pastoral, surrounded by thick stone walls, you can really get a sense of what life was like here in the 18th and 19th centuries.

Mission San Juan

Founded in 1731, this **mission** was once self-sustaining with orchards and gardens just outside the walls and farm fields further off. Take the **Yanaguana Trail** behind the church down to the river to see some of a natural ecosystem that was common before the arrival of the Spanish.

Mission Espada

The southernmost stop on the Mission Trail is also the oldest, dating from 1690. The **church** was built between 1745 and 1756. It's the best place to check out the historic *acequias*, which were dug by the mission inhabitants in the 1700s and used to water the farm fields.

TOP TIPS

- Mission San José is home to the main park visitor center, with free tours (10am and 11am).
- You can get here by cycling an extension of the River Walk.
- Mission San José's mariachi mass at noon on Sunday (in Spanish) is a San Antonio tradition.

PRACTICALITIES

- See *nps.gov/saan* for maps, opening hours and background information.

BEST STATE PARKS & SWIMMING SPOTS IN THE HILL COUNTRY

Garner State Park *(adult/child $8/free)* Float in a tube ($10) beneath limestone cliffs and rolling green hills.

Guadalupe River State Park (p286) *(adult/child $7/free)* Straddles a 4-mile stretch of the sparkling, bald-cypress-tree-lined Guadalupe River, and it's great for water activities and hiking.

Pedernales Falls State Park *(adult/child $6/free)* Trails wind through forests, atop ridges and along the churning riverside.

Lost Maples State Natural Area *(adult/child $6/free)* Summertime swimming, hiking amid limestone canyons and grasslands, and colorful leaves in autumn.

Jacob's Well Natural Area *(adult/child $9/5; jwna.checkfront.com/reserve)* A glorious setting for a swim, though you'll need to reserve ahead.

Blue Hole Regional Park *(adult/child $12/8; wimberleyparksandrec.com/blue-hole-swimming)* Leap into the spring-fed waters of Cypress Creek. Reserve ahead.

UNIVERSITY OF COLLEGE/SHUTTERSTOCK

Black's Barbecue

Texas Native Trail with three separate sections devoted to South Texas, the Hill Country and the eastern Pineywoods – which has a small lake ringed with bald cypress trees.

Historic Gruene's Fabled Dance Hall

Local crafts and live music

Settled by German farmers in the mid-1800s, the welcoming and historic town of Gruene (pronounced 'green') is the musical heart of the region. Pick up a cowboy hat from the **Gruene General Store** *(gruenegeneralstore.com)* and browse ceramics made by local artists at **The Barn** *(thebarningruene.com)*. Later, head to **Gruene Hall** *(gruenehall.com)*, an 1878 dance hall with free live music every night of the week.

Tubing in New Braunfels & Gruene

Waterside adventures

During the summer, nothing beats floating on the cool and easy-flowing waters of the Guadalupe and Comal rivers. When the sun gets to be too much, you can cool off with a swim, then hop back in the tube and continue along. Dozens of local outfitters rent tubes, and at the end of your trip, you'll be bused back to your starting point. **Texas Tubes** *(texastubes.com; $25)* is a recommended outfitter in New Braunfels, while **Rockin' R River Rides** *(rockinr.com; $25)* is the best choice in Gruene.

Eating Barbecue in Lockhart

Famous food spots

Back in 2003 the Texas Legislature officially named Lockhart the 'Barbecue Capital of Texas.' You can eat well at any of its barbecue restaurants. A good place to start is **Kreuz Market** (*kreuzmarket.com*). A local landmark since 1900, this barn-like eatery is famed for its dry rub meats – no sauce needed. Another stalwart is **Black's Barbecue** (*blacksbbq.com*), open since 1932 – and a favorite of President LBJ. This classic barbecue spot serves up buttery rich ribs and juicy sausage.

At **Barb's BQ** (*barbsbq.com*), the young pitmaster has turned the barbecue world on its head with her tender, delicately spiced brisket, ribs and lamb. It's open Saturday and Sunday only (11am to 3pm). Go early as they always sell out.

Strolling Boerne

Shops, restaurants and parks

Settled by German immigrants in 1849, the attractive town of Boerne (pronounced 'Bernie') has more than 140 restored historical structures.

The half-mile stretch of Main St between River Rd and Blanco St makes for some rewarding exploring. Start off the ramble at the **Main Plaza Park**. On its northeastern corner, stop in the **Dienger Trading Co** (*thediengertradingco.com*), a bistro, bakery and boutique in an 1884 grocery-store building. A few blocks south of there, the kid-friendly **Cibolo Creek Brewing Co** (*cibolocreekbrewing.com*) is a pleasant indoor-outdoor spot for craft beers and satisfying cooking.

A pleasant add-on to Main St exploring is a walk along the **Cibolo Creek Trail**, which follows a pretty creekside some 1.7 miles all the way to City Park. Once there, you can experience more fine scenery at the **Cibolo Center for Conservation**, which has short trails through native Texan woods, marshland and along Cibolo Creek.

Cowboy Culture in Bandera

Western lore

Bandera brands itself the Cowboy Capital of the World. While touristy, with staged gunfights (Saturdays at 10am and noon) and shops selling cowboy attire, Bandera still has an air of authenticity, particularly among the cowboy bars and honky-tonks. Near town, the 725-acre **Dixie Dude Ranch** (*dixiedude ranch.com*) offers horseback riding, campfire sing-alongs and other activities.

For a little perspective on bygone days in Bandera, stop by the **Frontier Times Museum** (*frontiertimesmuseum.org; adult/child $8/4*), which has displays of Western art and cowboy tchotchkes such as guns and branding irons.

BEST VINEYARDS OF HILL COUNTRY

Hill Country's wine destination is **Hwy 290** (*wineroad290.com*) which has over 50 wineries, many open to tastings and tours. Leave the driving to **290 Wine Shuttle** (*290wineshuttle.com; per person $50*).

Lost Draw Cellars Produces top-quality wines that showcase the terroir of the Texas High Plains.

Becker Vineyards One of the oldest and best wineries in the region, with a tasting room that's modeled on a German barn.

Grape Creek Resembles Tuscany with its spread of vineyards and stone buildings.

Ab Astris A boutique winery that produces handcrafted vintages, with a focus on lesser-known grape varieties.

William Chris Vineyards Hill Country's most famous winery with great views and premium wines.

EATING & DRINKING IN NEW BRAUNFELS & GRUENE: OUR PICKS

Gristmill River Restaurant: Get a deckside table and enjoy ribs, steak and catfish in an 1800s cotton gin behind Gruene Hall. *11am-9pm* $$

Gruene River Grill: The rustic dining room in Gruene makes a relaxed setting for American and Tex-Mex comfort food. *11am-9pm* $$

Naegelin's German Bakery: Pick up strudels and kolaches from this legendary New Braunfels bakery – the oldest in Texas. *6:30am-5pm Mon-Sat, 8am-2pm Sun* $

Pour Haus: Take a seat in the yard, and enjoy craft brews and delicious street tacos while catching live music in New Braunfels. *4pm-midnight Mon-Fri, 1pm-midnight Sat & Sun*

THE PERILOUS JOURNEY FROM GERMANY

In 1845 in Germany, overpopulation, low wages and widespread poverty inspired some to seek a better life abroad. Those that came to Texas faced a daunting journey that began with a two-month trip aboard a cramped, unsanitary ship to reach Indianola on the Gulf. Once there, the travelers discovered that war had broken out between Mexico and the US, and onward transportation was not available. This left 4000 people languishing on the beach with little shelter, impure water, contaminated food and soon-to-be-rampant disease. Over 1400 died that summer. As weeks passed, those who were able set out on foot, leaving behind many of their possessions as they trudged 200 miles through rugged lands to newly christened settlements where they would begin a new life.

Afterwards, sip a Shiner at the **11th Street Cowboy Bar** *(11thstcowboybar.com)*, billed as the 'Biggest Little Honky Tonk in Texas.'

Gallery Hopping in Wimberley

Galleries, markets and swimming spots

Small, charming Wimberley is famed as an artists' community. **Art on 12** *(arton12.com)* features works by dozens of local and regional artists. Nearby, check out the paintings and sculpture of **Pitzer's Fine Arts** *(pitzersart.com)*, another well-respected gallery. Afterwards, treat yourself to a meal at one of Wimberley's charming creekside restaurants like **The Leaning Pear**, with its elevated comfort fare, or the **Creekhouse Kitchen & Bar** with creative fare and a lovely forested backdrop.

From March to December, the first Saturday of the month is **Wimberley Market Day** *(wimberleymarketday.com)*, featuring live music, food stalls and more than 400 vendors selling arts, crafts and more.

German Roots in Fredericksburg

Pioneer architecture and schnitzel

One of the Hill Country's most vibrant towns, Fredericksburg is a former 19th-century German settlement with its history woven into the landscape. Its street signs proclaim 'Willkommen,' and you'll be welcome indeed along its main street, lined with historic buildings that house German restaurants, beer gardens, antique stores and wine-tasting rooms.

For insight into what life was like for Fredericksburg's first settlers, visit the **Pioneer Museum** *(pioneermuseum.org; adult/child $12/5)*, with its collection of restored historic buildings that you can wander through.

Music, dancing and schnitzel are on the menu every October, when Fredericksburg celebrates its German heritage with Texas' largest **Oktoberfest** *(oktoberfestinfbg.com)*. Families crowd around for oompah bands, kegs of German beer and schnitzels galore. On Saturday, join hands for the Chicken Dance!

Legendary Luckenbach

Music-loving enclave

Made up of a handful of Old West structures, tiny **Luckenbach** *(luckenbachtexas.com)* is big on Texas charm. By day, the main activity is sitting at a picnic table under an old oak tree with a cold bottle of Shiner Bock beer and listening to guitar pickers. On Friday nights, two-stepping couples whirl around the dance floor of **Luckenbach Dance Hall**.

STROLL FREDERICKSBURG'S PAST

Peer past the souvenir shops to discover Fredericksburg's immigrant past amid striking buildings from the late 19th century and early 1900s.

START	END	LENGTH
Nimitz Hotel	St Mary's Catholic Church	1 mile; 1½ hours

Start at the former 1 **Nimitz Hotel**, an 1860 building with a curious facade (meant to emulate a steamboat) that once hosted stagecoach travelers. Today it houses one big section of the National Museum of the Pacific War. Cross the street (carefully) and continue to 2 **249 E Main St**. The typical home, built in 1866, is the birthplace of Chester Nimitz, who would go on to command the US Naval fleet in WWII (and sign the Japanese surrender documents in Tokyo Bay). The hometown hero is the reason the museum resides in Fredericksburg.

The heart of town is 3 **Marktplatz**, a green space and centuries-old hub of the community. The octagonal building in the square's center is a 1935 reconstruction (and 2020 remodeling) of the 4 **Vereins Kirche**, which served as the town church, meeting hall and school.

Continue along Main St and turn down Milam. You'll soon spot one of Texas' original tiny homes. Known as a Sunday house, the 5 **Weber House** was used by early Fredericksburgers for their stay on weekends when driving in from the country to do their shopping, attend social gatherings and go to church. Around the corner, 6 **St Mary's Catholic Church** is one of the so-called 'painted churches' of Texas, its 1908 Gothic design replete with stained glass, artwork and stenciling.

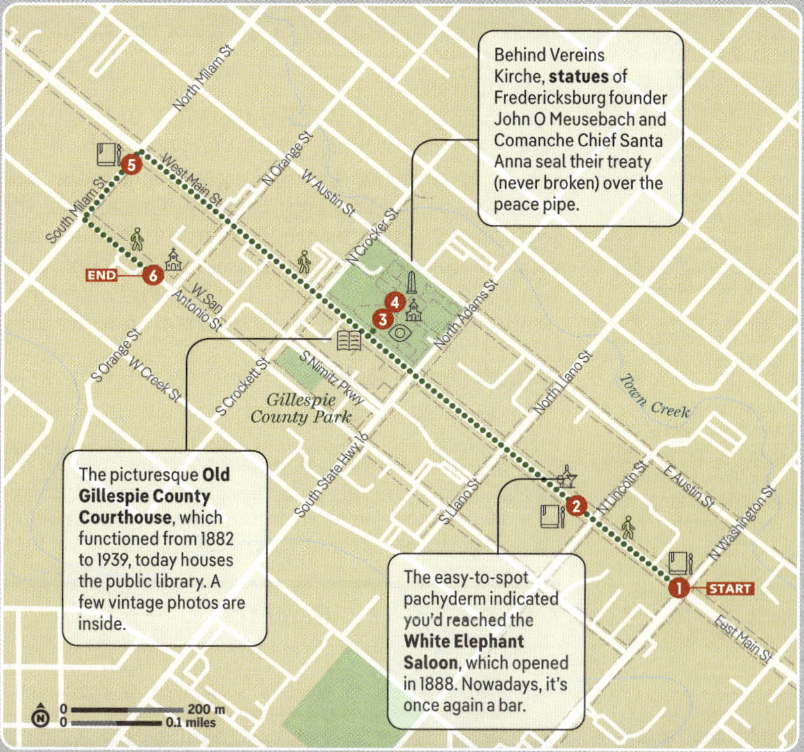

Behind Vereins Kirche, **statues** of Fredericksburg founder John O Meusebach and Comanche Chief Santa Anna seal their treaty (never broken) over the peace pipe.

The picturesque **Old Gillespie County Courthouse**, which functioned from 1882 to 1939, today houses the public library. A few vintage photos are inside.

The easy-to-spot pachyderm indicated you'd reached the **White Elephant Saloon**, which opened in 1888. Nowadays, it's once again a bar.

Dallas & Fort Worth

ARTS & CULTURE | CATTLE DRIVES | NIGHTLIFE

GETTING AROUND

Trinity Railway Express (TRE) makes the one-hour journey between EBJ Union Station in Dallas and Fort Worth Central Station every 30 to 60 minutes. Within Dallas, you can also take light rail lines operated by DART (Dallas Area Rapid Transit; *dart.org*), with the handy green line serving the Arts District, Deep Ellum and Fair Park.

In Fort Worth, buses operated by Trinity Metro connect areas of interest to most travelers. Travel between the Fort Worth Stockyards and Downtown is easy with the Orange Line. There are also myriad buses in Dallas operated by DART, plus a streetcar between Downtown Dallas and Bishop Arts.

Dallas, the 'Big D,' is Texas' most mythologized city, rich in the stuff of which American legends are woven – including oil barons, cowboys and cheerleaders. Excellent museums in the massive, recently developed Arts District downtown offer world-class displays of art and sculpture, while unmissable sites commemorate the city's rendezvous with history in 1963, as the site of President John F Kennedy's assassination. For the quintessential Dallas experience, explore its distinctive neighborhoods, like down-and-dirty Deep Ellum, pivotal in the stories of blues and jazz, or contemporary hipster hang-outs like the Bishop Arts District.

Famous as being 'Where the West Begins,' Fort Worth hasn't lost touch with its cowboy roots. It first rose to prominence during the great open-range cattle drives of the late 19th century. These days, the legendary Stockyards are the prime visitor destination, hosting cattle drives, rodeos and Billy Bob's, the world's biggest honky-tonk. Downtown Fort Worth, 3 miles south, is bursting with restaurants and bars.

A Dark Day in Dallas

MAP P293

The assassination of JFK

A good place to dive into one of America's most disturbing days is at the **Sixth Floor Museum** *(jfk.org; adult/child $25/21)*. Set in the former Book Depository where Lee Harvey Oswald fired those fateful shots, the museum gives a riveting account of the events that transpired on November 22, 1963.

TOP TIP

Plan your downtown Dallas visit around lunchtime, when you can enjoy wide-ranging global flavors at the Exchange Food Hall. There's also a festive happy hour buzz at the bars in the area in the early evening during the week – weekends are fairly dead downtown, but lively in Deep Ellum.

KIT LEONG/SHUTTERSTOCK

Dallas Farmers Market

Photographs, audio clips, news footage and eyewitness accounts make you feel almost as if you're experiencing it live.

Dealey Plaza, across the street from the museum, is where JFK was assassinated. The whole area is now a National Historic Landmark, with several signs detailing the day's events.

The Heart of Urban Life

MAP P293

Explore AT&T Discovery District

See the downtown renaissance of Dallas at the **AT&T Discovery District** *(discoverydistrictdallas.com)*, which features multimedia installations, concerts and an open-air plaza that has free movie screenings and big games shown on a 104ft video wall. By day, the best reason to come here is to munch your way around the **Exchange Food Hall**, with vendors serving tacos, pizzas, sliders, Indian curries, creative salads and Mediterranean fare.

The Best Food Hall in Dallas

MAP P293

Food stalls and shops

Since 1941, the **Dallas Farmers Market** *(dallasfarmersmarket.org)* has been a top spot for fresh provisions. These days,

BEST SHOPPING IN DEEP ELLUM

Dated Faded Worn: A pricey but well-curated vintage shop with T-shirts, denim and shoes.

Deep Vellum: One of Dallas' best indie bookshops (and small-press publishers).

Rocket Fizz: A kaleidoscopic selection of vintage and contemporary candies and sodas.

Jade & Clover: You'll find jewelry, candles and alpaca socks, along with a much-loved plant bar.

EATING & DRINKING IN DEEP ELLUM: OUR PICKS

MAP P293

Pecan Lodge: Dallas' best barbecue spot fires up mouthwatering brisket and smoky ribs, plus collard greens, okra and peach cobbler. *11am-8pm Tue-Sun, to 3pm Mon* $$

Velvet Taco: The taco is elevated to high art with fillings like beer-battered cauliflower and sweet chile shrimp. *11am-midnight Sun-Thu, to 4am Fri & Sat* $

AllGood Cafe: Art-filled street-corner diner with hearty breakfasts and Tex-Mex, plus a stage for live music Thursday to Saturday. *8am-3pm Sun-Wed, to 9pm Thu-Sat* $

Dot's Hop House & Courtyard: Has a charming courtyard, big beer menu and delicious comfort fare (like duck-fat fries). *4pm-1am Mon-Wed, noon-1am Thu-Sun* $$

BEST OF DALLAS' ARTS DISTRICT

The country's largest arts district stretches across some 118 acres just north of Downtown Dallas.

Perot Museum of Nature & Science *(adult/child $25/15)* A kid pleaser with five floors of interactive exhibits, plus massive dinosaur skeletons.

Dallas Museum of Art *(free)* One of Texas' best collections, with treasures that span centuries (and continents).

Klyde Warren Park Take a break between museum-hopping at this green space and community hub for outdoor yoga, movie screenings and markets. There are also food trucks and several restaurants.

Nasher Sculpture Center *(adult/child $10/free)* An impressive array of works by renowned sculptors past and present.

Crow Museum of Asian Art *(free)* Beautiful works in artfully designed exhibition halls.

the market has a capacious food hall where you can enjoy lattes, tacos, banh mi, sushi, thali platters, barbecue and juices.

On weekends, head to the nearby open-sided **Shed** for farm-fresh produce as well as handmade soaps, cutting boards, jewelry, and lots of other crafts and seasonal items.

Creative Deep Ellum

MAP P293

Music and art

Embodying the neighborhood's most creative aspect, **Deep Ellum Art Co** *(deepellumart.co)* is a spacious 5000-sq-ft multi-use venue that features an art gallery, concert stage and a back-yard of art installations, murals, food trucks and yard games.

Trees *(treesdallas.com; admission from $15)* has been a mainstay in Deep Ellum since its opening back in 1990. The wide-ranging lineup leans toward indie rock, hip-hop and EDM, with concerts four or five nights a week.

Uptown's Scenic Trail

MAP P293

Walking, running and cycling

To enjoy some see-and-be-seen walking, running or cycling, hit the tree-lined **Katy Trail** *(katytraildallas.org)*. The former railroad line stretches for 3.5 miles from N Houston St (just above the American Airlines Center) in the south to Airline Rd in the north. Post walk or run, stop in the Katy Trail Ice House, a scenic spot with outdoor tables for barbecue and craft beers.

Exploring Bishop Arts District

MAP P293

Crafts, records and books

One-of-a-kind boutiques, eye-catching galleries and an array of creative eating and drinking spaces line the streets of Bishop Arts District, Dallas' most walkable neighborhood.

Start your wander along Bishop Ave at **Mosaic Makers Collective** *(mosaicmakers.co)*, featuring beautifully made jewelry, clothing, stationery and housewares, all created by female artisans and designers. Across the street, **Spinster Records** *(spinsterrecords.com)* has a brilliant selection of new and used vinyl (plus a few CDs and old-school cassettes).

Continue along N Bishop Ave to **Dolly on Bishop** *(dollypythonvintage.com)*,which is crammed full of vintage apparel and curiosities dating from the 1940s to 1980s. Book lovers should definitely make the slight detour to W 8th St for **The**

EATING IN BISHOP ARTS: OUR PICKS

MAP P293

Tribal All Day Cafe: An inviting vegan-friendly spot with smoothies, seasonal vegetable bowls and breakfast burritos. *8am-5:30pm Mon-Sat, to 4pm Sun* $

Taco y Vino: A delightful mashup of creative Mexican fare, tacos and good wines with a lively ambience and a spacious backyard. *11am-10pm Mon-Sat, to 3pm Sun* $$

The Mayor's House by Selda: Excellent Turkish cooking in a historic building with multiple dining rooms and a breezy front porch. *noon-11pm* $$

Lucia: Reserve well ahead for a table at this award-winning restaurant serving up top-notch creative Italian fare. *5-10pm Tue-Sat* $$$

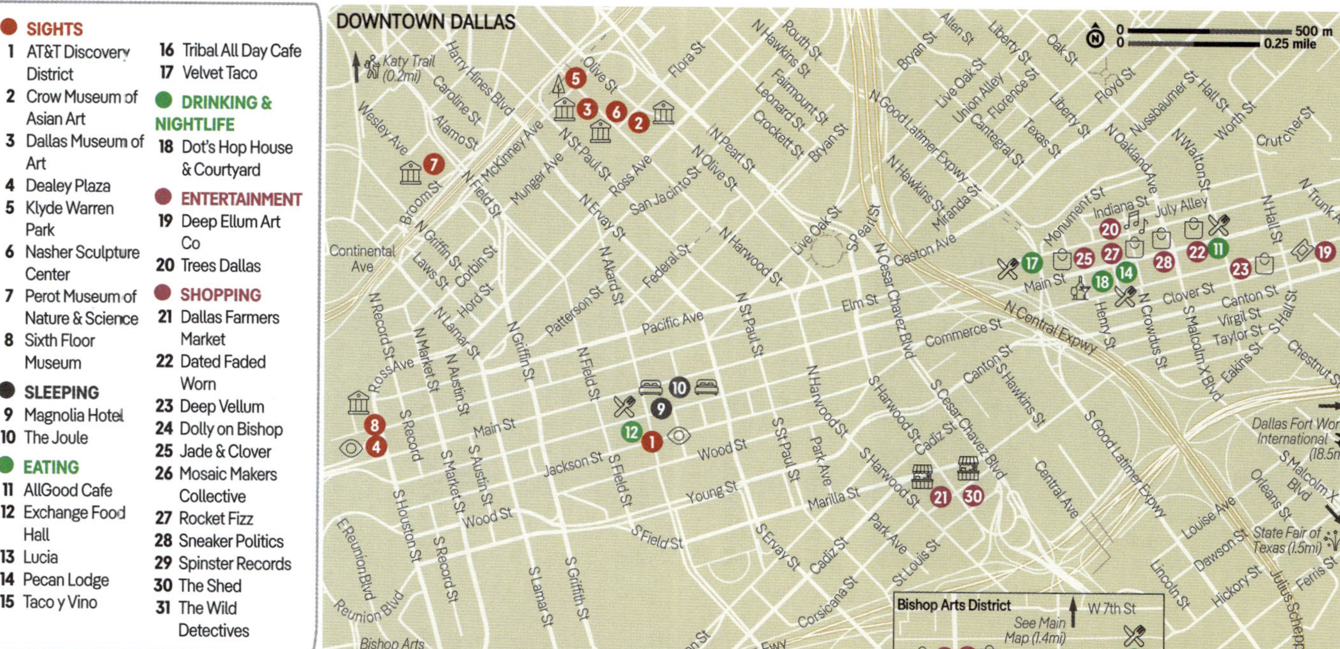

SIGHTS
1 AT&T Discovery District
2 Crow Museum of Asian Art
3 Dallas Museum of Art
4 Dealey Plaza
5 Klyde Warren Park
6 Nasher Sculpture Center
7 Perot Museum of Nature & Science
8 Sixth Floor Museum

SLEEPING
9 Magnolia Hotel
10 The Joule

EATING
11 AllGood Cafe
12 Exchange Food Hall
13 Lucia
14 Pecan Lodge
15 Taco y Vino
16 Tribal All Day Cafe
17 Velvet Taco

DRINKING & NIGHTLIFE
18 Dot's Hop House & Courtyard

ENTERTAINMENT
19 Deep Ellum Art Co
20 Trees Dallas

SHOPPING
21 Dallas Farmers Market
22 Dated Faded Worn
23 Deep Vellum
24 Dolly on Bishop
25 Jade & Clover
26 Mosaic Makers Collective
27 Rocket Fizz
28 Sneaker Politics
29 Spinster Records
30 The Shed
31 The Wild Detectives

BEST MUSEUMS IN FORT WORTH CULTURAL DISTRICT

Amon Carter Museum of American Art *(free)* Showcases works by some of the nation's most famous painters and sculptors.

Kimbell Art Museum *(free)* Has a small but surprising collection that allows you to hone in on single masterpieces like Caravaggio's *The Cardsharps* or El Greco's *Portrait of Dr Francisco de Pisa.*

The Modern *(adult/child $16/free)* Inside a building that appears to float above the surrounding reflecting pools, the Modern hosts groundbreaking contemporary exhibitions.

National Cowgirl Museum *(adult/child $12/6)* Explores the myth and reality of cowgirls in American culture, with interactive exhibits.

Fort Worth Museum of Science & History *(adult/child $16/12)* Kid-friendly galleries brimming with fossils, astronomy thrills and fun things to do.

MD GLOBAL/SHUTTERSTOCK

Ferris wheel, State Fair of Texas

Wild Detectives *(thewilddetectives.com)*, a tiny but well curated bookstore with good coffee and a small bar.

A Famous Fair

Rides, snacks and entertainment

Held from late September through mid-October, the massive **State Fair of Texas** *(bigtex.com; adult/child $25/18)* is a showcase for carnivalesque amusement. Come ride one of the tallest Ferris wheels in North America, eat corn dogs (invented here), and browse the prize-winning cows, sheep and quilts. You can also enjoy concerts, parades, fireworks and more. Admission varies by day (from $15).

Taste the Wild West in Fort Worth Stockyards

MAP P296

A world of cowboys and longhorns

Twice a day (at 11:30am and 4pm) in Fort Worth's famous **Stockyards** district, you can catch the legendary Cattle Drive. Cowboys wearing authentic 19th-century garb drive 17 or so longhorn cattle of the Fort Worth herd up the dusty road. Spectators line E Exchange Ave and an announcer gives insight into the cattle drives of old.

Come sundown, the place to be is **Billy Bob's Texas** *(billybobstexas.com)*, a former cattle barn that today houses the world's largest honky-tonk (stretching across 100,000 sq ft). Top country stars, DJs and house bands perform on two stages. Friday and Saturday nights see live bull riding in the indoor arena.

Alternatively, the 3400-seat **Cowtown Coliseum** *(cowtowncoliseum.com)*, built in 1908 to host the first-ever indoor rodeos, hosts live rodeo at 7:30pm on Friday and Saturday nights year-round.

WANDER THE HISTORIC STOCKYARDS

See why Fort Worth was the gateway to the West as you explore the hidden attractions of the Historic Stockyards.

START	END	LENGTH
Exchange Ave	Exchange Ave	3/4 mile; 1½ hours

Follow the sidewalk along brick-lined Exchange Ave past the ❶ **Fort Worth Stock Yards sign** that dates from 1910. Set back from the road is the ❷ **Cowtown Coliseum**, setting for weekend rodeos and other events. If the doors are open, wander inside for a look at photos and memorabilia from legendary rodeo performers of the past. Next door, the ❸ **Livestock Exchange** once served as the offices for cattle traders and occasional longhorn auctions are still held (nowadays via video-satellite feed). You can freely wander the old building; a small museum in back gives insight into the people and events that shaped the Stockyards. Head over to the ❹ **viewing deck** above the corral for a look at the Fort Worth herd. A signpost has pictures and descriptions of each animal. Across Exchange Ave, the ❺ **Stockyards Station**, which opened in 1876, was used to ship cattle by rail to markets in Kansas City. Though it's now a mall, peek down the corridors to see old photos from the past.

Continue to shop-lined ❻ **Mule Alley** and take the small lane down to ❼ **Marine Creek**, a trickling waterway where you can sometimes spot herons and other wading birds. Follow the peaceful ❽ **waterside path** under Exchange Ave before returning once again to the bustle of the Stockyards, with its myriad shopping and dining options.

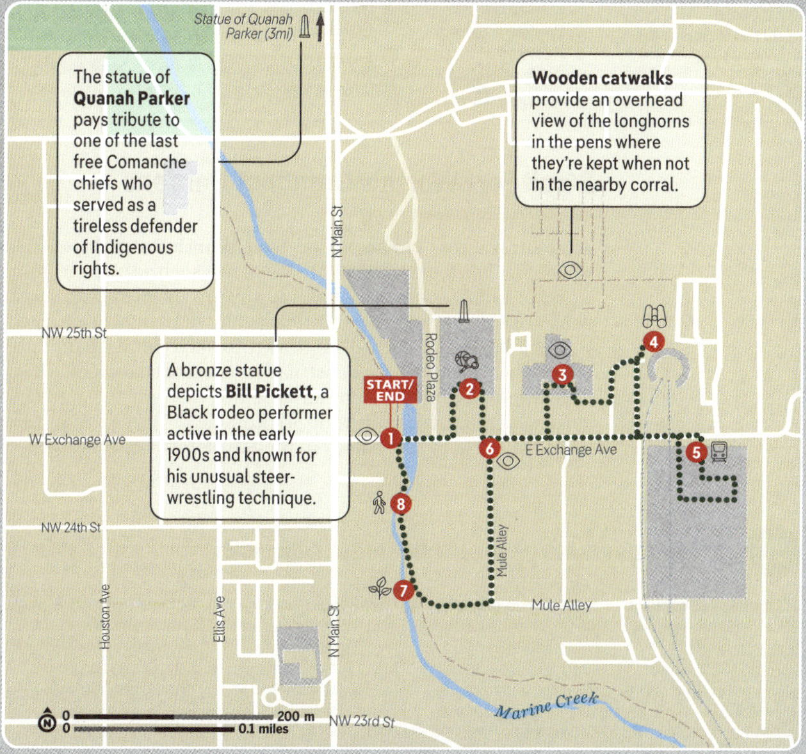

Statue of Quanah Parker (3mi)

The statue of **Quanah Parker** pays tribute to one of the last free Comanche chiefs who served as a tireless defender of Indigenous rights.

Wooden catwalks provide an overhead view of the longhorns in the pens where they're kept when not in the nearby corral.

A bronze statue depicts **Bill Pickett**, a Black rodeo performer active in the early 1900s and known for his unusual steer-wrestling technique.

NW 25th St
W Exchange Ave
E Exchange Ave
NW 24th St
NW 23rd St
N Main St
Rodeo Plaza
Mule Alley
Houston Ave
Ellis Ave
Marine Creek
START/END
0 200 m
0 0.1 miles

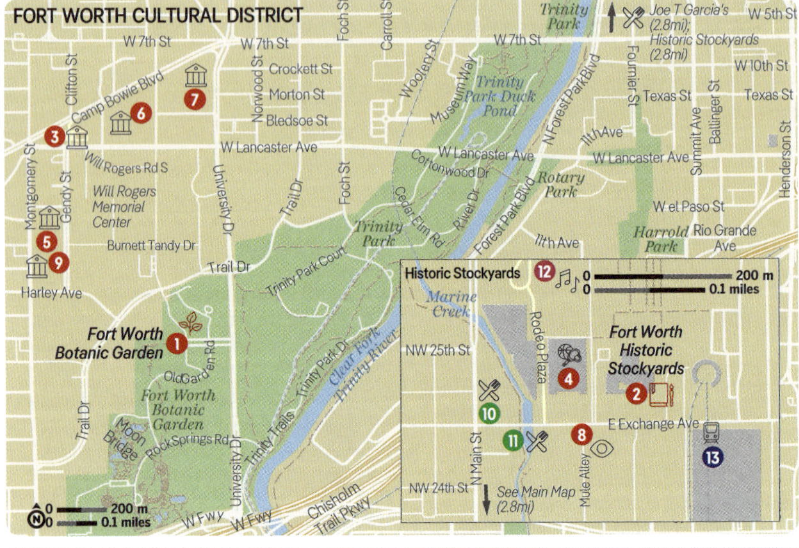

HIGHLIGHTS
1 Fort Worth Botanic Garden
2 Fort Worth Historic Stockyards

SIGHTS
3 Amon Carter Museum of American Art
4 Cowtown Coliseum
5 Fort Worth Museum of Science & History
6 Kimbell Art Museum
7 Modern
8 Mule Alley
9 National Cowgirl Museum

EATING
10 H3 Ranch
11 Love Shack

ENTERTAINMENT
12 Billy Bob's Texas

TRANSPORT
13 Historic Stockyards Station

Stroll Fort Worth's Grandest Gardens

MAP P296

Roses, orchids and cacti

Stretching across 120 acres, the **Fort Worth Botanic Garden** *(fwbg.org; adult/child $12/6)* are the oldest such gardens in Texas – and arguably some of its most beautiful. Its 23 specialty gardens are home to more than 2500 species of plants, not to mention the birds and butterflies drawn to such floral abundance. Stroll a boardwalk above dense native Texas species, look for koi in leaf-dappled ponds from an elegant bridge in the Japanese garden, get in touch with your prickly side in the cactus garden and take a trip to the tropics in the Rainforest Conservatory.

EATING & DRINKING IN THE STOCKYARDS: OUR PICKS

MAP P296

H3 Ranch: Atmospheric spot for mouthwatering steaks, tender ribs, smoked chicken and crispy fried catfish. *11am-10pm* **$$**

Joe T Garcia's: Famed place that serves Mexican fare in a photogenic courtyard of bubbling fountains and tropical foliage. *11am-2:30pm & 5-10pm* **$$**

Love Shack: Buzzing spot with a big patio for enjoying burgers and beers while listening to live music. *11am-9pm* **$**

Second Rodeo Brewing: Lively multilevel space with a huge patio, first-rate microbrews and live music. *11am-midnight* **$**

Houston & the Gulf Coast

ARTS & ENTERTAINMENT | CUISINE & COCKTAILS | BEACHES

Houston's massive size places it among the top 10 US cities in both area and population, encompassing a fair bit of everything that makes Texas great. Big Oil brings in major investment in fine arts and public spaces, though you can still find cowboy boots and Texas swagger even here in the big city.

The city would take a lifetime to explore completely, but with just a few days it's easy to enjoy the highlights: downtown's revitalized Main St of bars and restaurants, the Museum District's excellent art and cultural centers, plus the indie shops and nightlife of Montrose. It's also worth setting aside a day to see NASA's Space Center Houston.

Houston makes a great starting point for a road trip down the Gulf Coast, which has hundreds of miles of beaches, historic settlements like Galveston and plenty of outdoor adventures – both on and off the water.

Modern Arts in the Museum District

Cutting-edge art and artists

The Museum District is home to a number of top-notch modern-art exhibition spaces.

If time is limited, focus on the fantastic **Museum of Fine Arts** *(mfah.org; adult/child $24/free)*, with thousands of works of art spread across three main buildings connected by underground tunnels (each a work of art itself). You could easily spend a day exploring the museum's permanent collections and special exhibitions.

(continues on p300)

TOP TIP

Travelers exploring the Museum District in depth will benefit from the **CityPass** *(citypass.com/houston; adult/child $76/63)*, which includes entry to the Space Center Houston complex and the choice of four from the Museum of Fine Arts, Museum of Natural Science, Houston Zoo, Downtown Aquarium, Children's Museum and Kemah Boardwalk.

GETTING AROUND

Downtown is quite compact and walkable. To travel elsewhere within the city, Houston's three METRORail train lines converge downtown around the square formed by Main, Rusk, Capitol and Fannin streets. Regular services connecting the Theater District and downtown to the Museum District, Hermann Park and NRG Stadium are convenient for travel across the limited route network. Heading down the Gulf Coast, you'll want a car. It's about a six-hour drive (370 miles) if making a straight shot from Houston to South Padre Island, though you could easily spend a few days stopping at coastal enclaves along the way.

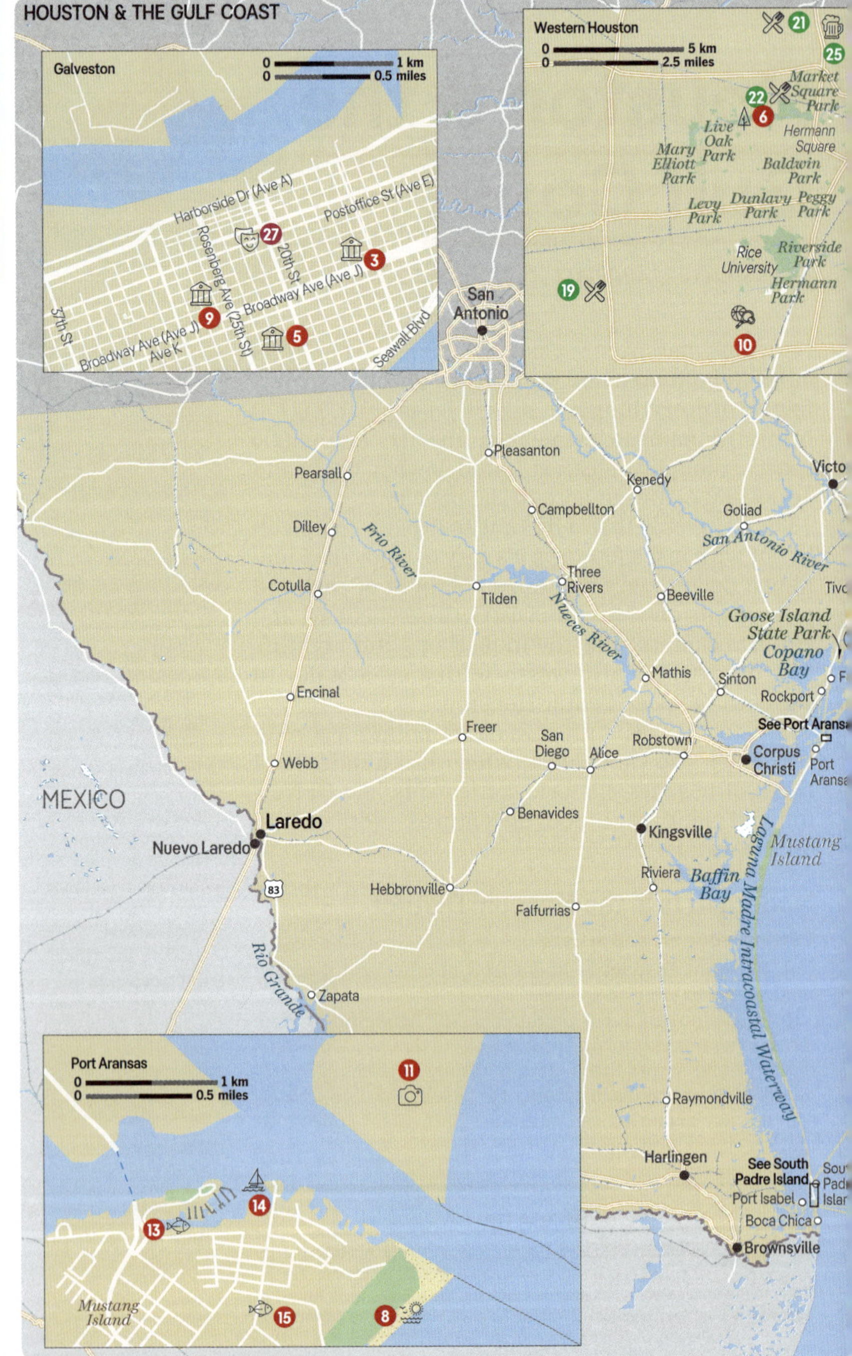
HOUSTON & THE GULF COAST
Galveston
0 1 km
0 0.5 miles
Harborside Dr (Ave A)
Postoffice St (Ave E)
Rosenberg Ave (25th St)
20th St
Broadway Ave (Ave J)
37th St
Ave K
Seawall Blvd
Western Houston
0 5 km
0 2.5 miles
Market Square Park
Live Oak Park
Mary Elliott Park
Hermann Square
Baldwin Park
Levy Park
Dunlavy Park
Peggy Park
Rice University
Riverside Park
Hermann Park
San Antonio
Pleasanton
Pearsall
Kenedy
Campbellton
Goliad
Dilley
Frio River
San Antonio River
Three Rivers
Cotulla
Tilden
Beeville
Nueces River
Goose Island State Park
Copano Bay
Mathis
Sinton
Rockport
Encinal
See Port Aransas
Freer
San Diego
Alice
Robstown
Corpus Christi
Port Aransas
Webb
MEXICO
Benavides
Laredo
Nuevo Laredo
Kingsville
Mustang Island
Riviera
Baffin Bay
Laguna Madre Intracoastal Waterway
83
Hebbronville
Falfurrias
Rio Grande
Zapata
Raymondville
Harlingen
See South Padre Island
Port Isabel
Boca Chica
Brownsville
Port Aransas
0 1 km
0 0.5 miles
Mustang Island

HIGHLIGHTS

1 Space Center Houston

SIGHTS

2 Aransas National Wildlife Refuge
3 Bishop's Palace
4 Brazos Bend State Park
5 Bryan Museum
6 Buffalo Bayou Park
7 East Beach
8 IB Magee Beach Park
9 Moody Mansion
10 NRG Stadium
11 San José Island

ACTIVITIES

12 Air Padre Kiteboarding
13 Deep Sea Headquarters
14 Fisherman's Wharf
15 Horace Caldwell Fishing Pier
16 Jim's Pier
17 The Original Dolphin Watch
18 Sonny's Beach Service

EATING

19 Blood Bros BBQ
20 Grapevine Cafe
21 Pinkerton's Barbecue
22 Truth BBQ

DRINKING & NIGHTLIFE

23 Louie's Backyard
24 Padre Island Brewing Company
25 Saint Arnold Brewing Company
26 Wanna Wanna Beach Bar & Grill

ENTERTAINMENT

27 Grand 1894 Opera House

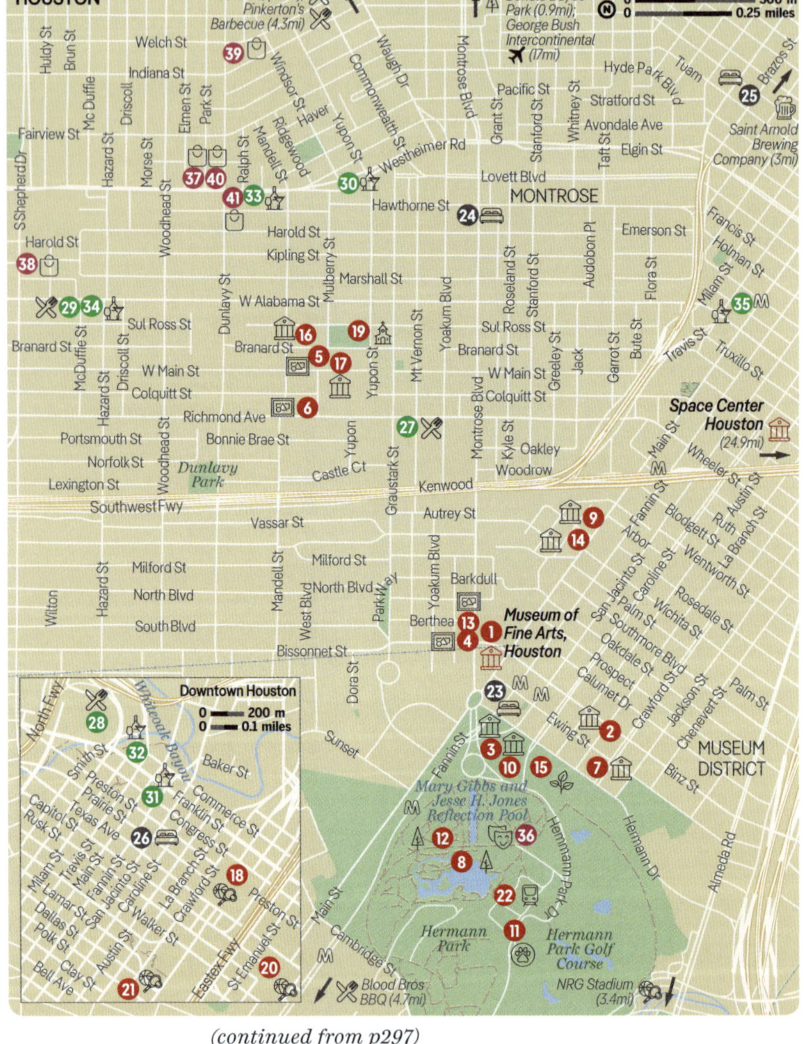

(continued from p297)

The **Jung Center** *(junghouston.org; free)* often features local and regional artists in its small exhibition hall; many of the works are for sale in the gallery. The **Contemporary Arts Museum Houston** *(camh.org; free)* hosts ambitious rotating exhibitions and several events each month; there's no permanent collection, so every visit is a new experience.

On the northern edge of the district, **Lawndale Art & Performance Center** *(lawndaleartcenter.org; free)* is home to interdisciplinary works of experimental music and boundary-pushing art. Next door, **Houston Center for Contemporary Craft** *(crafthouston.org; free)* is dedicated exclusively to crafts – the workers spaces here remain open in between rotating exhibits.

HIGHLIGHTS
1 Museum of Fine Arts, Houston

SIGHTS
2 Children's Museum Houston
3 Cockrell Butterfly Center
4 Contemporary Arts Museum Houston
5 Cy Twombly Gallery
6 Dan Flavin Installation at Richmond Hall
7 Health Museum
8 Hermann Park
9 Houston Center for Contemporary Craft
10 Houston Museum of Natural Science
11 Houston Zoo
12 Japanese Garden
13 Jung Center
14 Lawndale Art & Performance Center
15 McGovern Centennial Gardens
16 Menil Collection
17 Menil Drawing Institute
18 Minute Maid Park
19 Rothko Chapel
20 Shell Energy Stadium
21 Toyota Center

ACTIVITIES
22 Hermann Park Railroad

SLEEPING
23 Hotel ZaZa
24 La Colombe d'Or Hotel
25 La Maison in Midtown
26 Magnolia Hotel

EATING
27 Pit Room
28 POST Houston
29 Tacos Tierra Caliente

DRINKING & NIGHTLIFE
30 Anvil Bar & Refuge
31 Captain Foxheart's Bad News Bar & Spirit Lodge
32 Houston Watch Company
33 Poison Girl
34 West Alabama Ice House
35 Winnie's

ENTERTAINMENT
36 Miller Outdoor Theatre

SHOPPING
37 BJ Oldies
38 Buffalo Exchange
39 Guild Shop
40 Old Blue House
41 Pavement

Explore Buffalo Bayou

Art-lined trails and skyscraper views

Just northwest of downtown, the 2.3-mile-long **Buffalo Bayou Park** is dotted throughout with public art, dog parks, sporting grounds, and even 250,000 Mexican free-tailed bats that depart en masse at sunset from their roosts under the Waugh Drive bridge. The most interesting section for visitors stretches along the south shore from the Sabine Street Water Works to Waugh Dr, an easy one-hour stroll that takes in the bulk of the permanent art installations and nice views of the bayou.

Dine & Dance at POST

Renovated food and events venue

On the edge of downtown, **POST Houston** *(posthtx.com; 11am-9pm)* is home to over 30 restaurants ranging from West African **ChòpnBlok** to a branch of beloved Austin-based Japanese street food **Eastside King** as well as tacos, fancy grilled cheese and others. Atop the building the 5-acre **Skylawn** offers superb views of the downtown skyline, and POST hosts markets, DJ nights, film screenings and other events.

A Walk in Hermann Park

Outdoor art and natural surroundings

The lawns of **Hermann Park** *(hermannpark.org)* make an excellent sunny-day outing. Squirrels and ducks wander freely through the 445-acre expanse, much of which is encircled by the small-gauge **Hermann Park Railroad** *(full day $6)* that makes a loop every 25 minutes. Stop at the meticulously planned **Japanese Garden** and the sculpture-filled spaces of the **McGovern Centennial Gardens** before checking the schedule at the **Miller Outdoor Theatre** *(milleroutdoortheatre.com)* for open-air performances.

BEST FESTIVALS IN HOUSTON

Houston Livestock Show & Rodeo: Join 2 million locals for rodeos, carnival rides and live music each February/March at NRG Stadium.

Art Car Parade: April's biggest bash features hundreds of mobile masterworks cruising downtown.

Art Bike Parade: A newish take on the Art Car concept now for human-powered locomotion, each May.

Pride Houston: The Pride Parade left its historic Montrose roots in 2015 for the wider streets of downtown each June.

Freedom Over Texas: Houston's biggest July 4th celebrations take place in Eleanor Tinsley Park.

Bayou City Art Festival: Enjoy October's lower temperatures at the outdoor art fest in Memorial Park.

TOP HOUSTON ATTRACTIONS FOR FAMILIES

Children's Museum Houston: Activity-filled museum, where little ones can learn how stuff works, create inventions, play games or draw in an open-air art studio.

Health Museum: More play space than museum with an oversized crawl-through colon, a 12ft-tall beating heart and brain displays.

Houston Museum of Natural Science: (HMNS) Covers archaeology to zoology and plenty in between.

Cockrell Butterfly Center: Watch winged species all around you, inside this separate-admission space in the HMNS.

Houston Zoo: Zookeeper talks, a large children's zoo with playgrounds and petting zoos, and highlights like the World of Primates (buy tickets ahead; *houstonzoo.org)* with raised wooden walkways through the animals' habitats.

Wandering Montrose

The best way to explore

A mashup of trendy and countercultural, Montrose mixes fancy cocktail bars with Texas icehouses (open-air taverns that sell cheap beer), and is one of Houston's most walkable districts. Hit the pavement for a stroll amid antique shops and colorful consignment stores, refreshing over cold drinks along the way.

The intersection of Dunlavy St and Westheimer Rd is a good starting point, where both **Old Blue House** and **BJ Oldies** are reliable sources of antiques and oddities. Surrounding here are numerous small stores of varying quality – **The Guild Shop** *(theguildshop.org)* is large enough to appeal to all sorts, while **Pavement** *(pavement.store)* and national chain **Buffalo Exchange** *(buffaloexchange.com)* focus exclusively on clothing at somewhat higher standards and corresponding prices.

After shopping, stop at local classic **Poison Girl** *(poisongirlbar.com)* for an excellent whiskey selection and generous happy hour, or **Anvil** *(anvilhouston.com)* for one of the city's best selections of cocktails – don't miss poorly hidden 'speakeasy' Refuge around back. Expect pure Texas vibes at **West Alabama Ice House** *(westalabamaicehouse.net),* where outdoor seating and good cheap beer attracts a cross-section of Montrose and Houston locals – as does excellent taco truck **Tierra Caliente** *(tacostierracalientemx.com)* across the street.

Arts in Montrose

Building on the Menils' vision

Spread across 30 acres on the southern side of Montrose, the **Menil Collection** *(menil.org)* galleries and installations are curated from the private holdings of Houston-based French philanthropists Dominique and John de Menil, who relocated here in the early 1940s. The main building – designed by Italian architect Renzo Piano – houses an eclectic collection spanning cubism and surrealism, African and Pacific tribal cultures, and far more.

Nearby, the **Dan Flavin Installation** and **Cy Twombly Gallery** both house permanent single-artist exhibitions – the latter building was custom-built for the purpose. The smaller galleries inside **Menil Drawing Institute** display regularly changing drawing exhibits. Between gallery visits, look for large-scale sculptural installations throughout the shady campus.

DRINKING IN HOUSTON: COCKTAIL BARS

Houston Watch Company: Dimly lit favorite off Main St with engaging bartenders and a generous happy hour. *4pm-2am Tue-Sat*

Captain Foxheart's Bad News Bar: Speakeasy with a budget-friendly happy hour and even better list of handcrafted cocktails. *5pm-2am*

Winnie's: Craft cocktails just barely edge out the excellent oysters and lunch menu for top spot here. *11am-10pm Mon-Thu, to 11pm Fri-Sun*

Saint Arnold Brewing Company: The big name in Houston brewing, straight from the source at its Fifth Ward brewpub and beer garden. *11am-10pm Sun-Thu, to 11pm Fri & Sat*

Alongside the Menil collections, **Rothko Chapel** *(rothkochapel.org)* is a nondenominational sacred space hung with 14 large-scale monotonal paintings by abstract expressionist Mark Rothko. The quiet, meditative chamber evokes strong feelings among Houstonians, particularly within the art community. In early 2024 an expansion to the site was announced to include an event plaza, meditation garden and program center to be completed in 2026.

All these galleries are free to the public; note that they're all closed Monday and Tuesday.

Journey into Outer Space

Exploring NASA's Space Center

A 30-minute drive southeast of downtown, Johnson Space Center has served as mission control for all NASA space flights to the present day starting with the Gemini 4 mission in 1965. The **Space Center Houston** *(spacecenter.org/visitor-information; adult/child $45/40)* complex showcases interactive exhibits and short films on the history of space flight, and artifacts from the US space program, including moon rocks and numerous vehicles used by NASA astronauts.

The most popular aspect for many visitors – and the only way the public can access the actual Johnson Space Center campus – are the NASA tram tours. Three separate itineraries travel to Rocket Park, Historic Mission Control tours (additional $15 surcharge) and the Astronaut Training Facility (available on a first-come, first-served basis, with reservations made at Guest Services).

You can save a few dollars (and time spent in line) by buying tickets in advance.

Gators in the Grasslands

Walking trails and wildlife in Brazos Bend

Alligators lie along the lake shores, wading birds and waterfowl calls echo through the live oak, and bird-watchers hunker behind waterfront blinds trying to capture it all at **Brazos Bend State Park** *(adult/child $7/free)*, just 45 miles south of Houston. Here 37 miles of walking trails make this a popular weekend getaway. Reserve ahead for fall and spring weekends, when the park fills to capacity.

CATCHING THE BIG GAME

During home games (baseball, basketball, football) fans flood into downtown stadiums as well as bars and restaurants in surrounding neighborhoods.

Houston Astros *(mlb.com/astros)* See baseball games at **Daikin Park**, on the edge of historic downtown, late March to early October.

Houston Rockets *(nba.com/rockets)* From October to April, basketball games take over the **Toyota Center** on the southeast edge of downtown.

Houston Dynamo *(houstondynamofc.com)* Soccer fans can get their fix at **Shell Energy Stadium** in East Downtown (EaDo) from February to October.

Houston Texans *(houstondynamofc.com)* Biggest of all are the football games happening at **NRG Stadium** from September to January. Though far from downtown, the stadium is easily reached on the Red Line METRORail.

EATING IN HOUSTON: BARBECUE

Truth BBQ: Top-rated Texas barbecue joint. Expect a wait, but enjoy the views and smell of the smokers in the meantime. *hours vary* $$$

Pinkerton's Barbecue: Slow-smoked meat eaten at shared tables; a classic barbecue experience in the city. *11am-9pm Sun & Tue-Thu, to 10pm Fri & Sat* $$$

Blood Bros BBQ: Houston loves fusion; great meats here incorporate East Asian–inspired techniques and ingredients. *11am-3pm Wed-Sun, plus 6-9pm Thu-Sat* $$

The Pit Room: Neighborhood joint in Montrose equally popular for a lunch special or an after-hours cold one on the patio. *11am-9pm* $$

THE 1900 STORM

Once Texas' largest city and the nation's third-largest seaport, Galveston was dealt a devastating blow by a hurricane in 1900. Estimates show as many as one-fifth of the island's population died in the storm – making it the deadliest disaster in US history at the time – and around a quarter of the city's residents were left homeless.

In response, the city undertook massive public-works projects – raising the entire city by up to 11ft and constructing a 17ft seawall that would eventually extend 10 miles along the Gulf Coast. Galveston's economy never fully recovered, as ship traffic moved to nearby Houston and with it much of the income that made Galveston prosper.

DANITA DELIMONT/SHUTTERSTOCK

Spoonbills, Aransas National Wildlife Refuge

Coastal Charm in Galveston

Architecture and beach-hopping

Part historic Southern town, part sunburned beach resort, Galveston Island is Houston's favorite seaside bolthole.

Self-guided tours of the **Grand 1894 Opera House** *(thegrand.com; $5)* offer visitors a peek behind the curtains of Texas' official opera house, though not backstage access.

The former Galveston Orphans' Home is now the **Bryan Museum** *(thebryanmuseum.org; adult/child $15/free)*, with excellent exhibitions on Galveston and Texan history as well as an audio tour featuring residents' recollections of life in the Home.

Self-guided tours of both **Bishop's Palace** *(galvestonhistory.org; adult/youth $15/12)* and **Moody Mansion** *(moodymansion.org; adult/youth $15/7)* showcase the lifestyles of late-1800s Galveston elites, the latter boasting an excellent audioguide that adds familial context to the site.

After exploring the historic center, enjoy some downtime on the seaside. **East Beach** on the (eastern) tip of the island is party central in summer, but go west, and you'll pass miles of appealing beaches.

Hang out in Port Aransas

Texas' favorite coastal escape

On the northern tip of Mustang Island, Port Aransas is, for many lifelong Texans, the most appealing beach destination on this state's coast. The pace is relaxed, and daily life is dominated by beachgoing and sunset drinks. Connected to the mainland by a free ferry service, Port A feels like leaving real life behind.

IB Magee Beach Park and the **Horace Caldwell Fishing Pier** are great spots for swimming and fishing. Alternatively get in touch with outfitters like Texas Surf Camps *(texassurfcamps.com)* and Island Surf Rentals *(islandsurfrentals.com)* to add a bit of water-sports action to your trip. The latter has kayaks, beach bikes and paddle boards, in addition to surf gear, for rent.

Deep Sea Headquarters *(deepseaheadquarters.com)* arranges everything from half-day to offshore or overnight fishing trips. In addition, chartered trips of all sizes leave most days from **Fisherman's Wharf**, which is also home to dolphin tours, sunset cruises and the jetty boat that carries visitors across to the undeveloped **San José Island**.

Go Birding in Aransas NWR

A coastal driving tour

For bird-watchers, **Aransas National Wildlife Refuge** is a premier site on the Texas coast. More than 400 species have been documented here, and even people who don't carry binoculars and bird checklists get caught up in the frenzy. The scenery at Aransas NWR alone is spectacular. The blue Aransas Bay waters are speckled with green islets ringed with white sand. Native dune grasses blow gently in the breeze while songbirds provide background music. The easiest way to experience the refuge is by driving the 16-mile auto tour (starting on the road just past the visitor center), which features plenty of opportunities to stop and fish along piers, hike on nature trails or bird-watch from the observation tower.

Off-Shore Adventures in South Padre Island

Fun on the water

Near the southern tip of the Gulf Coast, the small resort town of South Padre Island is famed for its sparkling shoreline and clear waters. While the long beaches running through the city are built up and generally busy, miles and miles of undeveloped sand run to the Mansfield Cut channel at the north of the island.

The Laguna Madre is renowned for wind-powered water sports. You can take lessons or rent gear from **Air Padre Kiteboarding** *(airpadrekiteboarding.com)* or fly high with **Sonny's Beach Service** *(sonnysbeachservice.com)*, which offers parasailing.

For those looking for a more low-key adventure, there's kayaking and paddleboarding, along with a variety of boat trips. The **Original Dolphin Watch** *(theoriginaldolphinwatch.com)* heads out multiple times a day to get a glimpse at the pods of dolphins that call this area home.

FISHING ON SOUTH PADRE

No matter which chartered fishing guide you go with, there's a good chance you'll start and end your trip at **Jim's Pier** on the bay side of South Padre Island. This is the main dock at SPI for getting on and off boats, and it's also a fully stocked bait and tackle shop. In addition, if you need advice or help finding a guide to match what you want to do, the staff at Jim's Pier has a list of guides they can get you in contact with. They also offer fish-cleaning services after your trip. Prices vary depending on the type of fish you catch, but it's usually a couple of dollars per fish to have them fileted right there for you.

EATING & DRINKING AT SOUTH PADRE ISLAND: OUR PICKS

Padre Island Brewing Company: Burgers, pizza and seafood with freshly brewed beer on tap. *11:30am-10pm Mon-Sat, to 9pm Sun* **$$**

Grapevine Cafe: Great choice for breakfast and lunch with coffee beans roasted in-house. *7:30am-3pm* **$$**

Louie's Backyard: Iconic SPI hang-out on the bayside with fireworks every Friday during summer (June to August). *11:30am-2am*

Wanna Wanna Beach Bar & Grill: Longtime favorite tiki bar steps from the sand that's known for its turbo piña coladas. *11:30am-10pm*

West Texas & Big Bend National Park

OUTDOOR ADVENTURES | DESERT LANDSCAPES | ART-LOVING TOWNS

GETTING AROUND

Public transit is limited and inconvenient beyond El Paso, and it won't get you to Big Bend National Park. Amtrak trains stop in El Paso and Alpine, while Greyhound buses connect El Paso to Fort Stockton for buses to Marfa and Alpine.

You'll need a car to experience West Texas fully. Rent a vehicle at the airport in El Paso or pick up a Jeep rental in Alpine. You'll want a high-clearance 4WD vehicle if backcountry driving is on your itinerary. Fly into El Paso International Airport to minimize your drive time to Big Bend National Park.

West Texas is home to the tallest mountains in the state, some of the darkest skies in the world, two national parks and a vast canyon that's second in size to the Grand Canyon. The only major city in the area is El Paso, which is closer to San Diego, California, than it is to Houston or Dallas.

The region's biggest attraction is Big Bend National Park, where mountain peaks soar above a vast unforgiving desert, while the Rio Grande winds its ways past steep canyons carved out of limestone. Amid this 1252-square-mile wilderness, there are ample opportunities for hiking, camping, backcountry driving, stargazing and even paddling along the Rio Grande River.

Quirky small towns fill the gaps between large swaths of unspoiled nature and sprawling ranches. Visit art galleries, shop independent boutiques, listen to small-town jam sessions or dive deep into Texas history.

The Artistry of Alpine

Mural-filled town

Set at the foot of the Davis Mountains, the railroad and ranching town of Alpine might be West Texas' best-kept secret. Independent boutiques, antique stores and lively coffee shops line streets that feel like a movie set. Murals are everywhere – even in the alleys. And when the light hits the mountains around golden hour, it's easy to see why artists are drawn to this place.

TOP TIP

Big Bend is a hot desert park, and heat advisories are common, even in the fall. Avoid long hikes during the middle of the day, drink lots of water, use sunscreen and wear protective clothing, and carry extra water with you in case of an emergency.

Check out the **Welcome to Alpine** mural down the street from the historic **Holland Hotel** and the **Cattle Drive** mural across the street. Pop into the **Big Bend Gallery** *(facebook.com/bigbendartscouncil.org)* to shop for pieces from local artists that are more affordable than you might expect. Then go to the **Museum of the Big Bend** *(museumofthebig bend.com; adult/child $10/free)* for a hefty dose of West Texas–inspired fine art.

From the Springs to the Stars

Stellar highlights near Fort Davis

The **Fort Davis National Historic Site** *(nps.gov/foda; per vehicle $20)* protects a beautifully sited frontier fort established in 1854, at the northeast edge of modern Fort Davis (town). Staffed exclusively by Black soldiers between 1867 and 1881, it was abandoned in 1891, but today you can explore five of the remaining buildings set amid scores of ruins.

Thirty-three miles north of Fort Davis, **Balmorhea State Park** *(tpwd.texas.gov/state-parks/balmorhea; adult/child $7/free)* is a literal oasis in the West Texas desert. This state park is home to the world's largest spring-fed swimming pool (maximum depth 25ft), offering snorkelers and divers a chance to swim with turtles, catfish, minnows and endangered fish like the Pecos gambusia and Comanche Springs pupfish. If you're traveling during the summer, purchase day passes in advance online.

One of the best parties in West Texas starts after sunset high in the Fort Davis mountains. Here at the **McDonald Observatory** *(mcdonaldobservatory.org; adult/child $25/20)*, astronomers lead visitors on a guided tour of the constellations in the night sky. Guests at these Star Parties can peek

STARGAZING IN BIG BEND

Big Bend National Park is home to some of the darkest skies in the world, and it's one of best places in North America for stargazing. National park rangers offer regular night sky programs, including moonlight walks and star parties.

For the best views of the starry skies here, give your eyes a chance to adjust to the dark. It typically take about a half-hour for eyes to acclimate to total darkness, but once they do, you'll be able to see many more stars than perhaps you thought possible. Using a phone can disrupt your night vision, so keep it in your pocket and opt for a red LED light if needed.

BEST SHOPPING IN MARFA

Marfa Mood Mercantile: A tiny boutique selling gourmet pet treats, artisan jewelry and local gifts.

Raba Marfa: A stylish vintage store where the clothes and accessories will make you feel ready to grace a magazine cover.

Wrong Store: An impeccably curated indie shop that feels more like a gallery of unique treasures.

Cactus Liquors: Obscure spirits, unique beers, fine wines and a walk-up window.

Cobra Rock: Pick up a pair of custom-made handcrafted leather boots.

Texas Rose: Shop for West Texas–inspired art, clothing and accessories.

Garza Marfa: A chic furniture and textiles store.

at the Milky Way through powerful telescopes, check out exhibits in the visitors center, or just relax under a blanket of stars. Reserve ahead.

Marfa's Modern Art & Mystery Lights

Offbeat adventures in a desert town

Plonked down on the edge of the desert, the small town of Marfa is a wild mash-up of cowboy culture and cutting-edge art. Start off the Marfa experience at **The Chinati Foundation** *(chinati.org; adult/child $37/free),* an abandoned army base that now houses one of the world's largest permanent installations of minimalist art. Visits are by one of three guided tours, costing $15 to $35 (free for kids) depending on how much art you want to see. Reservations are essential. One of the best times to experience it is in mid-October, when **Chinati Weekend** *(chinati.org/chinati-weekend)* takes place. For two days there are gallery open houses with free-flowing wine, plus special exhibitions and events.

No matter when you visit, stop at **Ballroom Marfa** *(ballroommarfa.org),* a gallery that hosts rotating exhibitions in a former military dance hall. Across the street, **RULE Gallery** *(rulegallery.com)* shows contemporary abstract and conceptual photography, sculpture and paintings in a space that's also the curator's home. For the latest information on events and exhibits, check out the Marfa Gallery Guide *(marfagalleryguide.com).*

After sundown, keep an eye out of the **Marfa Mystery Lights**. For more than a century, people have watched unexplained glowing orbs appear on the horizon. Stop at the **Marfa Lights Viewing Area** (on Highway 90) east of Marfa and see if you can spot them for yourself.

Adventures in Big Bend National Park

Where the mountains meet the desert

Big Bend National Park *(nps.gov/bibe; per vehicle $30)* boasts more than 150 miles of hiking trails. An excellent introduction to the park's varied landscapes is the 4.8-mile round-trip Lost Mine Trail. The gently sloping switchbacks climb over 1000ft through a cool, shaded forest of juniper, oak and pine trees. Take in views of Juniper Canyon and Casa Grande Peak as you approach the main viewpoint, from where cliffs, craggy peaks and lush canyons are everywhere you look.

WHERE TO EAT & DRINK IN MARFA: OUR PICKS

Para Llevar: Wood-fired sourdough pizzas, sandwiches and salads in an upscale bodega and wine shop. *11am-8pm* **$$**

Angel's Restaurant: A casual spot for authentic Mexican food. Try the smothered burrito, chili relleno or enchiladas. *7am-8pm Mon-Sat, 8am-2pm Sun* **$**

Planet Marfa: A quirky beer garden with free peanuts and a surprisingly good menu. *1-10pm, to midnight Fri & Sat* **$**

Marfa Spirit Co: A distillery and tasting room that feels like a favorite neighborhood bar. *3-11pm Thu-Sat, 11am-7pm Sun*

After a day on the trail, head to **Boquillas Hot Springs**, a secluded 105°F pool overlooking the Rio Grande. Be prepared: it's a half-mile (round-trip) hike to the springs, and there are no changing facilities (bathing suits required).

River trips can range from a few hours to a few days. **Angell Expeditions** *(angellexpeditions.com)* offers guided raft, canoe and kayaking trips as does **Big Bend River Tours** *(bigbendrivertours.com)*.

Climb the Highest Peak in Texas

Trails of the Guadalupe Mountains

In a remote desert setting near the border of Texas and New Mexico, **Guadalupe Mountains National Park** *(nps.gov/gumo/index; adult/child $10/free)* has jagged peaks, spires and canyons. There are more than 80 miles of trails here, though most people have their sights set on climbing Guadalupe Peak, the state's highest point at 8751ft. Spectacular views await on the strenuous ascent (3000ft elevation gain) on the 8.5-mile round-trip hike.

SIGHTS
1 Ballroom Marfa
2 Chinati Foundation

EATING
3 Angel's Restaurant
4 Para Llevar

DRINKING & NIGHTLIFE
5 Marfa Spirit Co
6 Planet Marfa

SHOPPING
7 Cactus Liquors
8 Cobra Rock
9 Garza Marfa
10 Marfa Mood Mercantile
11 Raba Marfa
12 Texas Rose
13 Wrong Store

DISCOVER DOWNTOWN EL PASO

Visit free museums and a beautifully restored theater from the 1930, take in public art and shop for bargains in the heart of the city.

START	END	LENGTH
El Paso Museum of History	Plaza Hotel Pioneer Park	1.2 miles; 2-3 hours

Start at the 1 **El Paso Museum of History**, in the heart of the downtown museum district, to learn how city evolved from a railroad stop into a vibrant multicultural destination. Continue along N Santa Fe St to browse the Southwestern art at the 2 **El Paso Museum of Art** (admission free), founded in 1959 and housed in a former Greyhound station.

Next head to the nearby 3 **Plaza Theatre**. The 1930s single-screen movie theater is an impressive example of Spanish Colonial Revival architecture and was almost demolished in the 1980s. Schedule your visit around one of the theater's free tours.

Across the street, pop into the 4 **Hotel Paso del Norte** to admire the Tiffany Glass dome above the bar.

Check out the public art work 5 **Bienvenido**, a giant yellow door installed in 2021; it's one of many works you'll find in downtown. While here make a detour down 6 **El Paso St**.

Finish at the 7 **Plaza Hotel Pioneer Park**, where you can admire the Texas decor before heading up to its La Perla rooftop bar for a drink.

REGIS ST LOUIS; COURTESY OF THE CITY OF LUBBOCK, BUDDY HOLLY CENTER

Buddy Holly Center

The Canyons & High Plains of the Panhandle

Scenic drive through Texas' northwest

Home to wildlife-rich canyons, shortgrass prairies and empty highways stretching beneath big open skies, the Texas Panhandle makes a memorable setting for a road trip.

Start off in the sizable town of **Lubbock**. Learn about an early rock-and-roll legend on a visit to the **Buddy Holly Center** *(ci.lubbock.tx.us/departments/buddy-holly-center; adult/child $10/5)*. Afterwards, take a journey into the past at the **Museum of Texas Tech University** *(depts.ttu.edu/museumttu; admission free)*, which also displays textiles and pottery from some 20 different Southwest Native American tribes. Next door the **National Ranching Heritage Center** *(ranchingheritage.org; free)*, follow a 1.5-mile path around a historical park containing 19th- and early-20th-century buildings, including an old schoolhouse, a rural church and vintage windmills.

From Lubbock, get behind the wheel for the 100-mile drive up to **Caprock Canyons State Park** *(adult/child $5/free)*, home to 26 miles of rugged trails, plus prairie-dog towns and freely roaming bison.

Back in the car, drive 90 miles northwest to reach **Palo Duro Canyon State Park** *(adult/child $8/free)*, home to the second-largest canyon in the United States. You'll find some impressive hiking trails including the famous 2.8-mile (one way) Lighthouse Trail, which takes you to a 312ft monolith.

End your journey in the city of **Amarillo** (25 miles northwest of the canyon). Here you can refuel at the **Big Texan** *(bigtexan.com)*, a huge kitschy steakhouse. Nearby, you can explore some of the curious sites sprinkled along old Route 66, like the **Cadillac Ranch**, which features a row of Cadillacs, buried hood first, near a wheat field 10 miles west of Amarillo.

PALO DURO ESSENTIALS

Hiking Ample water is crucial. The park recommends one quart per person per hour. Start early. You'll beat the crowds and have a better chance to see wildlife by heading out around dawn.

Food The **Trading Post** (about 2.5 miles past the visitor center) has breakfast sandwiches, burgers, fries, ice cream and other snacks. Open 9:30am to 6pm.

Camping The park has four different camping areas ($16 to $26 per site), including one spot (**Fortress Cliff** area) for tent campers only. Several first-come, first-served permits for hike-in primitive camping ($12) are also available.

Cabins and glamping Cabins range from rustic to well equipped ($50 to $160). Several have stunning views. There's also luxury glamping tents ($300).

Places We Love to Stay

$ Budget $$ Midrange $$$ Top End

Austin

MAPS p271, p272, p275

Firehouse Hostel $ Hostel with shared dorms and private suites. Find the speakeasy behind the reception's bookshelf.

The Driskill $$ Legendary hotel on 6th Street that's been in business since 1886. The site of LBJ and Lady Bird's first date – and supposedly haunted, as well.

Hotel Van Zandt $$ Enjoy in-suite record players, live music in the restaurant and a rooftop pool, with quick access to Rainey St.

ARRIVE Austin $$ This chic 2019 build along the bars, restaurants and music venues of E 6th is a local landmark thanks to its unique exterior architecture.

Austin Motel $$ This historic 1938 spot has a riot of rainbow colors in its quirky rooms – and one of the most famous neon signs in town.

Hotel San José $$ Bungalow-style hotel with roots dating back to the 1930s. Rooms surround the courtyard lounge that's a favorite hang-out spot for locals.

Carpenter Hotel $$ Prime location that's a short walk away from Zilker Park, Barton Springs and Lady Bird Lake.

South Congress Hotel $$$ A hip boutique hotel with a sexy rooftop pool and the home of Café No Sé, one of the best dessert spots in all of Austin.

San Antonio

MAP P282

Hotel Havana $$ Quiet location set apart from other River Walk hotels by Cuba-inspired, boho-chic rooms from Texas design guru and hotelier Liz Lambert.

Menger Hotel $$ You can't get closer to the Alamo than this historic hotel, built next door just 23 years after the famous battle.

Ranch Motel & Leisure Club $$ On the edge of Brackenridge Park, this 1940s motel was given a contemporary makeover without losing its vintage charm.

Omni La Mansión Del Rio $$$ Luxe property in the middle of the River Walk born out of 19th-century religious-school buildings in the Spanish-Mexican hacienda style.

Hotel Emma $$$ The epicenter of the Pearl District blends Victorian-era decor with post-industrial edge, while guest rooms evoke a stylish but understated Texas ranch.

Hill Country

Peach Tree Inn & Suites $ Less than a 10-minute walk to Fredericksburg's Main St, this homey place offers good value for its quiet rooms and spacious suites.

The Vaquero Motel $ The rooms at this well-maintained Bandera motel have a rustic, Western design with chunky wood furnishings. It's an easy walk to bars and restaurants.

The Kendall $$ This charming Southern Colonial-style inn on Cibolo Creek in Boerne has one-of-a-kind rooms, including one set in a converted chapel.

Gruene Mansion Inn $$$ This cluster of buildings in Gruene is practically its own village, with atmospheric rooms in the mansion, a former carriage house and the old barns.

Dallas

MAP P293

Magnolia Hotel $$ In a 29-story 1922 building, the Magnolia is an old classic with good prices for the no-nonsense rooms and a great location.

Canvas Hotel $$ Rooms have exposed-brick walls and big windows in this former industrial space turned boutique hotel. Rooftop pool and other inviting common areas.

The Bishop Arts Hotel by Q Resorts $$ About a half-mile north of Bishop Arts, this good-value but unstaffed place has sunny rooms and a small dip pool.

The Joule $$$ Aside from well-equipped rooms with rain showers and spa amenities, this neo-Gothic beauty has an art-filled lobby, stylish eateries and cantilevered rooftop pool.

Fort Worth

Stockyards Hotel $$ This 1907 gem has Western-themed art, handsome cowboy-inspired rooms and a grand Old West lobby.

Miss Molly's $$ The former boarding house turned bordello currently enjoys a third act as an eight-room, possibly haunted guesthouse with antique Western-style decor.

The Ashton Hotel $$ Wide range of comfy rooms (including spa suites) in a six-story building dating back to 1915 with a great location off Sundance Sq.

Hotel Drover $$$ Fort Worth's best hotel has rustic-chic rooms, beautiful outdoor spaces, and atmospheric eating and drinking options.

Houston

MAP P300

Magnolia Hotel $$ Stylish velvet- and damask-layered rooms in this 1926 downtown favorite, once home to the *Houston Post & Dispatch* printers.

La Maison in Midtown $$ One of very few excellent B&Bs in Houston, surrounded by appealing dining and nightlife.

Hotel ZaZa $$$ Hip and flamboyant, from bordello-esque colors to zebra-accent chairs, ZaZa is good fun.

La Colombe d'Or $$$ A museum-like interior and refined French dining in the heart of Montrose keep this luxury suites popular.

Gulf Coast

Manor on 17th $$ Beautifully-renovated 1890 mansion in Galveston's East End with complimentary 4pm happy hour each day and nightcaps every evening.

The Tarpon Inn $$ Rebuilt after several hurricanes, this Port Aransas island mainstay has been operating in some form since 1900.

Dancing Dunes $$ Five funky beach cabins in Port Aransas around a connecting porch have a fun, ramshackle atmosphere.

Isla Grand Beach Resort $$ Longtime South Padre Island favorite on the beach with two great pools if you don't want to get super sandy.

Big Bend & West Texas

MAP P309

Ocotillos Village $ A collection of handsomely designed A-frame cabins in Terlingua, with outdoor showers and shared indoor bathroom facilities a few steps away.

Holland Hotel (p307) **$** This historic property in the heart of Alpine has a gorgeous courtyard, freshly renovated lobby and rooms full of character.

Maverick Inn $ This southwestern-style property in Alpine looks like it came out of an old Western. It has 21 guest rooms, a pool and is pet friendly.

El Cosmico $$ Designed by famed hotelier Liz Lambert, this camp-style bohemian property in Marfa rents teepees, trailers and safari tents with outdoor showers.

Hotel Limpia $$ This charming historic hotel in Fort Davis is the ideal place to lay your head after a Star Party at McDonald Observatory. Take your pick from Victorian-style rooms, 1920s-era guest suites or budget-friendly rooms.

Gage Hotel $$$ This luxurious southwestern-style hotel in Marathon is true Texas treasure and the closest hotel to Big Bend National Park.

Hotel Emma

TOOLKIT

The chapters in this section cover the most important topics you'll need to know about in the American South. They're full of nuts-and-bolts information and valuable insights to help you understand and navigate the South and get the most out of your trip.

Okefenokee National Wildlife Refuge (p159)

BOB POOL/SHUTTERSTOCK

Arriving

The South has many major airports that serve as both international and domestic gateways. You'll find the largest number of connections (and generally the most competitive prices) at the following major hubs: Atlanta (ATL), Dallas (DFW), Houston (IAH), Charlotte Douglas (CLT), Orlando (MCO) and Miami (MIA).

Visas

Citizens of many countries are eligible for the Visa Waiver Program, which requires prior approval via Electronic System for Travel Authorization (ESTA). Fill out the online form at least 72 hours prior to departure.

ATMs

Choose wisely when selecting an ATM at the airport. It's better to go with machines linked to a bank rather than currency-exchange ATMs, which tend to charge higher fees.

Border Crossings

Texas has numerous border crossings with Mexico. Make sure your documents are in order, and plan your arrival carefully – avoid peak times like weekends and holidays if possible.

Wi-fi

All major airports offer free wi-fi. Elsewhere, you'll find free wi-fi at hotels and many restaurants and cafes, as well as in public libraries; some cities and towns also have free public wi-fi hotspots.

Transportation From the Airport

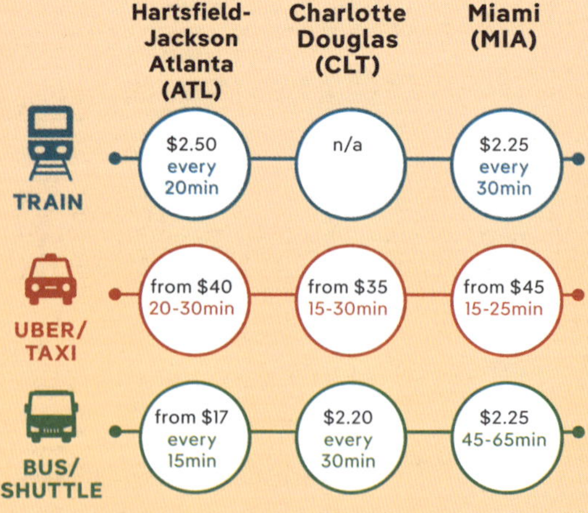

	Hartsfield-Jackson Atlanta (ATL)	Charlotte Douglas (CLT)	Miami (MIA)
TRAIN	$2.50 every 20min	n/a	$2.25 every 30min
UBER/TAXI	from $40 20-30min	from $35 15-30min	from $45 15-25min
BUS/SHUTTLE	from $17 every 15min	$2.20 every 30min	$2.25 45-65min

BRINGING ITEMS INTO THE US

The US has fairly strict rules regarding what you can bring into the country, so plan carefully before getting underway. In general, you're not allowed to bring any agricultural products (food, vegetables, plants etc) into the country. Bakery items and prepared foods (coffee, tea, honey) are permitted. You can bring in 1L of alcohol for personal use (but not if you're under 21). Although recreational or medical marijuana is legal in some states, it is illegal to bring marijuana and cannabis-infused products into the US. The exception is for CBD oil with less than 0.3% THC on a dry weight basis.

FROM LEFT: FUSE/GETTY IMAGES, GEORGE MDIVANIAN/EYEEM/GETTY IMAGES

Getting Around

Flights can get you to every state in the South, though the excellent highway system makes for memorable road trips. There are also trains and buses.

TRAVEL COSTS

Bus ride
$2.50

Car rental
from $40/day

Gasoline
$2.50–3.50/ gallon

Bike rental
from $20/ half-day

Public Transportation

In large cities, you'll find good public transit networks that may include buses, rail and streetcars. Most city networks now have dedicated transit apps, allowing you to purchase tickets; some also have real-time updates and maps to help plan your trip. Key apps include MARTA on the go (Atlanta), GoPass DART (Dallas and Fort Worth) and GO Miami-Dade transit (Miami).

Ferry

The North Carolina Ferry System *(ferry.ncdot.gov)* operates routes connecting the mainland with the Outer Banks as well as island-to-island transport. Several islands in Georgia, including Cumberland Island, can be reached via ferry *(cumberlandislandferry.com)* from St Marys near the Florida border. There's also daily boat service from Fort Myers to Key West aboard Key West Express *(keywestexpress.net)*.

TIP

You can save money on parking by putting in a little extra legwork. Prices at parking lots fall significantly if you're willing to walk 10 minutes or more to get to the town center.

GETTING BEHIND THE WHEEL

Renting a car (or bringing your own) is the most convenient option. But be prepared: traffic jams are common in built-up areas during peak hours and all along the coast in the summer.

DRIVING ESSENTIALS

Drive on the right

Speed limit is 25–30mph on city roads, and up 55–70mph on highways and interstates

.08
The blood alcohol limit is 0.08%

Flight

The domestic air system is extensive and reliable, with many competing airlines, hundreds of airports and thousands of flights daily. Flying is usually (but not always) more expensive than traveling by bus, train or car, but it's the way to go when you're in a hurry. If you're after a bargain, check rates with Spirit, Frontier, Allegiant or Breeze Airways.

Train

Amtrak *(amtrak.com)* has long-distance lines along the East Coast. There are also several key New Orleans trains that travel through Southern states. Compared to other modes of travel in the US, trains are rarely the cheapest or most convenient option, but they turn the journey into a relaxing, social and scenic all-American experience.

Bus

Greyhound *(greyhound.com)* is the major long-distance bus company, with an extensive network across the South. Ride with patience and/or a good sense of humor since problems sometimes arise (breakdowns, troubled fellow passengers). Other bus companies are Trailways *(trailways.com)*, Megabus *(megabus.com)* and FlixBus *(flixbus.com)*.

Money

CURRENCY: US DOLLAR ($)

Credit Cards

Credit cards are widely accepted throughout the US – and required to make reservations for hotels and car rentals. Only a handful of places (mostly mom-and-pop restaurants) accept cash only. Visa and Mastercard are the most common credit cards. American Express and Discover are less widely accepted.

Tipping

Tipping is not optional. Many service workers make minimum wage and rely on tips. Tip at least $1 per drink ($2 or more for fancier cocktails). Add about 15% to fares for cabs and ride-shares. At hotels and inns, $2 to $5 per day is typical for housekeeping.

ATMs

ATMs are ubiquitous in towns throughout the US. Most banks charge at least $2 per withdrawal. The Cirrus and Plus systems both have extensive ATM networks.

Taxes

Taxes vary by state, but up to 10% is added to the sticker price of retail goods, prepared food and beverages. Additional taxes at hotels tack on 2% to 10.5%.

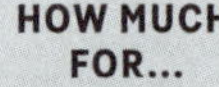

HOW MUCH FOR...

National Park entry
free–$35

museum admission
$15–35

a movie ticket
$12–24

live-music club entry
$10–20

HOW TO... Save Money

In many parts of the South, the high prices can quickly burn through your budget. There are plenty of ways to save cash, however. Inexpensive state parks can be a great way to immerse yourself in nature, and beaches are free everywhere (though parking not so much). Many towns host free first Friday or Saturday events (first of the month), with gallery openings, music and sometimes wine.

MOBILE PAYMENTS

No card? No problem. Many shops, cafes and restaurants – and some transit systems – accept mobile payments such as Apple Pay and Google Pay, so you can pay by tapping your phone.

FREE ADMISSION DAYS

Many major cities have designated days when entrance to museums is free or reduced for visitors, potentially saving hundreds of dollars for families or keen cultural tourists. In Texas, for example, San Antonio museums are typically free on Tuesdays, while Houston and Austin museums focus on Thursdays; several Dallas museums are free only on one day per month (typically the first Sunday). In Florida, Miami is a mixed bag, with free admission at some places on the second Saturday of the month. All national parks offer free admission on six days of the year.

Accommodations

Stay in a B&B

Intimate, family-run guesthouses are often contained in historic or architecturally interesting homes. Accommodations and amenities can vary widely, from the very simple and rustic to the luxurious (and prices vary accordingly). Many B&Bs require a minimum stay of two or three nights during high season, and some places do not welcome children under a certain age.

Camp Under the Stars

Available at private, state and national park campsites. The most basic have bathing facilities and electricity/water hook-ups, while some have pools, beaches and family activities. Most campsites open from mid-March to November (with year-round openings in Texas, Florida and the Deep South). If you prefer not to rough it, you'll also find glamping options, with safari-style tents, comfy beds and wilderness views.

Hotels & Resorts

Hotels, mostly found in cities, are generally large and full of amenities. Boutique hotels tend to have smaller footprints and lean toward the understatedly lavish. Resorts usually offer a wide variety of guest activities, such as skiing and water sports. Prices range from $200 upwards per night, though low-season discounts can bring substantial savings.

Save Money in a Motel

Motels, located along main roads, at interstate highway exits or on the outskirts of towns and cities, range from dowdy 10-room places to more stylish abodes. Motels offer standard accommodations: a room with a private entrance, bathroom, TV, heating and air-con. Some have small refrigerators, and many provide a simple breakfast at no extra charge.

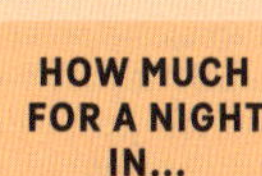

HOW MUCH FOR A NIGHT IN...

a B&B
$150–300

a campsite
$20–60

a motel
$85–160

Hostels

Budget-friendly hostels are disappearing from the US, but you will still find a small selection sprinkled across the South, including in Austin, Miami, New Orleans and Clarksdale. As elsewhere in the world, the big draw (apart from saving money in shared dormitories) is meeting other travelers, and many places organize inexpensive activities – dinners, bar-hopping and walking tours.

RENTALS & AIRBNBS

Across the South, you'll find thousands of vacation rentals for short- and long-term stays. Companies like Airbnb and Vrbo make it easy to find unique places to stay in all 13 Southern states. Not everyone is thrilled with the ever-growing expansion of homestays, which has only exacerbated the housing crisis. Locals cite the rise in housing prices and lack of affordable rentals as more properties are taken off the market to become Airbnbs. There's also the negative effect on communities as long-term residents are displaced by transients.

CLOCKWISE FROM TOP LEFT: RICHIR/SHUTTERSTOCK, PIXEL-SHOT/SHUTTERSTOCK, MIKELEDRAY/SHUTTERSTOCK, RHETT STANSBURY/SHUTTERSTOCK

Family Travel

Oceanside fun, woodland walks, horseback riding and deliriously fun theme parks are all part of the allure of travel in the American South. You can get a nature fix in the mountains, the rolling forests and on the seashore, or opt for a more urban itinerary. There are countless kid-friendly attractions in big and small cities all across the South.

Fun By the Water

Pencil in some water activities to keep everyone cool. The South has spectacular beaches on two coastlines, and there's never a bad season to visit (hit Florida in the winter and North Carolina beaches in the summer). If you're not near the coast, don't despair: you can cool off at creeks, streams, lakes and waterfalls, which you'll find sprinkled across the South.

Prams, Strollers & Babies

Urban areas are great for strollers but if you plan on enjoying the great outdoors, child carriers are definitely a better option. Some attractions offer rental strollers. Diapers and other essentials are available in supermarkets and drugstores (some open 24 hours), while organics and specialty items can be found at higher-end supermarkets. Bathrooms with changing facilities are common, as are family bathrooms.

Discounts

Children's discounts are available for everything from museum admission to movie tickets. The definition of a 'child' varies but usually means kids under 12 years old (kids under two are often free). Many restaurants also offer less-expensive children's menus.

Car Seat Laws

Laws vary state to state, but in general children up to thee years require federally approved car seats (rear-facing until one year or 20lb). Children four to five years need booster seats. Children under 13 must travel in the back seat.

BEST ATTRACTIONS FOR FAMILIES

Orlando theme parks (p238)
Immerse yourself in the fantastical worlds of Walt Disney World® and Universal Orlando Resort™.

Georgia Aquarium (p152)
Go eye-to-eye with magnificent creatures of the deep.

Great Smoky Mountains (p93)
Hop into the saddle at Smokemont Riding Stables or explore old homesteads on the Cades Cove Loop.

Cape Hatteras National Seashore (p82)
Discover life on the marsh at Hatteras Island Ocean Center, then enjoy some beach time.

Fort Worth Stockyards (p294)
Browse the Wild West stores and watch cowboys drive the longhorn cattle up the road.

BE A JUNIOR RANGER

Kids can earn a very cool badge through the Junior Ranger Program, available at numerous national park sites, and countless state parks. To earn the badge, kids complete an activity book with questions and games, and for some parks complete an activity (such as a hike, while making observations along the way). The program is aimed at five- to 12-year-olds. And some parks have a range of activities for younger vs older kids, as well as particular specialties – like nighttime stargazing, paleontology or sound exploration. Adults can enjoy it too, and everyone is likely to gain a deeper understanding of the surrounding environment.

Health & Safe Travel

INSURANCE

Travel insurance to cover theft, loss and medical problems is essential, especially for international visitors. Domestic visitors should confirm they have proper coverage. Some policies do not cover 'risky' activities such as scuba diving, riding a motorcycle and skiing, so read the fine print. Given upheavals like COVID-19, trip-cancellation insurance is a worthwhile expense.

Heat Dangers

During the summer (and even earlier in the South), you'll need to prepare for the heat, when midday temperatures can soar. Carry plenty of water to avoid dehydration, wear a wide-brimmed hat and use sunscreen. If you're out hiking or biking, know your limits: strenuous activity can lead to heat exhaustion.

Lyme disease

Ticks can be present in woodlands, so you'll want to check yourself carefully after visiting the park. Since some ticks can carry Lyme disease try to avoid them if possible. Using DEET repellent and wearing appropriate clothing (such as long pants and a hat) will minimize the risks.

POISON IVY

Remember: 'leaves of three, leave it be'. If you come into contact with poison ivy, wash the area within 30 minutes with soap and water.

WARNING FLAGS ON THE BEACH

Green flag
Calm conditions; safe to swim

Yellow flag
Waters may be rough: use extreme caution, watch for riptides

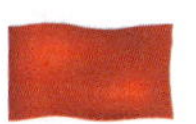

Red flag
Hazardous conditions: high surf or strong current

Purple/blue flag
Dangerous marine life (jellyfish, sharks) spotted

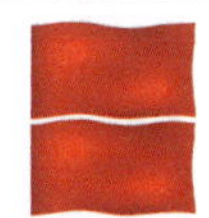

Double red flag
Extreme danger; do not enter water

Hurricanes & Tornadoes

Hurricanes can strike the Gulf and Atlantic coasts from June until November. The most active period tends to be in August and September. If you're in the path of a storm, follow all official directives. Tornadoes are also a concern (typically striking March through June). Stay weather aware by following alerts posted on weather.gov.

THOUSANDS WITHOUT HOMES

Despite billions spent annually to combat the country's homelessness crisis, the number of people living on the streets keeps inexorably growing. You'll see unhoused people – the current descriptor of choice – in large cities and small towns, living in tents, under tarps, in battered RVs etc. Solving the causes, which include housing costs, mental health and substance-abuse problems, is an elusive goal.

FROM LEFT: MOHAMADHAFIZMOHAMAD/SHUTTERSTOCK, STUDIO KIWI/SHUTERSTOCK

Food, Drink & Nightlife

When to Eat

Breakfast (7am to 10am, later on weekends) Tuck into pancakes and eggs at a classic diner or head to a cafe for pastries, sandwiches and good coffees.

Lunch (noon to 2pm) Anything from pork tacos off a food truck to veggie bowls or barbecue at a food hall.

Dinner (5pm to 9pm) Prime time for tucking into oysters, fresh-off-the-boat seafood and farm-to-table cooking.

Where to Eat

Cafes & bakeries Open during daytime, cafes are good for casual meals, sweet treats or coffee.

Food halls Typically six or more vendors offer a variety of diverse cuisines.

Food trucks Kitchen on wheels, parked where hungry pedestrians are found and often at breweries.

Crab, clam or lobster shacks Informal eateries along the East Coast serving simply prepared seafood.

Bars & pubs Many drinking establishments also serve food, from basic bar food to more innovative dishes (at gastropubs).

MENU DECODER

Entree Always confusing to non-Americans – the word for the main course. The course before it is an 'appetizer'.

Biscuits and gravy Homemade flaky yeast roll, similar to a scone, served warm and slathered with heavy sausage gravy.

Grouper sandwich The mild, meaty fish (best served blackened) is a favorite in Florida.

À la carte Choose anything you like from the menu; a side often must be ordered in addition to the main dishes.

Blue plate Special of the day in a diner.

Po'boy Large sandwich made on French bread and stuffed with a variety of fillings.

Brisket Beef that's been slow cooked for hours over a low-heat fire.

Grits Ground corn cooked to a porridge-like consistency and often served with butter or melted cheese.

Sweet tea Presweetened (and very sugary!) iced tea found on menus across the South.

HOW TO... Order Barbecue

Ordering at a barbecue counter is fairly straightforward, but first-time visitors might feel lost with the variety of choices. Popular restaurants typically have a posted menu with some kind of notes of what is already sold out.

Take your pick among the variety of meats on display, sometimes priced by weight, which are immediately cut and weighed in front of you. Most adults will want from a third to half of a pound of meat. Ideally, get a group together to order family-style and try a little of everything.

Next come the side dishes, often displayed buffet-style, making it easy to point and choose whatever looks most promising. They're normally served in a range of sizes: individual, pint and quart.

Pay up, then pick a seat. Many restaurants use shared tables, so don't be afraid to plop down next to a stranger if you need to. They won't bite.

CLOCKWISE FROM TOP LEFT: BAIBAZ/SHUTTERSTOCK, IMPACT PHOTOGRAPHY/SHUTTERSTOCK, NEW AFRICA/SHUTTERSTOCK

HOW MUCH FOR A...

coffee
$3–7

diner breakfast
$10–15

barbecue sandwich
$10–18

half-dozen oysters
$18–22

plate of shrimp and grits
$17–23

scoop of homemade ice cream
$4.50

pint of craft beer
$6–8

craft cocktail
$12–18

HOW TO... Pick a Craft Brew

The 13 states of the South have a wealth of microbreweries, and no matter where you are you'll likely find some unique options just up the road. IPAs enjoy widespread popularity, particularly American IPAs, which have a bold hop presence and varying touches of citrus, pine and floral notes. You might see hazy variants, with a more fruit-forward flavor and aroma.

On wintry days robust beers like porter and stout are good choices. Porters feature malted barley that's more likely to bring out chocolate notes. Stouts use unmalted roasted barley, showcasing a more roasty, coffee-like flavor.

True to their name, sour ales embody sour and tart notes. Brewers add acid-producing wild bacteria and yeast to achieve that lip-puckering taste. (Essentially, all ales were sour back in the day – that day being sometime in 4000 BCE, when the first beers were created.)

Farmhouse ales emerged in Belgium, and those produced in the South have a mix of spices, fruity yeast strains and complex malts, creating a unique but satisfying profile.

There are also traditional lagers and pilsners, good when you just want a clean, uncomplicated beer. You might also go for a classic APA (like IPAs, but more citrusy and containing less alcohol).

Head of Class

With over 400 breweries, North Carolina leads the South when it comes to craft beer. It's also an epicenter of the burgeoning spirit-making industry, with award-winning bourbons that have been on par with better-known Kentucky brands.

MOONSHINE: FROM BOOTLEGGERS TO NASCAR DRIVERS

The term 'moonshine' dates from the late 18th century, when the British levied an excise tax on liquor and people resorted to home distilling by the light of the moon to avoid detection. In 1862, in the midst of the Civil War, the US government passed the Revenue Act to help fund the Union army. Among other items was a tax on liquor, tobacco and similar 'luxury' items, and the first investigators were hired to catch tax evaders.

Moonshiners who refused to pay taxes had to develop new stratagems to avoid getting caught – particularly in the 1920s during Prohibition. Having a fast car was essential for outrunning law enforcement, and bootleggers tinkered with vehicles to give them an edge. In the 1940s, high-speed driving skills morphed into a new sport, Nascar, with some of the first drivers connected to moonshiners.

In more recent times moonshiners have gone legit. One of the first legal moonshine distilleries in the US (Belmont Farm Distillery) opened in Virginia in 1988. Distilleries in North Carolina, Tennessee and other Southern states followed in later decades. Moonshine, incidentally, is simply unaged whiskey. It can be made from a variety of grains, including rye, barley and, most commonly, corn. Owing to the simple taste, moonshine is often flavored with fruits and herbs.

Responsible Travel

Climate Change & Travel

It's impossible to ignore the impact we have when traveling; Lonely Planet urges all travelers to engage with their travel carbon footprint, which will mainly come from air travel. While there often isn't an alternative, travelers can look to minimize the number of flights they take, opt for newer aircrafts and use cleaner ground transportation, such as trains. One proposed solution – purchasing carbon offsets – unfortunately does not cancel out the impact of individual flights. While most destinations will depend on air travel for the foreseeable future, for now, pursuing ground-based travel where possible is the best course of action.

The **UN Carbon Offset Calculator** shows how flying impacts a household's emissions

The **ICAO's carbon emissions calculator** allows visitors to analyze the CO2 generated by point-to-point journeys

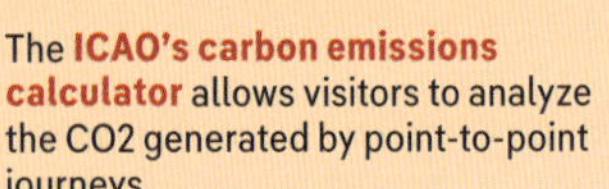

Travel by Train

Instead of flying or driving, take Amtrak. Travel on the *City of New Orleans* from New Orleans to Memphis through the Mississippi Delta, or chug along the eastern seaboard from Richmond, Virginia, to Miami, Florida, on the *Silver Meteor*.

Cycle the Sights

Skip the noisy double decker buses and rent a bicycle instead. Most cities have a good network of bike lanes and some towns are well connected to nature trails on former rail lines *(railstotrails.org)*.

Going strong since 1995, the nonprofit Seafood Watch *(seafoodwatch.org)* publishes guides that list sustainably harvested seafood. Download the guides to the Southeast and Southwest and bring them with you.

For high-quality jewelry, baskets, pottery and textiles made by Cherokee artisans, visit Qualla Arts & Crafts in Cherokee, in the far western mountains of North Carolina. It also displays a collection of historic pieces.

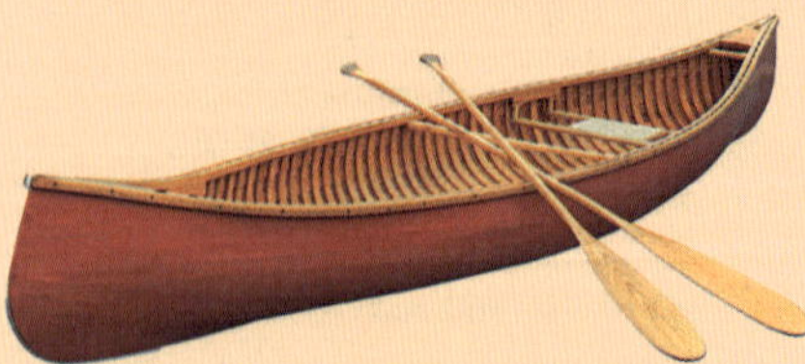

GREEN ADVENTURES

Consider taking a low-impact tour in the wetlands rather than a mortorboat or an airboat excursion. Kayaking and canoeing are more immersive, with fewer crowds and more opportunities to experience the plant and animal life.

BUY PICNIC FARE AT A FARMERS MARKET

You'll find farmers markets all across the South, with locally made cheeses, breads and other goodies along with seasonal temptations including berries and foraged mushrooms. Most markets are held on Saturday morning.

Go Electric

If you're renting a car during your stay, consider going electric. You'll find EV charging stations at a growing number of places, including hotels, grocery stores and campgrounds. Find the nearest charging station at chargehub.com.

Rest Your Head Wisely

Seek out hotels with sustainability policies certified by a credible organization like LEED or EarthCheck.

Sleep Under the Stars

Camping is a great way to go green while also immersing yourself in nature. You'll find many enchanting settings for pitching a tent, plus glamping spots for a dose of the outdoors without roughing it.

Respect the Wildlife

Stay at least 50yd away from all wildlife in national and state parks. Never approach an animal, and if your presence changes the animal's behavior in any way you're too close. Feeding wildlife is prohibited.

Tip Street Performers

Whether performing on the street or playing in a bar or restaurant, musicians are the lifeblood of many cities. Show your appreciation with a tip in cash or through an app.

Meat production in the US is a significant contributor to greenhouse gas emissions, accelerating climate change. Order plant-based dishes and visit vegan restaurants to reduce your carbon footprint.

Go secondhand shopping at flea markets, thrift stores and vintage shops instead of buying new. Every city and even small towns have secondhand stores packed with treasures waiting to be discovered.

Dark Sky Reserve

The McDonald Observatory outside Fort Davis is a Dark Sky Reserve, with the goal of protecting the night sky from light pollution. The observatory's popular Star Parties provide visitors with an up-close look at constellations.

RESOURCES

happycow.net
Vegetarian and vegan restaurants across the country.

environmentamerica.org
A citizen-based environmental advocacy organization.

thedyrt.com
Top campsites across the country.

CLOCKWISE FROM TOP LEFT: APATERSON/SHUTTERSTOCK, DAN THORNBERG/SHUTTERSTOCK

LGBTIQ+ Travelers

Attitudes vary from state to state, but prominent, welcoming LGBTIQ+ communities are found across the South, from Austin, Texas, to Miami, Florida. Unfortunately, bigotry still exists. In rural areas and conservative enclaves, it's unwise to be openly out, as violence and verbal abuse can sometimes occur. When in doubt, assume locals follow a 'don't ask, don't tell' policy.

Fabulous Florida Fests

One of the best ways to kick off the year is at **St Pete Winter Pride** held in February. South Florida hosts an action-packed **Miami Pride Fest** in early April, while Key West, Sarasota, Naples and Gulfport stage their Pride events in June. Also in June is Orlando's **Gay Days**, where everyone dons a red shirt and joins the throngs around theme parks. Key West features its one-of-a-kind five-day **Fantasy Fest** in October with its mix of colorful costumes and a massive parade.

THE SOUTH'S MOST VIBRANT 'GAYBORHOOD'

In Atlanta, Midtown is the heart of LGBTIQ+ life; the epicenter is around Piedmont Park and the intersection of 10th St and Piedmont Ave, where you can check out Blake's, Atlanta's classic gay bar, or 10th & Piedmont, good for food and late-night shenanigans, plus weekly drag shows. The town of Decatur, east of downtown Atlanta, has a prominent LGBTIQ+ community, especially lesbian couples.

New Orleans Nights

Bourbon St near St Anne marks the beginning of the so-called Lavender Line, with a dense concentration of LGBTIQ+ bars, lounges and nightclubs. If you're up for a wild party, visit during Southern Decadence (early September) with its mix of street parties and club nights.

LGBTIQ+ RESOURCES

Advocate *(advocate.com/travel)* News, LGBTIQ+ travel features and destination guides.

Damron *(damron.com)* Long-running, advertiser-driven gay travel guides and app.

LGBT National Help Center *(lgbthotline.org)* Counseling, information and referrals for people of all ages; special resources for youths.

Out Traveler *(outtraveler.com)* Free online magazine articles with travel tips, destination guides and reviews.

Gay Stays

The lodging website and app MisterB&B lists gay-friendly hotels, apartments, private rooms and vacation homes for rent. Hosts are well vetted to ensure all visitors are welcome.

LGBTIQ+ BUSINESSES IN TEXAS

The Lone Star State has many LGBTIQ-owned businesses, mostly in the major urban centers. Search business directories and LGBT Chamber of Commerce websites for North Texas, San Antonio, Houston and Austin to find out the latest openings and offerings. Popular LGBTIQ-owned restaurants include La Sicilia Italian Bakery & Cafe in Houston, Salum in Dallas and La Barbecue in Austin – the latter is Texas' first-ever lesbian-owned BBQ restaurant.

 NITO/SHUTTERSTOCK

Accessible Travel

If you have a physical disability, the Southern US can be an accommodating place, though you'll need to plan carefully. Bigger cities are generally more accessible, though you'll find accessible attractions sprinkled across the region.

Beach Accessibility in Florida

Florida has over 100 beaches with free or rentable wheelchairs designed for use on the sand. Find these beaches at visitflorida.com/travel-ideas/articles/wheelchair-accessible-beaches.

Airport

Most airports in the South provide barrier-free paths and accessible services throughout their terminals, including guided mobility assistance at designated locations. If a wheelchair is required upon arrival, be sure to request it in advance through your airline.

Accommodations

Hotels built since 1993 must meet modern accessibility requirements. Major chains usually have rooms adapted for accessibility needs, but you should book in advance and double-check they have what you require. Holiday rentals and older properties may not be accessible.

PARKS

Many national and some state parks and recreation areas have wheelchair-accessible trails. Most national park websites have an accessibility page giving complete details on the park's accessible attractions. Start your search at nps.gov.

Austin's Disability Film Festival

Cinema Touching Disability Film Festival is the top cinematic celebration of disability in Texas. Typically held in September in Austin, it features works by indie filmmakers, from documentaries to animated shorts.

Accessible Public Transit

In cities, many public buses are accessible thanks to 'kneeling' buses and automated ramps. Trains, including Amtrak, are generally accessible. Check local transport sites (like Norta in New Orleans) for accessibility options.

DISABILITY PRIDE

July is Disability Pride month. Look out for special events in big cities of the South. Atlanta's New Disabled South *(newdisabledsouth.org)* stages gatherings with food, drinks, music and discussions. In October, San Antonio hosts the AccessAbility Fest.

RESOURCES

AccessibleGO *(accessiblego.com)* Provides accessibility details and community reviews for hotels, flights and more.

Society for Accessible Travel & Hospitality *(sath.org)* Brings together organizations serving travelers with disabilities. It provides tons of helpful travel tips and access info.

Handiscover *(handiscover.com)* Useful for booking accessible accommodations.

Be My Eyes *(bemyeyes.com)* Excellent app that helps blind and visually impaired travelers navigate their environment through AI and live video.

Those who want to share that they have a non-visible disability should check out the Hidden Disabilities Sunflower Program *(hdsunflower.com/us)*. Users wear a sunflower-emblazoned lanyard, which alerts staff at airports and other places that they need extra help.

Snorkeling, Key West (p224)

Nuts & Bolts

OPENING HOURS

The following is a general guideline for opening hours. Shorter hours may apply during low seasons, when some venues close completely.

Banks and offices 9am to 5pm Monday to Friday; sometimes 9am to noon Saturday

Bars and pubs 4pm to midnight, some until 2am (3am in cities like Nashville and Atlanta)

Restaurants Breakfast 7am to 10am, lunch 11am to 2:30pm, dinner 5pm to 10pm

Shops 9am to 7pm Monday to Saturday; some open noon to 5pm Sunday, or until evening in tourist areas

Weights & Measures

The US uses the imperial system, with mountain heights measured in feet (0.3m) and road distances in miles (1.6km). Weights are measured in pounds (0.45kg) and gasoline is sold by the gallon (3.8L).

Internet

Mobile coverage is reliable in cities but spotty in rural areas. Many establishments offer wi-fi access.

Toilets

Free restrooms can often be found in malls, libraries, transportation hubs, gas stations, and government-run parks and beaches.

GOOD TO KNOW

Time zones
The Southern USA has two time zones: Eastern (GMT/UTC -5hrs) and Central (GMT/UTC -6hrs)

Country calling code
+1

Emergency number
911

Population
126 million

Electricity

Type A and B 120V/60Hz

PUBLIC HOLIDAYS

On the following holidays, banks, schools and government offices (including post offices) are closed, and transportation, museums and other services may operate on a Sunday schedule. Holidays falling on a weekend are usually observed the following Monday. There also local holidays (Mardi Gras in New Orleans, San Jacinto Day in San Antonio).

New Year's Day January 1

Martin Luther King Jr Day Third Monday of January

Presidents' Day Third Monday of February

Memorial Day Last Monday of May

Juneteenth June 19

Independence Day July 4

Labor Day First Monday of September

Indigenous Peoples' Day (aka Columbus Day) Second Monday of October

Veterans Day November 11

Thanksgiving Fourth Thursday of November

Christmas Day December 25

SIDEWAL
CLOSED
SIDEWALK
CLOSED
HERE

THE AMERICAN SOUTH

STORYBOOK

Our writers delve deep into different aspects of life in the American South

French Quarter (p184), New Orleans

FIIPHOTO/SHUTTERSTOCK

A HISTORY OF THE AMERICAN SOUTH IN 15 PLACES

The history of the South spans thousands of years, and features mysterious mound builders, Spanish missionaries, warring states and a people in bondage who helped build a nation. It's a story that's still being written, as communities lean toward a more just, inclusive society and cities reinvent themselves in the face of climate change. By Regis St Louis

'WE ARE NOT makers of history. We are made by history,' said Dr Martin Luther King Jr to his Montgomery, Alabama, congregation in 1954, a period that marked a major milestone in the fight for Civil Rights. That year the US Supreme Court made segregation illegal in public schools with the ruling Brown v Board of Education. And yet much work lay ahead, including bus boycotts, massive marches and countless acts of individual courage, such as the efforts of nine students to brave the angry mobs as they integrated Little Rock Central High School in 1957 (p122). King was undoubtedly shaped by his times, though he also played a vital role in pushing the nation toward a place of greater equality.

The story of the South is similarly a balance between agency and circumstance – of visionaries that fought for change amid often tumultuous times. Bold plans like the creation of the Civilian Conservation Corps helped preserve and showcase the landscape, while Southern innovations like the Higgins Boat helped the Allies win WWII. There were dreamers like the Wright Brothers, who launched into history from a beach on the Outer Banks, and astronauts who took one giant leap for mankind after rocketing from Florida's Atlantic Coast and into the history books.

1. Ocmulgee Mounds National Historical Park

EARLY CIVILIZATION

In Central Georgia, the Ocmulgee Mounds date back to around 900 CE, when an advanced Mississippian culture built a variety of earthworks. Leaders of the stratified society oversaw the creation of a seven-stage funeral mound, trenches (possibly used for defense) and a great temple mound complex where the chief and second in command would reside. An estimated 1000 people lived in the village, which was ringed by a palisade made of logs. Surprisingly, the Mississippian people weren't the first inhabitants here. In fact, archeologists have unearthed artifacts dating back to nearly 10,000 BCE, and the site was continuously inhabited for some 12,000 years.

For more on Ocmulgee Mounds National Historical Park, see page 158

2. Jamestown National Historic Site

THE ENGLISH PUT DOWN ROOTS

When the British established a settlement at Jamestown, Virginia, in 1607, the settlers were met with resistance from the Indigenous Powhatan Confederacy, as well as sickness and starvation. Nevertheless, the colony persisted: the new arrivals planted seeds for the Protestant religion to prosper, and in 1619, introduced British America's first representative government, a precursor to US democracy. That same year, the colony received a boatload of over 20 enslaved Africans – the beginning of an evil institution that lasted two centuries, forging a framework for racial inequality that reverberates around the nation today.

For more on Jamestown, see page 63

3. Mission Trail

COLONIAL SPANISH PRESENCE

A few miles south of downtown San Antonio, four Spanish Colonial missions provide a fascinating window into the past. Along with the Alamo, these beautifully preserved 18th-century complexes comprise the only UNSECO World Heritage Site in Texas. The San Antonio missions were constructed to both proselytize the Native American tribes and to provide a useful foothold for further colonial expansion to the north. Although farming and other Mission activities largely ceased less than 50 years after their construction, the buildings survived, and some of the descendants of those first converts still attend services at these now active parish communities.

For more on the Mission Trail, see page 285

Museum of the Cherokee People (p92)

SCULPTURE OF SEQUOYAH BY ARTIST PETER TOTH; PHOTO: SANDRA FOYT/SHUTTERSTOCK

4. The Cabildo

AMERICA'S BIGGEST LAND DEAL

On December 20, 1803, officials in New Orleans gathered in the Cabildo to complete the transfer of the Louisiana Territory to the United States. This marked the Louisiana Purchase – President Thomas Jefferson's $15 million deal with Napoleon Bonaparte for some 828,000 square miles of land. The transaction included the Port of New Orleans, a vital shipping hub that shifted between French and Spanish control for nearly a century prior. The real estate bargain doubled the size of the US for roughly 4 cents an acre, ended France's colonial ambitions in North America and kickstarted the nation's westward expansion.

For more on the Cabildo, see page 183

5. Museum of the Cherokee People

ANCESTRAL CONNECTION TO THE LAND

One of America's largest Indigenous groups, the Cherokee's roots in the Smoky Mountains date back over 1000 years. Excellent farmers, they lived in fertile river valleys in small villages with sturdy wooden houses and cornfields. Before the Trail of Tears exodus in 1838, a small group of Cherokee in western North Carolina received special permission to avoid relocation. Around 1000 stayed behind and worked to buy back their lands. Today, the Eastern Cherokee number around 15,000, with most living outside the national park in the Qualla Boundary, which is anchored by the town of Cherokee, NC. Learn the full history at the Museum of the Cherokee People, also in Cherokee.

For more on the Museum of the Cherokee People, see page 92

6. Whitney Plantation

LIVES OF THE ENSLAVED

In southern Louisiana, the Whitney Plantation, which began operating in 1752, flips the script on the old-fashioned plantation tour, and focuses on enslaved people rather than the wealthy inhabitants in the 'big house'. Original slave quarters show the meager state of the dwellings (freezing in the winters), while the sugar factory and fields give an idea of the brutality of the work. There's also a jail – where enslaved people would be held captive before being sold at auction – and a memorial wall of the victims. Most moving is the Field of

Angels, dedicated to the 39 enslaved children that died here.

For more on the Whitney Plantation, see page 195

7. Fort Sumter

SHOTS THAT IGNITED THE CIVIL WAR

In 1829 a large fort was built on an artificial island off Charleston to defend a fledgling nation from coastal invasion. Some 30 years later, however, the fort was attacked not by foreigners but by American insurgents. On April 12, 1861, soldiers now allied with the secessionist Confederate States of America bombarded the fort for 34 hours. Outgunned Union soldiers agreed to evacuate, and the Civil War was underway. Over 600,000 people would die during the course of the conflict, and whole cities – including Atlanta – were destroyed.

For more on Fort Sumter, see page 143

8. Delta Blues Museum

BIRTHPLACE OF AMERICAN MUSIC

Created by freed African Americans in the late 1860s, the music known as the Blues emerged from a place of farming and sharecropping in the sunbaked fields of the Mississippi Delta. This hardscrabble region is where greats like Robert Johnson, Muddy Waters and BB King got their start playing in dance halls and juke joints. Still packed with Blues clubs, Clarksdale is home to the Delta Blues Museum, which charts the importance of this uniquely American sound – one that would become the foundation for virtually all popular music of today, including rock, soul, R&B, hip hop and even country.

For more on the Delta Blues Museum, see page 175

9. Wright Brothers National Memorial

FATHERS OF AVIATION

Orville Wright and his older brother Wilbur had dreamed of creating a flying machine since childhood. After months of tinkering with their invention in the backroom of their Dayton, OH, workshop, they were ready to test it out. They settled on Kitty Hawk in North Carolina's Outer Banks for their first flight. It had steady winds (15mph to 20mph), soft areas for landing and isolation away from prying eyes. Beginning in September 1900, they spent several weeks a year at Kitty Hawk, and finally succeeded in December 1903, powering the world's first heavier-than-air machine some 120ft on a 12-second flight, and ushering in a new era in human history.

For more on Wright Brothers National Memorial, see page 84

10. Great Smoky Mountains National Park

PRESERVING WILDERNESS IN THE GREAT DEPRESSION

In 1929 the stock market crashed, and the economy collapsed. By 1932 one in four working-age Americans was unemployed. To help put people back to work, President Roosevelt launched a variety of New Deal programs, including the Civilian Conservation Corps (CCC), which provided work for over three million young men from 1933 to 1942. Active across the country, the CCC played a pivotal role working in conservation, particularly in state and national parks. The legacy of these laborers lives on in the Great Smoky Mountains, where CCC workers built fire towers, stone bridges, campgrounds and even hiking trails.

For more on Great Smoky Mountains National Park, see page 93

11. National WWII Museum

FROM THE BAYOU TO THE BATTLEFIELD

Before the outbreak of WWII, the US Army had just 174,000 troops, ranking it 17th in the world. The US was also woefully equipped when it came to war materials. After the attack on Pearl Harbor in 1941, the US transformed its economy and millions of men enlisted. Crucial to the war's success was the Higgins Boat, allowing soldiers to land directly on Normandy's beaches during D-Day. The vessels were developed and built in Louisiana – and modeled after the flat-bottom boats used in the bayous – which is why the nation's most important WWII museum resides in New Orleans.

For more on the National WWII Museum, see page 191

12. Dexter Avenue King Memorial Baptist Church

CHAMPION OF CIVIL RIGHTS

Martin Luther King Jr grew up in Atlanta, but Montgomery, Alabama, was where he first made his mark as a courageous defender of Civil Rights. Serving as pastor at

Wright Brothers National Memorial (p84)
ZACK FRANK/SHUTTERSTOCK

Dexter Avenue Baptist Church, King met Rosa Parks, a Black woman who refused to give up her seat for a white passenger. The year was 1955, and as King organized the Montgomery bus boycott, he insisted on nonviolent protest – no matter the abuse and beatings they endured. In the years that followed he inspired countless people to join his movement, won a Nobel Peace Prize and ultimately convinced a president to sign the Civil Rights Act.

For more on Dexter Avenue King Memorial Baptist Church, see page 169

13. Kennedy Space Center

ROCKETING INTO THE FUTURE

With the race to the future underway after the 1958 creation of NASA, aerospace engineers looked for the ideal location to build a rocket launchpad. They found the perfect place on Merritt Island, on Florida's east coast, whose closer proximity to the equator than many other US sites allows rockets to take optimum advantage of the earth's rotational speed. In the early 1960s crews set to work building facilities for an ambitious goal: to one day launch humans into outer space. Dozens of missions have since fired into the sky from Kennedy Space Center, some of which have changed our very idea of what lies beyond our tiny planet.

For more on the Kennedy Space Center, see page 245

14. Kentucky Derby Museum

FASTEST HORSE THAT EVER LIVED

The Kentucky Derby has electrified crowds since its premier back in 1875. Every year the 1¼-mile horserace brings thrills, but none quite as much as in 1973. That's when Secretariat, probably the fastest horse to ever live, stepped onto the track – and into the annals of racing history. The three-year-old thoroughbred broke the record, then went on to secure the coveted Triple Crown: he broke records at both the Preakness and the Belmont Stakes – winning the latter by an astonishing 31 lengths, a feat that's never been equaled.

For more on the Kentucky Derby Museum, see page 112

15. New River Gorge National Park

PRESERVING ANCIENT WONDERS

'New' might seem like a misnomer for North America's oldest river, which some geologists estimate to be 320 million years old. Its prehistoric stones have seen Cherokee tribes come and go, followed by railroads and coal mining towns. But in 2020, this 70,000-acre expanse became one of America's newest national parks – where coal-fueled ghost towns have been reclaimed by green vines, and forests once logged are now fully regrown. It's hopeful headway for a nation working to heal industrial scars.

For more on New River Gorge, see page 72

MEET THE SOUTHERNERS

No matter where you roam, you're bound to encounter people with a deep love for their community happy to smother you with Southern hospitality. REGIS ST LOUIS introduces his people.

LOCAL PRIDE HAS always run deep in the South, and these days Southerners seem to have more reasons than ever to celebrate their homeland. Some of the fastest-growing states are in the South, with Florida, Texas and South Carolina leading the US when it comes to population growth. Immigrants and new arrivals are enticed by a higher quality of life, a lower cost of living and a job market that routinely grows much faster than the rest of the country. Five of the country's 15 biggest metropolitan regions are in the South, and when it comes to music, food and celebrations, the South tends to outshine most other parts of the country.

Southerners are known for their fastidious politeness. We say 'yes, ma'am' and 'yes, sir', hold doors open for people, and pepper our speech with 'please's and 'thank you's. Outside of big city areas, we tend to greet one another on the street. It's not uncommon to engage in conversation with strangers – something that might be looked on with suspicion in other parts of the US. All of this human interaction means things sometimes move a little slower down here. Not surprisingly, patience is a virtue that's much-touted in Southern wisdom.

There are plenty of misconceptions about the South. Speaking with a heavy drawl doesn't mean someone lacks intelligence (see p338 for more on our accents). Some of America's most gifted orators spoke with a twang – indeed an accent is often a prerequisite for running for office in the South to show you're one of us (though we can tell when folks are putting it on). We are not all bible-beating Christians – though the top 10 most religious states are all in the South, led by Mississippi and Alabama with over 70% of residents describing religion as being important in their lives (according to recent surveys by the Pew Research Center).

Another mistaken belief revolves around our politics. Despite what you may have heard, Southerners aren't all conservative. While it's true the South reliably votes Republican in presidential elections, you'll find numerous cities and towns all across the 13 states that routinely elect Democratic mayors, from small mountain settlements like Eureka Springs, Arkansas, to big state capitals like Richmond, Virginia. At the community level, our beliefs are more complicated than most outsiders realize.

Speaking of community, this is something of utmost importance in the South. No matter our differing political or religious beliefs, we all tend to come together for the important things in life. This means following the home team when it comes to football (more zealously followed than most religions), taking part in the local festivals, and being a big supporter of our hometown food scene. Locals may argue endlessly over who does it best, though they'll agree on the heart of the matter: that this particular dish is simply the finest thing you'll ever eat.

Who & How Many

The American South is home to 126 million people living in an area nearly four times the size of France. Mississippi has the highest percentage of Black residents (38%), while Texas has the highest proportion of Latino/Hispanic residents (40%).

CLOCKWISE FROM TOP LEFT: YELLOW DOG PRODUCTIONS/GETTY IMAGES, CATHERINE LEDNER/GETTY IMAGES,MOMO PRODUCTIONS/GETTY IMAGES, KHOLOOD EID/GETTY IMAGES

PUTTING DOWN ROOTS IN THE SOUTH

I grew up in a small town just across the river from Henderson, Kentucky, and bumped around the US before moving to New Orleans back in 2015. I felt immediately at home, and not only because the muddy Mississippi reminded me of another big river (the Ohio) near the house where I grew up. I was also welcomed into this community with a level of heartfelt acceptance that I've never experienced anywhere else. Like some 10% of New Orleanians, I have French ancestry and I was also raised Catholic, a religion practiced by some 36% of the city's population. Similar to many other transplants, I've fallen in love with the region, the easygoing pace of life and the year-round celebrations that mark our calendars. It's easy to see why people find it hard to leave, which is supported by hard evidence: out of the entire US, Louisiana has the highest percentage of residents who were born in state.

SPEAKING SOUTHERN

The Southern accent appears in countless variations and provides surprising insight into regional history and culture. By Regis St Louis

IT'S BOTH A source of a pride and a stigma, a way to show rootedness and a stereotype used against them by outsiders. Southern American English is the most distinct and widely recognized collection of dialects in the US. Its origin stretches back to the first English settlers, and today it continues to evolve.

Silver-tongued Speakers

Southerners are sometimes known for having the gift of the gab. In his soaring oratory, Martin Luther King Jr employed Southern rhythms, grammatical features and vocabulary to create some of the world's most important and memorable speeches. He came from a long line of gifted preachers, raconteurs and storytellers – not to mention the abundance of great Southern novelists who channel the region's rich language into their writing.

The South's unique expressions (p35) have delighted and sometimes baffled those from outside the region. Never mind what the grammarians say, turns of phrase like 'might could' ('we might could go to the picnic') will never be abandoned as it adds an extra layer of meaning to one's discourse – 'we might could think about that' for instance carries the subtext of 'we'd rather not go, but we're too polite to say 'no' outright'.

Origin Story

When the first English settlers put down roots in Virginia some 400 years ago, English had yet to be standardized, and it was constantly mutating owing to the influx

Gullah-Geechee tour leader

of new immigrants. Influences from southern England tend to be most pronounced in the dialects of the Deep South. Speech in the Upper South was shaped more noticeably by immigrants from Scotland, northern England and northern Ireland. People from Africa and the Caribbean also shaped the language in dynamic ways.

No one knows precisely when the Southern accent became markedly different from speech in other parts of the country, but it was noted as early as 1801 by lexicographer Noah Webster, who railed against the variants of American English, especially Southern dialects.

THERE ISN'T REALLY A SINGLE 'SOUTHERN ACCENT', BUT RATHER MANY VARIATIONS

Regional Accents

Speaking of dialects, there isn't really a single 'Southern accent', but rather many variations. In addition to the following, there's Conch (Bahamian-influenced accents in Key West), Spanish-inflected Texas English, New Orleans English (sometimes mistaken for Brooklynese) and Chesapeake Bay English (with elements of a cockney-like drawl) among numerous others.

Charleston English

One of the oldest cities in the US, Charleston, founded in 1670, preserves unique linguistic features owing to the mixing of settlers from southern England, Scotland and Ireland along with enslaved people brought from West Africa. You might catch some extra syllables in certain words ('house' sounds like 'hah-oose' and 'state' becomes 'stay-it').

Gullah

Descendants of enslaved Africans, the Gullah (also called Gullah-Geechee) is a distinct group of people who live largely in the Lowcountry areas of South Carolina and Georgia. Their language is the only English-based Creole created and used (still today) in the US. Gullah retains elements of grammar and pronunciation that are heavily influenced by West African languages. There are those who are 'been ya' ('been here' meaning people native to the area and who identify as Gullah) and more recent arrivals known as 'come ya' ('come here' meaning people who moved to the area).

Appalachian English

The isolation of mountain communities in Appalachia (pronounced app-uh-LATCH-uh in these parts) has led to the retention of older elements of colonial American English that have disappeared elsewhere: words like 'holler' (a small sheltered valley between two mountains), 'bald' (treeless area of a mountaintop) and 'branch' (creek). 'Plumb' and 'right' are often used in place of 'very': 'you got here right quick'. The letter 'a' is sometimes affixed to verbs in the present participle ('She's a-tearin' up the hill') and 'you-uns' is preferred to 'y'all'.

Ozark English

Ozark English shares some similarities with Appalachian English. 'Done' adds emphasis in the past tense – 'I done told him not to pet that bear.' Switching around parts of compound words is also used: 'whatever', 'whoever' and 'whichever' becomes 'everwhat', 'everwho' and 'everwhich'.

Cajun English

The Cajuns are descendants of French-speakers who arrived in Louisiana in the 1760s. French words are still woven into the culture in terms like 'cher' (a term of endearment), 'fais do-do' (a Cajun dance party) and 'boudin' (a spicy sausage). Then there are uniquely southern Louisiana words like 'bayou' (small stream), which comes from the Choctaw language and entered English via Louisiana French. Cajun English tends to substitute 'd' or 't' for 'th' and drops 'r's and flatten vowels: 'there' becomes 'd'eh', 'corn' is 'cohn' and 'boils' is spoken more like 'bahls'.

Outer Banks English

The long chain of barrier islands off the coast of North Carolina is home to the unusual dialect known as Outer Banks Brogue or Hoi Toider (which comes from the local pronunciation for 'high tide'). Isolated for centuries, the islanders speak a dialect sometimes mistakenly identified as British English. Words like 'mommick' (to harass or bother somebody) date back to the time of Shakespeare. Sadly, a diminishing number of residents still speak this dialect.

GET OUTSIDE, SOUTHERN STYLE

The South's varied landscapes harbor some of the US's rarest and most socially and economically important ecology. By Bailey Freeman

THE SOUTH IS often omitted from the conversation when it comes to incredible outdoor adventures in the US, and what a shame that is. The region is actually the most biodiverse in the country, an enchanting tapestry of complex ecosystems spanning forested mountains, windswept seashores and internationally important wetlands.

A Land of Great Rivers

Rivers crisscross the South, the biggest of which producing sprawling deltas that encompass millions of acres of swamps, bayous and floodplains that define the Southern lowlands. Central to this sits one of the country's most important arteries, the mighty Mississippi River. This storied waterway is a thoroughfare for both man and beast: 60% of North American birds use the river basin as their migratory flyway. It's also home to a whopping 25% of all fish species in the country.

But each river in this region offers its own environmental and recreational value. To name a few, West Virginia's wild New and Gauley rivers deliver some of the world's most sought-after whitewater, Arkansas's

From top left: Fort Zachary Taylor Park (p228), Florida; Appalachian Trail (p44), North Carolina; Okefenokee National Wildlife Refuge (p159), Georgia; Gauley River rafting (p37), West Virginia

Buffalo River flows as one of the few remaining undammed rivers in the contiguous US, and the wide Rio Grande connects the Southeast and Southwest (and the US and Mexico).

CLOCKWISE FROM TOP LEFT: SIMON DANNHAUER/SHUTTERSTOCK, CVANDYKE/SHUTTERSTOCK, STEPHANIE ZELL/GETTY IMAGES, CAVAN IMAGES/ALAMY

Just Beachy

The coast here is a beautiful, varied thing. Virginia's grassy dunes give way to the golden beaches of North Carolina, South Carolina and Georgia. Florida's signature white sands and blue waters wrap their way around the gulf's edge until they meet the mouth of the Mississippi. Further west, the Texas coast opens back up to a lengthy network of barrier islands.

Of the 10 US National Seashores, seven are found in the South, and they protect an abundance of coastal ecosystems replete with life. These coastlines are also the first measure of defense against the increasingly strong storms that swirl up from the south and east.

The Swamps of the South

The South's wetlands are moody assemblages of cypress and tupelo trees draped in Spanish moss. These swamps are essential to the ecological health of the region, mitigating floods, improving water quality and providing a safe haven for many rare animal species.

Southern Appalachia

The Appalachian mountain chain is one of the oldest on the planet, forming 300 million years ago when the landmasses that would become North and South America collided. Believed to have once been as tall as the Himalayas, these mountains now form a gently undulating forest-covered landscape.

Southern Appalachia harbors some of the largest swaths of deciduous broad-leaf forests in the world, photogenic mountain balds, pockets of temperate rainforest, and a tangled network of rivers and streams that feed the valleys on either side of this eastern continental divide.

Ozarks Calling

While the rolling landscape of Arkansas and Missouri's Ozarks echo that of Appalachia further east, the geology here formed differently. The Ozarks are the result of prolonged erosion of an ancient plateau, rather than faulting and folding under pressure. This process created the numerous rocky bluffs the region is known for, and a largely riparian environment with few floodplains.

Threats to the Wild South

Unfortunately, one can't talk about the great ecosystems of the South without mentioning that they are some of the most at-risk biomes in the country. Numerous studies have shown that the South's already steamy temperatures are increasing thanks to climate change, not only putting vulnerable people in harm's way, but also disrupting the ecological balance of the region's forests and wetlands. Warmer oceans have led to an increase in the power and frequency of hurricanes that pummel the coast and sometimes push inland to catastrophic ends. Climate change has also shifted the heart of notorious Tornado Alley from the Great Plains to Arkansas, Mississippi, Louisiana and western Tennessee.

The South's natural spaces are also under threat from humans, as recent legislations have stripped back environmental protections across the region, and AI companies have targeted Southern states for resource-guzzling, air-polluting data centers.

The Good News

But things aren't all bad – locals are working hard to stem the tide of destruction. In 2025 environmental groups won a major battle to protect the Okefenokee from mining, while Glass Half Full *(glasshalffull.co)* rebuilds eroded Louisiana coastline with sand made from recycled glass. The Native Habitat Project *(nativehabitatproject.com)* fights to preserve prairie remnants in Alabama, and the Indigenous-led Appalachian Rekindling Project *(appalachianrekindlingproject.org)* is purchasing land in Kentucky for cultural revitalization and land stewardship.

Those passing through the South will find no shortage of volunteer organizations running river clean-ups, coast restoration and invasive-species removal – while it's impossible to list them all here, organizations like Tennessee's Cumberland River Compact *(cumberlandrivercompact.org)*, Louisiana's Restore the Mississippi River Delta *(mississippiriverdelta.org)* and Florida's Big Waters Land Trust *(bigwaterslandtrust.org)* are all doing great work.

SOUNDS OF THE SOUTH

Southern music is not just a regional thing – it's the soul of American music. By Bailey Freeman

YOU'VE HEARD SOUTHERN music even if you think you haven't – this region is the cradle of American music as a whole. Jazz, blues, ragtime, country, zydeco, cajun, bluegrass, and rock 'n' roll were all born here, and their rhythms have been shared, adapted and loved worldwide.

And while the history runs deep, this musical tradition isn't a thing of the past. The South remains a place of pilgrimage for music lovers, from Sun Studio in Memphis to Preservation Hall in New Orleans and the A3C Hip Hop Festival in Atlanta.

Origins

Southern music is as layered and complicated as the region itself, a product of European and African influences that comingled during centuries of colonization and slavery. This music was largely insular in the beginning, ringing through social halls, churches and juke joints and developing a distinctly regional flavor. After the Civil War, Black performers brought Southern music to the nation via touring shows, and popularity further skyrocketed following the invention of the radio; by the early 1900s, it had firmly entered the national and international zeitgeist.

It's worth emphasizing: Southern music is Black music. While cultural mixing did create uniquely Southern styles, Black musicians were most often on the frontline of innovation, despite the obstacles they faced. Early on, they were forced to tour in racist minstrel shows to be seen. Decades of American segregation greatly impacted the South's musical evolution, too, as many recording studios and radio stations would only market white artists to white audiences and Black artists to Black audiences. Black musicians were often passed over for opportunities in the genres that they created, with their legacies in country and bluegrass removed from discussion.

Despite this erasure, Black musicians continued to shape Southern music from the inside out, effectively defining Southern – and American – popular culture.

A Musical Timeline

The development of Southern music as we know it spans almost 150 years and encompasses 10 different genres. Let's explore them in chronological order:

The Blues

If Southern music as a whole is a garden, the blues could be considered its seeds. The blues emerged as a post–Civil War musical expression of the rural Black

South, an evolution of the field work songs from the slavery era, religious spirituals and narrative ballads that spoke to social inequalities and personal struggles. While the blues sprouted up all across the region during this time, the style that emerged from the Mississippi Delta was the most influential, a hard-hitting mix of gritty guitar, 'blue' or 'bent' notes that change in pitch while they're played, and emotive vocals.

In 1912, WC Handy released the 'Memphis Blues', one of the first blues pieces to be published as sheet music, introducing the genre to new audiences. In the following years, icons like Bessie Smith, Ma Rainey, Howlin' Wolf, Muddy Waters, John Lee Hooker and BB King cemented the blues in the national psyche and paved the way for jazz, R&B and rock 'n' roll to take the stage.

But blues isn't a thing of the past: neo-blues continues to make waves as new musicians blend old-school rhythms with modern subject matter. Some members of the new guard include KIRBY (Mississippi), who channels the Delta with her soulful voice; Adia Victoria (South Carolina), who melds blues, country and sharp social commentary; and Gary Clark Jr (Texas), who shreds hard on the guitar in blues-rock style.

ONE OF AMERICA'S MOST ICONIC MUSIC GENRES WAS BORN IN THE BLACK NEIGHBORHOODS OF NEW ORLEANS AT THE TURN OF THE 20TH CENTURY.

Trumpet player, New Orleans (p181)

SABME/SHUTTERSTOCK

Ragtime

We can't talk about Southern (and American) music of this era without mentioning ragtime, which emerged around the same time as blues but fell out of favor years before the first blues recordings were made.

Created by Black musicians in Southern bars and dance halls, ragtime was one of the first danceable American genres to use syncopated piano as a clear distinguishing element. Texan Scott Joplin, the 'King of Ragtime', settled in St Louis, where the genre reached its height in the 1890s. Sadly, ragtime was appropriated by white musicians who popularized (and made Black musicians perform) songs with racist lyrics reinforcing stereotypes about Black culture. This overtly racist trend waned in popularity in the early 1900s and the genre was on its way out, soon to be replaced by jazz.

Jazz

One of America's most iconic music genres was born in the Black neighborhoods of New Orleans at the turn of the 20th century. A fusion of ragtime and blues, jazz first emerged in the city's social houses and at public parades and events; Ferdinand 'Jelly Roll' Morton was the first to write down jazz sheet music in 1915.

From the beginning, jazz grew like a multi-limbed tree with a variety of artists of all backgrounds shaping it, but the common threads included syncopated rhythms, improvisation (particularly in solos), and 'bent' notes. From New Orleans, jazz exploded nationally after its first recordings in 1917 by the all-white Original Dixieland Jazz Band who, erroneously, also claimed to have invented the genre.

Appropriation aside, jazz took the world by storm via the speakeasies of the

Prohibition era and the salons of the Harlem Renaissance, fueling the Jazz Age of the 1920s and '30s and skyrocketing the talents of Duke Ellington, Louis Armstrong, Billie Holiday and Ella Fitzgerald into the history books. More icons followed – like John Coltrane, Miles Davis and Thelonious Monk – as the genre evolved into swing, bebop and modern jazz fusions.

Zydeco & Cajun

Often conflated but different in origin and sound, zydeco and cajun are the musical stylings of the Louisiana bayou and southeast Texas. Both genres are manifestations of African, French, Spanish, German and Indigenous influences, and together they paint a picture of life and culture along the Louisiana gulf.

Zydeco two-stepped into existence around the turn of the 20th century as a mix of French traditional music and Afro-Caribbean rhythms created by the region's Creole musicians (those of African heritage in French Louisiana). Zydeco always features an accordion and a washboard, a jaunty beat and blues-inflected lyrics. Amédé Ardoin made zydeco's first recordings in 1929, and it found wider audiences in the following decades thanks to the work of Boozoo Chavis and Clifton Chenier.

Alternately, cajun music was created by the white descendants of southwestern Louisiana's Acadians, French colonists that were expelled from Canada during the Seven Years' War in the mid-1700s. Cajun music features the accordion, but its central instrument is the fiddle, its pacing features longer notes, and the lyrics are in French. Like zydeco, the first recordings emerged in the 1920s, with the genre becoming more recognized nationally in the 1960s.

Country

Country music finds its roots in the dance and music of the Irish, Scottish and English immigrants that settled in the Appalachian Upper South (the Carolinas,

Sun Studio (p99)

FIIPHOTO/SHUTTERSTOCK

Kentucky, Tennessee, Virginia and West Virginia), and blues and gospel from the Deep South, particularly with the addition of the banjo, which originated in African and Afro-Caribbean cultures.

The genre began as an evolution of 'old-time' Appalachian music, a folk music largely used for social dancing since the beginning of European settlement in the area. First dubbed 'hillbilly music' somewhat pejoratively, it hit the radio waves in the 1920s (in part thanks to Nashville's nascent Grand Ole Opry radio show) and became a phenomenon in the rural South.

In the 1930s, Texas entered the chat, contributing a distinctly western sound influenced by Black swing jazz and the rise of the 'singing cowboy' image on the silver screen, and it was quickly answered with Nashville's honky-tonks in the '40s. With the success of local figures like Hank Williams and the Grand Ole Opry's move to the Ryman Auditorium, Nashville became the heart of country music, launching the careers of Johnny Cash, Merle Haggard, Loretta Lynn, Dolly Parton and more. Today country remains a Southern signature, with major stars regularly crossing over to pop charts, and a strong alt-country contingent making waves (Sturgill Simpson, Sierra Ferrell and Tyler Childers, to name a few).

NASHVILLE BECAME THE HEART OF COUNTRY MUSIC

Grand Ole Opry (p103)

GRINDSTONE MEDIA GROUP/SHUTTERSTOCK

Bluegrass

Bluegrass emerged from the same roots music combination as country – namely the music from Africa and the British Isles – and it functioned as a style revival for modern audiences.

Popularized by Bill Munroe in the 1930s and '40s, bluegrass speeds up old-time rhythms and highlights stringed instruments (banjos, mandolins and fiddles). Bluegrass banjo is also unique – old-time uses clawhammer style while bluegrass uses three-finger picking, a style popularized by Earl Scruggs in the 1940s. Bluegrass found its home at the Grand Ole Opry in Nashville during Munroe's rise to fame and has since frequently melded with folk, Americana and country.

Bluegrass has seen a resurgence in popularity, too. North Carolina artist and music historian Rhiannon Giddens has shed new light on bluegrass' past and present; the Virginia-based Infamous Stringdusters brings a contemporary flavor to their pickin'; and beyond the South, Billy Strings blends bluegrass and country in sold-out arenas.

Rhythm & Blues

The second Great Migration, the mass exodus of Black communities from the rural South to northern urban centers during and after WWII, led to the creation of rhythm and blues, a combination of classic blues, swinging jazz and gospel designed to get the people dancing. So while the rhythm and blues may not be an exclusively Southern phenomenon, it definitely has Southern roots.

Nat King Cole, the Ink Spots, Ray Charles and Etta James all ushered this new genre into the mainstream, and this era also introduced the smooth sounds of vocal ensembles like the Clovers and the Delta Boys, with MoTown supergroups like The Supremes and The Temptations emerging from this tradition later on.

Rock 'n' Roll

Rock 'n' roll was the next evolutionary step following rhythm and blues, upping the ante with driving rhythms, powerful electric guitar and exuberant piano. Its raucous debut defined pop culture in the 1950s and '60s, effectively creating a new national music scene that, for the first time, really transcended racial divisions.

Elements of rock 'n' roll manifested prior to its mid-century success; the

'Godmother of Rock 'n' Roll' Sister Rosetta Tharpe pioneered electric guitar on her gospel albums, while Big Mama Thornton bridged the gap between blues, R&B and rock 'n' roll with her iconic vocals. 'Rocket 88', by Jackie Brenston and Ike Turner and his band Kings of Rhythm, is credited as the first official rock 'n' roll single (released in 1951), and a few years later an explosion of predominantly Southern artists pushed the genre to new heights: Little Richard, Fats Domino, Bo Diddly, Chuck Berry, Elvis Presley and Tina Turner, to name a few.

Southern DJs like Memphis' Dewey Phillips and Nashville's William Allen (and those further north, like Cleveland's Alan Freed) delivered rock 'n' roll to ears all over the country, and the music shapeshifted almost as quickly as the singles hit the turntable. White artists began to emerge, covering songs by Black artists and adding country and western influences to create a rockabilly style now synonymous with artists like Buddy Holly, Jerry Lee Lewis and the Everly Brothers.

A NEW NATIONAL MUSIC SCENE THAT, FOR THE FIRST TIME, REALLY TRANSCENDED RACIAL DIVISIONS

And the rest, as they say, is history. As rock took the world by storm, Southern rock continued to develop its unique blues-and-country style, with bands like Lynryd Skynyrd, The Allman Brothers, ZZ Top and the Charlie Daniels Band paving the way for contemporary artists like the Drive-By Truckers, the Alabama Shakes, Chris Stapleton and the Revivalists.

Hip-Hop

While hip-hop didn't originate in the South, it has made itself at home in cities like Miami, Memphis, Houston and, of course, Atlanta, which today is one of the country's most important hip-hop hubs and the capital of the 'Third Coast'.

Hip-hop first emerged in the South as 'bass music' in Miami, a sub-genre defined by Latin and Afro-Caribbean beats pioneered by 2 Live Crew. Hip-hop came to Atlanta shortly after, but it didn't take off until the mid-1990s with the rise of Outkast and GOODie MOb (originator of the now ubiquitous term 'Dirty South') via LaFace Records and Organized Noize. A few years later, Ludacris exploded onto the scene, shortly followed by crunk sensation Lil Jon and the Eastside Boys. Atlanta hip-hop continued to grow in the 2000s, reaching its most recent milestone with the advent of trap music, the edgy musical style spearheaded by Shawty Redd, Young Jeezy, TI, DJ Toomp and Gucci Mane.

Other important Southern hip-hop milestones include the work of DJ Screw and the Geto Boys in Houston; Three 6 Mafia, 8Ball & MJG and Project Pat in Memphis; and the development of bounce music in New Orleans by DJ Jubilee and Big Freedia.

Today, hip-hop powers mainstream charts and Southern artists continue to be the tastemakers, particularly women rappers taking the helm like Megan thee Stallion (Houston), Doechii (Tampa) and Glorilla (Memphis).

INDEX

Map Pages **000**

N

O

P

R

Map Pages **000**

'An exclusive refuge for millionaires in the late 19th and early 20th centuries, Jekyll Island (p161) is a 4000-year-old barrier island with 10 miles of beaches. These include photo darling Driftwood Beach, famed for its fallen skeleton trees.'

"Thick with knobby bald cypress trees, moss-covered tupelos and tangled Spanish moss, the swampy interior of Congaree National Park (p148) is a Southern Gothic setting at its most elemental."

FROM LEFT: KELLY VANDELLEN/SHUTTERSTOCK, MARGARETW/GETTY IMAGES

Mapping data sources:
© Lonely Planet
© OpenStreetMap http://openstreetmap.org/copyright

THIS BOOK

The 1st edition of Lonely Planet's American South guidebook was written and researched by Regis St Louis and Jesse Scott. This guidebook was produced by the following:

Destination Editor Caroline Trefler

Coordinating Editor Andrea Dobbin

Production Editors Hannah Cartmel, Kate James, Robin Yule

Image Editor Carol Farrell

Cartographer Julie Dodkins

Assisting Editors Fionnuala Twomey

Cover Researcher Kat Marsh

Thanks Imogen Bannister, Kellie Langdon, Kate Mathews, Saralinda Turner

Paper in this book is certified against the Forest Stewardship Council™ standards. FSC™ promotes environmentally responsible, socially beneficial and economically viable management of the world's forests.

Published by Lonely Planet Global Limited
CRN 554153
1st edition – Feb 2026
ISBN 978 1 83758 818 3

10 9 8 7 6 5 4 3 2 1
Printed in China